Leopold and Loeb

The Crime of the Century

Nathan Leopold, Jr. (left), Clarence Darrow, and Richard Loeb before the bar at the arraignment

(Courtesy of the Chicago Historical Society, ICHi-21670; photograph © Chicago Tribune)

Leopold and Loeb
The Crime of the Century

Hal Higdon

University of Illinois Press
Urbana and Chicago

Illini Books edition, 1999

Reprinted by arrangement with the author
Manufactured in the United States of America
P 5 4 3 2 1

This book is printed on acid-free paper.

Previously published in the United States as
The Crime of the Century: The Leopold and Loeb Case
by G. P. Putnam's Sons (ISBN 399-11491-2) and
simultaneously in Canada by Longman Canada Ltd.

Library of Congress Cataloging-in-Publication Data

Higdon, Hal.
[Crime of the century]
Leopold and Loeb : the crime of the century / Hal Higdon. –
Illini books ed.
p. cm.
Includes bibliographical references.
ISBN 0-252-06829-7 (pbk. : alk. paper)
1. Leopold, Nathan Fruedenthal, 1904 or 5–1971.
2. Loeb, Richard A., 1905 or 6–1936. 3. Murderers–
Illinois–Chicago–Biography. 4. Murder–Illinois–
Chicago–Case studies. I. Title.
HV6245.H46 1999
364.15'23'0977311–dc21 99-10745
CIP

Contents

Preface to the 1999 Edition 7
Prologue 9

Part One: THIS CURIOUS COMING TOGETHER 11

1. Burglary 13
2. Chicago 16
3. Wednesday 29
4. Ransom 39
5. Hunt 48
6. Clues 56
7. Leads 64
8. Alibis 76
9. Interrogation 86
10. Confession 95

Part Two: THE MILLION-DOLLAR DEFENSE 113

11. Anguish 115
12. Evidence 125
13. Condemnation 133
14. Examinations 142
15. Plea 160

16. Prosecution 169
17. Mitigation 188
18. Alienists 206
19. Showdown 232
20. ABCD 249
21. Judgment 261

Part Three: NOTHING BUT THE NIGHT 271

22. Joliet 273
23. Life 282
24. Death 289
25. Light 304
26. Compulsion 321
27. Atonement 332

Epilogue 341
Acknowledgments 345
Notes 350
Bibliography 368
Index 369

Preface to the 1999 Edition

Despite all the mass murders since, this case somehow has retained its status as the crime of the century.

–ROBERT BERGSTROM

Christopher Meindl asked me, "Why was the Leopold and Loeb case called 'the crime of the century'?" We were seated in a house in Oak Park, a suburb west of Chicago. Meindl, a TV producer and director from California, had borrowed the house to use as a studio. He was filming an hour-long documentary for The History Channel, and the question he had just posed was central to the theme of his documentary. The Leopold and Loeb case was nearing its seventy-fifth anniversary. We were also nearing the end of the century for which it supposedly was *the* crime. My response would be broadcast months later to perhaps millions of viewers. I knew the question was coming and, in fact, had answered it many times before in promoting *The Crime of the Century*. At least on the surface, the answer was quite simple: Because that's the name reporters gave it at the time–and the name stuck.

In Meindl's trade, that's what they call a "sound-bite," a quick but relevant remark, which he could use or not use depending on how it fit with the narrative of his documentary. But the question begged a longer response. Other crimes have been given the label "crime of the century": for example, the Lindbergh kidnapping in 1932 and, later, the crimes committed by Heirens, Speck, Manson, and Gacy. Other crimes have equally captured the attention of the public: Son of Sam and O. J. Simpson. The musical *Ragtime,* set in 1906, includes a scene where a jealous husband shoots his wife's lover, prompting a song titled "The Crime of the Century." Was the Leopold and Loeb case *the* crime of the century? I told Meindl that I hated to believe we might all be meeting on December 31, 1999, to vote on which was the most heinous, or at least most publicized, crime of the last hundred years.

The Leopold and Loeb case earned the appellation "crime of the century" for several reasons. First, kidnapping is a frightening crime when it involves a young child. That the child was killed made it particularly frightening. The murder of fourteen-year-old Bobby Franks on the afternoon of May 21, 1924, was also a random killing. Chance was involved. Leopold and Loeb selected their victim at the last minute. That scared a lot of mothers: It could have been *their* child. All the families were wealthy, respected in their community. It was a thrill killing, pure and simple. It took several weeks for the police to uncover the killers, and how they were apprehended reads like a detective story. Chance again was involved. The two killers were geniuses with IQs of 210 and 160. Teenagers at the time of the killing, they already had graduated from college and were in graduate school. Why would they commit such a crime? What was their motive? The testimony of psychiatrists who attempted to answer that question at the trial fascinated the public. Leopold and Loeb were Jewish, so anti-Semitism may have been involved in the excesssive publicity given the case. There were sexual overtones, including rumors that the pair were "perverts," further titillating the public. There was room for 200 reporters in the courtroom, but triple that number appeared the first day. The case dominated front pages throughout the summer of 1924. But the ultimate reason why reporters referred to the Leopold and Loeb case as the crime of the century involved Clarence Darrow, the most famous attorney of the age, perhaps of any age. Decades later, a movie made from a fictionalized book about the case, *Compulsion,* would feature the enigmatic Orson Welles in the Darrow role. In my TV interview, I told Meindl, "Anything Darrow did made news–still does, or we wouldn't be sitting here talking about him."

Nearly a quarter century has passed since I wrote *The Crime of the Century.* The book sold well. It was well received by reviewers. The Oakland *Tribune* called it "a masterpiece of suspense," adding that *The Crime of the Century* outdid anything Alfred Hitchcock ever filmed, which certainly boosted my ego. Several Hollywood producers took options for movies based on the book. Scripts were written, although never committed to film. At least two plays were produced about the Leopold and Loeb case, though none involved my book. One of those plays is appearing off-Broadway as I write these words. Over the years, numerous historians and fans (yes, famous crimes have "fans") have contacted me for information or to ask if I had extra copies of the book. One professor at DePaul University chose *The Crime of the Century* as a text for his law class. I gave him permission to make photocopies, since the book was out of print, and only a few copies remained in my own library, not even enough for my grandchildren.

After Meindl contacted me about appearing in his documentary, I pulled one of those copies down from the shelf to review its contents. Since the book's initial publication, I have written a dozen more books and given little more thought to Leopold and Loeb. Writers spend weeks and months and years agonizing over every word that goes into their books and often are forced to reread them too many times for comfort; often they have never read the edition presented to the public. I was no exception, but enough time had passed that I was able to reread my book with a fresh mind, recalling facts long forgotten. Did Nathan Leopold or Richard Loeb wield the weapon that killed Bobby Franks? Each blamed the other, but what does the evidence suggest–and what did I think?

With the republication of *The Crime of the Century,* now titled *Leopold and Loeb: The Crime of the Century,* you can make up your own mind. Whether or not the murder of Bobby Franks deserves that appellation, the case continues to fascinate us.

Prologue

The mad acts of the fool in King Lear is the only thing I know of that compares with it.
—CLARENCE DARROW[1]

FIFTY YEARS later most of the scars are gone. The principal characters in the drama surrounding the crime of the century have died. The heart of one failed in a hospital in Puerto Rico. Another perished under more violent circumstances. The defense attorney was cremated, and his ashes were scattered in the Jackson Park lagoon not far from where his two most celebrated clients attempted to dispose of incriminating evidence. The state's attorney spent his last five years in a convalescent home, bitter to the end. The judge collapsed from a stroke, his health never quite the same after his ordeal during the summer of 1924.

The fashionable residences occupied by the three wealthy families no longer echo with the footsteps of servants. The sprawling Leopold house at 4754 Greenwood Avenue on Chicago's South Side disappeared first, the property cut up to accommodate several dwellings. The garage where Nathan Leopold kept his Willys-Knight remains, although it has been converted into a carriage house. The massive Loeb mansion three and a half blocks away at 5017 Ellis Avenue survived into the seventies, but on the fiftieth anniversary of the crime nothing remained of it but the brick wall guarding a yard overgrown with weeds. The Franks home down the block at 5052 Ellis Avenue still stands, although the family moved shortly after the crime. A nursery school now uses the place. Kenwood, which in the early twentieth century ranked among the city's most fashionable neighborhoods, has been surrounded, if not swallowed, by the ghetto. Unlike many big-city neighborhoods, however, it has aged reasonably well. New mansions have replaced some of the old ones, the trees have grown taller and shadier, but the Kenwood of today, in certain sections, looks much the same as it did in 1924. It still retains a certain exclusivity. Kenwood's most prominent recent residents have been the Honorable Elijah Muhammad, founder of the Black Muslims, and world heavyweight boxing champion, Muhammad Ali.

One of the least likely landmarks of the summer of 1924, curiously, remained standing until 1974: the Van de Bogert & Ross pharmacy at 1465 East Sixty-third Street. In this tiny drugstore, located strategically near the Illinois Central's Woodlawn station, the last act in the drama that came to be called the crime of the century was acted out.

Fifty years after that crime, urban renewal had swept most of the surrounding buildings from the vicinity. Elevated trains clattered above a scarred landscape. Only a few structures survived, awaiting death. One was a red-brick two-story building that formerly contained four narrow stores. The fixtures had been ripped out, but you could tell that the store on the corner had served as a pharmacy because the legend . . . PTIONS remained above the shattered front window.

Shattered dreams, shattered hopes, shattered lives: the former Van de Bogert & Ross pharmacy seemed a fitting monument for what Leopold and Loeb did—except it too soon disappeared, and all that remained was a bad memory, a very bad memory.

PART ONE:

This Curious Coming Together

1 Burglary

For some reason, back in 1924, the newspapers found in [our] particular case apparently something that would sell, something that would interest the public, whether it was [our] youth, the position of our families, the fact that we were college students, a combination of these things, I really don't know.

—NATHAN F. LEOPOLD, JR.[1]

Autumn had captured the land by the second weekend of November in Ann Arbor, Michigan. The few leaves that clung to the trees were brown, ready to fall. The acrid smoke from the fires of those that had fallen hung heavy in the air. Winter soon would be coming.

The ritual of fall in the Midwest includes burning leaves; it also includes football. Forty-five thousand appeared at the University of Michigan's Ferry Field on November 10, 1923: students, alumni, and ordinary fans. The Wolverines had the best team in the nation: undefeated, unscored on, led by All-American halfback Harry Kipke and center Jack Blott. Among those who traveled to Ann Arbor that weekend to see Michigan play the Quantico Marines was Secretary of the Navy Edwin Denby, class of 1896, who diplomatically divided his loyalties by watching half the game from the Michigan side and half on the side of the Marines.

The Marines scored first, the only touchdown Michigan would allow during a season in which they went undefeated.[2] Michigan quarterback Irwin G. Uteritz broke his ankle and had to be carried from the field. It was a brutal, rugged game, but the Wolverines eventually prevailed, 26 to 6. Afterward their fans wrote angry letters to the Michigan *Daily*, the school newspaper, demanding that the university never schedule those vicious Marines again.

The 45,000 fans dispersed following the game. Many returned to their homes. Others stayed for parties that night. The movie *Held to Answer* was playing at the Majestic. The stage play *The Circus Lady* could be seen at the Whitney. There were two dances on campus, an Armistice dance at Barbour gymnasium, an overflow dance at the School of Music auditorium.[3] Edwin Denby, who would resign his Secretaryship during the Teapot Dome scandal, probably attended neither movies, theater, nor dances, but if he followed the pattern of the typical alumnus, he might have stopped by his fraternity house to meet old friends, greet his fraternity brothers, and have a drink. Despite Prohibition, the constitutional act that made the manufacture and sale of liquor throughout the United States illegal between 1920 and 1933, most fraternity houses and their members had little difficulty obtaining bootleg booze for their parties, which began after games, lasted through the evening, and finally concluded in the early-morning hours when the last fraternity brother had passed out or fallen asleep.

The Phi chapter of Zeta Beta Tau sponsored its usual postgame party following Michigan's victory over the Marines. Zeta Beta Tau was exclusively Jewish, its roster of members including names like Schrayer, Weinfeld, Hirschman, Greenebaum. The big prestige fraternities on campus, such as Sigma Chi, refused to pledge Jews, so Jews formed their own fraternities. Other than the religion of its members, Zeta Beta Tau differed little from most other Greek societies on campus.

Perhaps because of anti-Semitism, the members of Zeta Beta Tau displayed considerable ambition. The Phi chapter of that fraternity recently had remodeled its house at 2006 Washtenaw Avenue, changing it from a simple barnlike structure into an impressive gabled home. It was laid out in the fashion of many fraternity houses: a living room, a dining room, a powder room, a kitchen on the first floor; individual study rooms, closets, and bathrooms on the second; and a large attic on the third where everybody slept.

The fraternity brothers, after a night of revelry on the first floor, would head upstairs to undress on the second floor (often dumping their clothes over chairs and desks, not bothering to secrete wallets or valuables), then ascend the final flight to sleep it off in double-decker beds.[4]

The party after the Quantico game followed the pattern of the usual football weekend on campus. It ended in the early-morning hours of Sunday, November 11, 1923. The last brother headed upstairs. The living room, its lights still blazing, stood empty. At approximately 3 A.M. the front door creaked open. In walked two men. Had anyone been awake to see them, he would have realized instantly that the two men had not come to Ann Arbor to party or watch football. The two men wore masks.

Each also carried a flashlight. One carried a chisel, its blade wrapped with tape. He had wrapped the blade that way to transform the chisel into a weapon for hitting people over the head.

The taped blade became the grip. The wooden handle became a bludgeon. The instrument could be used to render a person unconscious with a quick blow.

The other individual carried a rope which could be used to bind anyone discovering them. He also carried a revolver, as did his partner. Later the man with the rope would admit, "If anyone had recognized us, I would have shot to kill!"[5]

The two men eased the Zeta Beta Tau front door shut behind them. One tiptoed toward the powder room of the living room and cautiously looked inside. The powder room contained a bed. Weekend guests sometimes slept there. But the room was empty.

He motioned for his companion to follow him to the stairs. They moved up them, step by cautious step, listening nervously for the sound of anyone who might be awake above. After reaching the second floor, they tiptoed down the hall and slipped into one of the darkened study rooms, switching on their flashlights for light. Someone had emptied the contents of his pockets on his desk before hanging up his clothes. They grabbed what they found: money, a knife, an Eversharp pencil.

They moved from room to room. One removed a fraternity pin from the lapel of a coat thrown over a chair. The other came to a desk belonging to Max Schrayer, a graduate student living in the house. He took money, a watch, a medal. In another room they took a fountain pen, more money. One of them spotted a portable typewriter, an Underwood, that belonged to a freshman from Milwaukee named Pierce Bitker. He took it.

The two crept silently out of the fraternity house and returned with their loot to a car parked nearby. They counted the stolen money: $74. They drank from a bottle of liquor. The one who had wielded the chisel suggested they return home. The one with the rope insisted that they burglarize a second fraternity house, as planned.

The first burglar argued against it. Nobody had seen them, as they had hoped. His friend, however, insisted that they continue with their plan. It was a matter of honor. The first had wanted to burglarize Zeta Beta Tau, and he had cooperated. But they had also planned to burglarize a second fraternity, one of his choice.

The two headed there now.[6] On the first floor they found a camera, which they took. But hearing snores above, they did not go upstairs. Unlike Zeta Beta Tau, the second fraternity house contained a second-floor sleeping porch. The intruders became nervous. With the camera as their only loot, they fled to their car.

Soon they had vanished into the night.

2 Chicago

There is not a single act in this case that is not the act of a diseased mind, not one.

—Clarence Darrow[1]

On November 8, 1923, several days before the Ann Arbor burglary, the Chicago *Tribune* published a minor news story, datelined Munich, Germany, on the front page. It described the overthrow of the government of Bavaria by a gang of 600 men led by an obscure Austrian-born politician.[2] "I hope to lead the discouraged German people to better times," stated Adolf Hitler, a man so little known at the time that the *Tribune* spelled his name "Hittler." The newspaper learned the proper spelling within a few days, but the name soon faded from the news. Chicago had gangsters of its own to worry about.

Another minor news story appeared in the local briefs column on page three of the Ann Arbor *Times News* on Monday, November 13, 1924: "Police are investigating a reported robbery which took place between three and five o'clock at a fraternity house on Washtenaw Avenue. Watches, money, fraternity pins, and fountain pens were reported missing."[3]

It would be some time before the full significance of either news item became known.

The weekend following the Ann Arbor burglary Max Schrayer from the Phi chapter of Zeta Beta Tau encountered Richard Loeb, a former resident of the fraternity house. Loeb apparently had come to Ann Arbor to visit friends. He had been graduated from the University of Michigan the previous year at age seventeen, supposedly the youngest graduate in the history of the school.[4] That fall he was doing postgraduate work in history at the University of Chicago.

"Dick, guess what happened last weekend," Schrayer said the moment he saw Loeb.

Loeb said he couldn't imagine.

"We were robbed!" Schrayer told him. He explained to Loeb how he had awakened Sunday morning to find his watch and all the money in his wallet missing. In addition, the burglar had stolen several other items of seemingly little value to anyone but himself, including a medal he had been awarded for editing the yearbook. Schrayer was furious. He couldn't understand such a thing happening in Ann Arbor. "We never even bother to lock our doors," he protested.

Loeb, a sociable individual who seemed always to take an interest in those around him, had a dozen questions. He wanted to know more about the burglary. Schrayer showed him a list of stolen goods he had compiled for the police. A portable Underwood typewriter belonging to Pierce Bitker had also vanished during the burglary. The police appeared the next day but seemed to offer little encouragement that the culprits would ever be captured.

"I have a theory, though," Schrayer confided in Loeb. "Two colored kids were seen leaving Ann Arbor several days after the robbery carrying suitcases." Schrayer said he had given the fraternity house porter money for a bus ticket to Detroit to see if he could locate the two kids. Maybe the porter could recover the loot from them. Loeb agreed that had been a keen idea.[5]

Max Schrayer knew Richard Loeb prior to his becoming a member of Zeta Beta Tau. Both students came from Chicago. They had attended the University of Chicago Laboratory School, an academically oriented prep school affiliated with the university which was known both as the Lab School (kindergarten to eighth grade) and U-High. Schrayer was two years older than Loeb and had cared little for the younger man while at U-High. "He was just a young punk," Schrayer recalled. Loeb's father was one of the top executives at Sears, Roebuck and Company. The family had lots of money and tended to flaunt it. Albert Loeb had built one of the most impressive mansions on Chicago's South Side. He had also constructed a showplace summer estate in Charlevoix, Michigan.

Upon graduation from U-High, Max Schrayer had gone to Michigan, where he pledged Zeta Beta Tau. Two years later Richard Loeb, who had skipped several years in grade and high school, appeared on campus. Another Chicagoan, Irv Goldsmith, proposed Loeb for membership in the fraternity during the winter of 1921–22. At that time Loeb was rooming on campus with another South Side Chicagoan, Nathan Leopold.

Schrayer resisted accepting Loeb into the Phi chapter based on his previous acquaintance with him at U-High. There also were rumors concerning Loeb's relationship with Leopold. Nathan Leopold, though gifted scholastically, was considered arrogant and conceited. In contrast with the affable Loeb, Leopold was all but antisocial. "Nobody liked Leopold," Schrayer recalled. "Most people couldn't understand why Loeb hung around with him." Loeb fitted the fraternity pattern; Leopold did not. Finally, the members agreed to accept Loeb as long as Leopold not also be pledged. Goldsmith informed Loeb of his acceptance, and within fifteen minutes Loeb abandoned his closest friend and moved into the fraternity house. Leopold was affronted. He transferred to the University of Chicago at the end of the school year.

Nathan Leopold lived in the same South Side Chicago neighborhood as Richard Loeb: Kenwood, an area of imposing mansions north of the University of Chicago campus. Kenwood was not exclusively Jewish, but it did have its mink coat ghetto, an area of about a half mile square where lived the wealthiest and most socially respectable Jewish families in Chicago, These families included the Rosenwalds, the Adlers, the Blocks, the Epsteins, the Sulzbergers, the Loebs, and the Leopolds.

Many better families in this area, Jewish as well as gentile, sent their children to one of two prep schools. One was U-High; the other, the Harvard School, at 4731 Ellis Avenue. Loeb had attended U-High. He was only half Jewish. His mother had been Catholic. Leopold, meanwhile, attended the Harvard School. Leopold's mother was dead. His father and older brothers kept busy with their business interests. They were neither as wealthy nor as socially active as the Loebs. Whether Leopold and Loeb knew each other or not, they did not become close friends until age fifteen, when both were in college. Leopold, as precocious as Loeb, was graduated from the University of Chicago, a Phi Beta Kappa, in March, 1923. He was only eighteen, and although not Chicago's youngest graduate, he was academically far ahead of his peers—and knew it.[6] That fall he enrolled in law school at the university.

In addition to his academic accomplishments, Leopold developed an early interest in ornithology. He pursued this hobby with fanatic zeal, and kept nearly 3,000 bird specimens in the third-floor study of his home. As a young boy he had few close friends, but he did have his birds. He frequently toured woods and marshes around the Chicago area, looking for new specimens to add to his collection. On his own initiative he obtained permission from the city of Chicago to shoot birds in the public parks. He had several guns for this purpose.[7]

During the summer of 1923 Leopold had traveled into northern Michigan on an ornithological expedition where he uncovered the nest of a rare Kirtland's warbler. On the trip he met James MacGillivray of the Michigan Conservation Commission, who took motion pictures of him feeding the birds. (MacGillivray, a former reporter, had been the first one to publicize the legend of Paul Bunyan.[8]) In October Leopold traveled to Boston, where he delivered a paper, "The Kirtland's Warbler in its Summer Home," at the annual meeting of the American Ornithological Union.[9]

Leopold was also a linguist. He had studied fifteen languages and was able to speak at least five of them fluently. That same fall he was discussing the possibility of translating the works of Pietro Aretino, an Italian satirist, with Leon Mandel II, a wealthy department-store heir, who played bridge frequently with him and Loeb in high-stakes games of up to five cents a point.[10] Sums as large as $300 or $400 often changed hands. Leopold and Mandel planned to publish Aretino's *I Ragionamenti* in a limited edition of 200 to 300 copies for circulation only among people with a legitimate interest in literature. The work would be footnoted and documented with a lengthy preface "attempting some sort of justification of Aretino by looking at him in the spirit of the times," Leopold would explain. "Aretino has great literary value if one can get over the first feeling of revulsion and disgust, that it is absolute filth."[11]

Mandel and Leopold began to work on the translations that winter but never completed their work. Professor Wilkins, head of the Italian department of the University of Chicago, learned of the project and informed Mandel's parents. They sent their son packing to Europe to remove him from Leopold's influence.[12]

Other friends of Leopold from the University of Chicago were visiting his home regularly during this time. Despite his antisocial characteristics, he did attract a circle of friends who respected his scholastic achievements. Fellow law students met with him to study for exams, discuss different cases and pool their knowledge. Leopold typed study sheets for the group, giving each participant a carbon copy. The law students included Lester Abelson, Maurice Shanberg, Howard Obendorf, Nathan Kaplan, and Arnold Maremont.[13]

Maremont frequently argued philosophy with Leopold, particularly the ideas of the German philosopher Friedrich Wilhelm Nietzsche, who died in 1900 but whose ideas had become faddish on college campuses in the twenties. In Nietzsche's philosophy, the goal of the evolutionary struggle for survival would be the emergence of an idealized superior, dominating man. Leopold thought his friend Richard Loeb came as close to being that man as anyone he had met. "Leopold believed Nietzsche literally," Maremont would recall. "He was convinced Loeb was a superman, that he had a brilliant mind, was handsome and irresistible to women. I tried to tell him that he didn't know what he was talking about, that Loeb was glib, superficial, and lied to impress others. Leopold kept insisting I didn't understand Loeb."[14]

Leopold's friends could not understand Loeb; Loeb's friends could not understand Leopold. Yet despite basic differences in their personalities, the two were quite similar—at least superficially. Both were dark; both were slight; both were Jewish. Both wore their hair slicked back in the Valentino "sheik" style popular in the mid-twenties. Both dressed well, wearing suits and ties to classes. Both were wealthy; both lived in imposing houses in the same neighborhood on the South Side of Chicago. They drove expensive cars. They drank. They smoked. They had been graduated from college at an age when most boys were being graduated from high school. To add to the confusion, their names were similar, both starting with the letter *L*. Later, as they became known, many people would have difficulty remembering which one was Leopold and which one was Loeb. Even some acquaintances had difficulty separating the two in their minds at times. It made a difference, but on the other hand, it would make *no* difference. One was Leopold and one was Loeb, but they became Leopold and Loeb. Though possessing different personalities, they became the sum of those personalities.

During the year 1923, Cook County had 267 deaths caused by guns. Another 216 deaths were attributed to "moonshine," the often poisonous alcoholic beverages made in illegal stills.[15] The *Tribune* reported an acceleration of private drinking because the Eighteenth Amendment prohibiting alcohol, especially among previous abstainers and casual drinkers. The newspaper described the "spirit of non-observance," even among those supposedly charged with enforcing the law, quoting one individual: "In the last year I have had more drinks in [judges'] chambers than anywhere else."[16]

Yet when they had gone to the polling booth that same year, Chicagoans voted in favor of reform, electing as their mayor Democrat William E. Dever, a sixty-two-year-old former judge and alderman. He replaced the corrupt Bill Thompson. "I want to give Chicago as good an administration as I can," Dever claimed at a Chicago Bar Association banquet several months after his election. "The question now being discussed is whether the mayor of Chicago ought to enforce the Constitution of the United States. I have never taken part in propaganda either for or against Prohibition. I will not now attempt to mold public opinion one way or the other. But I will enforce the law."[17]

Dever tried hard to build a better Chicago. He revoked the licenses of hundreds of "soft drink" parlors for illegally selling liquor. He sought to restore fiscal integrity and sound management policies at City Hall. He attempted to eliminate dishonest policemen. He closed brothels and gambling resorts. He found the big-shot gangsters who had countless police and public officials on their payrolls and succeeded partially in harassing their operations. His decency campaign lasted one term. Four years later, in 1927, the voters of Chicago turned their backs on him and returned Big Bill Thompson to office.

Partly because of rampant gang warfare, Chicago began to gain a reputation as a city in which it was unsafe to walk the streets at night. Outbursts of violence occurred even in the quiet residential neighborhood surrounding the University of Chicago. At 2 A.M. on Tuesday morning, November 20, a Yellow Cab driver named Charles Ream descended from a streetcar and began walking near Fifty-fifth and Dorchester. Two men abruptly jumped from an automobile and pointed revolvers at him. "Hands up," they said. The pair searched his pockets, then ordered him into their car, driving to a prairie area south of the city. One of the men thrust an ether-soaked rag against Ream's mouth. Ream remembered nothing until he awoke at six in the morning. He was covered with blood. He staggered to the nearest house and was taken to a hospital. Ream had been castrated.[18]

Several days after the Ream castration, the body of Freeman Louis Tracy, a part-time University of Chicago student, was thrown from a car at three one morning at Fifty-eighth and Kimbark. The Chicago *Tribune* splashed the story across its front page: SLAIN IN AUTO NEAR MIDWAY. Police, finding $41 in Tracy's pockets, ruled out robbery as a motive. They suspected he might have been accosted by the same persons who had castrated Ream.[19]

The University of Chicago campus also experienced a rash of burglaries that fall. On Wednesday morning, November 21, the cook at the Beta Theta Pi house heard the back doorknob rattling. Opening the door, she confronted a tall man with a hook nose. When asked what he was doing, he displayed a star on the collar of his coat and said he was checking to see if the door was locked.

The star, however, was not an official police badge but rather one marked "Iroquois Special Police," an apparent relic of the aftermath of Chicago's famous Iroquois Theater Fire.

The intruder fled, and the Beta houseman, Louis, ran after the man, cornering him in an alley. According to the Chicago *Daily Maroon,* the student newspaper, Louis pointed a pair of pliers at the intruder and said, "Throw up yo' hands!"

"Look out, niggah!" the intruder reportedly replied, pointing a flashlight at the houseman.

Four policemen arrived and quickly arrested the intruder, who turned out to be I. W. Allen, alias Anderson, alias Rutledge, a paroled convict from the state penitentiary in Joliet. The police charged Allen with passing bad checks in various neighborhood groceries and clothing stores. They also suspected him of stealing items totaling more than $1,000 in recent burglaries of the Chi Psi and Sigma Chi fraternity houses.[20]

But Allen's arrest apparently failed to stem the fraternity house burglaries. Only five days later Max Thomas, a pledge at the Sigma Nu house, surprised two individuals rifling the house. One pointed a .32 caliber revolver at him; the other had a .45. They left with three watches and $150 in cash.[21]

There were other acts of vandalism on campus that winter. The Big Ten's largest drum—8 feet 1 inch in diameter—disappeared from under the Stagg Field stands. It eventually reappeared in the president's barn.[22] A fraternity shield vanished from the door of the Alpha Delta Phi house. A ladder by which freshmen pledges entered and left a second-floor room in the Phi Psi house disappeared one evening.[23]

Then on Sunday, February 3, following a formal initiation, the members of the Delta Sigma Phi house attended a banquet in honor of new pledges, leaving the house unattended. When they returned, they found their rooms had been ransacked by burglars, who had taken two tuxedos, a full-dress coat, a number of dressing gowns, a half dozen suits, and three suitcases. The burglars had shown some taste in their selection of clothing, passing up the opportunity to steal a slightly worn tuxedo and taking an overcoat instead.[24]

Later that night, around one, the members of the house noticed a five-passenger automobile stopped across the street, its motor idling. The fraternity members turned out the lights and waited; they could see two occupants of the car looking at the house. When someone walked out the front door, however, the occupants of the car hastily drove away, turning at the corner. Several members of the fraternity rushed through the backyard to the next street in time to see the car speeding by, but they could not spot the license plate.

The Chicago newspapers totally ignored the burglary in its editions the next day, as they ignored practically every other local news story in the city. They devoted almost their entire news sections to former President Woodrow Wilson, who had died that Sunday.

The following weekend two Delta Sig fraternity members, William Harrington and Eugene Potsock, surprised a man crouching under a card table. He gave his name as Williams, but after the police arrested him they identified him as Charles Conley. A search of his apartment uncovered a guitar taken from a Methodist church, a small Victrola removed from a public school, and stolen property from Northwestern University buildings, the Oak Park YMCA, and several homes in Hyde Park. The *Daily Maroon,* which reported the incident, did not mention the recovery of any of the goods previously stolen from Delta Sigma Phi or other burglarized fraternities. Nevertheless, apparently the fraternity burglaries ceased.[25] The student newspaper mentioned no more burglaries the remainder of the calendar year.

Meanwhile, a number of robberies occurred in the neighborhood around campus, including one on Monday, March 10, involving campus policeman Frank Skully. Two men descended from a car, pretended to examine its tires, then wheeled on Skully, guns in hand. They took his money. The following night the police arrested George Gilmore, an ex-convict, who, in addition to supposedly having robbed Skully, was identified as the perpetrator of three other nearby stickups.[26]

In April Melvin T. Wolf, a young man who lived at 4553 Ellis Avenue, only a half block from one of the stickup victims, set out one evening to mail a letter. He disappeared. A month later, in May, his body washed up on the beach at Sixty-fourth Street.[27]

Police had no inkling as to what had happened to cause Wolf's death. They also had not solved the Ream castration or the Tracy murder, but since violence was a continuing pattern in the Chicago of the twenties, they, and the public, soon forgot Ream, Tracy, and Wolf and shifted their attention to new and different crimes.

In April 1924, Richard Loeb received a call from Max Schrayer. Schrayer had dropped out of graduate school at the University of Michigan. His father was ill, dying of cancer. As the only son, he had to return home to Chicago to run the family business.[28]

Despite his early aversion to Richard Loeb, Max Schrayer gradually had come to accept him. "The reason I got to like Loeb,"

Schrayer admits, "was because he was an eager beaver. Here was a guy who could always be counted on to do something. If we needed someone to cut the grass, he was always the one to volunteer."

Schrayer's Zeta Beta Tau fraternity spirit remained strong even after his return home. Several dozen alumni from the Phi chapter in Ann Arbor lived in the Chicago area. He decided to gather them once a week on Wednesdays for lunch. "When I wanted to organize a luncheon group," said Schrayer, "who would be better to get to help than eager beaver Dick Loeb?" Loeb agreed to aid Schrayer with contacts.

Richard Loeb was involved in other activities in addition to his schoolwork and fraternity contacts. He and Nathan Leopold were involved in the beginnings of a rather curious adventure.

On Wednesday, May 7, 1924, Loeb visited the Hyde Park State Bank, where he had an account, and withdrew $100.[29] He then drove downtown to the Morrison Hotel, and while Leopold waited in the car, Loeb registered as Morton D. Ballard of 302 Elm Street, Peoria, Illinois. Loeb carried a suitcase which instead of clothes contained books. The bellhop escorted him to Room 1031. Loeb waited a reasonable length of time, left his suitcase, then rejoined his partner outside.

Later that day the two young men returned to the Hyde Park State Bank. This time Nathan Leopold walked into the bank posing as the fictitious Morton D. Ballard of Peoria. With the $100 his partner had withdrawn earlier from the same bank, he opened an account, giving his local address as the Morrison Hotel. Clerk Charles E. Ward asked if he knew anyone in the Hyde Park area, but "Ballard" admitted he did not. He did supply the names and addresses of several people in Peoria. Ward was suspicious. He allowed Morton D. Ballard to open the account but, after the man left, wrote on his card: "Be careful against uncollected funds."[30]

Before the pair left the vicinity of the bank, Richard Loeb cashed another check on his own account, for $400. Two days later, on May 9, just before noon, he and Leopold drove to the Rent-A-Car Company at 1426 South Michigan. Leopold went in and spoke with Walter L. Jacobs, who recently had sold his young car rental business to John Hertz, owner of the Yellow Cab Company. (In the twenties renting a car was considered a slightly dishonorable practice, and people who rented automobiles more than once usually requested the same car so their friends would not know they did not have money to buy one.)

Leopold introduced himself as Morton D. Ballard explaining that he was a salesman with the Chick Manufacturing Company who happened to be staying at the Morrison Hotel.[31] He had an account at the Hyde Park State Bank. He wanted to rent a car, would be happy to make a deposit, and offered four references, three in Peoria and one in Chicago: Louis Mason of 1358 South Wabash Avenue, whose number was Calumet 4568. Jacobs attempted to reach that number but learned it wasn't in service.

"I must have made a mistake," Leopold explained. "Try 4658."

Jacobs did, and a man answered who identified himself as Louis Mason. It was Richard Loeb. He was not at 1358 South Wabash, but rather 1352 South Wabash, the address of a lunchroom and cigar store operated by David L. Barish just around the corner from the car rental place.[32] Loeb had been waiting there, nibbling raisins and candy and chatting with Barish, from whom he had purchased a telephone slug asking for permission to await a telephone call.

Jacobs asked "Mason" if he knew anyone named Morton D. Ballard from Peoria. "I've known him for years," Loeb responded. "He's a good man, thoroughly reliable. He'll return the car. There'll be no problems."

Jacobs returned the phone to its cradle, smiled, and asked "Ballard" if he wanted to rent a Ford for fifteen cents a mile or a Willys-Knight for seventeen cents a mile. Leopold took the Willys-Knight. Jacobs instructed his assistant manager William G. Herndon to issue him the car. Leopold deposited $50 and signed the rental agreement, listing his age as twenty-three, his height as 5 feet 6-1/2 inches, his weight as 140 pounds, with gray eyes and black hair.

Leopold kept the car for several hours. He returned it at 4:37 P.M., having driven it only nine miles. He paid his bill, obtained the refund from his deposit, and, before leaving, asked Jacobs if an identification card might be sent to his hotel, the Morrison, so that the next time he wanted a car he would not have to provide references.

The two young men next went to the Morrison Hotel, where Loeb intended to retrieve his suitcase, pay his bill, and tell the clerk to hold any mail addressed to him. He went to his room, but the suitcase had vanished. Loeb panicked. He thought the maid probably had got suspicious because the bed had not been used and had confiscated the suitcase. He fled the hotel without paying or attempting to ask for the suitcase.

The pair drove to the Trenier Hotel. Leopold went in and introduced himself as Morton D. Ballard. He didn't register but told the clerk he had planned to do so before he had changed his mind. He asked the clerk to hold any mail that might come for him. They then called the Rent-A-Car Company and said he had moved to the Trenier Hotel and asked to have the identification card sent there instead of to the Morrison.[33]

The Phi chapter alumni continued to meet for lunch Wednesday noons, but the turnout disappointed Max Schrayer. The number of those in attendance had trickled down to a loyal few. Schrayer told Richard Loeb after their luncheon on May 14, "Listen, let's either make this thing go, or let's quit it. How about calling everybody to come next Wednesday?" Loeb promised to help with calls to ensure a good turnout.[34]

On Saturday Richard Loeb encountered Bobby Asher, a small boy in the neighborhood. He spent several minutes playing catch with him. "You ought to come out to the university and see a real baseball game," suggested Loeb.

Asher seemed interested. "How can I get there?"

"I'll give you a lift in my car."

Asher wanted to know when. Loeb suggested next Wednesday, May 21. Bobby looked disappointed. He had to go to the dentist that day. "Well, maybe we could make it some other time," suggested Richard Loeb.[35]

On Tuesday Loeb visited a hardware store at 4236 Cottage Grove Avenue. While Leopold waited outside, Loeb purchased a chisel and thirty-five feet of rope. Then he and Leopold drove to Leopold's home to write some letters.

Life went on in Chicago. People were born; other people died. On April 2 a man named Bertrand Van de Bogert had committed suicide by swallowing eight grams of strychnine. The newspapers noted his passing only briefly, identifying him as a "wealthy Woodlawn druggist." Van de Bogert was one of the coowners of a small drugstore on the corner of Sixty-third and Blackstone where his son, Percy, continued to serve as clerk.[36]

The day before Van de Bogert's death, Cicero, a blue-collar community of about 60,000 west of Chicago, held a municipal election. Mobster Johnny Torrio feared that a reform movement similar to the one that had displaced Big Bill Thompson the previous year might sweep out of office friendly politicians, including city president Joseph Z. Klenha. He dispatched Al Capone to Cicero to see that their side won. Capone and his gang raided polling places. They bullied voters. They kidnapped election workers. Gun battles erupted, causing four deaths and forty injuries. Eventually Chicago police arrived to provide protection.

At dusk Al Capone and his brother Frank engaged in a shoot-out with police outside one polling place. Frank was shot and killed. Capone, fleeing down Cicero Avenue, encountered another group of policemen and, gun in hand, fought them off until darkness came, permitting him to escape. But he had accomplished his mission: Klenha's group won the election. Cicero became an underworld capital under Capone with whores patrolling the streets instead of police and 160 saloons and gambling houses operating on twenty-four-hour schedules. Capone had such control over the city that on one occasion, in daylight, he kicked Klenha down the city hall steps because the town president had displeased him.

A week after the Cicero election Illinois held a primary election with considerably less bloodshed. Judge Robert E. Crowe, a former ally of Big Bill Thompson, who had broken with him when he sniffed the winds of change, was renominated on the Republican ticket to run for state's attorney for Cook County.[37] Crowe, an ambitious politician, would soon find thrust in his lap a cause that would present him with the opportunity to spread his name nationally.

And in early May two men walked into a saloon on the South Side and pumped four bullets into Joseph L. Howard, a reported dynamiter and gang murderer. Witnesses identified Al Capone as the killer, although later they would decide maybe their vision had been faulty. GUNMAN KILLED BY GUNMEN, headlined the Chicago *Tribune*.[38] Life was rarely dull in Chicago of the twenties if you were a reader of newspapers and particularly if you were a newspaper reporter.

Chicago during this gangster era was a journalist's paradise. Ben Hecht, Charles MacArthur, John Gunther worked for Chicago newspapers at the time. The people of the city, disillusioned after the end of the war to make the world safe for democracy, sought titillation, excitement, diversion, entertainment. The Chicago newspapers were anxious to please and served up great gobs of print about crime, scandal, and juicy divorces.

Chicago newsmen, a tough and daring breed, did whatever seemed necessary to get a scoop. They wiretapped, impersonated law officers, stole, and committed burglaries. Any means justified the end.

Of the six daily newspapers, the two Hearst publications, the morning *Herald and Examiner* and the *Evening American*, paid the highest salaries and produced the most sensational stories. "A Hearst newspaper," Arthur James Pegler, a Hearst reporter, claimed, "is like a screaming woman running down the street with her throat cut." Nothing gave the Hearst crew more pleasure than whipping "The World's Greatest Newspaper," as the *Tribune* had proclaimed itself in 1911.[39]

The *Tribune* and *Herald and Examiner,* when not complaining on their editorial pages about crime, engaged in a bloody circulation war in which their hired thugs (including gangster Dion O'Banion) terrorized newsdealers, newsboys, and even readers into taking their papers. Ben Hecht would comment, "Each publication sent stern and muscled minions through the rush-hour street-cars to snatch the rival paper out of passengers' hands, and, on resistance, toss the reader into the gutter." During a three-year circulation battle prior to World War I twenty-seven persons were killed and many more injured. Life was cheap in Chicago.

"Nobody moved even to the water cooler except on a dead run," commented Bob Casey, a reporter for the *Evening American.* "The city editor and his crew yelled at the copyreaders, the copyreaders yelled at the copyboys, and the copyboys yelled at each other. Each story, from a triple murder to a purse-snatching in the ghetto, was a big story and was greeted with quivering excitement by everybody who had anything to do with it."

The vibrant press of Chicago soon would have a story related neither to politicians nor to gangsters which would command such attention that it would completely dominate the front page almost until the end of the summer.

3 Wednesday

Life? Bah! It has no value. Of the cheap things it is the cheapest. Everywhere it goes begging. Nature spills it out with a lavish hand. Where there is one life, she sows a thousand lives, and it's life eats life till the strongest and most piggish life is left.

—Wolf Larsen[1]

Wednesday, May 21, 1924, a heady time to be young, a time when old taboos and traditions were being swept aside by the shock troops of "flaming youth," who guzzled bathtub gin from hip flasks at their notorious "petting parties." Women, recently given the vote, asserted themselves, wearing ever-shorter skirts, rolling their stockings below the knees, painting themselves with rouge and lipstick, bobbing their hair, smoking. The flapper was born. "Here was a new generation," F. Scott Fitzgerald proclaimed, "grown up to find all Gods dead, all wars fought, all faiths in man shaken."[2]

Sex, long a forbidden subject, became a national obsession. Everyone, young and old, talked about it. It was a time of fads: Mah-Jongg, marathon dancing, six-day bicycle racing, the crossword puzzle craze. Radio, first used commercially four years earlier, had begun to take hold. It was also a time of disrespect for the law because of the Eighteenth Amendment banning liquor. Jack Dempsey ruled as heavyweight champion of the world. Bobby Jones dominated golf. Babe Ruth slugged home runs. Johnny Weissmuller seemingly broke a new swimming record every weekend. Bill Tilden beat all rivals in tennis. And it was a time of increasing prosperity—Coolidge prosperity—as the country waxed fat under the frugal, honest, laconic, and immobile President Calvin Coolidge.

On Wednesday, May 21, 1924, authorities prepared to follow up their immensely successful raid two days earlier at the Sieben Brewery where gangsters Johnny Torrio and Dion O'Banion had been seized along with twenty-six others and truckloads of beer. It had been one of the most successful beer busts in the city since the start of Prohibition. Encouraged, the raiders planned to hit more breweries that night.[3]

At the City Council meeting members memorialized one of their fellow aldermen, "Bathhouse" John Coughlin, as the "best dressed man in the City Hall, if not in the city." Coughlin had begun his career as a masseur in a Turkish bath and attracted attention with his flamboyantly colored outfits.

That Wednesday State's Attorney Robert E. Crowe announced a drive to prevent private citizens from carrying guns. "The promiscuous issuance of permits to carry firearms by Justices of the Peace is one of the most vicious practices permitted by our state law," Crowe complained. The city soon would be averaging one killing a day.

Elsewhere in town on Wednesday people lined up in front of a downtown movie house to see Cecil B. DeMille's *The Ten Commandments.* The best-seller list included H. G. Wells' *The Dream.* The stage play *Abie's Irish Rose* attracted large houses. The newspapers informed their readers that Rudolph Valentino was vacationing in Florida.

At 7:30 A.M. Wednesday, Sven Englund, chauffeur for the Leopolds, as was his custom every weekday, descended from his room over the garage behind the family home at 4754 Greenwood, started the engine of the red Willys-Knight used by Nathan F. Leopold, Jr., allowed it to warm up for several minutes, then parked it near the side door on the driveway.[4] Shortly afterward young Nathan appeared, climbed into the car, and drove to the University of Chicago for his eight o'clock class in criminal law.[5] At nine he attended a class in French (one in which he was not enrolled) with a friend named Susan Lurie. At ten he had another law school class. At eleven, classes over for the day, he met Richard Loeb, and they drove downtown in Leopold's car to the Rent-A-Car Company.

Loeb waited parked several blocks south of Sixteenth Street, while Leopold, in his guise as Morton D. Ballard, rented a car. He again chose a Willys-Knight touring car, similar to his own, but a different color. The rental car was dark blue with Illinois license plate 701917. "Ballard" paid a $35 deposit before obtaining possession of the automobile.[6]

Loeb waited until Leopold passed in the rental car, then followed him to Kramer's Restaurant on the corner of Thirty-fifth and Cottage Grove Avenue. They parked both cars. Before entering the restaurant, they raised the side curtains on the rental car. Then they ate lunch. It was 12:15 P.M.

At a downtown restaurant the Zeta Beta Tau alumni were also eating their noonday meal. Max Schrayer, looking around, congratulated himself on the large turnout that day. The telephone campaign had proved successful, and everybody had come. That is nearly everybody.

"Guess who's not here?" Schrayer commented to a friend.[7]

"Who?" asked the friend.

"Dick," said Schrayer. "Dick Loeb. He does all the work in getting everybody to come; then he doesn't show himself."

"He's probably busy at the university," the friend suggested.

At 1 P.M. Leopold and Loeb finished eating and returned to the cars parked outside. Leopold drove his own car, while Loeb climbed into the rental car. They headed for Leopold's home and pulled both cars into the driveway. Sven Englund noticed their arrival and came down to meet them.[8] Leopold explained to the chauffeur that he wanted to transfer some gear from his car to his friend's car.

With the transfer completed Leopold commented to Englund that his brakes had been squeaking lately. "Can you do anything about it?"

The chauffeur said he had read recently in a motor magazine how you could cure squeaky brakes by oiling the brake bands, but warned, "You better be careful to use the emergency brake the first few times you stop after I do it, or you may run into somebody."

"I'd rather run into somebody than have squeaky brakes," commented Leopold.[9] He and Loeb climbed into the blue Willys-Knight they had rented and drove away. After they left, Englund moved one of the family's Packards out of the garage so that he could work on the brakes of Leopold's car inside.

Leopold and Loeb drove to Jackson Park, the long lakefront park on Chicago's South Side. They parked near the Jackson Park golf course. The day was cloudy and chilly.

After waiting in the park for nearly an hour, the pair drove back into Kenwood, parking on Ingleside Avenue, a block west of the Harvard School. It was two thirty, and classes had ended for the day. Bobby Asher, to whom Loeb had spoken the previous Saturday about riding with him to a baseball game at the University of Chicago, left school and went straight to his dentist's office to keep his appointment.[10]

Loeb left Leopold waiting in the car and walked toward the school. Many of the boys remained hanging around the red-brick building, waiting to begin baseball games in the playground. Loeb walked behind the school to the playground and noticed Johnny Levinson. Nine years old, he attended the same fourth-grade class as Loeb's younger brother Tommy. Johnny was the son of Salmon

O. Levinson, a distinguished attorney who worked with the American disarmament delegation following World War I and who in 1927 would aid in drafting the Kellogg-Briand Peace Pact.[11]

Loeb greeted young Levinson pleasantly: "What are you doing after school?"

Johnny responded indifferently: "I'm going to play baseball." He wasn't eager to linger long talking to Loeb. He didn't like him, even feared him. At a birthday party for Tommy Loeb recently, Richard Loeb had spanked Johnny hard. There had been something peculiar about the way he had done it, or so Johnny thought.

While Loeb talked with Johnny Levinson, trying to uncover his plans, J. T. Seass, an instructor at the school, walked over to say hello.[12] They talked briefly, then Seass went to supervise the afternoon play of his students. Johnny Levinson disappeared to play baseball at a lot nearby. Loeb walked around to the front of the school where he saw his brother Tommy. They talked for a while, then parted. Loeb looked across the street to where he saw Leopold waiting. Leopold whistled for his friend to join him.

The two disappeared. In the playground a baseball game involving freshmen at the Harvard School began. Several hours later a fourteen-year-old boy who had been umpiring that game, rather than playing in it, left the playground and began to walk south on Ellis toward his home two and a half blocks away. He wore a tan jacket, belted, with patch pockets, knickers, wool golf stockings with checkered tops, a necktie, and a tan cap. He carried a lightweight overcoat of rough English material.

His name was Bobby Franks.

He was reportedly a distant relative of Richard Loeb's. The Franks family lived down the street from the Loebs in a large yellow-brick house at 5052 Ellis Avenue. Bobby occasionally played tennis on the Loeb court, sometimes with Richard Loeb.

Bobby Franks' father was Jacob Franks, former head of the Franks Collateral Loan Bank: a pawnshop. Mr. Franks, then sixty-seven, a somber man with few interests beyond his family and his investments, later would complain that the newspapers overemphasized that part of his life. "I only did that for two years," he protested.[13] Possibly because of his pawnbroker background, "Honest Jake" (as his customers one time called him) had never been accepted by the leaders of Jewish society in Chicago, most of whom were his neighbors in Kenwood. They never asked Jacob Franks to join their clubs—the Standard in the city and the Lake Shore and Ravisloe in the suburbs. They rarely saw Franks and his wife socially.

Though born Jewish, Jacob Franks now professed the Christian Science faith, as did his family. Nevertheless, he would be identified and remembered as a Jew, as would his son Bobby.

The Franks family had moved to Chicago before the Chicago fire.[14] When Jacob Franks' father died, his mother became a partner with Simon Goldberg in a loan office and clothing store on Chicago's West Side. In 1874 she and her young son opened a pawnshop west of the river.

Chicago then was a wide-open gambling town. The gamblers would visit the Franks Collateral Loan Bank to hock their watches, rings, and diamond studs. Honest Jake offered generous allowances, so his customers multiplied. While the fortunes of the gamblers rose and fell, the fortunes of the Franks Collateral Loan Bank rose.

"He ran the business strictly on the square," Alderman Michael "Hinky Dink" Kenna would tell a Chicago *Tribune* reporter later, "and he had the respect of every man who ever made a loan. I know of instances where Jake Franks loaned 90 per cent of the value of the stuff pawned."[15]

Jacob Franks eventually abandoned the pawnshop and became president of the Rockford Watch Company. He also acquired part ownership in the Elgin Watch Case Company. In 1914, anticipating a slump in watch sales, he turned his attention to managing real estate investments in the Loop, which he had been accumulating. He also wanted to spend time with his growing young family.

At one time he and several other speculators purchased stock in the Ogden Gas Company (a rather notorious firm in the history of Chicago graft) and resold it to the People Gas, Light and Coke Company at a reported profit of $1,000,000.[16] The Chicago *Tribune* estimated Honest Jake's fortune in 1924 at $4,000,000, although four years later, when he died, his estate would be probated at $1,500,000.[17] Jacob Franks served as a member of the library board and actively engaged in Democratic politics, although never as a candidate for office. Once a woman described as a "French modiste" sued him for breach of promise, but everyone assumed it to be a shakedown attempt.

Jacob Franks and his wife, Flora, had three children: Josephine (seventeen), Jack (fifteen), and Bobby (fourteen). Franks continued to live in Kenwood, instead of moving to the increasingly prestigious northern suburbs, because he wanted his two boys to complete their educations at the Harvard School, then go to Dartmouth.

The Harvard School had been founded just before the turn of the century on the corner of Twenty-first Street and Indiana Avenue to provide quality education for boys whose families could afford it. When the moneyed families moved south into Kenwood, the Harvard School followed them, consolidating with two other preparatory institutions, the Princeton-Yale School and the South Side Academy. Charles E. Spence now served as headmaster.

Spence considered Bobby Franks one of his most brilliant students. Two weeks previously Bobby, a member of the debating team, had taken part in a debate on the subject of capital punishment. Bobby was against capital punishment. His older brother, Jack, argued with the team favoring it. "I believed that murderers should be hanged," his brother, Jack, later would comment. "Life prisoners can get out too easily."

Bobby Franks, on his way home from school the afternoon of May 21, reached Forty-eighth Street and crossed it, continuing south on Ellis. A car passed heading north. He did not notice it at first, nor did Irving Hartman, Jr., the nine-year-old son of a wealthy furniture merchant, who was walking nearby. Young Hartman paused in his walk to examine some tulips in a flower bed. The car which had passed turned at the corner of Forty-eighth and came back toward him. Hartman continued to look at the tulips, oblivious to any danger.

When he looked up, Bobby Franks had disappeared. A car was speeding south on Ellis, but Hartman hadn't seen Bobby get in, nor had he seen anyone get out. One minute Bobby Franks was there—and the next he was gone.

By six thirty Bobby Franks had not returned home, nor had he called to explain his delay. His parents, Jacob and Flora Franks, became concerned.[18] Bobby had said nothing about going anywhere or doing anything when he had left for school after lunch and had not warned anyone that he might be late. Neither of the older children, Jack or Josephine, knew his whereabouts. Jack had stayed home that day because he was sick. "Maybe he's playing tennis across the street and forgot the time," Jack suggested.

Jacob Franks walked across the street to the Loeb tennis court, but saw nobody playing there. When he returned, his wife, Flora, telephoned several of Bobby's classmates. The mothers she spoke to said Bobby wasn't there. She spoke with several boys who knew Bobby, including Bobby Asher, who had been at the dentist that afternoon. "Do you know where my son is?" asked Flora Franks.

Bobby Asher said he would try to find out. He called two or three of his friends but could learn nothing more than that Bobby had remained at school for a while.[19] Bobby's friends said he had umpired a baseball game after school, then left with the game uncompleted. Justin Cohen recalled Bobby leaving the ball game but had not seen him after that. He and the other boys had no idea where Bobby had gone afterward. They assumed he went home but had not paid much attention.

Jacob Franks and his wife tried to remember anything their younger son might have said that might give them a clue to his whereabouts. Flora Franks had last seen Bobby when he had come home for lunch at noon. He failed to say anything about plans for after school. Jacob Franks had seen him for only a minute that morning. Bobby had already finished breakfast before his father had got downstairs. They talked briefly, and then Bobby left. The picture of his son dashing out the door to go to school would haunt Jacob Franks.

By seven Bobby Franks still had not returned. A maid entered the room to ask if they wanted dinner served now. Flora Franks told her that they would wait a little longer. Her husband frowned. He didn't know whether he should be angry at the boy for being so late or worried because some harm might have happened to him. As minutes ticked away, he became less angry and more worried. He rose and went outside. He walked to the street and looked north, down Ellis toward the Harvard School, three blocks away. He couldn't see the school. There were too many trees in the way. A car came down the street. He glanced at it as it approached, hoping it would pull over to the curb, stop, and let his son skip out to run into the house, to a good scolding. The car passed and continued down the street. Jacob Franks continued staring down Ellis. Where could Bobby be? he wondered. Why hadn't he called? What had happened to him? He shivered. He turned around and walked back into the house.

He suggested they eat dinner without waiting for Bobby to return. Jacob Franks continued to worry about the whereabouts of his son, even while assuring his wife that probably nothing had happened. After dinner he called Samuel A. Ettelson, a family friend and a prominent attorney. Ettelson, aged fifty, had served as state senator for seventeen years as well as corporation counsel under Big Bill Thompson.[20] When Thompson lost the mayor's office to Dever in 1923, Ettelson lost his political position, too. Franks explained the situation to Ettelson over the telephone. The attorney replied that he would come over.

Ettelson arrived at the Franks home about nine.[21] He talked with Jacob Franks, discussing possible reasons for Bobby's disappearance. At one point they decided he inadvertently might have become locked inside the school, so they called Headmaster Spence to ask about obtaining a key to the building. Spence, who lived on the rural outskirts of the city, suggested that they contact the janitor. They tried but could not find him. They called Walter Wilson, Bobby's math teacher, who lived in the neighborhood. He had gone out. They called Richard P. Williams, the school's athletic director. Williams was also out, but they located him at the home of another family in Hyde Park, where he was giving a young boy gymnastics instructions. Williams said he too had last seen Bobby leaving the baseball game walking toward his house but admitted he might have doubled back and reentered the building. He said he would come by and assist them in the search. He arrived shortly afterward accompanied by Thomas Skillman, a sixteen-year-old Harvard pupil.

At the school they tried the front door, but it was locked. They walked around the outside of the building until they found a basement window left open. They clambered inside. If they could get in the building this easily, surely Bobby could have got out. Nevertheless, they continued to go through the motions, searching the building on every floor, shouting Bobby's name. They found no sign of him.

"There must be some explanation," mumbled Jacob Franks.

There was, and it was about to be offered. Back at the Franks' home the telephone rang. Flora Franks answered and heard the person on the other end of the line ask for her husband. She said Mr. Franks was not home.

"Your son has been kidnapped," the voice said. "He is all right. There will be further news in the morning."

"Who is this?" asked Mrs. Franks, trembling.

"Johnson," the voice replied.

"What do you want?" Mrs. Franks screamed. "What do you want?"

There was no reply. The person at the other end hung up. Flora Franks fainted, falling to the floor.[22]

She was still unconscious when her husband returned with Samuel Ettelson from their unsuccessful search of the Harvard School. They carried her to a sofa and revived her. She told them what happened, crying as she did. Jacob Franks took his wife upstairs and put her to bed.

Downstairs her husband and Samuel Ettelson debated whether or not to inform the police. Worrying that the resulting publicity might force the kidnappers to harm Bobby, they decided to do nothing and await further word. Samuel Ettelson contacted the telephone company and asked that all future calls be traced.

At about ten thirty Walter Wilson arrived at the door. The instructor said he had just learned they had been trying to reach him. Samuel Ettelson regarded him dourly and said they had been looking for a key to the school but no longer needed one. Without revealing the reason for his question, Ettelson asked Wilson when he had last seen Bobby. Wilson said not since three fifteen. That had been the time he had left school for his rooming house. Ettelson thanked him for his trouble, said they might want to ask some further questions later, and shut the door. Wilson left to return to his rooming house.[23]

At approximately the same time Nathan Leopold and Richard Loeb arrived at Leopold's home, parking their rented Willys-Knight on the street in front of the house. They went inside, where Leopold's aunt and uncle awaited a ride home. Leopold got his own car out of the garage and obliged them. The brakes, which Sven Englund had oiled that afternoon, no longer squeaked.

Leopold soon returned. He and Loeb sat around the living room talking with his father, having a drink. Nathan Leopold, Sr., decided to go to bed around eleven thirty, but his son and Loeb remained downstairs playing casino and having a few more drinks. Later Leopold drove Loeb home.

At one thirty in the morning Bernard Hunt, a night watchman, saw a car going south on Greenwood toward Forty-ninth Street. The car slowed, and a man sitting in the rear seat of the car raised up, leaned from the window, and threw out an object. Hunt, puzzled, walked to where he had seen the object thrown and searched in the gutter until he found it: a chisel with tape wrapped around the blade. He examined the chisel more closely under a streetlight and saw what he believed to be blood on the handle. He kept the chisel, planning to turn it over to the police.[24]

At 2 A.M. Jacob Franks couldn't stand his feeling of helplessness any longer. The kidnappers had not called again. He suggested to Ettelson that they go to the police, despite the danger of publicity. Ettelson said he knew Chief of Detectives Michael Hughes and Captain William Shoemacher well. He thought they could be trusted with news of the kidnapping.

Franks and Ettelson drove to the police station downtown but did not find either Hughes or Shoemacher on duty at that late hour. They talked instead with Lieutenant Welling. "I'll be glad to get the detective bureau working on a search," Welling offered.[25]

Ettelson hesitated. He said he would rather they wait until

4 Ransom

Without doubt it is the most terrible criminal offense that has been perpetrated in this generation.
—Robert E. Crowe[1]

On Thursday morning Nathan Leopold arose as usual at seven fifteen and drove to the University of Chicago to attend his eight o'clock class. After class he telephoned George Porter Lewis, a friend who shared his interest in birding. On Sunday he and Lewis had visited a number of bird habitats in and around Chicago. They had ended the day near Wolf Lake on the city's Southeast Side, where Leopold fired several shots at a rare bird.

"I'm going to be busy this afternoon," Leopold told Lewis over the phone. "I wonder if you would take my bird class today?"

Leopold regularly took groups on guided tours to look for birds, sometimes earning several hundred dollars a week. Lewis agreed to handle Leopold's Thursday class, which consisted of thirteen young girls from U-High. Lewis obtained directions on where to find the girls and what to show them, then hung up.[2]

At about the same time Lewis was speaking with Leopold, a Polish immigrant named Tony Mankowski was walking through the prairie and marsh area near Wolf Lake that Leopold and Lewis had visited four days earlier. Tony Mankowski lived at Ice House Number Two on the shores of Wolf Lake, a relatively small lake about a mile inland from Lake Michigan astride the Illinois/Indiana border. He worked as a reel runner in the millhouse for the American Maize-Products Company, a producer of corn products, where he was known by the name Tony Manke.[3] Having just completed work on the night shift, Manke planned to walk to Hegewisch, a blue-collar community in the southeastern corner of Chicago, to pick up a watch he had left for repair. Manke's walk brought him along a path that paralleled a channel that connected Wolf Lake with shallower Hyde Lake to the west. A single track belonging to the Pennsylvania Railroad crossed the channel at about what would have been 118th Street, had that street extended that far. A culvert permitted the water in the channel to pass beneath the track.[4]

Nearing the track, Manke glanced down into the culvert. He stopped, startled at what he saw. He moved to the water's edge for a closer look. Manke stood still as though rooted to the ground, uncertain what to do. Then he heard a noise in the distance. He ran up onto the railroad embankment and looked north.

Manke saw two gasoline-powered handcars approaching. Four signalmen rode on the handcars. They were a railroad crew under the direction of Paul Korff. Like Manke, Korff was an immigrant. He had migrated to the United States from Germany in 1911 and, because of his previous training as a locksmith, had been able to obtain work on the Pennsylvania Railroad repairing signals.

Korff's crew, which included John Kaleczka, George Knitter, and Walter Knitter, was headed toward Hegewisch to service some railroad equipment. As they approached the channel between Wolf and Hyde lakes, Paul Korff looked ahead and saw Tony Manke standing beside the track, waving frantically at them. He alternately waved his arms over his head, as though wanting them to stop, and lowered them to make slicing motions across his knees. Korff's first thought was that someone might have been hit by a train and had his feet sliced off.[5]

Korff halted his handcar. Manke was shouting to him in Polish, which he couldn't understand. Manke pointed down toward the channel that ran beneath the railroad track. Korff jumped down from his handcar and moved down the embankment to the water's edge. He looked at where Manke pointed.

"My God!" he exclaimed.

"What's wrong?" asked Walter Knitter from above.

"It looks like somebody drowned," said Korff. He pointed toward two bare feet which protruded from the culvert pipe. Without waiting for the others, Korff stepped into the knee-deep water and waded toward the culvert. Knitter and the others helped him pull the limp body from the pipe and place it on dry land. They turned the body over. It appeared to be a young boy. Korff had hoped that the person might still be alive, but he could see now the boy was dead. He had no clothes on.

John Kaleczka scrambled up the embankment to get a tarpaulin from one of the handcars. Korff asked Manke what had happened. Manke attempted to explain with signs and broken English how he had come to notice the feet sticking out while walking past. He shrugged as though to indicate no further knowledge or responsibility.

They placed the tarpaulin on the ground and rolled the body onto it. As they carried it up from the water's edge to the handcar, Paul Korff tried to imagine what might have happened. Maybe the boy had drowned while swimming. He could have been there with friends who ran off and left him. If he had been swimming, his clothes might be nearby. While the others waited near the handcars, Korff looked around the area, but he saw no clothes. He did notice something lying on the ground: a pair of eyeglasses. He bent and picked them up. They could have belonged to the boy, or they could have been dropped there at another time by someone else. Without mentioning the glasses to his friends, he stuck them into the pocket of his work suit and rejoined the others. The four signalmen and Manke climbed onto the handcars to continue their journey to Hegewisch, now with the body of an unidentified young boy.

At the Jacob Franks residence ten miles to the north, the doorbell rang. A servant opened the door and discovered a mailman waiting outside with a special delivery letter in his hand. The servant accepted the letter and took it to the library, where Jacob Franks, unable to sleep, was attempting to pass time by reading a magazine.[6]

Franks hurriedly opened the letter and found two typewritten sheets, containing a message that began "Dear Sir." He quickly scanned the contents and realized it was exactly what he had feared. Bobby had been kidnapped. He read the letter again, more slowly. It read:

> Dear Sir:
>
> As you no doubt know by this time, your son has been kidnapped. Allow us to assure you that he is at present well and safe. You need fear no physical harm for him, provided you live up carefully to the following instructions and to such others as you will receive by future communications. Should you, however, disobey any of our instructions, even slightly, his death will be the penalty.
>
> 1. For obvious reasons make absolutely no attempt to communicate with either police authorities or any private agency. Should you already have communicated with the police, allow them to continue their investigations, but do not mention this letter.

2. Secure before noon today $10,000. This money must be composed entirely of old bills of the following denominations: $2000 in $20 bills, $8000 in $50 bills. The money must be old. Any attempt to include new or marked bills will render the entire venture futile.

3. The money should be placed in a large cigar box, or if this is impossible, in a heavy cardboard box, securely closed and wrapped in white paper. The wrapping paper should be sealed at all openings with sealing wax.

4. Have the money with you, prepared as directed above, and remain at home after one o'clock. See that the telephone is not in use.

You will receive a further communication instructing you as to your final course.

As a final word of warning, this is an extremely commercial proposition and we are prepared to put our threat into execution should we have reasonable grounds to believe that you have committed an infraction of the above instructions.

However, should you carefully follow out our instructions to the letter, we can assure you that your son will be safely returned to you within six hours of our receipt of the money.

Yours truly,[7]
GEORGE JOHNSON

GKR

Flora Franks insisted on reading the letter. When she did, she fainted again. Jacob Franks sent for a doctor, then telephoned Samuel Ettelson at his office downtown and read him the letter. Ettelson later would recall: "Its deliberate tone struck terror into our hearts."[8] The attorney advised his friend to go to the bank and obtain the money in denominations suggested by this George Johnson. In the meantime he would confer with Chief of Detectives Michael Hughes. Ettelson assured Jacob Franks that the kidnapper only wanted money and that Bobby would be all right.

At that same moment a small crowd had begun to form at 133d and the Pennsylvania Railroad tracks where the four signalmen and Manke had stopped to phone the police. The men nervously awaited the arrival of a squad car. The body, still covered by the tarpaulin, had been removed from the handcar. It lay on the ground nearby.

While he waited, Paul Korff remembered the glasses he had found near the culvert. He removed them from his pocket and examined them. They had circular lenses and dark frames. He tried putting them on, but they didn't fit. The lenses were too strong for his eyes.

"What have you got there?" asked Walter Knitter.

"I found these glasses," Korff responded.

"Let me see," said Knitter. The signalman examined them closely and noted they were dirty from having lain on the muddy ground. He removed a bandana from a pocket in his work suit and carefully cleaned the glasses, polishing the lenses. Then he tried them on. Though somewhat small, they fit. "Hey, I can use these," said Knitter.

"Keep them," Korff told him.

The police arrived, including Officer Tony Shapino (born Anton Szcziepanek), who had no difficulty communicating with Manke in Polish.[9] Shapino lifted the tarpaulin and examined the body. He noticed cuts on the head. The face was discolored. Shapino asked the five men about the condition of the body when they found it. He thought perhaps the scratches had occurred when they dragged the body out of the culvert. He was unhappy that they had moved it before calling the police.

"We thought he still might be alive," explained Paul Korff.

"Did you see anything else?" Shapino asked.

Korff said he had looked around for the boy's clothing but had not seen anything. Then he remembered the eyeglasses.

The policeman asked for them.

"I gave them to Walter," Korff told him, pointing to his friend.

Walter Knitter reluctantly produced the eyeglasses. Shapino examined the glasses and put them in his pocket. Knitter later would complain to Korff, "Why did you have to tell him about the glasses?"

The policemen lifted the body into their squad wagon and drove to a nearby funeral home at 133d and Houston Avenue owned by Stanley Olejniczak. His wife greeted the policemen and received custody of the body. Shapino also handed the glasses to Mrs. Olejniczak. Presuming they belonged to the dead boy, she placed them on his head.

Jacob Franks drove downtown to his bank and asked for $10,000 in $20 and $50 bills, as specified in the ransom note. He also asked that the bills not be new ones.[10] It was hardly the kind of request that even a large downtown bank gets very often. The Chicago *Tribune* would describe the reaction this request engendered the next day: "The young teller looked in surprise at the tired man at the cage. He dropped the crisp bills he had reached for and counted out old worn bills. The teller shook his head as the patron walked away."[11]

James Mulroy, a twenty-four-year-old reporter, was sitting in the back corner of the newsroom at the Chicago *Daily News* when the city editor called his name. Mulroy rose from his chair to see what the editor wanted. "We just got a tip that Sam Ettelson knows something about a kidnapping," said the editor. "Get over to his office and check it out." The tipster never would be identified.[12]

Mulroy went immediately to Ettelson's office but found the attorney reluctant to talk and indignant that Mulroy should know about the kidnapping. Ettelson finally admitted everything he knew in exchange for a promise of silence. As soon as Mulroy left, Ettelson telephoned the *Evening American,* giving them the same information already known by the *Daily News.* He also elicited from that paper a pledge of silence, pleading that the information not be published because it might imperil the life of the boy.

Meanwhile, Mulroy relayed what he had discovered to his editor, who told him to go to the Franks home and await further developments. The newspaper had learned from a contact at East Side police headquarters that a boy's body had been discovered in a marsh near Hegewisch. The boy supposedly had drowned.

Ordinarily the newspaper might have paid little attention to a drowning, what at first glance seemed like a minor news story. In a city of 3,000,000, deaths occur by the hundreds each day. Most people who die rate little more than a death notice paid for by their family. Others will rate a paragraph or two, depending on their public visibility, their social reputation, or their jobs. Previously prepared obituaries of important public figures sit in newspaper morgue files, awaiting the day when they can be used. Very few individuals are important enough so that their death makes front-page news. The circumstances surrounding the death of even an unknown person, of course, may cause that person's death to be announced in eight-column headlines. Such would be the case with the boy found "drowned" in the marsh near Hegewisch, although the city editor at the *Daily News* had no way of knowing that yet. Nevertheless, his instincts as a newsman were such that he assigned Alvin Goldstein, another young reporter, to go to Olejniczak's funeral home and try to determine the boy's identity.

The paper had leads on two items. A dead boy had been found in a culvert, presumably drowned. Another boy from a wealthy family had been kidnapped. The two items might be connected; the two boys might be one. The kidnappers might be apprehended in their attempt to collect ransom for a boy they already had murdered. If so, it would make a major story.

Alvin Goldstein of the *Daily News* arrived at the funeral home by one that afternoon. A reporter from the *Evening American* also had been sent to the home. Goldstein examined the body, then called his office to give them a description.

"From what we know, it might be the kid," said the *Daily News* city editor. "Mulroy's at the Franks home. Why don't you phone him there, tell him what you told me, and see if he can talk one of the members of the family into making a positive identification?"

Mulroy had talked his way into the Franks home by saying that his newspaper had promised not to break the kidnap story prematurely. He requested the opportunity to wait with the family during their ordeal. It would look suspicious if the kidnappers should pass by and notice reporters waiting outside on the sidewalk, so Jacob Franks allowed Mulroy to enter but told him to be discreet. After he had been at the home awhile, one of the servants informed Mulroy that he had a telephone call. It was Goldstein, speaking from the funeral home.

Goldstein described the dead boy as about ten or eleven years old, five feet tall, and weighing maybe 100 pounds. His face seemed discolored and he was wearing horn-rim glasses.

"I'll see what Mr. Franks has to say," Mulroy responded.

Mr. Franks seemed certain from the description that the dead boy could not be his son. Bobby was older. He didn't weigh that much. But most important, Bobby didn't wear glasses. "It's not Bobby," said Jacob Franks, unwilling to consider the possibility of his son's death. He was still negotiating with the kidnapper. The kidnapper wouldn't have killed his son before receiving the ransom. Why should he endanger his chances of receiving the money by dumping him in some culvert?

But as the afternoon wore on, the family still had heard no more from the kidnappers. At 2:30 P.M. Samuel Ettelson asked Mulroy to take Franks' brother-in-law, Edwin M. Gresham, to the undertaker's in Hegewisch to make certain the dead boy was not Bobby: "It's probably not him, but we better not take a chance."[13]

At the Franks home the telephone rang. Samuel Ettelson answered. The person on the line identified himself as Johnson and said, "I am sending a Yellow Cab for you. Get in and go to the drugstore at 1465 East Sixty-third Street."[14]

"Just a minute," said Ettelson. "I'll let you talk to Mr. Franks."

Franks took the phone, and "Johnson" repeated the message, giving the address of the drugstore a second time. Jacob Franks hung up the telephone and, in a state of shock, immediately forgot the address of the drugstore. Franks asked Ettelson if he recalled the address. The attorney could not remember it either. The two men looked at each other in panic.

The phone rang once more, and Franks grabbed at it, thinking it might be the kidnapper calling again. Instead, it was his brother-in-law, Edwin M. Gresham, calling from the funeral home. He had seen the body. The dead boy was Bobby Franks.

Near Hegewisch police had begun to investigate what now quite obviously was a murder, not a drowning. Officer Edward F. Anderson went with Manke and the signalmen to where they had found the body. Anderson was irritated because the men had not called the police first. In removing the body from the culvert, they had inadvertently obliterated any tracks that might have been left by the murderers.

Nevertheless, he began to examine the area, hoping to find some clue. Several hundred feet northeast of the culvert he picked up a single knee-length golf stocking. It had a checkered top. Officer Anderson continued to search but found nothing more. The nearest houses were about a mile away, but several people had been attracted to the scene by the presence of police. He asked if they had heard any unusual noises the previous evening. Most had not. Even the dogs of the neighborhood had been quiet all night, they said.[15]

One man, Michael Barrett, did remember something unusual. He had returned to his home on Avenue F from work at the Ford assembly plant around 12:40 A.M. and he recalled seeing three men walking along the railroad tracks talking to one another. He couldn't understand what they were saying during their muffled conversation. They soon had vanished in the night. Officer Anderson noted the information. It was the first of many false leads which would divert the attention of the police from the track of the real killers.

At 3:30 P.M. Yellow Cab driver Charles Robinson arrived at the Franks home. Leaving his cab running at the curb, he rang the doorbell. The maid who answered the door said she didn't think anyone had ordered a cab. The driver insisted someone had. Wasn't this 5052 Ellis? Didn't Jacob Franks live here? The maid told him to wait and went inside. Samuel Ettelson soon appeared at the door. "Who sent for you?" he asked the driver. "Where are you supposed to go?"[16]

"A Mr. Franks called for the cab," insisted Robinson. "He didn't say where he wanted to go."

Ettelson disappeared inside the house to discuss the matter with Jacob Franks. Bobby's father wondered whether he should get in the cab anyway. Ettelson advised Franks not to do so. He already knew that Bobby was dead, so there was no sense endangering his life through a possible confrontation with the kidnappers. But there was a more important factor: Nobody knew where the cab was supposed to go!

Samuel Ettelson went outside to speak to the driver again, but the cab had left. Another friend of the family, William Taylor, a stockbroker, had paid the cabdriver fifty-five cents and instructed him to leave.[17]

At the Van de Bogert & Ross drugstore at 1465 East Sixty-third Street some minutes later the telephone rang. James C. Kemp, a porter employed at the drugstore, was sweeping the floor near the phone booth when he heard the bell. He picked up the receiver.[18]

"Is Mr. Franks there?" asked the person on the other end.

"No, there is no Mr. Franks here," said the porter. "I probably have the wrong number," said the person and hung up.

Kemp returned the receiver to its cradle and continued sweeping the floor. Five minutes later the telephone rang once more. This time Percy Van de Bogert answered.[19] "Is Mr. Franks there?" asked the caller.

"Who?" asked Van de Bogert.

"Mr. Franks," the caller repeated.

"I don't know a Mr. Franks," said the druggist, whereupon the caller gave him a detailed description of Jacob Franks, including the information that he probably would be smoking a cigarette. The caller asked him to look around the store. The druggist looked, saw no one, and returned to the phone booth. The caller thanked him and hung up.

5 Hunt

Police call the crime the strangest and most baffling homicide in Chicago's history.

—ASSOCIATED PRESS[1]

Late in the afternoon of Thursday, May 22, Mott Kirk Mitchell, an instructor at the Harvard School, left that institution and walked north on Ellis to the streetcar stop at Forty-seventh Street a half block away. The school had been abuzz all day with talk about the mysterious disappearance of Bobby Franks, one of his pupils. Finally they had received the sad news: Bobby's body had been identified in a mortuary on the far South Side of the city.

Mitchell thought of Bobby as he walked down the street, trying to picture in his mind the last time he had seen the boy. But his thoughts were interrupted at the corner when he saw Nathan Leopold, a graduate of the Harvard School, and Richard Loeb, whose younger brother attended there. They were emerging from the drugstore on the corner. Each was carrying late editions of the afternoon newspapers. They waved at him as he approached.

"Isn't that terrible what happened to poor Bobby Franks?" Loeb said to Mitchell. "He used to play tennis all the time on our court."

Mitchell, a man in his fifties, stood talking to the two young university students for several minutes about the crime, then boarded a streetcar to head home.[2] Leopold and Loeb were also en route home after having stopped for sodas at the drugstore. Leopold drove Loeb home, then went home himself.

Loeb, however, decided to walk from his house up the block to where a crowd of reporters and curiosity seekers had gathered in front of where the Franks family lived. He saw *Daily News* reporter Alvin Goldstein, whom he knew from the University of Chicago. Goldstein, a member of Zeta Beta Tau, later would recall a conversation he had with Loeb about this time: "He inquired about the nature of the crime. I described to him, and to two or three others that were standing around there, the condition of the body when I was out at the morgue. Then he, with several others, shook their heads and said something about it being a terrible crime and that punishment certainly should be meted out. I believe the expression they used was that whoever committed the crime should be strung up."[3]

Another individual who for the next several weeks would haunt the vicinity of the kidnapping was a senior at Crane Tech High School. He would enroll the following semester at the University of Chicago in quest of a law degree. Although Elmer Gertz could not predict it at the time, his life would intermesh with one of the principals of the Franks murder case. Gertz's father owned a clothing store at Thirty-ninth and Cottage Grove, and the Gertz family lived nearby, in what he referred to as "the shabby gentile periphery of the wealthy German Jewish neighborhood, only a few blocks away from the Rosenwald mansion and all those magnificent homes."[4]

Every evening in late May, Elmer Gertz and his brother Robert would rush home from school and wander up and down Ellis Avenue near the Franks home, seeking fresh details about the case. "The sidewalks were full of people," Gertz remembers. "Everybody was talking. There was an air of excitement. People were literally on the prowl. My brother and I were just filled with the case. Loeb himself was up and down the street getting into conversations, volunteering ideas, and for all I know I may have talked to him."

Later that evening Richard Loeb spoke with one of his former girlfriends. "Come on, let's go for a ride in the park," he suggested. She thought it funny that he should be interested in her. He had not called her in two months. She told him she had to go to a school meeting.[5]

When Nathan Leopold returned home, he telephoned Susan Lurie, with whom he had attended the French class the previous morning. He asked her for a date for the following evening, and she accepted. He ate dinner and spent the rest of the night studying for his law exams. At 7:30 P.M. George Porter Lewis called to inform Leopold that the bird-watching class had gone successfully.[6]

At approximately that same time, Samuel Ettelson stood on the lawn before the Franks mansion, sadly shaking his head. "It all happened in such a short time," he told reporters. "The events swept before us like a rushing river. We did the best we knew how."[7]

With the news of the murder public knowledge, the Franks home was placed under special guard. Jacob Franks offered a $5,000 reward for information leading to the capture of the kidnapper/murderers. Police Chief Morgan A. Collins pledged $1,000 and the rival morning newspapers, the *Tribune* and *Herald and Examiner,* each said they would pay $5,000 for exclusive information. Few tangible clues seemed to exist, but tips and suggestions flooded into police headquarters. The authorities established a special headquarters at the recently built Drake Hotel to coordinate their efforts. Police Chief Collins and State's Attorney (for Cook County) Robert E. Crowe mobilized resources in the search for the guilty person or persons. Collins ordered several hundred detectives to search the area near Wolf Lake, the neighborhood around the school, and other likely places. "It is one of the worst crimes in the history of the city," he said. "We must and will clear up the murder."[8]

State's Attorney Crowe pledged quick justice: "If the slayers of Robert Franks are caught, they will be brought to trial within the shortest time permitted by law." He assigned one of his top assistants, Bert A. Cronson, to the case. Cronson, Samuel Ettelson's nephew, was one of three assistant state's attorneys who had been dubbed the "three aces" by the Chicago newspapers because of their previous successes in solving crimes. The other two were Milton Smith and William Smith.

Cronson lived in an apartment building at 4605 Woodlawn Avenue, only a few blocks from the Harvard School. He telephoned his wife, Ethel, briefly told her about the murder of Bobby Franks, and said he might be several hours late getting home that day. Cronson underestimated the time he would have to devote to the case. It would be ten days before he returned home.

Ethel Cronson hung up the telephone and sighed sadly. She often had heard her husband's aunt, Samuel Ettelson's wife, speak about Flora Franks. Ethel Cronson was pregnant, and she began to think of how Bobby Franks' mother must feel. "I sat out on our balcony that night," she recalled years later, "and just stared off in the distance in the direction of the Franks home. It was dusk, and I was thinking about that child, and I heard a church bell in the distance tolling mournfully. It just seemed to signify death."[9]

The Chicago *Evening American* tried to describe that death by assigning "the world's youngest reporter," Horace Wade, to the case. Horace dutifully re-created the tragedy as though he were Bobby Franks reincarnated: "I had turned for a final, lingering breath of the flower-scented air when, like a flash, a rough hand was clasped over my hot lips, white with terror, to halt any outcry, and my arms were pinioned behind my back. I matched my strength, born of desperation, with that of my fiendish captors, with the tides of hell running like molten lava through their accursed veins."

Everybody had a theory to explain the crime. Some called it a kidnapping for ransom in which Bobby Franks died accidentally. Others suggested the murder was an act of revenge against Jacob Franks by someone he had offended during his pawnbroker days. Many believed the boy to have been attacked by a pervert who unintentionally killed him, then devised the kidnap plot to mislead police.

One early theory suggested that Bobby had been roughed up and accidentally killed by players he had displeased in the baseball game he had umpired immediately before his disappearance. That theory was quickly discarded. Many found it difficult to understand why the kidnappers would kill the boy so soon, thereby jeopardizing their attempts to collect the ransom. Coroner Oscar Wolff believed the kidnappers unwittingly killed the boy during the struggle of capturing him, then proceeded with their original plans to collect the money.

Typewriter experts examined the ransom letter and decided it had been written on a portable Corona or Underwood. H. P. Sutton, an expert with the Royal Typewriter Company, eventually identified the machine as an Underwood. He also felt the typist did not know the touch system. "A person using the touch system strikes the keys pretty evenly, with an even pressure on the keys," he explained. "The man who wrote this letter was either a novice at typing or used two fingers. Some of the letters were punched so hard they were almost driven through the paper, while others were struck lightly or uncertainly." Other experts examined the hand lettering on the ransom letter envelope and identified it as having been done by an accomplished draftsman trying to disguise his ability by printing poorly.[10]

The police asked Chicago oculists to check their records to try to determine the owner of the horn-rim glasses found by Paul Korff near the body—an admittedly monumental and seemingly impossible undertaking. The glasses were quite small. Experts believed they might have belonged to a woman. The frames were made of Xylonite. Their tips had been chewed, indicating nervousness on the part of their owner. There did not seem to be anything particularly distinctive about them, however.

One oculist quickly reported he had prescribed just such glasses for a Mr. Johnson. "He was nervous and high strung," the oculist said. "He seemed intelligent, yet of such a nature as would stop at nothing—cruelty, crime, anything. Instinctively on looking at that face one would know the possessor capable of murder."[11]

The newspapers published photographs of the spectacles. Soon the police received a call from a telephone operator, who had seen a woman pass her at the corner of State and Madison (Chicago's busiest corner!) wearing those glasses. The telephone operator claimed she would recognize the woman if she saw her again.[12]

At noon on Friday, Richard Loeb stopped by the Zeta Beta Tau fraternity house on the University of Chicago campus to have lunch. He encountered Howard Mayer, campus correspondent for the *Evening American,* the Hearst afternoon paper. Mayer had known Loeb for about a year. Loeb had several theories about the murder which he volunteered to Mayer. Loeb said he didn't believe the kidnapper would have met Mr. Franks at the drugstore, but merely would have left word for him there to meet some other place with the money.[13]

"The kidnapper wouldn't meet a man on a busy street," Loeb insisted. "That's common sense."

Mayer agreed that Loeb had a good point.

Loeb suggested that the two investigate: "Why don't we make the rounds of some of the drugstores on Sixty-third and see if we can find one where word was left for Mr. Franks?"

Mayer hesitated. He planned to study for approaching exams. His paper had not assigned him to the story. Besides, it was raining.

Alvin Goldstein walked into the fraternity at about that time with his partner on the *Daily News,* James Mulroy. They had just come from the home of Irving Hartman, Jr., the nine-year-old student at the Harvard School, who had been walking about a hundred feet behind Bobby Franks at the time of the kidnapping. With no immediate assignments, the two young reporters had stopped by Goldstein's former fraternity house to relax.

Loeb also knew Goldstein and asked Mayer for permission to suggest his idea to canvass drugstores to them. Mayer said, go ahead. Goldstein and Mulroy immediately liked the idea, but they had no car. They finally persuaded Mayer to chauffeur them on their rounds in his father's car.

The three reporters, with Richard Loeb accompanying them, drove to Sixty-third and Stony Island. They started checking drugstores, beginning at that corner and working west. It began to rain harder. At Blackstone, Mulroy remained in the car while Goldstein went into a cigar store, Loeb and Mayer entered the drugstore on the southwest corner, one identified by its sign as Van de Bogert & Ross. They asked the black porter whether any calls had been received the day before for a Mr. Franks.

The porter said yes. There had been two calls on the public telephone. He had taken one. Percy Van de Bogert, the pharmacist, had answered the other, but nobody by the name of Franks was in the store at that time. Loeb seemed thrilled by the discovery. "You see, I told you we could find it, Howie. Now you have a scoop." He suggested to his friend that he keep the information for himself rather than tell the reporters from the *Daily News.* Mayer said it would not be fair to do that since they all had been working together. Loeb ran out to inform the other two reporters.

"This is the place!" he yelled as he approached the car. "This is the place!" They later would remember him as being ecstatic. "This is what comes from reading detective stories," Loeb boasted.

Back in the drugstore, the reporters phoned the news to their offices, then called the police. Loeb wandered over to a table and introduced himself to a pretty girl, joining her for a soda. While they waited for the police, Mulroy thought it might be a good idea to have the calls traced, if that was possible. He headed toward the telephone. Loeb followed him, grabbing him by the arm. "For God's sake," Loeb said, "don't use my name." The calls, however, could not be traced.

When Chief of Detectives Michael Hughes arrived at the drugstore, the reporters explained their discovery, then left in Mayer's car. At one point they stopped so Loeb could purchase several newspapers. He refused to let the others look at them, saying he had promised to bring all the papers to his mother. Because of her interest in the Franks case, he wanted to keep them intact.

Mulroy, seated next to Loeb in the back of the car, asked whether he had known Bobby Franks. Loeb said he had. The reporter wondered what kind of boy he had been, whether he would have struggled. Loeb glanced out the car window for a moment, then turned toward Mulroy, a slight smile on his face. "If I were going to murder anybody," he said, "I would murder just such a cocky little son of a bitch as Bobby Franks."[14]

The four drove to Furth Undertakers at 934 East Forty-seventh Street to attend the coroner's inquest. Coroner's physician Joseph

Springer, who conducted the autopsy, reported that there was a small, sharp wound three-quarters of an inch in length on the right side of the head near the hair, its upper surface flattened. Another wound, about a half inch in length, was found on the left side in the same region running longitudinally—that is, straight down the face, as if delivered by a downward blow. Springer found bruises and swelling on the left and right side of the back of the head, caused by external violence. On opening the scalp, he found a large amount of blood in the tissues underneath. On opening the forehead, he discovered that the cuts were sharp and to the bone. The two cuts to the forehead were caused by "some blunt instrument," possibly the same weapon which also caused two wounds on the back of the head.[15]

The coroner's physician also found some small scratches extending from the right shoulder to the buttocks and a few superficial scratches on the forehead. These could have been made if the body had been dragged any distance along rough ground. The face was copper-colored as far down as the mouth, caused by some irritant having been poured on it. On opening the body, Springer found dark discoloration extending down the windpipe into the right lung as far as the diaphragm, caused by absorption of fumes and suffocation. "He came to his death from an injury to the head, associated with suffocation," the coroner's physician decided. Springer also said rigor mortis had not yet set in and concluded, mistakenly, that death had occurred within two to five hours before his examination.

He and other doctors present at the inquest admitted to the assembled reporters and officials that the cause of death had baffled them most of the previous day, but finally Coroner Oscar Wolff in conference with Dr. Joseph Springer and Dr. William D. McNally decided that the boy died of suffocation, either while the abductors held their hands over his mouth or after a handkerchief had been forced down his throat. Wolff believed the boy's struggle with his captors had been violent, causing an internal hemorrhage, which accounted for discoloration of the heart, lungs, liver, and other organs. He said that the dead boy had not been abused, apparently ruling out the theory that the crime had been committed by a pervert.[16]

Wolff said in an interview with a reporter from the Chicago *Tribune:* "They must have been educated to have drafted that ransom letter in such perfect English. That would signify intelligence, a dangerous attribute in a criminal, and render him devoid of either conscience or the ability to feel remorse. Greed would be the controlling passion and, dead or alive, they intended to cash in on Robert Franks, the millionaire's son." Wolff suggested further that the murderer was probably familiar with the neighborhood where the boy had been hidden and said that a check was being made on a particular disorderly house in the vicinity. "If the killer is a degenerate, he may have frequented the house I have in mind."

At the conclusion of the coroner's inquest several reporters, including Howard Mayer, interviewed Jacob Franks in the parlor. Richard Loeb listened nearby, excited by his participation in the event. Mr. Franks told the reporters he could not imagine *who* would want to kill his son. He could not understand *why,* particularly when they could have had "everything he had" just for producing him alive.

Mayer, Goldstein, and Mulroy left the funeral home. Mayer gave a policeman friend a ride. Loeb asked the officer, who had a late edition of the *Evening American,* whether he could have the paper. It already carried a story about their discovery earlier that afternoon of the drugstore. The officer obliged him.

That night Loeb met Germaine K. Reinhard, his current girl, a pretty flapper with a slender figure whose hair was cut in a fashionable Egyptian bob. Called Patches or Bud, she was self-assured and uninhibited, considered "pretty much of a shocker." She worked as a model and secretary.

Loeb had known Patches for a few months. At first he dated her on "off" nights: Tuesdays and Thursdays. Recently, however, she had been getting the big nights: Fridays and Saturdays. They made the rounds of the smart places like the Edgewater Beach Hotel and Rainbow Gardens. Occasionally they went to a casino where Loeb played roulette. He bragged to others that he was having sexual relations with her.[17] Loeb, however, was a chronic liar and could not always be believed.

That Friday night they went dancing at the Edgewater Beach. Loeb was in good form, bubbling with charm. They stayed until the band left at midnight, hardly missing a dance, then went to a nearby waffle shop for a snack. Then he took her home.

Meanwhile, the search for the murderers of Bobby Franks continued.

6 Clues

There is no scoffing at clues and the wildest rumor, the slightest abstract occurrence, is given as much police attention as though it were the preferred theory of a master criminologist.

—Chicago Herald and Examiner[1]

Although the police were having trouble uncovering positive leads, the Chicago *Tribune* discovered that the kidnap letter mailed to Jacob Franks bore an amazing similarity to one that had appeared in a story called "The Kidnap Syndicate" in the May 3 issue of *Detective Story* magazine. The fictional kidnap letter read:

> Your wife is in our custody, and, so long as your conduct toward us warrants, she shall be treated with every courtesy and respect, and, in so far as the circumstances permit, will be made comfortable. Any change in this attitude will be the result of your own defiance to our terms which are:
>
> That you make no appeal to the police or to any private detective agency. In that event the amount stated below is automatically doubled, and, let us assure you, it will avail you nothing and only bring great anguish to yourself and your wife.
>
> Upon receipt of $50,000 in bills of $10 and $20 denominations delivered at the place, the time and under the conditions which you will receive later, Mrs. Griswold will be returned to you within a very few hours thereafter.
>
> Acceptance of these terms are to be conveyed to us as follows: You will leave your home tomorrow morning wearing a white carnation on the lapel of your coat and wear it all day.
>
> Following this we shall send you further instructions as to how, when, and where the money shall be paid.
>
> The Kidnapping Syndicate[2]

The discovery of the similarity between the real and fictional kidnap notes proved of no help in locating the killers, although it did suggest they might have been detective magazine fans.

In attempting to uncover suspects, the police focused their attention on three teachers at the Harvard School. The three included Mott Kirk Mitchell, English teacher and assistant headmaster, whom Leopold and Loeb had encountered the day after the murder; R. P. Williams, athletic instructor, who had helped Jacob Franks and Samuel Ettelson search the school building the night of Bobby's disappearance; and Walter Wilson, mathematics teacher, whom Franks had called the same night. The police could not find Wilson home late Thursday afternoon, but a *Tribune* reporter who appeared at his door later that night had no difficulty locating him.[3]

Wilson, reportedly a pock-faced virile man, greeted the *Tribune* reporter at the door dressed in a bathrobe. He appeared nervous. He admitted having taken Bobby and his brother to Riverview, a North Side amusement park, a year ago. Mr. and Mrs. Franks had been worried at the time because they had not returned until 1 A.M., but the park was on the other side of town. Wilson claimed he had no theories on who might have committed the crime.

Of the three teachers, the prime suspect was Mott Kirk Mitchell. Charles Edgar Spence, the headmaster at Harvard School, tried to defend his instructor: "He has always impressed me as being a very fine man. He was always big hearted and was interested in his work and his pupils. Why, whenever one of his boys was ill at home, he always sent flowers."

That remark hardly did much to help Mitchell, an effeminate man, whom the police suspected of homosexual tendencies. Thinking the murder the work of perverts, they focused their attention on him. While riding with Mayer, Mulroy, and Goldstein, Richard Loeb had accused Mitchell of once having tried to proposition his younger brother, Tommy. Others would make similar accusations.

The police questioned Mitchell and Williams about what they were doing at the time Bobby Frank was kidnapped, and finally decided to take them to the Wabash Avenue police station. It was then 3 A.M. The police continued to grill them until the early hours of the morning trying to break their alibis and make them confess their guilt. Eventually the police released them, telling them to report back later that day. Lieutenant Michael O'Grady admitted to a reporter from the United Press that they were being released so they might be followed.[4]

While they were detained, the police searched their rooms. Lieutenant O'Grady discovered what appeared to be four bottles of liquid poison in Williams' room. Later a United Press reporter spoke over the telephone with the instructor. Williams, born in

Cornwall, England, in 1874, had grown up in Lebanon, Ohio. He had been featured in Ripley's *Believe It or Not* for his sprinting achievements. (He once ran the 100 yard dash in 9.0 seconds—although with a running start.[5]) The athletic instructor insisted he was innocent of the crime and claimed that despite what the police had said about the contents of the four bottles, they did not contain poison. "One bottle contained tincture of iodine," he insisted, supposedly saying he used it for rubbing sore muscles. The other bottles contained other lotions that might be used by an athletic trainer. "During the time the boy is said to have been taken up in the auto, I was walking home with another student."

Mott Kirk Mitchell also defended himself. He had been home all evening in Morgan Park, a section of the city on the far South Side, entertaining friends.

The police also suspected Fred Alwood, the Harvard chemistry teacher, the only reason being that during the early stages of investigation they believed Bobby Franks had died from some sort of poison. They also sought N. C. Starren, a former Harvard instructor who had been dismissed from the school after several boys had complained about him. Supposedly he owned a Corona typewriter and wore shell-rimmed glasses.

Other teachers fanned the rumors that the murderer might be a member of the faculty. One woman teacher claimed that another teacher (unidentified in reports) was constantly talking about Robert Franks' wealth and his own need for money because of his low $160-a-month salary. A male teacher corroborated her story, claiming this individual once had remarked after Bobby Franks had passed, "His father has nothing but money. He would be good pickings for someone."[6]

Police soon released Williams but continued to hold Mitchell and Wilson. Wilson boarded at the home of Mr. and Mrs. George D. Chase of 4757 Ingleside. The Chases, as well as a sister-in-law, Florence Quigg, informed police that Wilson had been home between 3:15 and 9 P.M. and thus could not have committed the crime. The police refused to accept the alibi, however, still suspecting that one of the Harvard instructors had masterminded the murder even if he had not committed it. The telephone call to Mrs. Franks had come after nine, so conceivably Wilson might have left his boardinghouse at that time to make it.[7] Percy Van de Bogert came to the police station, as he would on several occasions during the next week, and listened to the telephone voices of the instructors but said none sounded familiar.[8]

At midnight Saturday State's Attorney Robert Crowe called a meeting of all law enforcement officials involved in the case to discuss clues. "The progress being made tonight is encouraging," he said at the meeting's end. "The process of elimination will not fail us in this case."

The investigation was being divided into areas of responsibility by Crowe. The state's attorney's office's part of the investigation would be supervised by Bert Cronson, who was still so busy he had not got home to see his wife. Lieutenant O'Grady would trace automobiles: the Winton connection. Lieutenant John Joe Farrell would consider the theory that mental defectives might have committed the crime. Sergeants William Crot and Frank Johnson would follow up kidnapping angles. Sergeants Charles Egan and Philip Moll would consider the home and past life of Jacob Franks on the theory that revenge might have been the motive. Police Chief Morgan Collins would serve as overall director.

The division of duties seemed an efficient method of tracing the murderer from an organizational standpoint, but it proved troublesome for the family of Paul Korff, the railroad signalman who had found the eyeglasses. The glasses were the main clue, and since Korff had found them, it was he to whom the police turned again when they had questions to ask. Korff had no telephone and no automobile, so every time the police wanted to question him they would send a squad car to where he lived at 6453 South Carpenter Avenue. His son Claude, who was thirteen at the time, would remember how his family would sit down to dinner only to hear a clanging bell in the distance. The police department used Cadillac squad cars painted bright orange and in lieu of a siren had a large bell mounted on the side. "We could hear them coming from blocks away," Claude Korff recalled. "Clang! Clang! Clang! Then there would be a squeal of brakes as they pulled in front of our house. My father would have to go down to the police station to answer what he considered some screwball question. They would bring him back, and he would sit down at a cold dinner, and almost before he finished it, we would hear the clang-clang-clang again. He had to go downtown again to answer questions for some other investigator. Sometimes he would go in for questioning two or three times a day. He never had a moment to relax."[9]

Claude Korff also recalled going to the movies and seeing his father appearing in the Pathé newsreels. In one shot Paul Korff, dressed nattily in his Sunday suit and tie, walked down the railroad tracks and descended into the ditch, looked around, then acted surprised as he picked up a pair of eyeglasses from the ground. It was a staged reenactment of the actual event, and young Claude thought it amusing that his father did not have on his usual work suit. "It was a big deal, though," he remembers. "It's not every day you see your father in the movies."

Korff also had his photograph taken by newspaper photographers—along with John Kaleczka and the Knitter brothers. "Four suspects in the case" read the caption under their picture.

Irving Hartman, Jr., the nine-year-old Harvard student who had been walking behind Bobby Franks at the time of the kidnapping, provided one lead. He told police how he had been strolling south on Ellis beyond Forty-eighth Street when he glanced at some tulips. By the time he looked up Bobby had vanished and a Winton automobile was speeding away. His story was partially corroborated by Philip Van de Vorrse, a chauffeur for Miss Agnes M. Fay of 4854 Ellis. Van de Vorrse reported seeing a Winton cruising near Harvard School the day before the kidnapping and also just before Bobby left the school the next day. The car was dirty gray, rusty, with the curtains drawn. It contained two men in front and a woman in the back seat.[10] As a result of these two eyewitness accounts, the police began an intensive hunt for a "ghost gray" Winton. They immediately received a series of reports about such cars.

One woman saw an auto of that description at 113th and Michigan at eight the night of the murder. There was a woman in the car and a bundle in the rear. William Lucht, an employee in the assessor's office, saw two human forms on the floor of a Winton that passed the streetcar on which he was riding at Sixty-seventh and Cottage Grove.

Frederick G. Eckstein, a watchman who worked at one of the Wolf Lake ice plants, claimed to have encountered two "suspicious-looking" strangers driving a gray Winton a week before the kidnapping on May 14. They stopped at this building, he said, and asked if they could drive through the marsh to Hegewisch. The watchman told them no, but they drove on anyway. "The driver had a prominent adam's apple and a skinny, corded neck," the watchman said. "Perhaps I could identify him." He also saw the car two other times: the following night on May 15 and the night of the kidnapping (May 21) between ten and twelve.[11]

With the car so positively identified the police seemingly had a lead to the identity of the killers more valuable than that of the glasses. The officials of the Winton Company pledged their cooperation, saying they would turn over their books listing car owners. The police were looking for a car with license plates between the years 1922 and 1924, that had "11" as its first two numbers.

Anyone owning a Winton suddenly found the eyes of all Chicagoans focused on him. A man named Joe Klon was arrested at the instigation of two citizens who reported that Klon not only owned a gray Winton, but also wore horn-rim glasses. "This has got to stop somewhere," a disgruntled Klon said after being released. "I'm going to have that car painted black or trade it. I have to wear glasses to see, but I'm doing away with these tortoiseshell rims. This is the third time I've been arrested for murder in as many days!"

Another citizen similarly picked up took his arrest more philosophically. "I expected it. Everybody with a gray car is being taken in," said Adolph Papritz, who incriminatingly was known as Johnson.[12]

Late one evening police received a tip from Waukegan, north of Chicago, that a man in a gray Winton had been spotted picking up a portable typewriter from a person in another car. Detectives dashed to Waukegan, obtained the license number of the gray Winton, and traced it to Aurora, west of Chicago. They quickly found the owner of the car: a typewriter repairman.

Of the many letters received concerning the case, several would seem significant, at least temporarily. One was addressed to Jacob Franks and threatened his daughter Josephine. Police viewed it as an attempt by the kidnapper to halt the massive manhunt, and it also strengthened their theory that Franks' son had been murdered out of revenge. Later they eventually dismissed it as a hoax. Also considered a hoax was a note found near the culvert where the body had been deposited. The note read:

> DEAR OFFICERS:
> Find me quick. I'm in danger. Find me quick.
> ROBERT FRANKS

Police Chief Morgan Collins received a letter that he thought at first might have been written by the same person who sent the ransom letter to Jacob Franks. It read:

> I am the murderer and kidnapper of the Franks boy. When you get this letter I will probably be a dead man. I intend to commit suicide. I am very sorry I did that inhumane piece of work.
> A SORRY MAN

The morning the letter arrived a man jumped in Lake Michigan and drowned. Police identified him as Sylvester Wenjenski, also known as Went, a typographer. They investigated to determine any involvement in the kidnapping but could find none. Later they also investigated a man whose body was found in a drainage canal in Cicero.

In Kenosha, Wisconsin, a well-dressed man who had stripped himself of all means of identification committed suicide by throwing himself in front of a Chicago and Northwestern train. Because he wore a watch set on Chicago time, police theorized he might have been the person who wrote the note.[13]

On the day of Bobby Franks' funeral a wreath of tiger lilies from a "Mr. Johnson" arrived at the Franks home. The police canvassed florists on the South Side and discovered that the flowers had been purchased from W. Laube at 365 West Forty-third Street. Laube described the purchaser as between thirty and thirty-two, just under six feet, and weighing about 160 pounds. The man wore horn-rim glasses, a dark overcoat, and a gray hat. "If I had only known, I could have held the buyer for the police," Laub said when he learned for whom the flowers had been intended.[14]

Later a man fitting the description given by Laube was seen at the Tyson Apartments at 4259 Grand, on the West Side of town. He entered the building and told the manager, A. L. Kaska, that he needed a room "in a hurry," because he had to "get off the street." Kaska told the man, nattily dressed in a gray felt hat and checked suit, that he could have one in half an hour, but the man could not wait that long and left.

"I wonder if you are thinking the same thing that I am?" Kaska remarked to the switchboard operator. The manager dashed into the street, but the man had vanished. Nearby the operator of a garage saw a man pass and also noted his resemblance to the person described by Laube. He watched him enter an apartment building and walk up the stairs. The tenants heard someone run through the halls. The police arrived, but the man was nowhere to be found.

Most of the similar leads and clues uncovered in the early police investigation of the Franks killing would lead, as this one had, to dead ends.

On Saturday, May 24, a letter arrived at the Morrison Hotel addressed to Morton D. Ballard, who had checked out, having failed to pay his rent.[15] The letter contained an authorization from the Rent-A-Car Company attesting to Mr. Ballard's credit and allowing him to do business without further identification. The hotel held the letter, as they had also held the book-filled suitcase.

The person who had abandoned those books, Richard Loeb, continued to follow the Franks case closely. He talked about it constantly, speculating about who might be responsible for the murder and how it had occurred with anyone who would listen to him. At dinner one night Loeb's mother suggested that whoever did the crimes should be tarred and feathered. He agreed with her. His father, who was recovering from a recent heart attack, said little about the crime.

Nathan Leopold continued to attend classes at the University of Chicago, rising each morning at seven fifteen for his eight o'clock law school class. He had altered his pattern of living slightly, however. One of his friends, Sam Goldfarb, later would recall that about the time of the murder Leopold began sitting in the rear of the classroom by himself. Previously he had sat up front.[16]

Other acquaintances of Leopold would recall attending a party with him at the time of the murder and seeing him in a gay mood. He said that if he were to be struck by lightning and die at that moment, he would not regret it. "I already have experienced everything that life has to offer," boasted Leopold.[17]

Saturday night Leopold and Loeb went to a black-and-tan nightclub at the corner of Sixty-third and Cottage Grove with a classmate from the University of Chicago, Abel Brown. (Brown and Leopold were planning to tour Europe together that summer. They had reservations to sail on the *Mauretania* in several weeks.) Leopold was with Susan Lurie; Loeb had a date with a girl named Lorraine Nathan. During the evening Brown introduced Loeb to someone else in the club. Loeb shook the person's hand, then commented, "You've just enjoyed the treat of shaking hands with a murderer." Brown considered the comment merely another example of Loeb's madcap sense of humor.[18]

7 Leads

Swift, implacable justice is the only remedy that will cure Chicago of its malady of crime.
—ROBERT E. CROWE[1]

In their continuing search for leads, the police questioned the game warden at Eggers Woods, the forest preserve on the northwest shore of Wolf Lake, asking him for names of frequent visitors to the area. The game warden mentioned the name of a young ornithologist from the University of Chicago.[2]

At 11 A.M. on Sunday, May 25, two policemen from the Eighth District station rang the bell of a home in Kenwood seeking that ornithologist. When a servant appeared at the door, one of the officers asked to see Nathan Leopold, Jr. The servant awakened young Nathan, who greeted the policemen dressed in pajamas and robe.

The policemen wanted to know if he was the Nathan Leopold who sometimes visited Wolf Lake. Leopold admitted he was. "Then I'd appreciate it if you'd accompany us to the police station for questioning," they said.

Leopold did not want to go; he had a date to meet Susan Lurie for lunch. The officers finally convinced Leopold that by bringing his car to the station, he could return home quickly.

At the station Captain Thomas C. Wolfe asked Leopold if he wore glasses. Leopold said he occasionally did, but apparently Wolfe did not insist that he produce them. The officer asked for the names of others who visited the area around Wolf Lake, particularly those who wore glasses.[3]

Leopold offered Captain Wolfe the names of several persons. He also wrote and signed an official statement:

> I have been going to the general locality of 108th Street and Avenue F for six years. I have been in the locality about five or six times this year. The last two times were Saturday, May 17th,

and Sunday, May 18th. On May 17th, George P. Lewis and I drove out through the forest preserve and down south along the east shore of Wolf Lake to about 126th Street. We then returned, arrived about 2:30 P.M. and left again about 5:00 P.M.

Sunday, May 18, at the conclusion of a day's birding, Mr. Sidney Stein, Jr., George Lewis, and I drove along the road to the forest preserve and out to May's shack between Wolf and Hyde Lakes. We arrived about 6:30 or 6:45, walked east to the ice house, back to the railroad track and left by the same road about 7:20 or 7:30.

The purpose of all these trips was the observation of birds.[4]

As they parted, Captain Wolfe apologized to Leopold for getting him out of bed. Leopold told the officer he was sorry he had not been of more help. Captain Wolfe later would say that Leopold's answers seemed so ready, and his demeanor so innocent, that he regarded him without any suspicion. Leopold's statement concerning his trips to Wolf Lake was filed and forgotten.

Captain Wolfe undoubtedly deferred to Nathan Leopold because of his wealth and social position. The Leopold family was well respected in Chicago. Louis Leopold had come to the United States from Germany. He arrived on Mackinac Island in 1843 and opened a store to trade with fishermen. His brother Henry followed him in 1844 to help in the business, and two years later another pair of Leopold brothers appeared: Aaron and Samuel. Samuel Leopold was the grandfather of Nathan F. Leopold, Jr.[5]

The Leopold brothers entered into partnership with another family of German Jews named Austrian. For many years the Austrians and Leopolds ran a chain of stores along the southern shore of Lake Superior. Samuel supervised stores in Eagle River, Eagle Harbor, and Hancock in Michigan's Upper Peninsula. Twice he was appointed postmaster. In 1867 he moved his family to Chicago, where brother Louis and Joseph Austrian had started a shipping company to haul goods to and from their stores.

Samuel Leopold became a pioneer in lake transportation, and under his direction the business expanded. By the turn of the century the company (initially the Lake Superior Peoples' Line and later the Lake Michigan & Lake Superior Transportation Company) had ten ships hauling grain, copper, and other materials as well as passengers between Chicago and Duluth, Minnesota.

Samuel and his wife, Babette, had four daughters and two sons, including Nathan F. Leopold, born in 1860 in Eagle River. At the age of sixteen, Nathan, Sr., began working in the family business. In 1892 he married Florence Foreman, member of a German

Jewish banking family. She was considered a warm and gentle person, and she spent considerable time in charitable work. "Happiness is a perfume you cannot sprinkle on others without getting a few drops on yourself," Mrs. Leopold was quoted as saying.

Nathan F. Leopold's family attained prominence and respectability within the Chicago Jewish community. One of his wife's brothers, Edwin Foreman, founded the Associated Jewish Charities. Another brother-in-law, Oscar Foreman, became head of the Illinois State Bankers' Association. His sister Helen married Henry Everett Greenebaum, who founded his own bank at age twenty-three and built it into one of the best in the city. His sister Celia married Philip D. Block, whose father founded Inland Steel.

Nathan, Sr., quiet, soft-spoken, and stocky, remained in the shipping business, helping organize the Inland Steamship Company to haul iron ore for Inland Steel. He acquired mining interests in New Mexico, as well as in the copper country of Michigan. But later he fought with the Blocks and was forced out of the business. Several lawsuits resulted.[6] In 1916 he and another brother-in-law, Leo Strauss, purchased a paper company, Morris Paper Mills. Leopold eventually bought out Strauss' interest and converted the company into a manufacturer of boxes and cartons so his sons could have a business of their own. His eldest son, Foreman M. Leopold, known as Mike, born in 1895, eventually became president of Morris Paper Mills, which prospered under his management. In addition to Mike, the Leopolds had two other sons: Samuel and Nathan, Jr.

Nathan F. Leopold, Jr., was born on November 19, 1904. He was a precocious boy who reputedly spoke his first words while only four months old. Because of his being the youngest in the family, he soon was given the nickname Babe. He was a sickly child. Medical examinations showed young Nathan had a diseased and overactive thyroid and also a disorder of the nervous control of the blood vessels. He suffered from a retrogression of the pineal glands, which by the time he was nineteen had already calcified. He also suffered from an adrenal insufficiency and would become a diabetic. Medical examiners anticipated that he probably would not live to old age.[7]

His mother had died relatively young, having suffered from ill health from the time of the birth of her youngest son. Nathan was seventeen at the time of his mother's death in 1922. It had a profound effect on him. It also meant there no longer was a woman in the house. Other than servants, only men occupied the three-story Leopold family house on the northwest corner of Forty-eighth Street and Greenwood Avenue: the father, three sons, and a cousin named Adolph Ballenberg. Mrs. Leopold's sister Mrs. Birdie Schwab (who lived nearby) supervised the household. All the men in the house worked at Morris Paper Mills, except young Nathan, who still attended school.

After leaving the police station, Leopold returned home and assured his father not to worry, explaining, "The police merely feel they have to follow every lead." He telephoned Susan Lurie, saying he would be late for their lunch date. He also phoned George Lewis to admit he had revealed Lewis' name to the police, apologizing for having done so. "By the way, George," Leopold inquired, "did you lose your glasses when you were out there last Sunday?"

Lewis said he had not.[8]

Later that afternoon Leopold picked up Susan Lurie at her North Side home, and they went to a small country inn for lunch. He ordered for both of them. After lunch they rented a canoe for a ride on the Des Plaines River. He paddled while Susan, a shy but pretty girl with bobbed dark hair and bright brown eyes, sang quietly, accompanying herself on a ukulele. The sun shimmered on the water. The afternoon was dazzling, dreamy, a hint of summer to come. He noticed a clearing in the woods and beached the canoe. They sprawled on the grass, Nathan resting his head in her lap. She had brought the book of French poetry he had given her for her birthday the week before. Susan opened the book and began reading softly. He considered it a perfect afternoon, one he long would remember.[9]

The Franks family also would remember Sunday, May 25, 1924, because it was the day they buried their son.

The funeral service, held at the Franks home, was conducted by two Christian Science readers. Hymns sung were those of Mary Baker Eddy.[10] Six motorcycle policemen guarded the procession of twenty-five cars to Rosehill Cemetery. The pallbearers were Bobby's Harvard classmates, one of them Bobby Asher. They placed the coffin covered with rosebuds in a mausoleum. The Chicago *Tribune* described the scene in its Monday morning edition: "Mrs. Franks, assisted by her daughter and son, stood for a long time at the door looking down at the coffin where her boy lay. She trembled, turned away and went back to the car where she gave way to her grief in pitiful little moans and sobs. Her daughter and husband tried to comfort her, although he too was on the verge of breaking down."[11]

One of those who was an accidental witness to the funeral procession was Richard Loeb, who passed by at the moment the coffin was being carried from the Franks home.[12]

In its editions that same Monday, the Chicago *Herald and Examiner* offered a prize to the reader who wrote the best theory as to how the crime was committed. The newspaper asked:

> How and why was Robert Franks, a fourteen-year-old heir to $4 million, killed? Police investigators may clear that up. But have you a theory now? Can you write a logical theory, telling step by step how the crime was committed and what motivated the participants? The *Herald and Examiner* will give a prize of $50 to the reader who writes the best theory. The winner also will be eligible for a share in the $10,000 reward if his theory should aid in the solution of the slaying. The judgment will take place when the slayers are apprehended, if they are, and if they are not, upon the logic and probability of credence obtained in the written theory. The theories should be written in condensed, concise form, cleanly written or typed, on one side of the paper, and should be addressed to the City Editor, *Herald and Examiner.*
>
> Somewhere in Chicago, behind a desk, or in a street car, or in a foundry, may be a keen analytical mind adapted but not trained to detection and the reconstruction of past events, as a hunter reconstructs the story of the chase from the muddy records of the spoor. It may be yours. Send in your theory.[13]

Within three days the newspaper announced that it had already received 3,000 letters.[14] People from more than forty states would eventually respond, an outpouring of interest that "exceeded the most sanguine expectations" of the newspaper.

On Monday, May 16, Nathan Leopold took his law exams, passing them easily. He asked his instructors to forward his test results to Harvard Law School, where he planned to continue his law education in the fall.[15]

Also on Monday the newspapers revealed that Gertrude Barker, a seventeen-year-old from Yakima, Washington, had disappeared the same day as Bobby Franks. According to the girl's aunt, she would have passed near the Franks home at about the time of the kidnapping on her normal route home from St. Xavier's, a Catholic girls' school. Authorities concluded that she had been apprehended to prevent her from identifying the person who had captured Bobby Franks. Efforts to find the kidnapper intensified.

The newspapers published her photo, and several people reported they might have seen Miss Barker. One described seeing a gray Winton at 113th and Michigan on May 21 at 8 P.M. The person noticed an "excited woman" and an "excited man" in the car and a bundle in the rear that might have been a "huddled human form." The excited woman might have been Miss Barker, the bundle a dead Bobby Franks. Other Winton sightings had included mention of a girl.

A farmhand reported he had been paid a dollar to help a man close the door of a freight car that contained Miss Barker. He did not know her at the time but said he recognized her after her pictures appeared in the newspapers.

The missing girl, however, miraculously appeared. She had not been kidnapped. She had been keeping house for Bert Jeffrey, who had an apartment over the stable he ran at 1030 East Forty-third Street. Miss Barker claimed to have tired of her schoolwork, so she ran away.

Police Chief Morgan Collins called, meanwhile, for help from the people of Chicago. He said:

"The person or persons who committed this crime must necessarily have smeared themselves with mud when they got down into the ditch to push the body into the pipe. Some of the mud and dirt must have been carried into the automobile. The clothes were taken from the boy's body and the persons who took them must have hidden them around near where they reside. This person or persons was doing no other work that Wednesday afternoon and was away from home part of the time Wednesday night when the body was secreted. I would ask everybody in Chicago to look around him and note whether his neighbors, friends, or acquaintances showed signs of muddy clothes, shoes, and so forth, or muddy and dirty automobiles and who was away from his usual haunts and callings Wednesday afternoon and night. All information will be treated as strictly confidential, thoroughly analyzed, and run down to the end. Some one of Chicago's three million people other than the person or persons who committed this crime must know or have some suspicion of the one who did it. I hope by this means to enlist the aid of everyone in Chicago for the solution of this crime."

A group of citizens went to the area where the body was found and reported they discovered part of a sheet and a penciled note signed "George Johnson." They said they recovered the sheet in the culvert and the note a short distance away. The note reportedly read: "You dirty skunk—George Johnson. I will get you yet." Both discoveries were taken to the temporary police headquarters at the Drake.

A cabdriver told police he had been hired at 12:30 P.M. the day of the kidnapping by two well-dressed men who had him drive to the Franks home. He said they sat in the cab for fifteen minutes, "looking over" the place, then had him drive to Sixty-third and Cottage Grove, where they got out. He identified them as being in their early twenties, with dark complexions and wearing dark clothes.

A railway switchman, John Shackleford, reported he had been driving in the area near Wolf Lake the night Bobby Franks was kidnapped when a strange car, a blue or black sedan, approached and halted in front of him. It made him suspicious, he said, so he stopped. Three men and a woman jumped out of the sedan. One of the men clutched a bundle under his arms. The four of them walked into the woods, then returned without the bundle. They got back in the car but became stuck in the mud as they had to leave. Shackleford, who had chains, towed them out. In doing so, he broke the sedan's front bumper. "They did not explain why they were there," he observed. "I am confident now the four were the slayers and that the bundle contained the boy's clothes." State's Attorney Crowe pronounced the switchman's story "an important clue." Police unsuccessfully searched for the mystery bundle and began hunting for a sedan with a broken bumper.

Simultaneously, the police combed the city, arresting known perverts and dope addicts. A theory had developed that the crime had been committed by cocaine addicts acting under the direction of a mastermind. Crowe stated, "We shall by process of elimination try to find some one user of drugs who was sufficiently well acquainted with the habits and movements of the Franks family to have contrived a kidnapping plot. That someone would not have attempted the crime himself. He would have engaged someone else to do it for him. The killing was an accident and everything that followed was undertaken to cover that accident. Dope will be found at the bottom of it all."

The police darted about the city, pursuing all leads and possibilities and making more arrests. Acting on a tip, the police corralled two men who were staying at the Sheridan Plaza Hotel. They gave their names as De Witt White, twenty-three, and Edward Wellington, thirty-eight. White identified himself as a salesman, Wellington, a chiropractor. Both admitted to being bootleggers but emphatically denied killing Bobby Franks. The police decided to detain them anyway. "These fellows have no record that we have found yet," Captain Shoemacher commented, "but they don't look good to me and they brazenly admit bootlegging. I think we'll hold them a while to do a little checking up."

Following another tip, police arrested two blacks and a white man at dawn as they sat in a dilapidated car near Forty-fourth and Cottage Grove. As police approached, the men tried to conceal a bundle containing a dismantled typewriter. They also had some white powder, a withdrawal slip from the South Side Trust and Savings Bank, and a collection of papers, some of which had been partially burned.

The police seized three sisters one morning. They were packing after having been out all night. One of the sisters, Mrs. Lillian Borena, had told her neighbors that she knew all about the Franks case. When the police arrived, she quickly tore up a letter and attempted to throw it away, but the officers collected the fragments. They also recovered a thick package of newspaper clippings about the murder and a hammer that Mrs. Borena had put in her luggage.

All suspects were duly questioned—and eventually released.

The police continued, however, to hold the two Harvard instructors, Walter Wilson and Mott Kirk Mitchell, applying pressure to make them confess. Wilson later would claim that two officers held him while another worked him over with a rubber hose. Another time, he asserted, a policeman grabbed him by the throat and told him he would be strangled—just the way he strangled Bobby Franks—unless he confessed. He also charged that an officer threatened to push him out a fifteenth-floor window if he didn't tell the truth.[16]

Wilson retained some of his composure, but Mott Kirk Mitchell wilted under the pressure. One of the pupils at the Harvard School accused Mitchell of attacking him, and Mitchell did confess—although not the Franks murder. A spokesman for the state's attorney's office issued a statement authorized by Robert Crowe: "Mitchell confessed he had been guilty of numerous acts of perversion, and that he had been a psychiatric case since the age of seven."[17]

Monday afternoon shortly before five, attorneys Charles S. Wharton and Otis F. Glenn appeared in the court of Judge Frederick De Young to apply for a writ of habeas corpus to free Wilson and Mitchell. The judge said that because of other engagements, he would be unable to give them a hearing and asked them to return the following afternoon. The police took handwriting samples of the two instructors so that expert James Ennis could compare their writing with that on the kidnap letters. The comparisons proved inconclusive.[18]

Tuesday the attorneys appeared again in court, still seeking a writ of habeas corpus. "Our investigations have reached a critical stage," Assistant State's Attorney Gorman pleaded with the judge.

He asked that the case be continued until the next day. Over the vigorous objections of Wharton and Glenn, the judge granted a continuance.

Chief of Detectives Michael Hughes admitted to reporters afterward that they probably would have to book Wilson and Mitchell for murder on Wednesday or free them. Despite having no concrete evidence against either of the instructors, Hughes considered them the most likely prospects. It had been learned that Mitchell had a semiannual interest payment on his mortgage for his Morgan Park home due the day of the kidnapping. The mortgage was for $10,000, the same sum asked for in the kidnap note.[19]

Squads of policemen began excavating the sewer in front of Mitchell's home, hoping to find some of the still-missing clothing from the dead boy. Samuel Ettelson, meanwhile, supposedly told reporters that one instructor at Harvard had killed Robert Franks, while another wrote the polished note demanding $10,000. The quote didn't mention either Mitchell or Wilson, and the following day Ettelson vigorously denied having made the statement.

On Wednesday, May 28, Richard Loeb appeared at the weekly luncheon for the Phi chapter members of Zeta Beta Tau. "Where were you last week?" Max Schrayer asked. Loeb claimed he was busy at the university.

Reporter Alvin Goldstein was at the meeting, which was well attended because of interest in the Franks case. Schrayer remembered everyone's quizzing him about the progress of the investigation. Loeb offered Goldstein his latest theories on the case and suggested they check some more drugstores, this time on Fifty-fifth Street, to see if anyone remembered persons making suspicious telephone calls. Goldstein had learned to pay attention to Loeb's hunches. The two left before lunch ended.[20]

That same noon Nathan Leopold lunched with Susan Lurie. They met on campus and walked to the Cinderella Tearoom nearby. En route Leopold purchased two newspapers, giving one to Susan. At the table, he opened his newspaper. "Let's see what has happened in the Franks case." Susan remembered him smiling, almost laughing, as he said it. When Leopold came to an item about an anonymous letter calling Jacob Franks a "dirty skunk," threatening the life of his daughter, he chuckled, commenting, "That's a good one."

Susan joked with him, suggesting lightly that he should go to the police, confess to the crime, and collect the $16,000 reward. Leopold laughed.[21]

That same day Leopold visited his criminal law professor, Ernst W. Puttkammer, and asked some questions about murder and kidnapping, mentioning the Franks case as an illustration. Puttkammer had attended the Harvard School, and they discussed whether Mott Kirk Mitchell, the prime suspect of the three teachers who had been arrested, might have been involved in the crime.

"It's inconceivable to me," Puttkammer said.

"I don't know," argued Leopold. "I'm not sure. You know Mitchell has made improper suggestions to several boys!"

"Are you certain? That kind of rumor always springs up when someone is arrested in a case like this."

"He made that sort of proposition to my brother. That's reliable enough, isn't it?"

The conversation drifted to other subjects. As Leopold rose to leave, they discussed Mitchell again. "I would like to see them get him," Leopold said at the door. "But I don't say he did it."[22]

That afternoon attorneys Wharton and Glenn once more attempted to obtain a writ of habeas corpus for their clients, Wilson and Mitchell. Several of Wilson's college classmates appeared to testify to his good behavior, as did the Chases, at whose home he roomed.

Without any concrete evidence against the two instructors, Crowe found it difficult to justify their continued detention. Nevertheless, he appeared personally before the court to ask for more time.

"It is true we are holding them with no warrant," Crowe admitted. "They are so held because we think they can help us in clearing up this murder. Our investigation is not complete."

Glenn told the judge, "I don't think anything need be said in view of what you have just heard."

Judge De Young apparently finally agreed. "Under the law there is only one thing I can do. There is no escape from it."

"You might continue the case," Crowe suggested.

But the judge refused to do so. "The relators are dismissed." Wilson left the courtroom accompanied by Mr. and Mrs. Chase and his college classmates, pausing only long enough to make a purchase from a girl selling poppies on the steps of the courthouse. Detectives continued to trail the two suspects, hoping they might uncover some fresh clue that would crack the case.[23]

Several weeks later the Harvard School announced that Mitchell had decided not to remain at Harvard. Wilson left the city in June, supposedly broken by his ordeal, although he returned to teach at the school the following year.[24] According to a later rumor, unconfirmed, one of the pair had to be committed to a mental institution.[25]

After almost a week of ceaseless activity, the police had made no headway. All their leads had proved worthless. The crime remained a puzzle. Hope for an early solution faded.

One possible suspect had been Freddie Gresheimer, a ne'er-do-well brother-in-law of Jacob Franks, who had vanished. He became the object of an intense search that ended when police officials discovered that Gresheimer had been in the San Diego County Jail since February 26.[26]

Eugenie Dennis, a psychic from Kansas, had a vision while discussing the case in Detroit. She telegrammed her vision to the frustrated Chicago police. As she saw it, the crime had been committed by two men and a woman with red hair. She said, "One of the men is in custody now and the other one, the light-complexioned one—he has a sort of gray streak in his hair—is hiding. He's in a big place, not a hotel, somewhere in the southwest part of the city. The Franks boy's clothes are there. At least some of them are hidden there."

Samuel Ettelson was astounded by Miss Dennis's account, especially by her statement that a red-haired woman was involved. "She was seen hanging around Ellis between Forty-eighth and Forty-ninth streets the afternoon Robert was kidnapped," he said. "We're looking now for a certain man who can identify her. If we find him, we've solved the case."

The man was found, Robert Orr, gardener for Charles H. Swift, of the meat-packing Swifts, who lived across the street from the Harvard School. Orr said Mrs. Charles Chase had been loitering on Ellis about the time young Franks was kidnapped and had been peering under the shrubbery at the Swift house. According to Orr, she told him she had lost her cat and offered him $5 if he could find it. Mrs. Chase denied any connection with the murder. Her husband acknowledged that they owned a cat. They had lost him on May 5.[27]

The next day Chicago police learned that Charles Heath, a druggist who had eluded them, had been discovered in Louisville. Earlier he had attempted to poison himself, a highly suspicious act since it happened at the time Chief Collins received the letter from a writer admitting to being the Franks killer and saying he planned to take his life. Police had held Heath under surveillance at Mercy Hospital in Chicago, but somehow he had escaped.

In Louisville, Heath was found unconscious in his room at the Coker Hotel. He had taken an overdose of drugs. Police discovered a batch of clippings about the Franks case stuffed in his pockets. They rushed him from the hotel to a hospital. "This certainly looks good," Collins said after learning of Heath's capture. "I'll have a conference with my officers at once and probably will send detectives to Louisville." Detectives were sent to Louisville, but Heath never regained consciousness. He died several days later.[28]

On Thursday, May 29, the *Tribune* carried an interview with Jacob Franks, whom they described as a "gray ghost" who hovered around the corridors of the Criminal Court's Building, wearing glasses, a black derby hat, and smoking cigarettes. "They tell me I bear up under the strain very well," Franks told a *Tribune* reporter, "but they do not know. I know it will not help that baby any to keep brooding. I try to put things out of my mind, but they come back. My wife keeps showing me pictures of him. And I lie awake until dawn thinking about it all, thinking about that baby." Franks admitted that Bobby had not liked it when his parents continued to refer to him as their baby, even at age fourteen.

"I have been racking my brains trying to think who they could be," theorized Franks. "Robert knew the murderers. That is why they choked him to death. And since Robert knew them, I must know them. Whoever it was who kidnapped my boy did so for the ransom. It was the money they were after. They knew his habits. They knew my love for him, and that I would willingly pay any sum to have him back. But Robert recognized them, and they grew afraid, and strangled him."[29]

Later that same day the police finally made their first major breakthrough in the Bobby Franks murder case.

8 Alibis

The man who kills is society's greatest enemy. He has set up his own law. He is an anarchist—the foe of all civilized government. If anarchy is not to be met with anarchy, it must be met by the laws, and these laws must be enforced.

—Robert E. Crowe[1]

"By phone, telegraph, and cable, patrons of Almer Coe & Company order eyeglasses, and have them delivered with signal promptness," read one of that firm's newspaper advertisements in 1924. "An efficient system of records makes it possible to duplicate any lenses that have been made or registered in the Almer Coe stores. If you bring in your present lenses, or even the broken pieces, they may be duplicated at once or at any time in the future and delivered to you anywhere, at your order."

The ad concluded with the slogan "Always the best in quality but never higher in price."

Among the patrons of Almer Coe the previous fall was a wealthy young patient of Dr. Emil Deutsch. The patient had gone to Dr. Deutsch because of eyestrain-induced headaches. The optometrist prescribed eyeglasses to be used while reading, so the wealthy young patient took his prescription to the firm that promised in its ads "always the best in quality" without realizing that that same firm's similarly advertised "efficient system of records" would bring the Chicago police to his door.

When State's Attorney Crowe delegated assignments, he asked his assistant Joseph P. Savage to trace the eyeglasses discovered by Paul Korff. Savage began by showing the eyeglasses to several optical companies. The eyeglasses proved much easier to trace than most people might have suspected. Almer Coe easily identified the glasses as having been purchased at one of their stores by a faint diamond mark on the lenses. The firm checked the prescription and found it to be common, as were the Xylonite frames. The hinges on the frames, however, had been made by the Bobrow Optical Company of Brooklyn. Almer Coe, in fact, was the only Chicago distributor carrying the Bobrow line.[2]

After checking 54,000 records, Almer Coe discovered it had

sold three pairs of the Bobrow horn-rims. One of the purchasers had been an attorney named Jerome Frank (later a successful judge and author of the book *Courts on Trial).*[3] A woman bought the second pair. The final pair had been sold for $11.50 in November, 1923, to Nathan F. Leopold, Jr.

State's Attorney Crowe directed that Leopold be picked up for questioning. (He may not yet have realized that Captain Wolfe had spoken to Leopold the previous Sunday about the young man's birding visits to Wolf Lake.) Knowing Leopold came from a socially prominent family, Crowe found it difficult to believe he could be implicated in the crime. The state's attorney ordered Leopold brought to a room at the LaSalle Hotel instead of to his office, where reporters would spot him. Crowe wanted to spare him and his family any notoriety if it became known he was being questioned about the Franks case. The treatment afforded Leopold would differ strikingly from the way police had handled school teachers Wilson and Mitchell.

Thus at 2:30 P.M. on May 29, eight days minus a few hours after the death of Bobby Franks, Detective Sergeants William Crot and Frank A. Johnson arrived at the Leopold home. Nathan Leopold was in his room preparing for one of his bird classes when the detectives arrived. Elizabeth Sattler, the maid, answered the door and ushered the detectives, dressed inconspicuously in street clothes, into the library. Within a few minutes, Leopold appeared to ask what they wanted.[4]

Crot and Johnson introduced themselves and said the state's attorney wanted to talk to him.

"Johnson?" Leopold asked, puzzled. "Let me see your credentials."

The detectives produced identification. Leopold examined the credentials and laughed, saying he thought the person might be the "Johnson" involved in the Franks case. The detectives seemed unamused. They wanted to know if Leopold wore glasses. He said he did but did not have them on at the moment. "Did you lose your glasses?" asked the detectives.

"No."

"Have you got them?"

"No, but I'm sure they're around here someplace."

The detectives did not want to take time for a search at that moment and asked Leopold to accompany them downtown. He protested, saying he had to meet a bird class at U-High. The detectives said the class would have to wait. Leopold called the school, apologized, and postponed his class. The detectives escorted him to their car and they drove downtown.

Robert E. Crowe, the state's attorney, a jut-jawed, forty-five-year-old Irishman with a shock of brown hair and thick glasses, awaited their arrival in Room 1618 of the LaSalle Hotel. For the past week Crowe had devoted almost all his time and the time of his key assistants to the Franks case. "Fighting Bob" Crowe, as the pugnacious Republican liked to call himself, was up for reelection in the fall and knew it would help his campaign to crack the case.

Born in Peoria in 1879, he attended Yale Law School, graduated in 1901, and opened an office in Chicago.[5] He became assistant state's attorney eight years later, then chief justice of the Circuit, and later Criminal, Court. In 1919 as judge, he sentenced a janitor, Thomas R. Fitzgerald, to hanging for assaulting and strangling a five-year-old girl named Janet Wilkinson.

He proudly referred to that decision while running for election as state's attorney the following year. His slogan was: "To make life, children, and property safe in Cook County, vote for Judge Robert E. Crowe."[6] He also listed, among his accomplishments, the development of a special calendar for murder cases so that within two months thirteen men were convicted by juries and sentenced to death, while twenty others received long penitentiary sentences.

Early in his political career, Crowe allied himself with Chicago's notorious Mayor "Big Bill" Thompson. Thompson aided him in his run for state's attorney in 1920. (The Chicago *Daily News* noted that in a survey of forty underworld hangouts along one street, thirty-five contained Crowe literature.[7]) But in one of the many scraps that would mark his career, Crowe clashed with the mayor's police chief, Charlie Fitzmorris. Crowe wanted to close some vice dives, Fitzmorris told him to mind his own business, so Crowe broke with the Thompson machine. Thompson called Crowe a rat; Crowe in turn labeled Thompson a skunk. The Republican Party split into rival factions.[8]

The state's attorney soon appeared before a grand jury with evidence that Fred Lundin, the mayor's mentor, and other Thompson men had defrauded the school board. The day before the return of indictments Big Bill bowed out as a candidate for a third term in the 1923 election. Thompson would return to run successfully for mayor in 1927, and Crowe would support him, but in 1924 Bob Crowe was driving hard to establish himself as the Republican boss of Cook County. The Franks case presented him not only with a great challenge, but also with a priceless opportunity. The eyes of all Chicagoans were focused on the Bobby Franks case.

Crowe greeted Leopold when the young man was escorted into

his suite. He began to question him. He showed him the glasses, asking whether they might be his. "They look like mine," Leopold replied. "If I didn't know mine were at home, I'd suspect they were."

"Yours are at home?"

"Yes."

The questioning continued. Crowe decided eventually that one way to determine whether Leopold owned a similar pair would be for him to produce them. Sergeants Crot and Johnson drove Leopold back to his home. James Gortland, secretary to Chief of Detectives Hughes, accompanied them. It was nearly 6 P.M. when the group arrived again at the Leopold home.[9]

Nathan's twenty-nine-year-old brother Mike greeted them. Nathan explained his problem, and they began to search the house for the glasses. Everybody helped, but the glasses could not be found. "This place where they found the body is right where you often go looking for birds," Mike finally suggested. "Maybe you dropped them out there without noticing it."

Nathan Leopold conceded that might be so.

Mike suggested they contact Sam Ettelson. Ettelson lived in the neighborhood, knew the Leopold family, and had known Nathan since childhood.

Mike called, learned Ettelson was visiting Jacob Franks, and the two Leopold brothers and the three detectives went to the Franks home to see him. They entered the parlor, where Ettelson and Franks were talking. Nathan Leopold, Jr., who had not known Bobby Franks, met Jacob Franks for the first time. The group spoke with Ettelson, and Mike explained that his brother must have dropped his glasses near the culvert on one of his birding trips; he had been in the area only three days before the kidnapping.

The story did seem plausible. Ettelson apparently could not picture young Leopold as being involved in the crime and believed him merely a victim of circumstances. Nevertheless, he said Leopold should go with the detectives to clear the matter. He politely informed Detective Crot, however, that he would take an interest, as an attorney, in what happened: "You tell Mr. Crowe to let me know before he makes another move."

Mike telephoned home that he would be unable to attend a dinner party that night, then accompanied his brother and the officers back to the LaSalle Hotel. Mike waited in an anteroom while two of Crowe's assistants, Joseph Savage and John Sbarbaro, questioned his younger brother.

At this point Leopold acknowledged ownership of the glasses.

He stated he probably lost them while birding near Wolf Lake on Saturday or Sunday, May 17 and 18.[10] He said that on Saturday he visited the area with George Lewis. They noticed three Wilson's phalaropes, a bird rarely seen near Chicago. He wanted to get a specimen for his collection, so he left Lewis watching the birds and ran to a nearby shack to pick up a gun and boots. Lewis dashed up to the shack within a few minutes to say the birds had flown west over the railroad tracks into Hyde Lake. The two ornithologists ran through the marsh to the lake, and Leopold fired three times, "missing like a tenderfoot," before the gun jammed and the birds flew away. He failed to notice the place where Bobby Franks' body later would be found.

"I didn't know there was a pipe there," he claimed. "I knew that this little channel flowed from one side of the tracks to the other. I knew, of course, just where it went under, but I never bothered to investigate to see how it got under there."

Leopold said he visited the same area with Lewis and Sidney Stein on Sunday. They spent the entire day at the marsh, from five in the morning until seven thirty that night. Again, he did not particularly notice the culvert but thought he must have been right next to it at the end of the day.

He told his questioners, "At 7:30, after parking our car and going east almost to the Indiana line, we got up on the railroad tracks and tried to see some ducks which we thought might be in Hyde Lake, but the sun was so low it made it almost impossible to see at that angle. I should say I passed right over the pipe, probably about on a level with it. I would guess, oh, within ten or twenty feet of it anyhow and Saturday it was the same, because a path leads almost from the drain."

Savage and Sbarbaro inquired why he had his glasses with him. Leopold earlier had said he had not worn them for months.

Nathan Leopold had a ready answer: After he stopped using them, he lazily left them in a breast pocket of his coat. Perhaps he would have removed the glasses had the suit been sent out for cleaning, but normally he wore his worst clothes for birding, not having them cleaned for months. He had not missed the glasses because he had not been wearing them and did not even know he had them with him.

"How do you think you lost the glasses?" asked Savage.

Leopold responded that they probably fell out when he stumbled.

"When did that occur?" Savage probed. "Saturday or Sunday?"

"Usually, I have a pretty good memory, but I don't recall having fallen at that spot on Saturday or Sunday," Leopold answered.

"May I add that Saturday, you must remember, I had a pair of large rubber boots that didn't fit me, and therefore the probability of my stumbling was greater than if I had been just normal."

Savage handed him the pair of glasses, asked him to put them in his breast pocket, and demonstrate how he tripped and lost them.

Leopold did so, falling to the floor. The glasses remained in his coat. He repeated the performance, again stumbling to the floor. The result was the same: The glasses did not fall out.

The interrogators asked him to remove his coat, lay it on the floor, then pick it up from the hem. As he did, the glasses tumbled onto the carpet. The demonstration proved little. Leopold could have lost the glasses in that manner on his weekend birding trips or on the night the body was stuffed in the culvert. Savage and Sbarbaro undoubtedly realized this. After finally achieving a key breakthrough and identifying the owner of the glasses, they found that he had visited the spot, apparently innocently, days before the crime. Nevertheless, they proceeded with their questions.

The two questioners asked Leopold where he had been the day of the murder and what he had been doing. At first Leopold could not remember. Nothing distinguished that particular day from any other. So much had been happening. He had been very busy, particularly with his exams. It was very difficult to pinpoint his actions on any one day. He had no special reason to do so, until now.

For more than an hour they tried to get him to remember as best he could. Their questioning grew sharper. They became annoyed at his vagueness, his uncertainty, about a day on which someone that lived only a half mile from him had been kidnapped and killed. It really was not that long ago: just eight days, barely more than a week. Surely, he had some idea. Then gradually, piece by piece, he began to reconstruct what he had done. Leopold was somewhat embarrassed, as the story unfolded, but he did tell all. It involved a close friend of his, Richard Loeb, and he had not wanted to involve him with the police.

He and Richard Loeb ate lunch that day at Marshall Field's Grill. Afterward they drove in his car to Lincoln Park on the North Side to look for birds. They brought a flask of gin and a flask of scotch along and drank through the afternoon. "I should say we might have been a little bit happy by the end of the day, but neither of us was drunk," Leopold admitted. Loeb's father disapproved of his son's drinking. Because of the alcohol smell on their breath, they decided to eat dinner before going home. They ate at the Cocoanut Grove Restaurant at Fifty-third and Ellis.

After dinner they cruised along Sixty-third Street, looking for "a couple of girls with nothing to do." They soon found two and coaxed them into going for a ride. They drove the girls around for a while; then he stopped at a drugstore at Sixty-third and Stony Island to call his aunt and uncle, who were at his house. He was supposed to drive them home. He told them he would be delayed about forty-five minutes. After that they went to Jackson Park and stopped the car. "Then we sat around and had a few drinks. We couldn't come to an agreement with the girls. They wouldn't come across, so we asked them to leave. And then we went home."

Sbarbaro and Savage questioned him about details of the story. The names of the girls? He knew them only as Edna and Mae. He could not recall their last names. Their descriptions? They were between nineteen and twenty-two, rather short. Exactly where did they pick them up? What time was it? How far did the girls permit them to go? Did they kiss them? Where did they drop them off? What time was that? Where did they go in Lincoln Park? What birds did they see? What did they have for dinner? How much did they have to drink? What time did they get back to his house? Who was there? How late did Mr. Leopold stay up? What time did he take Loeb home? The names of the girls again? Was he sure he didn't know their surnames? The questioners wanted all the information they could get, every last detail, so the story could be checked as closely as possible.

As the hours passed, Savage and Sbarbaro alternated in the interrogation. At times one remained in the room, while the other stepped outside. Leopold remained unruffled. He did not appear concerned. He answered each question willingly and without hesitation. His alibi seemed a bit implausible, but it could be true.

Asked about his background, Leopold told Sbarbaro that he had attended both the University of Michigan and the University of Chicago. He had started at Chicago but after one year transferred to Michigan. A year later he transferred back to Chicago, where he was graduated in March, 1923, with a bachelor of philosophy degree. He had done graduate work for a short time in comparative philology before he began law school last fall.

He had studied a number of languages. He knew fifteen, including Greek, Russian, Hawaiian, Latin, and Sanskrit, and could speak five in addition to English fairly fluently. "My father thought I was mature enough to study just exactly what I pleased, and that was my choice," he answered when asked about his studies. He had been interested in ornithology since the age of five and had been teaching the subject to various groups of women and children for the past three years.

Yes, he owned a typewriter, a Hammond Multiplex which he had used for a few years, but he did not have a portable. Earlier he had owned a Corona. Years earlier he might have had an Oliver. He typed fairly well and easily could have typed the ransom letter.

Yes, he had read the letter in the newspapers and agreed the person who drafted it must have had considerable education, though not necessarily a college degree. A high school graduate or a man with some college training could have written the letter. He himself, "no doubt," could have composed it.

Yes, he noticed the writer used certain legal phrases and thought he probably had some knowledge of the law, but it was hard to say how much.

No, he did not know Bobby Franks, but he knew of his family. Young Franks had not been interested in ornithology. He would have known if he had been, because most of the boys at Harvard with an interest in the subject were his students. He agreed it was "extremely likely" that the kidnapper was familiar with the area where the body was concealed; otherwise, he would never have been able to find the culvert at night. It appeared he knew exactly where he was taking the body.

Yes, he had been following the case closely in the newspapers, ever since he first heard about it a week ago. He had read "everything I could find" about the case. He knew that a pair of horn-rim glasses had been found near the body, had seen pictures of them in the papers. But he "never for a moment" thought they might be his until he was picked up and questioned.

No, he had no religious beliefs. He did not believe in God. When you die, "your ashes return to ashes and dust to dust." There is no life after death, no hope of reward, or threat of punishment. And there is no difference between the death of a man and the death of a dog. "It's all the same." He had felt that way for seven or eight years, since the age of eleven.

Yes, he knew who Sappho was, "a great Greek writer of old, a homosexualist." Yes, a pervert. He knew of the work of Havelock Ellis, the English author who wrote about sex. Yes, Oscar Wilde also was a pervert. As a matter of fact, he himself had studied perversion, though he never practiced it. He described his abandoned plans to translate the works of an Italian author who treated thirty-two forms of perversion. He never had committed any acts of perversion with Richard Loeb, although it was true he had written him a letter the previous fall in which he seemingly had referred to his friend and himself as "cocksuckers."[11]

Leopold had written the letter because the two had a misunderstanding, he insisted, and he was referring to a rumor which had been spread about them three years before. Because of the rumor, he and Dick had been very careful for more than a year not to be alone, always to have someone with them wherever they went. But the rumor was malicious and unfounded, started by a mutual enemy.

Yes, their friends called each other names. No, they didn't resent it. "Certainly not," explained Leopold. "Hasn't an old friend ever come up to you and slapped you on the back and said, How are you, you old son of a bitch, or you old bastard, or something like that?"

While the questioning continued, Detective Sergeants William Crot and Frank A. Johnson returned for a third time to the Leopold home with brother Mike, arriving around twelve-thirty in the morning. They had come to get the Hammond typewriter which Leopold admitted owning to compare its typing with that of the ransom note. While there, the detectives made another thorough search of the house. Sergeant Crot found a leather glass case with the Almer Coe label. In the attic study where Leopold kept his bird specimens, the detectives found a large can of ether, a bottle of strychnine, and a bottle of arsenic. Those materials seemed incriminating but actually were part of Leopold's ornithological equipment. They picked up different copies of typewriting and handwriting. They searched Leopold's red Willys-Knight and found in the trunk a copy of the Chicago *Daily News,* dated April 24, 1924, with a string tied around it. The detectives suspected it to be some sort of cudgel. In the side pocket of the left door of the car were several Illinois Central and Michigan Central timetables. Searching a bookcase, Sergeant Johnson found a copy of Robert Lewis Stevenson's *Kidnapped,* which he considered suspicious.

Back at the LaSalle Hotel, the interrogators pressed on, probing from all angles, testing the suspect, hunting for inconsistencies, leads, attempting to break down his alibi, trying to measure the man and evaluate his statements. More questions. More answers. Food and drinks arrived at the room. There was a short break while all parties ate. Then more questions, more answers. It was getting stuffy. The questioners began to tire. Nathan Leopold, however, seemed to maintain his alertness despite lack of sleep. Shortly before 4 A.M. Savage and Sbarbaro called a halt for the night. Leopold, weary but unshaken in his story, was taken to the central police station for a rest before the interrogation could be resumed. Mike was sitting in the anteroom, still waiting, and saw his brother led away.

Earlier that same day a letter arrived at the Hotel Trenier at

409 Oakwood Boulevard addressed to Mr. Morton D. Ballard. As had been the case with the previous letter sent to the Hotel Morrison, it contained an identity card from the Rent-A-Car Company stating that hereafter Mr. Ballard would be permitted to rent cars without having to produce further references. The hotel clerk, Frank B. Tuttle, as instructed by a man he thought to be Mr. Ballard, held the letter for the time when it might be claimed.[12] It would be several days before he realized the true identity of Morton D. Ballard.

9 Interrogation

I am talking now about the cold-blooded type of crime, the like of which has never been seen before, by two young men who pushed all decency aside and committed the crime of the century.

—Benjamin Adamowski[1]

On Thursday afternoon, shortly after they arrested Nathan Leopold, the police also picked up Richard Loeb and brought him to another room in the LaSalle Hotel for questioning. State's Attorney Crowe wanted to ask Loeb, as Leopold's constant companion, about their whereabouts on Wednesday, May 21. Loeb insisted he could not remember. "That was more than a week ago," he claimed. The interrogators refused to accept his excuse and questioned him into the early hours of the morning.[2]

Friday at 7 A.M. the telephone awakened Howard Mayer. His editor at the *Evening American* directed him to go to the Loeb mansion—fast! Mayer quickly dressed and arrived by seven fifteen, in time to see Richard Loeb stepping out of a police car, a Marmon. The police were planning to search his home. Loeb greeted Mayer jovially: "You know, Howie, I've always wanted to ride in one of these Marmons, and now I'm getting my ride."[3]

During the visit to the Loeb mansion, Mayer spoke with Sergeant Johnson, who told him Loeb and his friend Nathan Leopold were suspected of the murder of Bobby Franks. "That's impossible," Mayer snorted.

"No, it's not," said the police officer. "They're telling different stories. These boys are in deep trouble." According to Johnson, Loeb admitted being with Leopold the afternoon of the murder but claimed he had left him around dinnertime. Leopold, however, was telling a story about their picking up some girls and going to a Chinese restaurant near the university.

Mayer figured that this was what he might expect from Leopold and Loeb: Leopold, being brash and arrogant, telling it all; Loeb, being more circumspect, more the gentleman, not wanting to provide details of such an escapade. After the police left with Loeb, Mayer decided to go downtown to see if he could help his two friends establish their innocence.

Leopold had been moved from the LaSalle Hotel to Crowe's offices at the Criminal Courts Building, a massive white stone edifice at the corner of Dearborn and Hubbard, just north of the Chicago River. Mayer was given a chance to talk with Nathan Leopold. "I'm telling the truth, Howie," Leopold insisted. He admitted to Mayer that the glasses found at the murder site had been his but had been dropped during one of his birding trips to Wolf Lake the previous weekend. Leopold repeated that he and Loeb had been out with some girls the night of the murder.

"That's not Dick's story," Mayer told him. "According to the police, he can't recall what happened that night."

Leopold looked up at Mayer imploringly. "Tell him to remember what happened on Wednesday. He'll understand."

Mayer apparently did not realize he was being used. He left Leopold and asked if he might see Loeb. Loeb, however, was now being held incommunicado at another police station at Forty-eighth and Wabash. Mayer contacted the coroner's physician, Dr. Joseph Springer, who happened to be a friend of his parents. The reporter explained that he believed Loeb innocent and wanted to give him a message from Leopold. Springer unwittingly agreed to help. He soon appeared in a police car and took Mayer to where Loeb was being held. Mayer was allowed to enter his cell. He told Loeb, "Dick, if you want to clear yourself, you've got to tell the truth."

Loeb appeared hesitant. "I don't want to talk at this time."

Mayer, still believing Loeb's hesitancy stemmed from a reluctance to confess a drunken orgy with two cheap girls, tried to persuade his friend to talk. The reporter explained that Leopold had sent a message.

Loeb suddenly became alert. "What did he say, Howie?"

"Babe said to tell the truth about the two girls. Tell the police what you did with them. You can't get in any worse trouble than you are now. He said you'd understand."

Loeb nodded. He suggested that Mayer ask the questioners to return.

Howard Mayer still had not awakened to the fact that he was being used to break the police security surrounding the two accused men. He left, walking out with Dr. Joseph Springer. The coroner's physician shook his head. "That boy's no murderer."

Mayer decided to call Loeb's older brother, Allan, and tell him what was happening. He suggested that Allan get a lawyer. Allan brushed him off, saying he understood the situation and would take care of matters.

After the reporter left, John Sbarbaro returned to Loeb's cell, accompanied by Bert Cronson. Loeb began telling the same story that Leopold had used, saying that because of being under the influence of alcohol, he could not remember many details. Mayer, because of his friendship with Loeb, never used what he heard during the interview as a news story, but later said, "In general, what he said followed Leopold's story very closely."

Loeb's story only reinforced the growing belief among the state's attorney's staff that maybe they had two innocent men.

James Doherty, a reporter for the Chicago *Tribune,* recalled seeing Leopold while he was being held. "I sat down with him and he very quickly displayed his superior education—in a nice way. I thought I would outfox him. I called a friend, a distinguished psychiatrist, who talked to Leopold. His conclusion: 'This boy certainly had no part in the murder.' He later denied having made such a statement, but I remember it."[4]

During the day Crowe allowed Leopold and Loeb to speak with members of their families. He offered them privacy, but they asked him to stay. That evening he took the suspects and his staff to the Drake Hotel for dinner. "The bill for our small party there alone was $102," Crowe recalled, "so it may be that they got the best of everything."[5]

After their dinner at the Drake, the two men were returned to the state's attorney's office. Later that evening Leopold again chatted with newspapermen. "I don't blame the police for holding me," he told a *Tribune* reporter. "I was at the culvert the Saturday and Sunday before the glasses were found and it is quite possible I lost my glasses there. I'm sorry this happened only because it will worry my family. But I'll certainly be glad to do what I can to help the police."[6]

Reporters peppered him with questions about literature, philosophy, politics, art, sports. Leopold would puff on a cigarette, pause, then issue a decisive pronouncement in stilted legal language, occasionally flashing a sardonic smile.

Some of his favorite authors, he informed reporters, were Wilde, Nietzsche, Haeckel, and Epicurus, but "I won't add Socrates, for I never thought such a lot of him."

Leopold claimed to be a profound student of the past, particularly the sixteenth century, the "wickedest century the world has ever known." He denied being a radical, Communist, or Socialist: "On questions of reform my temperature is decidedly normal."

Though an admitted atheist, he did not recommend that view for everyone. A belief in God was a good thing to keep the common people under control, to keep them in their place.

The reporters, scribbling rapidly in their notebooks, took down every word, mesmerized by the young man.

They also spoke that same day with Nathan F. Leopold, Sr., who told the press he believed his son blameless. "While it is a terrible ordeal both to my boy and myself to have him under suspicion," he explained, "our attitude will be one of helping the investigation rather than retarding it. And even though my son is subjected to hardships, he should be willing to make sacrifices, and I am also willing for the sake of justice and truth until the authorities are thoroughly satisfied that this supposed clue is groundless. I probably could get my boy out on a writ of habeas corpus, but there is no need for that sort of technical trickery. The suggestion that he had anything to do with this case is too absurd to merit comment."

Richard Loeb's father, having been confined to his bed with heart trouble for nearly two weeks, did not talk to reporters. Mrs. Loeb expressed confidence in her son. "The affair will so easily straighten itself out."

Meanwhile, Goldstein and Mulroy, the two *Daily News* reporters, continued their own investigation. They learned about Leopold's membership in a small study group of freshman law students who met once a week to work at his house and prepared "dope sheets" to help them prepare for exams. The reporters decided to obtain some copies of these dope sheets, which were typed on Leopold's typewriter, to compare the typing with that of the ransom letter sent to Mr. Franks.[7]

About nine thirty on Friday morning, Goldstein visited study group member Arnold Maremont at his home, 5216 Ingleside. Maremont had been studying for exams late the night before, and Goldstein had to rouse him from bed. The reporter explained his mission. Maremont said he understood the ransom letter had been written on a portable Underwood or Corona; Leopold usually used a large Hammond.

Nevertheless, he offered the reporter copies of his notes. In looking at them, Goldstein noticed that some appeared to have been typed on a different machine from the others.

Then Maremont remembered. On one occasion in early February they had worked in the library on the first floor instead of in Nathan's study, where he kept his Hammond. On that day there was a different typewriter, a portable, in the corner of the room on the desk near the window. Nathan had got the typewriter and put it on the card table where they were working. He used it to prepare the dope sheets that night.[8]

Goldstein could barely restrain his excitement. He felt certain he had stumbled onto an important break in the case. He borrowed some of Maremont's notes, thanked the student for his help, and hurried away, hardly daring to believe that, after only two years as a reporter, he might have uncovered evidence that could crack a sensational murder case. He brought the notes to the *Daily News* The newspaper contacted H. P. Sutton, the expert employed by the Royal Typewriter Company. Sutton examined some of the specimens and decided they had come from the same machine on which the ransom note had been written. In comparing dope sheet notes with the kidnap note, he pointed out that on both the *t* printed heavy at the top and light at the bottom. The *m* and *t* were somewhat slanted. The *i* was slightly twisted. The typewriter had fingers with prints just like a human being, and they pointed at Nathan Leopold![9]

The *Daily News* presented State's Attorney Robert E. Crowe with the evidence it had uncovered. He summoned the members of Leopold's study group: Maurice Shanberg, Howard Obendorf, Lester Abelson, and Maremont. Savage questioned them in the presence of Leopold. Each of the students remembered using a portable typewriter at one of their sessions, and each stated it did not belong to him. Leopold, who still denied ownership of a portable, interrogated his friends. When did they see the machine? Where was it? Was he, Leopold, in the room at the time they entered and saw the machine? Were they positive one of them didn't bring it? At one point Leopold turned to Shanberg and asserted that the typewriter belonged to him, that he had brought it with him. Shanberg angrily denied ownership of the machine.[10]

Finally, Leopold conceded that they may have used a portable typewriter, but he denied ownership of it. He suggested it belonged to his friend Leon Mandel. Mandel unfortunately was away in Europe. When Leopold and Mandel worked together on some Italian translations, they had used Mandel's portable. If so, Leopold acknowledged, the machine still would be at his house.

So Savage, Captain Shoemacher, and several other detectives returned with Leopold to his house on another search.[11] They could not find the portable typewriter. They knocked on the door of the maid's room and awakened Elizabeth Sattler. The night before, she had told Shoemacher about the presence in the house several weeks ago of a portable machine. She repeated her statement.

"I think you must be mistaken, Elizabeth," said Leopold, troubled.

Shoemacher asked, "You are sure about that, are you, Elizabeth?"

"Yes," she replied, embarrassed at the trouble she was causing.

The group returned to the state's attorney's office, where Leopold continued to proclaim his innocence, as did Loeb. The questioning continued with no further progress. Despite the feeling on the part of Crowe's men that they had the guilty persons, their evidence was mainly circumstantial. The glasses belonged to Leopold, but he could have lost them on another trip to Wolf Lake. The typewriter seemed to have been Leopold's, but they could not locate it.

As the night continued, Crowe called his staff into his office and admitted that their interrogation had stalled. "We can't hold these boys any longer," he said. "They've got wealthy parents. We've got to either book them or release them." The state's attorney set midnight as a deadline, adding that the investigation would continue whether they held Leopold and Loeb or not.

While Crowe talked, his assistant Bert Cronson pondered the alibi offered by the suspects. He suggested finally, "I'd like to talk to the Leopold chauffeur."[12]

"What do you think you'll find out?" asked Crowe.

"I don't know," Cronson admitted. "I'd just like to talk to him."

Cronson delegated a policeman to visit the Leopold home and bring the chauffeur in for questioning, then forgot his request as he became involved once again in the interrogation of the two suspects. The midnight deadline was imminent when Cronson realized he still had not seen the chauffeur. "He's been sitting out in the waiting room for the last two hours," a policeman admitted.

"Why didn't somebody tell me?" The assistant state's attorney sighed.

Cronson asked Sven Englund to step into his office. He began questioning the chauffeur about the events of May 21. Englund remembered the day clearly and told how Leopold arrived home that afternoon driving his red Willys-Knight. He wanted his brakes repaired, because they had been squeaking. Englund took the car into the garage and began working on it.

"Then when you were finished, they took the car and left?" suggested the assistant state's attorney.

"Oh, no," replied the chauffeur. "I worked on the car all day. They used some other machine."

Cronson's eyes widened. Leopold and Loeb claimed they had

used Leopold's car to pick up the two girls. Yet, according to Englund, the car remained in the garage.

"Are you sure of the date?" asked Cronson.

"Very sure," the chauffeur responded. "My wife had to take my daughter to the doctor because of a cold."

"Can you prove it?"

"Well, we were given a prescription."

The assistant state's attorney asked Sven Englund to call home and ask his wife to find the prescription. She did. "What is the date on it?" Cronson had him ask her. Mrs. Englund identified the date as May 21. Englund said further that Leopold's Willys-Knight remained in the garage until late that evening.[13]

Cronson walked into Crowe's office and told his boss that the suspects had lied about using Leopold's car that day. Crowe asked Cronson how he knew. When Cronson explained, the state's attorney smacked his palms with delight. "God damn! I think we've got them!"

Later Crowe would kid Bert Cronson about the prescription that had provided the corroborating link in the chauffeur's testimony. Sven Englund was Swedish, and Bert Cronson's wife also happened to be Swedish. "When you are a Swede you're bound to remember when you spend money on your daughter," insisted Bob Crowe.[14]

He told his assistants to intensify their questioning. The midnight deadline passed and was forgotten. Sbarbaro interrogated Loeb in one room. Savage and Hughes grilled Leopold in another. Sbarbaro urged Loeb to confess for the sake of his conscience, that there was no point in pretending anymore, because they knew he and Leopold were guilty. They did not go birding in Lincoln Park. They had not picked up two girls in Jackson Park. There had been no two girls; just one small boy, Bobby Franks. Their alibi had been revealed as a lie because Leopold's car was in the garage that afternoon.

Loeb looked up and frowned. "Who told you that?"

"Englund," Sbarbaro replied.

Loeb trembled. His face became ashen. He slumped back in his chair. He tried to speak, but the words stuck in his throat. Sbarbaro handed him a glass of water. Loeb gulped it down. "My God!" Loeb said at last, his voice barely audible. "He told you that?"

"Yes, he did."

"Shit!" said Loeb, and asked for a cigarette.

For a moment, Loeb said nothing. Blankly, he gazed out the window. He shivered, although it was hot in the room. Then he turned to Sbarbaro and slowly said he would like to see State's Attorney Crowe.

It was 1:40 A.M. on Saturday morning, May 31. Sbarbaro summoned Crowe to the interrogation room. For more than an hour, while court reporter E. M. Allen recorded his words, Loeb talked, confessing an entirely new version of the events of ten days previous.

Savage and Hughes, however, found Nathan Leopold still unwilling to admit anything. He stoutly maintained his innocence despite what Englund had said. The chauffeur had the date wrong, Leopold insisted, because he and Loeb had used his car on May 21. He recalled the time when Englund fixed the brakes, but that was another occasion. He was positive. The Englunds simply had confused the days. The prescription with that date on it meant nothing.

It was almost 4 A.M. when Crowe walked into the room. He was having a difficult time suppressing his excitement. "Well," said the state's attorney, "your pal has just confessed, told us the whole story."[15]

Leopold laughed. "Do you think I'm stupid? I'm not going to believe that. Anyhow, it's impossible. There's nothing to confess."

Crowe smiled. He had good reason to do so. After more than a week of frustration following frustration, after groveling for scraps of information which proved useless, after seeing lead after lead disintegrate, Crowe had the killers in his grasp—and he could prove it. Tomorrow the entire world would know their identity, as well as the identity of those responsible for their capture. The Bobby Franks case had become a *cause célèbre*, and when the public learned that the boy had been killed by his neighbors, sons of wealthy and prominent families, and most astounding, the *reason* the crime had been committed, the public would be shocked. What had been until this moment a good local story would soon transfix the attention of the entire world.

Crowe moved forward, his jaw raised, his teeth clenched in a tight smile. He removed his thick glasses and carefully polished them with a handkerchief from his pocket. Replacing the glasses he fixed his gaze on Nathan F. Leopold, Jr. "What about your getting the other automobile at the Rent-A-Car Company because your car was red and too conspicuous? What about the false identity at the Morrison Hotel? What about waiting in hiding on Ingleside Avenue for Johnny Levinson to appear? Your friend says you planned the kidnapping. He says you were the one who killed Bobby Franks."

Leopold flushed with anger. Only Dick Loeb could have furnished that sort of information. No one else knew, no one! Leopold snuffed out a cigarette and lit another. Crowe filled in more details. Leopold listened intently.

He began to talk at four twenty in the morning, making an official statement before E. M. Allen, the same court reporter who previously recorded the confession of Richard Loeb. Leopold talked for an hour.[16]

Outside the office, word spread that the case was near solution. Reporters had been gathering through the night, including Goldstein and Mulroy, who later won a Pulitzer Prize for their work, the first received by the Chicago *Daily News.* Howard Mayer also waited anxiously, and fearfully. He had begun to realize how he had been used as a dupe to transmit information from one accused killer to the other. Rumors spread that Loeb and Leopold were confessing, but no official announcement was given.

More newsmen arrived as morning approached. Several card games were started. Reporters clustered in groups, discussing the case, swapping stories, joking. Some sat on the floor and dozed; others read the papers. Time passed slowly. Maybe it was a false alarm. Perhaps the two youths were not confessing after all. The group finally decided that someone should peek through the transom of Crowe's office. They chose Jack McPhaul, a copyboy for the *Herald and Examiner.* Several reporters boosted him up to where he could look into the room. He saw Leopold and Loeb seated at a long table with prosecutors and policemen ranged about them. Leopold was talking, but McPhaul could not hear anything. He climbed down, and they continued to wait.[17]

10 Confession

The crime, in its commission and in its background, has features that are quite beyond anything in my experience or knowledge of the literature. There seems to have been so little normal motivation, the matter was so long planned, so unfeelingly carried out.

—Dr. William Healy[1]

While the reporters waited impatiently, the two killers were having their confessions read back to them by court reporter E. M. Allen.[2] They listened intently, and angrily, as they heard each other's words. Listening with them were State's Attorney Robert E. Crowe, his staff, and assorted members of the police who had helped break the case. It struck Crowe at this point how callously and unfeelingly the two had decided that a person must die. Nathan Leopold in his confession spoke of the "problem" of getting a victim to kill. "This was left undecided until the day," Leopold admitted. "We decided to pick the most likely-looking subject that came our way." Richard Loeb commented in his version: "The plan was broached by Nathan Leopold, who suggested that as a means of having a great deal of excitement, together with getting quite a sum of money."

As the state's attorney heard those words repeated almost impassively by the court reporter, he felt a shudder run down his spine.

The pair had been planning the kidnapping for some time: Leopold said since November, Loeb admitted to at least two months of preparation. The identity of the victim had been one of their early considerations. The two met frequently to discuss who it might be. It almost became a game with them—pick the victim—and added pleasure to their meetings and conversations.

Gradually they developed the qualifications for their candidate. His father would have to be wealthy, capable of paying a sizable ransom without flinching. He should be someone they already knew, since it would be easier to approach an acquaintance and lure him, or her, into their trap. The fact that they would have to kill the kidnap victim to prevent their being identified did not seem to bother them.

At one stage they discussed kidnapping—and murdering—their own fathers but vetoed the idea not from filial devotion, but rather from the fact that it would cause them to be under too close scrutiny. They had to be free to collect the ransom. For that same reason they also discarded the idea of kidnapping Loeb's younger brother, Tommy. (Loeb later claimed he liked his younger brother and had not been serious in suggesting him.[3])

Leopold at one point proposed that they kidnap a girl and rape her the way he had imagined German soldiers attacked defenseless French girls. Loeb said no, girls were more closely watched than boys and would be more difficult to capture.

Loeb suggested their mutual friend Dick Rubel. He fantasized himself being asked to serve as a pallbearer, giving him a tremendous thrill. But Rubel's father reportedly was a tightwad and might not post the ransom to redeem his son. They considered Hamlin Buchman, an older boy who had worked summers in Charlevoix, Michigan, where the Loebs had a summer home. Several years before, Buchman had spread rumors about the relationship between Leopold and Loeb. They could murder him for revenge. They eventually decided that because of his size, Buchman might be difficult to subdue. Loeb was slender and at five feet ten inches was only slightly taller than average. Leopold was two or three inches shorter and disdained physical activity.

It would be easier to kidnap someone younger and smaller, such as Billy Deutsch, grandson of Julius Rosenwald, the head of Sears, Roebuck & Company. But Loeb's father was a Sears vice-president, second-in-command to Rosenwald. They did not want to injure the family business. They considered Irving Hartman, Jr., whose father owned Hartman Furniture Company, and Johnny Levinson, whose father was a prominent attorney. Other candidates included the sons of Clarence Coleman and Walter Baer.

Leopold and Loeb eventually decided not to choose a victim. They would allow the victim to choose himself—by his presence. They would go to the Harvard School on May 21, 1924, and grab whoever could be most easily nabbed, whoever offered the easiest and most convenient target. They would wait until the last second before making the decision as to who would die.

State's Attorney Crowe, in taking Leopold's confession, had questioned him on this point. "Your original plan," Crowe asked, "when you were thinking it out as late as last November, Nathan, did you have anyone at that time that was to be the victim?"

"Nobody in particular," Leopold replied.

Crowe probed further: "When was the plan finally effected whereby you considered the Franks boy?"

"When we saw him—by pure accident."

It was perhaps this single element that elevated their deed to crime of the century. The sheer randomness of it. The fact that the identity of the victim was decreed by chance, much the way chance dictates which slot on the roulette wheel the ball drops into. As the facts of the Franks case eventually became clear, every mother in the city of Chicago would realize that she too had been playing roulette over the life of her son with Leopold and Loeb.

But the plot was not hatched as an act of violence. The choice of the victim, the kidnapping, the murder were merely incidental to the scheme in which the ransom would be collected. This was the part of the game that appealed most to Loeb. Leopold in his confession also conceded that the ransom collection scheme was their most difficult problem. "We had several dozen different plans," he admitted, "all of which were not so good for one reason or another. Finally we hit upon the plan of having money thrown from a moving train after the train had passed a given landmark."

The pair spent several afternoons over a period of weeks during early 1924 walking railroad tracks outside the city, seeking a pickup point. Finally, they discarded the idea of collecting the ransom in the country, deciding instead on the middle of the city, where they could lose themselves more easily. They chose a site near the Champion Manufacturing Company, a large red-brick factory on the east side of the Illinois Central tracks at Seventy-fourth Street.

They rolled up a newspaper, tying it to simulate a package of money. (This was the "cudgel" found by Sergeants Crot and Johnson in the trunk of Leopold's car.) On several occasions Loeb purchased a train ticket, boarded a train heading south, and moved to the rear platform to hurl the "ransom" toward his waiting friend. Leopold picked up the simulated ransom package, then drove to meet Loeb at the next train stop. Once a conductor told Loeb that he could not go back onto the rear platform, but they proceeded with their rehearsals anyway.[4] Finally, they determined that if the person with the ransom package counted five as he passed the Champion factory, the package would land near Seventy-fifth Street, where it quickly could be retrieved.

Collecting money thrown from a moving train offered the plotters some security, but not enough. If the victim's father received his instructions too soon before the ransom attempt, he might alert the police, who could move in to encircle the kidnappers. So Leopold and Loeb devised a number of fail-safe devices with split-second timing which not only would confuse efforts to trace them, but also increased the complexity of the plot and their pleasure from the challenge of plotting it.

Ultimately they decided to notify the victim's father by telephone that his son had been kidnapped. They then could warn him not to contact the police or risk having the boy killed. They next would send instructions by mail telling him that to secure his son's release, he should obtain a sum of money in small denominations and used bills. He should place the money in a cigar box, wrap the box securely, then await further instructions. Finally, they would call and direct him to a trash can on which he would find an envelope starting him on a bizarre scavenger hunt.

The envelope would contain a note directing the victim's father to a drugstore near the Illinois Central's Woodlawn station. They would call him at a public booth at the store and instruct him to go quickly to the station and board a certain train which would be due in a few minutes. He would be given just enough time to make the train so that he would not be able to notify the police. Once aboard the train, he would find a note in the telegraph box of the last car giving him instructions to throw the ransom from the train. Leopold and Loeb would watch the collection point through field glasses to see that the money was properly thrown. If the train was late or slowed down (suggesting that the police had been notified), they would have time to escape.[5]

If they succeeded in collecting the ransom, they planned to keep it hidden in a safe-deposit box. None of it would be spent in Chicago, at least not for a year. Loeb planned to go to Mexico, where he thought it might be safe to use some of the money. Leopold decided that he might spend some in Europe. They figured on a straight fifty-fifty split.[6]

Since they planned to kill the victim, they needed to dispose of the body quickly. They could hardly drive around with him in the trunk of their car until after the ransom had been collected. They had to select some area where the body would not immediately be found and identified. Leopold knew of the perfect spot.

Early that spring he drove Loeb to 108th and Avenue F and to a dirt road that led into the wilderness area near Wolf Lake. They parked their car and walked along the Pennsylvania railroad tracks, scouting for a place to hide a body. They could have selected almost any place within the desolate area to dig a hole for burial, but they chose a culvert running beneath the tracks. Water flowed through the culvert from one lake to the other. Leopold had never noticed the culvert during any of his birding trips, so he assumed that no one else knew of the culvert's existence either. It would save them the bother of digging a grave.

Other details needed to be arranged, specifically the kidnap vehicle. They did not want to use one of their cars for fear it might later be identified. Leopold's Willys-Knight was bright red, much too noticeable; Loeb's car was being repaired following an accident. They could have stolen a car, but to keep it for the necessary length of time would involve too much additional risk. Finally, they decided to rent a car, using a fictitious name, and further disguise it by covering the license plate.

Thus came into being Morton D. Ballard, the Peoria salesman who opened a checking account at the Hyde Park Bank, checked into the Morrison Hotel with a suitcase full of books, then went to the Rent-A-Car office with $400 in his pocket (in case they needed a deposit) and the number of a public telephone where the other waited to provide a phony recommendation.

(A case study in how news gets distorted grew out of this incident. Immediately after the identity of the killers was made public, the United Press released a story saying that several weeks before the murder Leopold traveled to Peoria and deposited $400 in a bank as a getaway fund. Loeb reportedly deposited a similar sum in a bank in Morris, Illinois. The confusion probably arose because the fictitious "Ballard" supposedly came from *Peoria* and stayed at the *Morrison.* Or it may have been due to the Leopold family ownership of the Morris Paper Company. The Peoria *Evening Star* initially printed the item on faith, then, checking with local banks, discovered no accounts under the name "Ballard." Loeb eventually admitted neither of them had gone anywhere near Peoria.[7])

Several days before the planned kidnapping the pair composed kidnap letters to be mailed to the victim's father, to be attached to the trash can, and to be placed in the telegraph box of the train. They purchased ordinary stationery from a store near the University of Chicago. On the kidnap eve, Leopold typed the letters on a portable typewriter in his study.

While Leopold confessed, Crowe quizzed him about the preparation of the kidnap note. "Now this letter, Nathan, that you had already prepared in an envelope without any address on it, you had prepared that letter some time prior to that time?"

"Yes," Leopold responded.

"Just when did you prepare that letter?"

"Four or five days ahead of time."

"No one, definitely, as to whom you were going to send it to?"

"No, just 'dear sir.' "

"But the address you placed on later on?"

"Yes. It was not addressed inside. It was just 'dear sir.' "

Dear sir—an anonymous greeting to the father of a victim that had not even been selected at the time it had been written.

On May 21, 1924, after his morning classes at the university,

Leopold met Loeb at eleven o'clock, and they drove downtown to rent a car, a blue Willys-Knight. They returned to the South Side, stopping to eat and also to purchase some additional items for their plot: rope, hydrochloric acid. They raised the side curtains of the rental car. They stopped at the Leopold home and left Leopold's red Willys-Knight in custody of Sven Englund, who planned to repair the brakes. They drove to Jackson Park, where they waited for school to let out. In his confession, Loeb claimed that Leopold wrapped adhesive tape around the blade of a chisel; Leopold claimed Loeb wound the tape.

At two thirty they returned to the vicinity of the Harvard School, parking their car on Ingleside Avenue. Loeb, apparently unworried that he might be seen and remembered, wandered over to the school playground and talked to Johnny Levinson, instructor J. T. Seass, and his brother Tommy. Then Nathan Leopold, standing across the street, whistled for him to return. (One of the puzzles of the Leopold and Loeb case is why J. T. Seass did not inform police that Richard Loeb was prowling around the Harvard schoolyard only hours before the kidnapping. Reportedly police questioned all members of the Harvard faculty, but if Seass told then, Loeb never was brought in for questioning. Johnny Levinson could also have led police to Loeb had he been questioned.)

Loeb crossed the street, and the two started back through the alley to Ingleside. "There are some children playing on Ingleside who might be possible prospects," Leopold explained to his partner. The two watched the children for a while, considered them, then rejected them as potential victims. They continued walking west to Drexel Boulevard, where they spotted another group of children playing in a vacant lot at the southwest corner of Forty-ninth and Drexel. Johnny Levinson was in this group.

They returned to their car and drove down Drexel, heading south on the opposite side of the street from where the group of boys were playing but found it hard to recognize anybody from a moving car. They parked the Willys-Knight again and walked down Fiftieth Street and through an alley to a point where they could observe the baseball game. They still could not get close enough to see anything without risking being seen.

Leopold suggested they go to his home and get a pair of field glasses he used for watching birds. While he did, Loeb went to a drugstore at the corner of Forty-seventh and Ellis and looked up Johnny Levinson's address in a telephone directory. Levinson lived at Fortieth and Lake Park, nearly two miles away. Loeb thought Levinson might be interested in a ride home. "I incidentally bought a couple of packages of Dentyne chewing gum at the drugstore," said Loeb in his confession.

He left the drugstore and met Leopold. They returned to the alley, where they used the field glasses to watch the children playing baseball. They considered several others in the group, in addition to Levinson, as kidnap victims, but Johnny still looked like the best prospect.

Time passed; the group of boys at Forty-ninth and Drexel continued their game. At about four thirty, with the game still in progress, Leopold and Loeb noticed Johnny Levinson and several others walk down the alley out of sight. They became concerned when Levinson and the boys failed to return. "I went to look for him in the alley," stated Loeb, "but didn't see him. I saw Seass leaving with the rest of his children."

Leopold and Loeb drove to Forty-eighth and Greenwood, where another group of boys were playing across from Leopold's home. The group included the sons of Clarence Coleman and Walter Baer. The pair watched them for several minutes. Then they drove north on Lake Park to Fortieth Street, where Levinson lived, to see if they could locate Johnny in his neighborhood. Unfortunately, he was nowhere around. They wondered what had happened to him. Maybe someone in the family had picked him up by car. He could have gone to the home of one of his friends. They did not know when, or *if*, he might reappear.

Leopold and Loeb returned to Kenwood, driving south on Greenwood Avenue past the group playing near the Leopold home. They continued to Forty-ninth Street, where they turned right, then turned right again at the next corner to return north on Ellis Avenue. It was getting late, near dinnertime. If they did not find a victim soon they would have to abandon their plot—at least for that day. And if they did not consummate their plot that day, who knows when they might find the time—or the courage—to try again.

At that moment, shortly after 5 P.M. on Wednesday, May 21, 1924, they saw another boy.

"We caught a glimpse of Robert Franks coming south on the west side of Ellis Avenue," confessed Richard Loeb. "As we passed him he was just coming across us past Forty-eighth Street. We turned down Forty-eighth Street and turned the car around."

Nathan Leopold also described the scene. "About the time that we had turned around and given Robert a chance to get a sufficient distance from another pedestrian on the street, he was almost at Forty-ninth Street. It was here that we picked him up."

The other pedestrian apparently was Irving Hartman, Jr., who had been one of their earlier candidates. Either they did not recognize him or discarded him in favor of Bobby Franks. Hartman stopped and bent to examine some flowers, so did not notice the dark blue Willys-Knight that passed him.

In their confessions the two kidnappers differed in their version of the next several minutes.

"Richard was acquainted with Robert and asked him to come over to our car for a moment," Leopold told Crowe. "This occurred near Forty-ninth and Ellis Avenue. Robert came over to the car, was introduced to me, and Richard asked him if he did not want to help him."

"Richard who?" inquired the state's attorney, seeking an exact identification for the record.

"Richard Loeb. He replied no, but Richard said, well, come in a minute. I want to ask you about a certain tennis racket. After he had gotten in, I stepped on the gas, proceeded south on Ellis Avenue to Fiftieth Street. In the meantime Richard asked Robert if he minded if we took him around the block to which Robert said no. As soon as we turned the corner, Richard placed his one hand over Robert's mouth to stifle his outcry, with his right beating him on the head several times with his chisel, especially prepared for the purpose. The boy did not succumb as readily as we had believed, so for fear of being observed Richard seized him and pulled him into the back seat. Here he forced a cloth into his mouth. Apparently the boy died instantly by suffocation shortly thereafter."

Loeb, however, insisted he had been driving, not Leopold, and it was Leopold, not he, who struck the death blow. "At this time I was driving," said Loeb in describing the last few minutes of Bobby Franks' life. "Leopold got in the back seat. I drove the car then south on Ellis parallel to where young Franks was, stopped the car, and while remaining in my seat opened the front door and called to Franks that I would give him a ride home. He said, no, he would just as soon walk, but I told him that I would like to talk with him about a tennis racket, so he got in the car. We proceeded south on Ellis Avenue, turned east on Fiftieth Street, and just after we turned off of Ellis Avenue, Leopold grabbed his mouth and hit him over the head with a chisel. I believe he hit him several times. I do not know the exact number. He began to bleed and was not entirely conscious. He was moaning." Loeb further described how Leopold grabbed Franks and carried him over the back of the front seat and threw him on a rug in the car. "He then took one of the gags and gagged him by sticking it down his throat, I believe."

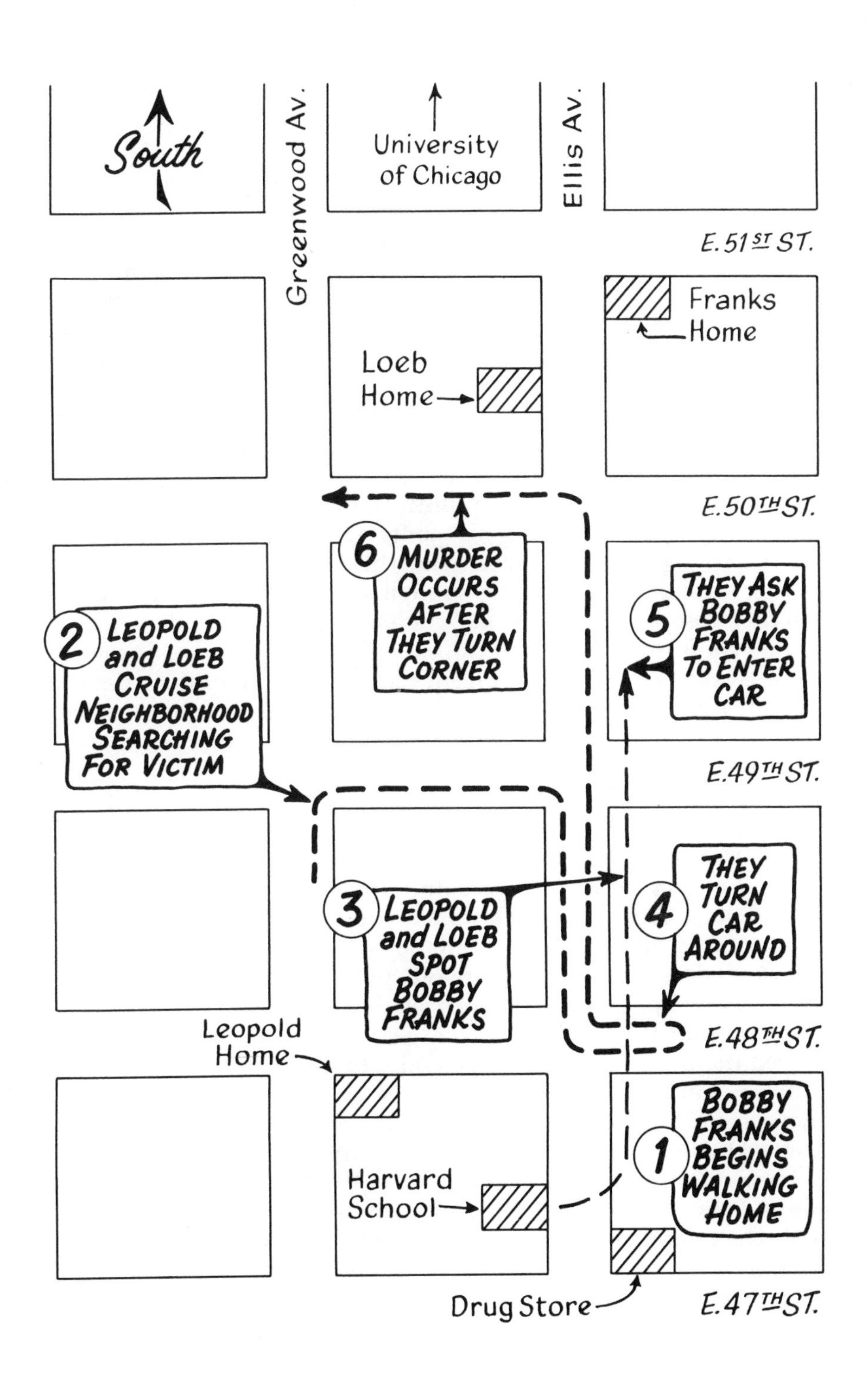
South
Greenwood Av.
University of Chicago
Ellis Av.
E. 51ST ST.
Franks Home
Loeb Home
E. 50TH ST.
6 MURDER OCCURS AFTER THEY TURN CORNER
5 THEY ASK BOBBY FRANKS TO ENTER CAR
2 LEOPOLD and LOEB CRUISE NEIGHBORHOOD SEARCHING FOR VICTIM
E. 49TH ST.
3 LEOPOLD and LOEB SPOT BOBBY FRANKS
4 THEY TURN CAR AROUND
Leopold Home
E. 48TH ST.
1 BOBBY FRANKS BEGINS WALKING HOME
Harvard School
Drug Store
E. 47TH ST.

The question of which one of the boys told the truth about the killing of Bobby Franks would become one of the puzzles of the Leopold and Loeb case.

With Bobby Franks now lying motionless on the floor of their rented car, Leopold and Loeb continued driving east, passed through the viaduct under the Illinois Central tracks, and entered Jackson Park. They drove south toward Indiana, crossing the Calumet River, following U.S. Highway 12 as it twisted south and east along the edge of Lake Michigan.

They reached Indiana near the city of Hammond, and as they drove along Michigan City Road through a wide fallow prairie that had not yet been claimed by man, they slowed the car and pulled off on the shoulder. It was quiet. They were alone.

Looking both directions along the road to see that no cars were approaching, they began to pull the clothing off Bobby Franks' limp body. "We removed his pants and stockings," confessed Loeb. Leopold mentioned removing the same items of clothing, as well as his shoes. "We did this so we might be saved the trouble of too much undressing later on," claimed Loeb. Before they drove off, they left several items of clothing: the shoes on one side of the road, the belt on the other. The question of whether or not Bobby Franks was still alive, maybe even still conscious, at the time the clothes were stripped from his body would become another one of the puzzles of the Leopold and Loeb case.

They began cruising in their rented car, killing time, waiting for night to fall. When they came to a hot dog stand at the corner of Fifteenth Street and Calumet Avenue in Hammond, the Dew Drop Inn, they decided to get some sandwiches. Leopold went inside to place the order. Loeb waited in the car. Leopold returned with hot dogs and root beers, and they sat eating.

Eventually it grew dark enough to proceed. They drove to 108th Street and Avenue F and took the dirt road into the marshlands around Wolf Lake. "Having arrived at our destination, we placed the body in the robe, carried it to the culvert where it was found," admitted Leopold. "Here we completed the disrobing, then in an attempt to render identification more difficult, we poured hydrochloric acid over the face and body."

Loeb claimed that this was when they both realized that Bobby Franks was already dead. He insisted in his confession: "Our original scheme had been to etherize the body to death. The scheme for etherizing him originated through Leopold, who evidently has some knowledge of such things, and he said that would be the easiest way of putting him to death, and the least messy."

But the pair had abandoned plans to etherize Franks, deciding to strangle him with the rope purchased the day before.

State's Attorney Crowe attempted to pry more details out of Leopold. "Just how did you place the body in the drainpipe; just explain how you placed the body there?"

"I think it was head first," Leopold replied. "I had a pair of rubber boots." He said they were his own boots, and he had brought them from his home. He sat down on the railroad embankment, donned the boots, stepped into the water, and took the feet of the body while Loeb took the head. He shoved the body into the culvert.

"Was it much of a job, Nathan, to push the body in?"

"At first I thought it was rather doubtful whether it would fit at all, but after it once started, it was not hard at all."

"Then after you pushed it in as far as you could with your hands, Nathan, you used your feet and pushed it up further?"

"Yes."

Leopold climbed out of the water and sat down on the embankment to remove the boots. He was concerned because when the body struck the water, it had splashed his clothes. Loeb went to the other end of the culvert, where he could more easily get at the water. "I washed my hands," said Loeb, "which had become bloody through carrying the body." Loeb had also got some blood on his clothes, as had Leopold.

With their task completed they prepared to go. "We gathered up all the clothes, placed them in the robe, and apparently at this point the glasses fell from my pocket," said Leopold. He would claim that his partner handed him his jacket upside down, causing the glasses to fall unnoticed onto the ground. While carrying the robe and clothes back to their automobile, one of the stockings also dropped from the bundle.

As they drove past 104th Street en route home, they stopped the car by a roadhouse. Leopold went inside to telephone his father and explain he had been delayed and would be late. His father told him his aunt and uncle were visiting and suggested he could give them a ride home. Leopold agreed to do so as soon as he returned.

The pair stopped again at a drugstore at 6734 Stony Island Avenue. They went in and bought a slug for the telephone. In the phone book they located the name of Jacob Franks, his address, and his phone number. They wrote Franks' name and address on the envelope containing the kidnap note. Leopold picked up the phone and asked the operator for Drexel 8938.

They waited for the operator to make the connection, but there was a delay. Fearful that the call was being traced, they hung up. The call, however, was not being traced. Only a handful of people at that time knew of Bobby Franks' disappearance. None dared suspect what actually had happened.

The pair returned to the car and continued their journey. Passing a mailbox on Fifty-fifth Street, they halted again and dropped the kidnap letter through the slot. The letter, with six two-cent postage stamps attached, was marked "special." The word was underlined.

At a drugstore at 1200 East Forty-seventh Street, they decided to telephone the Franks home again. This time the connection was made more promptly. "I spoke to Mrs. Franks," admitted Leopold, "and told her that my name was George Johnson, that her boy had been kidnapped but was safe, and that further instructions would follow."

They next drove to Loeb's house. "When you got to Dick's house, what did you do?" Crowe inquired.

"We went in the basement and burned the clothes," Leopold responded. "We intended burning the robe, but it was too large to fit in and would have caused an awful stench."

They hid the robe in some bushes near the Loeb greenhouse, then attempted to remove the bloodstains from the floor of the rental car, using soap and water. Because of the late hour, they worked only briefly, then drove to Leopold's home. They parked the blue Willys-Knight to the north of his driveway and went inside. Leopold's aunt and uncle were waiting for a ride, so Leopold took his red Willys-Knight from the garage and drove them home. The brakes, which Sven Englund had oiled that afternoon, no longer squeaked.

Leopold soon returned. He and Loeb sat around the living room, talking with his father, having a drink. Nathan Leopold, Sr., decided to go to bed around eleven thirty or twelve o'clock, but his son and Loeb remained downstairs playing cards. "We played two games of casino for fun," recalled Leopold. When they finally decided the elder Leopold was asleep, they left and drove the rental car toward Loeb's home. "It was then we threw the chisel out."

The following day they proceeded with their plans to collect the ransom money. At 11 A.M., following his classes, Leopold met his partner at the University of Chicago. They ate lunch at the Cooper-Carlton Hotel with Dick Rubel, a friend who under another scenario might have been the one lying in the Hegewisch mortuary. Rubel later would remember Loeb as being in an extremely good mood and talking about playing bridge that night. Leopold said he planned to study instead.

After lunch, the pair left Rubel and stopped briefly at the Loeb mansion, where Loeb picked up a pair of glasses and an overcoat and a hat belonging to his father. They went next to Leopold's house, where, obtaining soap and brush, they began cleaning the rental car. As they worked, chauffeur Sven Englund came outside to ask what had happened. Loeb told him they had been drinking wine the night before and had spilled it in the car. Englund offered to help, but they said they were just about done. Englund thought their actions curious since he never had seen either of the boys clean their automobiles before. They rarely did any work.

When they finished their task, Leopold went to his bedroom where he had secreted the kidnap letters written several days before. While his friend was upstairs, Loeb noticed an overcoat in the hall that seemed more suitable than the one he had borrowed from his home. He tried on the coat and saw that it fitted reasonably well. He decided to use it.

Leopold appeared with the kidnap notes and they drove to the corner of Vincennes Avenue and Pershing Road, several miles to the northwest. Using adhesive tape, the two plotters attempted to attach one of the kidnap notes to a "Keep the City Clean" trash can. To their consternation the note would not stay attached. The can was too slick. Despite months of preparation, they had not realized that small details such as this might foil the scheme they considered so clever.

Since the note merely would direct Jacob Franks to another contact point, they decided to eliminate this part of their plan. One of the two crumpled the note and threw it in the trash can. They drove downtown to the Illinois Central railroad station at Twelfth Street and Michigan Avenue. Loeb, wearing glasses, the borrowed overcoat, and his father's hat, approached the ticket window. He asked for a ticket on the next train to Michigan City, Indiana. The train was scheduled to leave at 3 P.M, Central Standard Time. (Chicago was on Central Daylight Time, so the train would actually leave at 4.) Ticket seller George C. Fry sold Loeb seat number four in car 507 for 75 cents.[8] Loeb took the ticket and boarded the last car of the train which already stood at the platform. It would not be leaving for another hour, but Loeb had no intention of traveling to Michigan City that afternoon. He placed the second kidnap note in a telegraph box on the last car, then returned to the waiting room, where his friend waited next to the phone booth.

Leopold next called the Franks home and gave Bobby's father

the address of the Van de Bogert & Ross drugstore. "I told him a Yellow Cab would be at his door to take him," Nathan Leopold confessed. "I repeated the number twice, and he asked if he couldn't have a little more time, to which I replied no, it must be immediately. About the time I was phoning, Richard had returned from the train and we started out south intending to call the drugstore from Walgreen's store, Sixty-seventh and Stony Island. We chanced to see a newspaper lying on the stand with the headlines: UNIDENTIFIED BOY FOUND IN SWAMP.

"We deliberated a few minutes as to what to do, Dick thinking that the game was up. I, however, insisted that it could do no harm to call the drugstore. This I did, but was told that no Mr. Franks was in the building. We then went to Sixty-eighth and Stony Island, another drugstore, and again telephoned; we met with the same reply. Then we gave it up as a bad job and returned the car to the place where it had been rented."

Richard Loeb also discussed in his confession this final moment when the two had realized their grandiose scheme had failed. "I was not very anxious to go on with the matter, but Leopold persuaded me to go ahead," Loeb said in describing their futile attempt to phone Franks. "We then realized that the body had been identified as that of Robert Franks and that any further attempt to get the money would only result in failure."

Loeb concluded his confession with a statement apparently designed to shift as much of the responsibility from his shoulders as possible: "I just want to say that I offer no excuse, but that I am fully convinced that neither the idea nor the act would have occurred to me had it not been for the suggestion and stimulus of Leopold. Furthermore, I do not believe that I would have been capable of having killed Franks." It was a self-serving statement. But as the facts of the case were made known, most members of the public, in 1924, were willing to believe it.

Following the confessions, State's Attorney Crowe brought the two boys together in one room. By then it was early in the morning, but the room was packed. Crowe was there. Cronson, Savage, Sbarbaro, Hughes, Ettelson, detectives, policemen, and stenographers. Outside, the press continued to wait eagerly for the major story to break.

After court reporter E. M. Allen concluded his reading of Loeb's confession, Nathan Leopold said he wanted to talk. "I have some corrections. First of all, we started planning this thing as early as November, 1923. In the second place, the suggestion was his, not mine. The Rent-A-Car is at Fourteenth Street, not Sixteenth. The little restaurant he refers to is at Thirteenth, not 1538 Wabash. The hardware store was not at Forty-seventh Street, but between Fifty-fifth and Fifty-sixth on Cottage Grove. I did not bind the chisel with tape, but he did. The hip boots are not my brothers, but my own. At the time the Franks boy entered our car, I was driving, not Mr. Loeb, and Mr. Loeb was in the back seat. It was Mr. Loeb who struck him with the chisel, not I. We made the phone call to my father at nine forty-five from 104th and Ewing. Loeb got home at one o'clock, not ten thirty as he seems to think."

Loeb wanted to argue: "No, I never said that. I said I went to your house at ten thirty."

Leopold continued: "And as far as that suggestion is concerned, again, I am sure it was Mr. Loeb that made it and it was his plan and it was he who did the act."

After Leopold's confession had been read, Loeb wanted to speak. "There are certain corrections that Leopold has made in mine that are not important, such as Fourteenth Street and the boots being his instead of his brothers, which don't amount to a damn. I mean, it doesn't make any difference, are not important, and don't affect the case. However, I would like to say this: In the first place, he says that the chisel was wrapped by me. It was wrapped by him and wrapped by him in Jackson Park. He brought it in and put it in the car, and he wrapped that chisel while there in Jackson Park in that little nine-hole golf course.

"In the second place, he mentioned that the idea of the thing, that the main thing was to get the place and the means of throwing that package, and he stuck on that thing in the train, and it was his idea. But he doesn't mention the method of the killing, that he had that very well conceived and planned out as evidenced by the ether in the car, which was absolutely the notion that he followed through. The boy was to be etherized to death, and he was supposed to do that, because I don't know a damn thing about it and he does. He has a number of times chloroformed birds and things like that and he knows ornithology. I don't know a damned thing about that.

"He said it was November when the idea was conceived. I believe I said two months in my statement. I know it wasn't November. It may have been two and a half months, but certainly not any longer than that."

State's Attorney Crowe asked Loeb who hit Bobby Franks with the chisel.

"He did," responded Loeb, pointing at Leopold. "Nathan Leopold, Jr. He was sitting up in the front seat. I said, he was sitting up in the front seat. I mean *I* was sitting up in the front seat. That is obviously a mistake; I am getting excited. This Franks boy got up in the front seat. Now he was a boy that I knew. If I was sitting in the back seat he would have gotten into the back seat with me. He was a boy I knew and I would have opened the door and motioned him in that way. As it was, he got in the front seat with me because I knew the boy and I opened the front door.

"He didn't see Babe until he was inside the car. He stood at the same place. I introduced him to the Franks boy and then took him into the car. I took him into the car and when he got in the car, I said: 'You know Babe? This is Bobby Franks.'"

The question of which one of the pair actually wielded the chisel on Bobby Franks thus was not resolved by their confessions. Leopold said Loeb did it; Loeb said Leopold did it.

Which one told the truth? In his remarks, Loeb had stumbled when he said: "He [meaning Leopold] was sitting up in the front seat." Loeb immediately corrected himself, but was that an inadvertent slip that revealed the true identity of the driver?

Internal evidence suggests that Richard Loeb may have been telling the truth when he insisted that he had been driving and that Leopold struck the death blow. According to the version agreed on by both young men, after spotting their victim, they turned at the corner of Forty-eighth Street to approach from behind. They were driving south on Ellis when they stopped and hailed Bobby Franks. Bobby was walking on the *west* side of the street, which put him on the right, or passenger, side of the automobile. One of the kidnappers was sitting in the front seat, driving. His partner was in the rear. To determine which one was where, their previous movements have to be considered.

The two had eaten lunch earlier that day. After their meal they raised the side curtains of the Willys-Knight. In that particular model of Willys-Knight those were *isinglass* curtains, what might be described as plastic windows. They could be seen through, but not as clearly as through glass. Someone outside the car would be able to see a person through the curtains but would not be able to converse with him easily unless the door were opened. Isinglass curtains did not roll up and down as easily as do windows in modern cars.

Only Loeb knew Bobby Franks. It was he who lured him into the murder vehicle. But considering the known facts concerning the moment Bobby Franks climbed into the car, it seems most probable that Richard Loeb was driving. As Loeb himself insisted, it would be natural for him to open the front door so Bobby Franks could slide in beside him—with Nathan Leopold poised behind his back.

Yet it is possible that Loeb was sitting in the rear. In such a case he would have had to lean forward over the front seat in order to be able to call to Bobby through the right front window. He then could have reached down and opened the front door (the handle was toward the rear), causing Bobby to take that seat. It was *possible*, but it did not seem *probable*, and the impression held by most who studied the case early would be that Nathan Leopold struck the death blow. Indeed, as the facts of the crime became known to Chicagoans, Nathan Leopold appeared to be the more evil of the two, the smug, self-satisfied conniver who had been the brains behind the entire affair. Richard Loeb, the social-minded fraternity boy, liked by all, may have stood equally guilty under the law, but he seemed to be under the domination of his intellectually superior partner. Leopold and Loeb: two wealthy Jewish boys, so similar in many respects. The public would have a hard time differentiating one from the other. Partly for this reason it did not seem vital which had struck the death blow. In the Franks case they had become one individual, not two.

Loeb continued to rage at his partner, complaining that he had been made a fish. The fact that Leopold had used their previously prepared alibi about drinking and two pickup girls named Edna and Mae disturbed him the most. After learning about the glasses being discovered by police, they had invented the alibi in case they were picked up and questioned. Loeb felt they should not use the alibi if they had not been picked up within a few days. Leopold thought they should offer the alibi if picked up any time. Finally, they settled on seven days from the time of the crime as the point after which the alibi would not be used.

A problem arose, however, concerning the time of the crime. Loeb reckoned the time interval from the time of the murder, or around 5 P.M. on Wednesday, May 21. Leopold reckoned the time interval from the time of the last telephone call, or around 3:30 P.M. on Thursday, May 22. When the police picked up Loeb the following Thursday, he figured the seven days were up, so did not use the alibi. Leopold, however, had been picked up at two thirty on Thursday, only an hour before the seven day time limit (as figured by him) would be over. He used the alibi, and the difference between their stories became the opening wedge between the pair.[9]

"I tried to help you out," Loeb blurted at his partner, "because I thought that you at least, if the worse comes to the worst, would admit what you had done and not try to drag me into the thing in that manner. Well, now, that is all I have to say."

Leopold had his points to score. "Those are all absurd dirty lies," he complained. "He is trying to get out of this mess. I can explain to you myself exactly how I opened the door to let the Franks boy in, and he got up from the back seat and spoke to the boy from the back. I was driving the car. I am absolutely positive."

Leopold then directed his attention to his partner. "I am sorry that you were made a fish of and stepped into everything and broke down and all that. I am sorry, but it wasn't my fault." Leopold gave Loeb a stony glance, then turned back toward Crowe. "All the rest of the corrections he made, with the exception of that one of the car, are lies."

"Now listen, boys," Crowe interrupted.

Leopold replied: "Yes?"

"You have both been treated decently by me?"

"Absolutely," agreed Leopold.

"No brutality or roughness?"

"No sir."

"Every consideration shown to both of you?"

"Yes sir."

"Not one of you have a complaint to make, have you?"

"No sir."

"Have you, Loeb?"

"No."

Finally, at 6 A.M., State's Attorney Robert E. Crowe emerged from his office. He appeared exhausted—his tie askew, his shirt rumpled, deep circles beneath his eyes. But he was beaming. The jutting jaw was held high.

"The Franks murder mystery has been solved," Crowe announced, having difficulty suppressing his joy. "The murderers are in custody. Nathan Leopold and Richard Loeb have completely and voluntarily confessed. The kidnapping was planned many months ago, but the Franks boy was not the original victim in mind."[10]

Pandemonium erupted as reporters scrambled for telephones to inform their offices of the news. Others pressed for more details. Within minutes the Chicago *Herald and Examiner* began to grind out extra editions carrying the first news of the confessions. The newspaper later claimed that it distributed 100,000 copies of the confession extra within ten minutes of when the papers appeared in front of the Hearst building.[11]

Later in the day Crowe again talked to the press. He spoke of his plans, of his determination to proceed without delay. "I have a hanging case," said the state's attorney, "and I would be willing to submit it to a jury tomorrow. I shall present the facts to the grand jury early next week."

PART TWO:

The Million-Dollar Defense

11 Anguish

We have striven to free our youth, to put upon them little or no responsibility; we have permitted and encouraged the casting off of restraints, a contempt for old codes and morals. We have become supine before the spirit of experiment and the sneer at not being "new." And two of the most gifted and brilliant products of the experiments of today are held by the state's attorney, charged with the most revolting crime of the century.

—EDWIN BALMER[1]

After learning that Leopold and Loeb had confessed, the Chicago *Tribune* devoted practically its entire news section to the story, a double column on the front page explaining the reason for the extensive coverage:

> In view of the fact that the solving of the Franks kidnapping and death brings to notice a crime that is unique in Chicago's annals, and perhaps unprecedented in American criminal history, the *Tribune* this morning gives to the report of the case many columns of space for news, comment, and pictures.
>
> The diabolical spirit evinced in the planned kidnapping and murder; the wealth and prominence of the families whose sons are involved; the high mental attainments of the youths, the suggestions of perversion; the strange quirks indicated in the confession that the child was slain for a ransom, for experience, for the satisfaction of a desire for "deep plotting," combined to set the case in a class by itself.[2]

The Hearst papers—the morning *Herald and Examiner* and the *Evening American*—cried for blood. "The people of this city, whom this thing has shaken with its horror, have a right to immediate procedure," editorialized the *Herald and Examiner*. "This is not a case the details of which anybody cares to cherish in his memory. It should not be allowed to hang on, poisoning our thoughts and feelings. Every consideration of public interest demands that it be carried through to its end at once."[3]

The newspapers reported that "never has public opinion in Chicago been at such a white heat of indignation." It contended there were "insistent demands" that the state take every step necessary to "inflict the full penalty of the law."

In an editorial the *Evening American* cited the Old Testament to support a similar demand that the youths be executed: "Society requires that there be no slipping in the wheels of justice in this case. It demands that punishment be meted out with the rigorous impartiality of the old law that recognized no new-fangled 'mental psychosis':

"'And thine eye shall not pity; but life shall go for life, eye for eye, tooth for tooth, hand for hand, foot for foot.'"[4]

With the identity of the killers now revealed, the greatest shock occurred within the Chicago Jewish community—indeed, among Jewish communities all over the United States. The fact that the murdered boy had been Jewish was painful enough, another example of the endless persecutions inflicted on Jewish people. But to learn that the killers were *also* Jewish was an embarrassment that the Jewish community had to suffer together. It would be inaccurate to suggest that the Jews of America shared the *guilt* of Leopold and Loeb. More accurately, the Jews of America shared the *anguish* of the Leopold and Loeb families, that their children could be capable of such a crime.

Perhaps the most crushing blow to the Jewish psyche was that this horrible crime had been committed by, and among, the so-called best people, the German-Jewish aristocrats. Had such a murder occurred in the West Side ghetto, among the desperate and impoverished Eastern European Jews, it would have been almost understandable—and probably never would have been granted more than token coverage. But to have the crime occur among the wealthy and cultured Jews of German background was incomprehensible—and therefore front-page news.

Yet if the Eastern Jews were tempted to gloat over the catastrophe suffered by their social superiors, any smugness was tempered by the knowledge that the *goyim*, the non-Jews of Chicago, saw little distinction between the two classes of Jewish society. To the Protestants and Catholics, Jews were Jews. The Leopold and Loeb murder case for years would be regarded by them as "the great *Jewish* crime." And among Jewish families of Chicago, Leopold and Loeb would provide a subject for dinner-table conversations for many, many years. Several generations of children would rise to maturity remembering their parents and grandparents arguing the pros and cons of the case.

"In the Jewish community," wrote Meyer Levin in *In Search*, "there was one gruesome note of relief in this affair. One heard it uttered only amongst ourselves—a relief that the victim too had been Jewish. Though racial aspects were never overtly raised in the case, being perhaps eclipsed by the sensational suggestions of perversion, we were never free of the thought that the murderers were Jews. And I believe that beneath the very real horror that the case inspired, the horror of realizing that human beings carried in them murderous motives beyond the simple motives of lust and greed and hatred, beneath all this was a suppressed sense of pride in the brilliance of these boys, sympathy for them in being slaves of their intellectual curiosities, a pride that this particular new level of crime, even this should have been reached by Jews."[5]

The effect of the case on non-Jewish Chicago was less profound, but no less apparent. Author Edwin Balmer described the general reaction of Chicagoans to the confessions. Despite their having become accustomed to gangster killings, the people of Chicago were not prepared for wanton murder by wealthy aristocrats.

"No single event in our memory has cast such fear and awe over all classes of people," Balmer wrote. "The murder has become more than a mere crime. It has become a portentous and ominous social fact. The deed confessed by Nathan F. Leopold, Jr. and Richard Loeb meets no parallel in the police records of this nation."[6]

Huge crowds continued to flock to Kenwood, but now they had three homes, instead of one, at which to stare. People rode slowly past in cars, walked along the streets, stood for hours in front of the Leopold, Loeb, and Franks residences, hoping to catch a glimpse of the families. All the shades were drawn, but one time the gate at the Loebs' opened and a large black limousine, a chauffeur in front, a single passenger in back, drive out, and turned north on Ellis.

"It's Mr. Loeb," someone in the crowd said. "It's Mr. Loeb," others in the crowd repeated. The car drove away. "It's the father of the boy." A muted cheer arose, an expression of sympathy for the family. (The crowd may have been mistaken in its identification. Albert Loeb still was seriously ill following his heart attack.)

The Loeb family had arrived in the United States from Germany about the same time as did the Leopolds. Moritz Loeb, Richard's grandfather, went to Rockford, Illinois, where he met and married Johanna Unna, who had emigrated with her parents in 1856. They had four sons: Sidney, Julius, Albert, and Jacob. Moritz Loeb moved to Chicago after the birth of his third son and opened a shoe store. His wife, a bright and vital woman, plunged into charitable work. The shoe store prospered.[7]

The third son, Albert Loeb, attended public school, then studied political science and history at Johns Hopkins University in Baltimore. After graduation he returned to Chicago and studied law during the day while teaching school at night. Admitted to the bar in 1889, he formed a legal partnership with a friend, Sidney Adler.

Loeb and Adler practiced together for nearly a decade, specializing in corporate law and developing a good reputation. In 1901 Julius Rosenwald retained the law firm of Loeb and Adler to handle some incidental legal matters for the growing mail-order company in which he and his brother-in-law, Aaron Nusbaum, recently had purchased a half interest. The other half interest belonged to Richard Sears. The company's name: Sears, Roebuck & Company.

Rosenwald persuaded Albert Loeb to become a Sears executive. Loeb later became vice-president and also served as Sears, Roebuck's chief officer while Julius Rosenwald worked for the government in Washington during World War I. As the mail-order company's fortunes prospered, so did those of Albert Loeb, and by 1922, when he was forced into partial retirement because of heart trouble, Loeb had become a millionaire.

He built a summer estate near Charlevoix in northern Michigan and also chose the fashionable Kenwood neighborhood on Chicago's South Side as site for a spacious red-brick mansion, Elizabethan in style. The grounds, surrounded by a brick wall, contained a greenhouse, goldfish pond, and tennis court, one of the few in the neighborhood. The Loebs allowed neighboring children to use the court and even made their own children wait in line on crowded days.

In 1894 Albert Loeb married Anna Bohnen, a member of a large (eleven children) German Catholic family. She had been a secretary, and in those days it was unusual for a member of the upper class to marry a secretary. The fact of the mixed marriage also caused a mild scandal in the Catholic parish to which the Bohnens belonged. Parishioners considered it a sin that Anna left the faith—especially to marry a Jew. Some members of her parish later would claim that Anna openly bragged that she was marrying a millionaire to enable her to live a life of ease.[8] Members of the Jewish community, however, apparently welcomed Albert Loeb's new wife. She would be remembered as "well thought of."[9]

The Loebs had four children, all of them boys: Allan, Ernest, Richard, and Thomas. The third now stood accused of murder.

When the two families received the news, neither the Leopolds nor the Loebs apparently could believe that their sons had confessed the murder of Bobby Franks. Reporters immediately swarmed to their homes in Kenwood, but found only Nathan Leopold, Sr., willing to communicate with them. The *Tribune* pictured him as an aged millionaire invalid who stood on the front porch of his house crying, saying over and over again his son could not have done the things attributed to him. The newspaper described him as trying to smile through his tears at reporters who gathered about him.[10]

The Loeb family made itself inaccessible to the press. Albert Loeb, ill from his heart condition, was in no condition to talk to reporters. Of Richard's three brothers, Allan worked in Seattle, Ernest managed the family farm in Charlevoix, and Tommy was too young fully to comprehend what was happening. Only the mother remained to communicate the family's feelings to reporters, and she saw no need to do so. Women in that era were more inclined to remain in the background. Supposedly she was not yet willing to concede her son's guilt.

Richard Rubel also denied the facts. "It's a damned lie," he informed reporters. "I'm Dick Loeb's best friend, and he couldn't have done it. For a ransom?" Rubel suggested that reporters look around them at the symbols of his friend's wealth: the mansion, the limousines, a tennis court. With such money available the thought of committing murder for $10,000 seemed ridiculous.

Julius Rosenwald appeared at the state's attorney's office, saying he had come because his grandson had been mentioned in the confessions as a potential victim. "It does not seem possible that two boys with so much money at their command should do a thing like this, especially for the motive assigned to them."

"My wife and I dined at the Loebs' a month ago," commented Salmon O. Levinson, father of Johnny Levinson. "Richard was there and delighted us by his charming personality. I regarded him as one of the finest youths I've ever known. His confession of this awful crime is simply unbelievable to all who knew him."

Other friends of the Leopolds and Loebs questioned their children to determine whether they had any knowledge of the kidnap plot. Many parents hastily made plans to send their sons and daughters away for the summer to shield them from further exposure to the case. The teenage children of wealthy Jewish families suddenly discovered trips to Europe being planned for them.

Bobby Franks' mother, now a recluse, pale and listless in her grief, still refused to believe her son lay dead. She kept saying his abductors had only hidden him, that one day he would return to her. It was a common theme among all three involved families—they were not yet ready to believe.

"Young Leopold has said that he is an atheist," Jacob Franks bitterly commented. "Now, perhaps, he will realize that there is a God, that God alone would have caused him to drop those glasses and lead the way to my son's murderers." Franks suggested that to have done what they did, the two youths might be insane and perhaps should be confined in a mental institution. But he added, "The law must take its course."

State's Attorney Robert E. Crowe moved quickly to strengthen his case and make his evidence absolutely irrefutable. Hardly had the confessions been announced than Crowe hustled Leopold and Loeb on a tour to corroborate their statements and recover evidence. The youths, once close friends, now avoided all contact with each other.

A caravan of seven cars pulled away from the Criminal Courts Building at 8 A.M. Saturday, May 31, only hours after the identity of the murderers had been revealed by Crowe. The caravan crossed the Chicago River, passed through the Loop, and stopped at the Rent-A-Car Company at 1426 South Michigan Avenue, where Leopold had obtained the kidnap car under the alias of Morton D. Ballard. He was readily identified, and the rental contract he had signed was found and taken as evidence.[11]

The group visited the restaurant at 1352 South Wabash Avenue, where Loeb had waited to be called by the car company as a reference for "Ballard" in early May. "Let's eat," Leopold said when they arrived. Mrs. Gertrude Barish, who owned and operated the restaurant with her husband, pointed to Loeb and identified him as the "Louis Mason" who had waited there for a call earlier in the month. Loeb suddenly turned pale, staggered, and crumpled to the floor. Several police officers picked him up as Leopold looked on in disdain at his former friend's weakness under pressure. Loeb may have been exhausted from the all-night interrogation, or he merely may have been faking. The police took him to the Windermere Hotel in Hyde Park and put him to bed.

Meanwhile, the rest of the group proceeded with Leopold to the hardware store at 4236 Cottage Grove Avenue, where the murder weapon, the chisel, had been purchased. A clerk, Albert Hubinger, remembered selling a chisel recently but failed to identify Leopold as the buyer. (Actually Loeb, not Leopold, had bought the chisel.) A half block farther south on Cottage Grove on the corner of Forty-third, they stopped at a drugstore where Leopold had attempted unsuccessfully to obtain hydrochloric acid, then went to the drugstore at Forty-fifth and Cottage where he finally had succeeded in making the purchase. The clerk who sold it remembered the acid as the first such bottle he had sold in several years.

They headed west to the vacant lot at Forty-ninth and Drexel Boulevard where the two killers had watched a group of boys playing before they finally selected Bobby Franks. They stopped at Leopold's home and looked around his garage. Inside the house he gave the police the rubber hip boots he had worn while stuffing Bobby Franks' body in the culvert. At the Hyde Park police station Leopold viewed the chisel that night watchman Bernard Hunt had seen thrown from a car the night of the murder.

The group drove into Jackson Park, stopping at the bridge near a golden statue of Columbia erected at the time of the Columbian Exposition in 1893. Leopold got out of the car, walked to the bridge, and pointed down into the water.

(On Saturday after the murder he and Loeb had gone out on dates along with their friend, Abel Brown. After taking their girls home, the two murderers met at 2 A.M. in a restaurant on Fifty-first Street. Leopold brought along his portable Underwood typewriter on which the ransom notes had been typed. Loeb brought a blood-soaked robe which had been used to cover Bobby Franks' body. During a time when the police had frantically been searching for clues, it had lain undetected in the bushes behind the Loeb family greenhouse. The two murderers had burned most of Bobby's clothes in Loeb's furnace the night of the murder, but they had feared incinerating the blanket because its burning might have caused an unpleasant and detectable odor.

(That night, as Leopold drove them through the park, Loeb had taken a pair of pliers and pried off the tips of the typewriter keys. When they reached the bridge near the Columbian statue, Loeb had scattered the keys into the water. Next, they had continued south until they reached the outer drive bridge that crossed the channel connecting the inner lagoon with Jackson Park harbor. There Loeb had hurled the typewriter into the water.)

After Leopold had reconstructed his actions of a week previous for the benefit of police, Captain William Shoemacher ordered several police officers to remain at the spot where the typewriter had sunk from sight until a diver arrived.

The caravan next drove south along South Shore Drive, still following Leopold's lead. The day had been sunny when they started, but rain now threatened. A brisk wind blew from the east. As they neared Seventy-third Street, Leopold told the police to turn left. "Pull in here and I'll show you where the robe is. We used it to cover the body." They found the remnants of the bloodstained robe, mostly ashes, in a pile of debris under a pier.

The caravan continued south and east into Indiana to try to find the place where the murderers had discarded Bobby's shoes, belt, and buckle. They drove through Hammond and past a Russian cemetery to Michigan City Road, turned right, and drove another half mile to a prairie area.

"Stop here," Leopold said abruptly. He got out of the car and looked around. "This looks like the place," he announced. "The shoes were buried on one side of the road and the rest of the things on the other." They searched the area but failed to find anything. The police finally took Leopold back to the Windermere, while two squads under the direction of Sergeant Joseph Bernounsky remained to look for the clothes.

As dusk fell, one of the officers found two tan Oxfords under some leaves. He took the shoes to the Franks home. Bobby's older brother, Jack, identified them. "I remember them perfectly," he told policemen. "Bobby bought them six weeks ago at Marshall Field's. I was with him at the time."

Later that day State's Attorney Crowe announced himself pleased with the day's work. "We have the most conclusive evidence I've ever seen in a criminal case, either as a judge or prosecutor," he said. "We have the shoes young Franks wore when he was murdered as well as other evidence. We found these things in every instance where Loeb and Leopold led us, places where they told us they'd be found. The case against these two young men is absolutely conclusive. I can't see how they can get away from it. Our whole afternoon was spent in checking and organizing the evidence. I have no hesitation in saying I would be ready to go to trial tomorrow."

He added that only one loose end remained: Each of the boys continued to accuse the other of having struck the blow that killed Bobby Franks. It was a moot point under the law, of course. Each shared equal guilt in the murder.

At the Windermere Hotel the police put Leopold in a room by himself. Thoroughly exhausted, he immediately went to bed. While he slept, one of the family servants came to the hotel and left pajamas and a change of clothing for both boys. At 1 A.M. the police awakened the pair and transferred them to the Wabash Avenue police station near the Loop for the remainder of the night. After four hours' sleep, Leopold became restless and played rummy with his guard. In the morning he sent out for candy and magazines. Loeb continued to sleep.

During the day Mike Leopold had visited Crowe's office to see his brother. Accompanying him were Jacob Loeb, Richard's uncle, a handsome and dynamic man who had headed the city's school board for five years, and Benjamin C. Bachrach, a trim forty-nine-year-old attorney. During his career Bachrach successfully defended aldermen and gangsters. He obtained an acquittal for vice boss Mike Heitler on a murder charge. (The Capone gang later killed Heitler.) Bachrach also had won a reversal of a Mann Act conviction of Jack Johnson, the first black heavyweight champion.

The three men tried to learn the whereabouts of the two accused murderers. The person in charge of the state's attorney's office told them that Leopold and Loeb no longer were there and it was not known when they would be returned, probably not until the next day. The three men left, irritated at being so brusquely dismissed.

Later that night Jacob Loeb visited Attorney Clarence Darrow, who lived with his wife in the Midway Apartments, a spacious apartment building near the University of Chicago. The Darrows were asleep when Jacob Loeb rang their bell. Ruby Darrow came to the door. Loeb insisted on seeing her husband, even though she told him he was ailing and in bed. Undeterred, Jacob Loeb barged into the bedroom, aroused the attorney, and pleaded with him to represent his nephew and young Leopold.

"Get them a life sentence instead of death," he said. "That's all we ask." Jacob Loeb reportedly fell to his knees beside the bed. "We'll pay anything, only for God's sake, don't let them hang."[12]

At sixty-seven Clarence Darrow was plagued with rheumatism, neuralgia, and plain fatigue. A large, rumpled, homespun man—philosopher, and author, as well as lawyer—he long had been the champion of the poor and the oppressed. He had left his job with the Chicago and Northwestern Railroad thirty years before to represent Eugene V. Debs and other union leaders who were plunged in a bitter fight with the railways and the federal government. He had traveled the country in defense of the defenseless, earning a reputation as a master orator and a devastating cross-examiner. His voice was a marvelous instrument, which he played to perfection. He could rumble in anger, soothe with compassion, needle with scorn. He rarely took notes during a case, yet almost never forgot a fact.

Ben Hecht wrote of Darrow: "The picture of Darrow drawling in front of a jury box was a notable scene: the great barrister artfully gotten up in baggy pants, frayed linen, and string tie, and 'playing dumb' for a jury as if he were no lawyer at all, but a cracker-barrel philosopher groping for a bit of human truth."[13]

Darrow decorated the walls of his office with the portraits of his heroes: John Brown, Leo Tolstoy, Thomas Hardy, Arthur Schopenhauer, Henry D. Lloyd, John Ruskin, Karl Marx, Walt Whitman, Henry George, William Morris, and John Peter Altgeld. Altgeld was his friend and mentor, who as governor of Illinois brought about the end of his political career by pardoning the three survivors of the eight men convicted of causing the Haymarket Riot in 1886. The large library in Darrow's home, bulging with books on a multitude of subjects, was where the Evolution Club held its weekly meetings to discuss biology, archaeology, anthropology, paleontology, sociology, comparative religion, almost everything. Visiting scholars made it a point to drop by and address the club when they came to Chicago. One of Clarence Darrow's most famous cases would be his defense of a twenty-one-year-old teacher named John T. Scopes, arrested for teaching Darwin's theories of evolution in a small school in Tennessee.

"He was a sentimental cynic," biographer Irving Stone wrote of Clarence Darrow. "He was a gullible skeptic. He was an organized anarchist. He was a happy pessimist. He was a modest egocentric. He was a hopeful defeatist. And was perhaps aware of the various contradictions he was housing under one dome."

Darrow believed in a mechanistic philosophy: that a man was formed and his actions determined by his birth and environment, that he had no free will, thus could not be held responsible for what he did. He considered it barbarous to punish a man for a crime because man cannot control his behavior. Over the years Darrow had fought in behalf of countless causes, but his greatest and most enduring battle had been against the death penalty.

Clarence Darrow finally decided to accept the defense of Leopold and Loeb, not for any promise of wealth or to please a worried uncle, but because he believed that in defending these two confessed killers, he would have a rare chance to strike a blow against capital punishment.

"No client of mine had ever been put to death," he wrote later in *The Story of My Life,* "and I felt that it would almost, if not quite, kill me if it should ever happen. I have never been able to read a story of an execution. I always left town if possible on the day of a hanging. I am strongly—call it morbidly, who will—against killing. I felt that I would get a fair fee if I went into the case, but money never influenced my stand one way or another. I knew of no good reason for refusing, but I was sixty-seven years old, and very weary. I had grown tired of standing in the lean and lonely front line facing the greatest enemy that ever confronted men—public opinion.

"But I went in, to do what I could for sanity and humanity against the wave of hatred and malice that, as ever, was masquerading under its usual *nom de plume:* 'Justice.' "[14]

12 Evidence

Tell Loeb for me that it makes no difference which of us did the actual killing.

—NATHAN LEOPOLD[1]

In its Sunday edition on June 1 the Chicago *Tribune* published what is probably the most incredible photograph taken during the entire Leopold and Loeb case, one that said more about that case than the hundreds of thousands of words printed in the American newspapers the preceding week. The photograph shows no brutalized body, no ghastly details of the murder. It is a posed portrait, taken most likely in the several hours following the confessions but before the caravan left for the south side on its Saturday morning hunt for evidence.

The photograph shows Nathan F. Leopold, Jr., and Richard Loeb, fashionably attired in suits and vests as though their valets had arrived at the state's attorney's office with fresh clothing only a few minutes before. They are seated in an office along with Robert E. Crowe and his assistants: John Sbarbaro, Joseph Savage, Milton Smith, and Bert Cronson. Crowe's secretary, Lawrence Cuneo, also joined the group. The police are represented by Chief of Detectives Michael Hughes, Captain William Shoemacher, and Sergeants Thomas O'Malley, William Lang, James Gortland, William Crot, Frank Johnson, and John Q. Johnson. The final member of the group was Samuel Ettelson, Jacob Franks' attorney.[2]

The participants sat properly posed, comfortable, looking out at the camera. It suggested the type of executive portrait you might expect to encounter in the boardroom of a multibillion-dollar corporation. The photograph bespeaks elegant distinction—except two of the men in the picture were confessed murderers, while the others were responsible for bringing them to justice.

Clarence Darrow later would see that and other pictures featuring Crowe and the murderers and comment, "When I first saw them I believed it showed a friendship for the boys, but now I am inclined to think he had them taken just as a lawyer who goes up in the country fishing has his picture taken with his catch."[3]

On Sunday morning the police and the two murderers resumed the search for evidence. This day, however, a full contingent of reporters also accompanied the caravan, some even being allowed to ride in the car with Leopold and Loeb and ask them questions. Their answers would fill the newspapers the following day.[4]

The caravan went from the police station at Forty-eighth and Wabash to Daley's Restaurant on Sixty-third Street for breakfast. They visited the bridge at Jackson Park, where a large crowd had gathered to watch a diver hunting for the typewriter. Loeb offered suggestions as to where he might find the machine. One of the reporters advised Loeb to stay back so the crowd would not see him. Loeb straightened up and said, "I'll look the world in the face. I'll look them straight in the eye. I'm not afraid."

They continued south, Leopold chain-smoking cigarettes, and passed the South Shore Country Club. Leopold looked contemptuously out the window as they drove past the club's nine-hole golf course. "Aren't golf players nuts?" he commented.

Leopold noticed that Chief Hughes, bothered by arthritis, seemed uncomfortable and asked whether his wife had been kicking him around. "You know, Caesar married an Irish woman," Leopold announced.

Hughes, a bespectacled, scholarly-looking man, said he had not heard that before. "Yes," Leopold continued. "In the nineteenth chapter, fourth paragraph, you can read that he married a woman by the name of Bridget, and that's a good Irish name, isn't it?"

He seemed surprised to learn that neither Wallace Sullivan, a *Herald and Examiner* reporter riding with him, nor apparently any of the other newsmen in Chicago knew shorthand. "In that case," he commented, "it would be a good idea to have a memory like mine. For instance, you can give me a list of twenty-five words and I can repeat them, forward or backwards." Reporters also noted he could recite Milton's "Il Penseroso" by heart.

Asked his opinion of the ransom letter, Leopold said he thought it better than average. "There was nothing flamboyant in that letter," he boasted. "It was concise and well phrased. It instilled terror. And it certainly impelled action."

Leopold seemed proud of his crime, telling a *Tribune* reporter, "Why, we even rehearsed the kidnapping at least three times, carrying it through in all details, lacking only the boy we were to kidnap and kill."

He also remarked, "It was just an experiment. It is as easy for us to justify as an entomologist in impaling a beetle on a pin."[5]

Afterward Leopold seemed more disturbed about that quotation attributed to him than any of the many other incriminating statements he would make. He fell back on the old ploy used by public figures caught saying what they actually meant and claimed he had been misquoted. Leopold wrote later: "What I meant was, of course, that no doubt they, the reporters, could ease their consciences for the prying, probing, questioning of me they were doing on the grounds of scientific curiosity. For they were asking me the most personal questions: Did I have a girl? How did I feel about the crime now? Was I mad at Dick? I was being sarcastic. I was telling them that they were showing me, a human being—and a human being in a tough spot—no more consideration than a scientist showed an insect or a microbe."[6]

When they arrived at the Indiana prairie where the two murderers had disposed of some of Bobby Franks' clothes, Loeb asked Sergeant Bernounsky where the shoes had been found. Bernounsky gave Loeb a rake, and he began to dig in the sand, finding a blue and white web belt. He gave it to Detective Hughes, saying that the clasp and buckle could be found within twenty feet or so. After the caravan left, police officers uncovered a clasp and buckle, as well as Bobby Franks' class pin.

"This thing will be the making of me," Loeb said while riding with Captain Shoemacher. "I'll spend a few years in jail and I'll be released. I'll come out to a new life. I'll go to work and I'll work hard and I'll amount to something, have a career." Shoemacher stoically told Loeb that Crowe wanted him hanged and that the best he could hope for was to spend the rest of his life in a mental institution. Loeb remained quiet for a long time after that.

Later he discussed his feelings about the crime: "My mother wouldn't believe me. I told her it was true, but she wouldn't believe me. What hurts is that she won't believe. Even now I'm sure she doesn't think I did it. That hurts—a mother's faith, the disgrace to the family. I could have carried this secret in my mind the rest of my life. It didn't bother me much. A thought or two at times. That's all."

A *Tribune* reporter asked whether Loeb had been dominated by Leopold? Loeb rose cautiously to the bait, responding, "Well, I wouldn't say that exactly. Of course, he's smart. He's one of the smartest and best educated men I know. Perhaps he did dominate me. He had nothing on me. He knew nothing that I wouldn't have the world know, but maybe I just followed along." When reports such as these appeared in the newspapers, it helped establish the belief held by many at this time that Nathan Leopold was the more evil member of the duo.

At one stop Wallace Sullivan of the *Herald and Examiner* tried to play Leopold and Loeb against each other, moving back and forth from one to the other one. Sullivan seemed determined to learn which one actually struck the blow that killed Bobby Franks. "Did you kill Robert Franks, or did Loeb kill him?" Sullivan asked Leopold.

"Loeb killed him," snapped Leopold.

Sullivan moved to the car containing Loeb. Loeb, ever at ease socially, seemed to get along well with the reporters. Sullivan goaded him: "Nathan said you killed Bobby Franks; is it true?"

"No," said Loeb.

By 2:30 P.M. the caravan returned to the Criminal Courts Building, and a *Tribune* reporter described Richard Loeb as beginning to lose his composure. His hands wavered. He puffed rapidly on a cigarette. "I've an appreciation of the thing now," Loeb conceded. "Not all the time, but every once in a while the realization of what we have done comes to my mind. I don't see how that little bastard can sit in that other car and laugh over the whole thing."

The reporter described Loeb's big brown eyes as glassy as he entered the state's attorney's office. Waiting for him and Leopold were his Uncle Jacob, Benjamin C. Bachrach, and Clarence Darrow. They wanted to see the two accused killers, but Crowe refused. The attorneys protested, but Crowe would not relent. They left, promising to take the matter to court Monday morning.

Crowe, meanwhile, had further plans for that afternoon. He had asked three of the city's foremost specialists in mental illness to come to his office: Dr. Hugh Patrick, a past president of the American Neurological Association, professor emeritus of nervous and mental diseases at Northwestern University Medical School; Dr. Archibald Church, author of a well-known textbook on mental illness and head of the department of nervous and mental diseases at Northwestern; and Dr. William O. Krohn, also an author, then in private practice. They would become well known that summer in their alternate role as alienists, a term used at that time to describe forensic psychiatrists, those who testify in court.

All three alienists were traditionalists. Like many of their colleagues, they dismissed as too radical the new psychoanalytical theories being developed by Sigmund Freud in Vienna. Crowe wanted the three to observe Leopold and Loeb to attest to their sanity. He had employed the psychiatrists quickly—before Clarence Darrow had an opportunity to hire them to testify on the side of the defense.

Leopold was brought into the room first. He jumped at the opportunity to display his intelligence and engaged Dr. Patrick in a conversation about psychology. He compared the psychology of animals and humans, referring to a paper he had written on the change in migration routes of certain birds he had studied. Later he discussed the Stanford-Binet intelligence test with Dr. Krohn, saying, "I don't believe there is any unit or standard by which you can measure intelligence. There's no unit that will be applicable to the study of the mind in all its parts."[7]

Loeb appeared next, and the doctors asked that he and Leopold tell how they committed the crime. They largely repeated what they had already admitted in their confessions. But at one point, Nathan Leopold said his friend always had been the natural leader among their acquaintances, that in any group they did what Dick decided even if all the others wanted to do something else. Loeb bristled at the inference that he had led Leopold to commit the crime against his will. "Well, I'll leave it to you gentlemen to say who has the brighter mind here. I'll leave it to you to judge who has the dominating mind." Loeb made an important point, which many people later would overlook. Although on the surface it appeared that he was the leader, because of his superior social presence, Leopold was probably able to achieve a more subtle dominance because of the force of his will and superior intellect.

Later Crowe had them taken to the courtyard of the Cook County Jail, just behind the Criminal Courts Building, to view a Willys-Knight automobile believed to be the one rented for the kidnapping. Newsmen and photographers filled the courtyard. Loeb inspected the car but said he could not be sure it was the one. Leopold walked around to the right side of the vehicle and bent down. "Yes, this is the car," he said. "I know it by these scratches on the front door."

He agreed to pose behind the wheel, but Loeb refused to climb in the car. "Not with him there," he said bitterly. Loeb agreed to pose only if he could sit in the driver's seat. A little later a flashbulb popped and he stumbled back against the wall, unnerved. "Poor weakling," Leopold murmured, turning away with disdain.

The youths returned to Crowe's office, where Drs. Patrick and Krohn gave them a quick physical examination. "You won't be able to find anything in this that will help us, not a thing," Leopold remarked to Dr. Church before the three physicians left.

That evening the police took the two young men to separate restaurants for dinner. Loeb, now relaxed and in a genial mood, chatted pleasantly throughout the meal. Only once or twice did he seem preoccupied and worried.

At Weiss' Restaurant on North Clark Street, Leopold ordered herring and discussed some of the exotic foods he liked. "I presume you've never eaten seaweed or bamboo shoots," he said to Sergeant Frank Johnson. "Then you evidently haven't been to Hawaii. I wanted to try something of everything. And I did." Leopold admitted he had cramps after eating the seaweed but quickly added that this did not stop him from continuing a planned trip.[8]

At a nearby table, a woman leaned over to whisper to her husband. She glanced toward Leopold, then began to stare. Leopold arose and walked over to the couple. "I beg your pardon, madam," he said, "but I'm not Nathan Leopold. I've been embarrassed several times by being mistaken for him." He smiled graciously at the startled pair and returned to his table.

"How'd you like to be able to lie like that?" he said, chuckling, to Johnson.[9]

After dinner the police brought the pair to the Wabash Avenue station to spend the night. Leopold did not feel like retiring early. "Hey, Sergeant," he called to jailer William Klockzien, who approached his cell. "Be a good fellow and have this delivered, will you?" Leopold handed him a note addressed to his home. Klockzien said he would take care of it at once and walked into another room, where he opened the note, which read: "Please give the bearer a pint of gin or whiskey."

On Monday morning, June 2, before nine, Clarence Darrow and Benjamin Bachrach appeared at Crowe's office. Darrow had access to his clients, and he now demanded that Leopold and Loeb be moved to the county jail, where he and their families could see them. Crowe refused. He wanted more time for his alienists to examine them and obtain positive evidence of their sanity. He suspected Darrow might have the murderers plead not guilty, by virtue of insanity, to escape hanging. And Darrow, indeed, was considering exactly that tactic.

Darrow and Bachrach brought a writ of habeas corpus against Crowe before John R. Caverly, chief justice of the Criminal Court, who would later figure prominently in the case. Crowe argued, "I realize these boys have rights, but if the court will grant me a continuance until two, I will release them to their attorneys for as long as they want."

Darrow snorted. "Now there's an extraordinary statement. These boys are minors and have rights."

"A cold-blooded, vicious murder has been committed, and these boys have confessed to it," Crowe replied.

"Another most astounding statement," Darrow retorted. "It matters not how cold-blooded the murder was. There is only one place for them to be held, in the county jail, in the custody of the sheriff. The question is not debatable."[10]

Following the brief hearing, Judge Caverly permitted Darrow and Bachrach to confer with their clients and ordered Crowe to relinquish control of the pair and have them confined in jail. However, Caverly said Crowe could take them to the inquest scheduled for later in the morning.

Following the brief hearing, Leopold and Loeb finally met with their attorneys in the lockup behind the judge's courtroom on the sixth floor of the Criminal Courts Building. It was an area that they would come to know well during the next several months. The meeting lasted only a few minutes, but it produced a marked change in the attitude of Leopold and Loeb toward their captors. Darrow and Bachrach told their clients not to furnish any more information. "Be polite. Be courteous," Darrow instructed. "But don't give Crowe any more help. Just keep quiet and refuse to answer questions."

Thereafter the two accused murderers, who had up to then been open to the point of garrulity with policemen and reporters, pleaded the Fifth Amendment to all questions addressed to them, almost making a game out of it. When asked if they wanted a drink or a cigarette, they would respond, "I respectfully decline to answer." Later, when a clerk in the jail attempted to gather routine information in a standard procedure, Loeb identified his religion as Jewish, but Leopold replied, "I refuse to answer except by advice of counsel."[11]

Clarence Darrow previously had helped 102 clients avoid the death penalty. Leopold, however, seemed unawed. He would later describe Darrow as one of the least impressive-looking human beings he ever had seen. "The day was warm," Leopold would write later, "and Darrow was wearing a light seersucker jacket. Nothing wrong with that, surely. Only this one looked as if he had slept in it. His shirt was wrinkled, too, and he must have had eggs for breakfast that morning. I could see the vestiges. Or perhaps he hadn't changed shirts since the day before. His tie was askew.

"He wore no hat, and his unruly shock of lusterless, almost mousey hair kept falling over his right eye. Impatiently he'd brush it back with his hand. He looked for all the world like an innocent hayseed, a bumpkin who might have difficulty finding his way around the city. Could this scarecrow know anything about the law? He didn't look as if he knew much of anything!"[12]

A reporter stopped Bachrach as he was leaving the building following his and Darrow's meeting with the two accused killers. The reporter asked Bachrach what he planned to do, what his approach would be. "My concern now is to render the confessions inadmissible in court," Bachrach said, striding away.

Leopold and Loeb went under custody to the judicial inquiry necessary for them to be held for trial. After a continuance they returned to the Criminal Courts Building. Awaiting them was Charles Ream. After the Saturday morning confessions Crowe's staff and the police had sought to determine whether they could connect Leopold and Loeb to a number of other unsolved, seemingly motiveless crimes. One of these involved Ream, who in the fall had been kidnapped on the South Side and castrated.

Ream identified the two as his two assailants, saying he had recognized them the moment he saw their pictures in the newspapers.[13]

Several days later a woman filed a $100,000 suit against Leopold and Loeb, charging them with kidnapping her, assaulting her, and throwing her from a car.[14] The authorities doubted her story. Joseph Savage said he considered her case weak—but they did suspect Leopold and Loeb might have killed Freeman Louis Tracy, whose battered body had been discovered in the gutter at Fifty-eighth and Woodlawn, five days after the Ream castration. The previous November police had said they believed the same persons were involved in both the Ream and Tracy cases. Asked about these crimes, Leopold and Loeb, replied as one: "I must respectfully decline to answer."

Late that afternoon Crowe finally transferred them to jail, where they filled out the required forms, received routine physical examinations, took showers—and still refused to talk to each other. Leopold became number 50, Loeb, 51. Attendants at the jail served them dinner on soggy cardboard plates.[15] The two wealthy murderers, who had eaten lavishly the previous evening, gave the unappetizing food away. Later, their parents sent them meals from Joe Stein's Court Restaurant. Leopold fell asleep on his cot by ten thirty. Loeb read a newspaper for another hour before going to bed.

13 Condemnation

Loeb and Leopold were merely the first bits of flotsam carried along by a swift stream which had originated deep in the springs of changing thought and which was destined to rise to flood. Those muddy waters are still rising, and the flotsam being swept along in increasing quantities is frightening.

—Erle Stanley Gardner[1]

For the first few days in jail, the two accused murderers remained hostile and uncommunicative, each blaming the other for their predicament. Finally, however, they settled their differences and decided to face the gallows together. "What the hell's the use?" Loeb supposedly decided. "We're both in for the same ride, so we might as well ride together."

Leopold agreed, according to the *Tribune*, in these words: "Yes, Dickie. We have quarreled before and made up, and now when we are standing at the home stretch of the greatest gauntlet we will ever have to run, it is right we should go along together. Shake."[2]

So Leopold and Loeb resumed their friendship—except they still could not agree on who killed Bobby Franks.

Nathan Leopold adapted slowly to the prison routine. The jail officials assigned him to Cell 604 with Thomas Doherty, an accused bandit. Leopold kept to himself, rarely speaking to anyone during his two hours in the bullpen, the exercise cage. He sat on the sidelines of the indoor baseball court, watching the other prisoners play. "He better lay off that ritzie stuff and get down to earth, or he'll find himself in a hell of a situation," snorted another prisoner.[3]

Loeb adjusted more readily. He was assigned to Cell 717 with accused robber Edward Donker. Loeb mingled easily with the other inmates, joined their bullpen games, and quickly picked up their jargon. He talked about how he might "get the rope" or "get the street," and he knew how to say "bum rap." He was contemptuous of his former companion for not picking up the language of the prison. Even though he always had been a meticulous dresser, he did not mind wearing the shabby prison uniform. He made certain his hair was always combed, however. Loeb did not seem depressed by his surroundings. He almost enjoyed being in jail; he felt comfortable, as though he belonged there.[4]

The two wealthy killers did not adjust their tastes to the prison food served on the cardboard plates; they never had to. They continued to receive their meals from Stein's Restaurant, complete with cigarettes.[5] Despite Prohibition, they also received liquor with their dinner through a special arrangement with Tyrell Krum, a *Tribune* reporter, who did not mind subverting the law if it meant he could obtain exclusive material. Krum appeared every afternoon, two four-ounce bottles filled with Jacob Loeb's choice bourbon stuck under his belt. The *Tribune* reporter would visit either Leopold or Loeb, lean against the cell bars, and the prisoner would remove one of the bottles and quickly pour the bourbon into his tin cup. Later Krum would supply the other prisoner in the same manner. (The Cook County jail was not known for its stringent security. Two big-shot bootleggers imprisoned there in this era were discovered to have paid $20,000 in bribes to be allowed to come and go as they pleased. They went shopping, dined in fancy restaurants, attended the theater, and made the rounds of cabarets, one with his wife, the other with his mistress.)

On Thursday, June 5, only two weeks after the discovery of Bobby Franks' body, the grand jury of the Criminal Court of Cook County, having heard seventy-one witnesses in three days, voted indictments for eleven counts of murder and sixteen of kidnapping against Nathan F. Leopold, Jr., and Richard Loeb. Demands began to rise that the state's attorney bring the confessed slayers to immediate trial. Few doubted their guilt. The day after the indictment the Chicago newspapers published their confessions in full.[6]

Sheriff Peter Hoffman (who soon would be in jail himself for misadministration of the prison) called the Franks murder the most revolting and gruesome case that ever had come to his attention, in Chicago or in any other part of the country. The *Herald and Examiner* worried that by pleading the accused murderers insane, the "million-dollar defense" would succeed in preventing their hanging. "The general consensus seemed to be," reported the Hearst paper, "that it would be a battle of wealth versus the law."[7]

Billie Sunday, the popular evangelist and former outfielder for the Chicago White Sox, believed Leopold and Loeb should be hanged—if indeed they killed Franks: "I have absolutely no sympathy for them. I think this hideous crime can be traced to the moral miasma which contaminates some of our 'young intellectuals.' It is now considered fashionable for higher education to scoff at God."[8]

Numerous authorities called the crime unprecedented. "As far as I can observe at this time," commented Walter B. Pillsbury, director of the Psychological Laboratory at the University of Michigan, "the crime does not fit into any of the groupings of abnormal conduct. I cannot recall a single crime parallel to this one."[9]

Dr. William A. McKeever warned: "Another partial explanation of the Loeb-Leopold case is the fact of chronic dissipation. The digestive tracts of thousands of youths today are clogged with the poisons and impurities of a constant supply of too much rich food. This heavy mass thrown into the stomach, washed down with bad drinks and smokes, this chronic poison, actually changes the chemistry of the blood which surges through the brain and initiates the thinking."

Leopold and Loeb, meanwhile, continued to have their meals shipped in to them from Stein's Restaurant.

The city's clergy drew different lessons from the case. "The Franks murder has startled the nation," commented the Reverend Alva Vest King. "The only cure for youthful crime, boy brigands, and bobbed-hair bandits is the thorough training of the children in the principles of the Christian religion."[10] The Reverend S.P. Long declared, "Only the love of God could conceive of the law that would let the murderer know that at a certain hour he must meet God whom he denied and so be led to repentance. Capital punishment is God's last act of love to save a man from eternal punishment."

The city continued to seethe over the crime. The shock, the horror, the bewilderment would not disappear. "The Haymarket riot, the firing of the guns that opened the great war, and the confessions of Leopold and Loeb are the three events that during my own lifetime have thrown this town into a tumult," commented author I. K. Friedman. "The town is shocked to its indurated core. It wants a motive, for in the motive lies the explanation and not one that satisfies can be found. Even the one given by these boys themselves takes us nowhere. All of us, save the experts, are up in the air, screaming for the parachute that will make our descent to the ground easy."

And something else developed: the conclusion drawn from the hiring of Clarence Darrow as defense attorney that the Leopolds and the Loebs would use their millions to subvert justice and save their sons from hanging. Word spread that the two families had lured the famed attorney into the case by the promise of the largest fee ever paid an American criminal lawyer: $1,000,000.

Darrow was thoroughly denounced, more so than in any of his other controversial cases. He was accused—he, the champion of the underdog—of selling out for a fat fee. People called him a hypocrite, and worse. His wife, Ruby, went to buy a dress and, as usual, chose an inexpensive one."Oh, Mrs. Darrow," the saleslady protested, "you'll want something better now that your husband is earning a million dollars for one case."[11]

MILLIONS TO DEFEND KILLERS, the *Tribune* trumpeted in a banner headline. "If your father had $10 million," the story quoted a spokesman from the state's attorney's office, "he'd spend at least $5 million to prevent you being hanged. The fathers of these boys have an estimated combined fortune of $15 million and we suppose it will be millions versus the death penalty."[12]

It would be the People of Illinois against the Leopold and Loeb fortunes. The *Tribune* probably exaggerated the fortunes of the two families by a factor of three. Nathan Leopold, Sr., apparently had a fortune of around $1,000,000. Albert Loeb, about $4,000,000. They were rich, but not quite as rich as everyone believed. The charges stung the two families, wounded by publicity from the crime, yet still proud of their past and of their place in the community. That their sons had confessed to a brutal murder was searing enough. It was something they never would forget; the families would be marked and would suffer for years. They needed no further aggravation, so, at Darrow's urging, Loeb and Leopold, Sr., issued a joint statement to combat the rumors and defuse public opinion:

> In view of the many statements that large sums of money will be used in defense of Nathan F. Leopold, Jr., and Richard A. Loeb, the families of the accused boys desire to say that they have lived in Chicago for more than fifty years, and the public can judge whether they have conducted themselves in their relations with this community in such a way as to earn a standing as truthful, decent, upright, law-abiding citizens, conscious of their duties and responsibilities to the community in which they live. They have not the slightest inclination or intention to use their means to stage an unsightly legal battle with an elaborate array of counsel and an army of high-priced alienists in an attempt to defeat justice.
>
> Only such defense as that to which every human being is entitled will be provided for their sons. Assuming that the facts in this case are substantially as published, then the only proceeding they favor is a simple, solemn investigation under the law, touching the mental responsibility of their accused sons. They

> emphatically state that no counsel for the accused boys will be retained other than those lawyers now representing them, with the possible, but not probable, retention of an additional local lawyer. There will be no large sums of money spent, either for legal or medical talent.[13]

The families succeeded in blunting some of the criticism directed against them which may have been unfair, but in selecting Clarence Darrow they were hardly obtaining an ordinary public defender. As for whether any large sums of money would be spent in defense of their sons, it depends on what one considers "large." The legal bills would exceed $100,000.

As his first move, Darrow sent Benjamin Bachrach's younger brother Walter, an attorney interested in modern psychology, to attend the American Psychiatric Association's eightieth annual meeting in Atlantic City, New Jersey.[14] Darrow felt he had to go out of state to engage psychiatrists to examine his clients because Crowe already had acquired the best-known alienists in the Chicago area. The question of whether medical experts should be hired independent of either defense or prosecution would be aired frequently in medical and legal journals following the Leopold and Loeb trial. Darrow suggested a single panel of medical examiners whose fees would be paid by the court rather than by either side, but in this, as with many of his ideas, he was ahead of his time.

Bachrach persuaded three of the country's most eminent psychiatrists to conduct an examination of the two accused killers. He obtained Dr. William Alanson White, president of the American Psychiatric Association and superintendent of St. Elizabeth's Hospital (the government mental institute) in Washington, D.C.; Dr. William Healy, a pioneer in criminal psychiatry and in the study of juvenile delinquents; and Dr. Bernard Glueck, who had established an innovative psychiatric clinic at Sing Sing Prison in Ossining, New York. All three men, unlike the traditionalists who had observed Leopold and Loeb at Crowe's request, were receptive to the new psychological theories of Sigmund Freud.

The traditionalists concerned themselves with the conscious. They believed mental illness and insanity to be caused by an impairment of the intellect. "In the vast majority of cases," wrote Dr. Hugh T. Patrick, one of Crowe's neurologists, "the exhaustive and intricate corkscrewing methods of the Freudians are unnecessary. Sometimes they are harmful."

The new-school psychiatrists concerned themselves more with subconscious motives. They felt that mental illness resulted from deep emotional and instinctual drives. "The new analytic psychology," claimed Dr. White, "goes much deeper in its analysis of motives and delves beneath the surface of the obvious into the region of the so-called unconscious where reside those primitive tendencies of which the individual himself may be quite unaware and yet which, in their efforts at expression, avail themselves of all manner of devious byways which are calculated to obscure their real meanings."

While the three psychiatrists hired by the defense prepared to come to Chicago, Leopold and Loeb appeared in court for arraignment. The date was June 11, Loeb's nineteenth birthday and the day Leopold would have sailed for Europe on the *Mauretania*.[15] It also was the day when Al Capone surrendered himself to police for the restaurant murder he had committed several months previous.[16] Capone had chosen the day deliberately, realizing that the public's attention was focused too closely on the two wealthy Jewish thrill killers for it to worry much about a gangster slaying, done for pure business motives. Capone never would go to jail for the murder he committed a month before the Franks slaying. Witnesses, who had previously identified him, had sudden memory lapses and decided they hadn't seen Big Al after all.

The day of the arraignment a crowd began to gather at the Criminal Courts Building at 7 A.M., three hours before the scheduled start of the hearing. When the courtroom door opened, the mob stampeded for seats. Spectators packed the room, sitting on windowsills and standing wherever they could, while hundreds more milled in the corridors outside, hoping to catch a glimpse of the "sheik defendants." Supposedly the largest crowd ever to come to the Criminal Courts Building, it was merely a harbinger of events to come.

"Loeb and Leopold had prepared themselves well," a *Daily News* reporter described the hearings in that afternoon's paper. "Their clothes had been brushed. They had shaved and their hair was slicked down. They entered handcuffed to deputies but bore themselves well."

In a short session, the defendants pleaded not guilty to all charges. Crowe asked that Judge Caverly set the trial for July 15, but Darrow urged a later date because of the intensity of the public feeling against his clients. The judge ordered that all motions be filed by July 21 and said the trial would begin on August 4, unless the defense requested and convinced him of the necessity for a continuance.

During the hearing Constance Lazelle, an attractive girl from the South, kept smiling familiarly at Leopold and Loeb, trying to attract their attention. She later told reporters that the defendants had picked her and her roommate, Mabel, up the night Bobby Franks was kidnapped. She got in the front seat of the car with Loeb, she claimed, and Mabel got in back with Leopold. "I'd like to see them," Miss Lazelle told an assistant state's attorney. "Maybe I can help them in the trial." But her request was denied, and the defense attorneys showed no interest in her either. Miss Constance Lazelle quietly slipped from the pages of history.

Another person attending the arraignment that day was a young University of Chicago student named Meyer Levin, who served as campus correspondent for the Chicago *Daily News.* Levin followed developments in the case closely, because he usually occupied a desk near those of Mulroy and Goldstein. He often saw them rushing into the newsroom, shouting news of their latest scoop. He discussed the case with them between deadlines. More feature writer than reporter, however, he had not yet written anything about Leopold and Loeb.

The newspaper finally assigned Levin to attend the arraignment, and he produced a feature article centering on Nathan Leopold's father, confused, overwhelmed, muttering to the reporters, "Why come to me? What did I do? Why come to me?"[17]

Levin's editor liked the story and hinted that when the trial began that summer, he would be assigned to it on a regular basis. This faced Meyer Levin with a quandary. He planned to spend the summer traveling in Europe with a friend of his from the University of Chicago named Will Gehr, who was active in campus dramatics. (Gehr, his name changed to Will Geer, fifty years later would achieve fame for his portrayal of the grandfather on the hit TV show *The Waltons.*) Unlike Nathan Leopold who had reservations on the *Mauretania* and $3,000 spending money, Levin and Gehr were going by cattle boat. Levin did not want to miss the trial, but he also did not want to miss the trip. What he feared most, however, was waiting around Chicago all summer for a trial that would be delayed again and again by attorneys seeking continuances. Darrow already was pleading for more time to prepare his defense. Deciding that the trial would not begin until the fall, Meyer Levin went ahead with his European plans.[18]

The impending trial provided Chicago newspapers with a battlefield on which a new circulation war could be fought. The publishers of the Chicago *Tribune* and William Randolph Hearst, owner of the *Herald and Examiner* and the *Evening American,* attempted to employ Sigmund Freud to commentate on the trial. Hearst was the first to approach Freud. He offered the famous psychiatrist any amount he wanted to come to the United States. Knowing Freud had been ill, he offered to charter a special liner so other passengers wouldn't bother him. The *Tribune* sent Freud a telegram offering him $25,000—or "anything he named"—to come to Chicago and psychoanalyze the two defendants. Freud turned down both offers, for "reasons of health" and because "I cannot be supposed to provide an expert opinion about persons and a deed when I have only newspaper reports to go on and have no opportunity to make a personal examination."

Nevertheless, both the *Herald and Examiner* and *Tribune* offered their readers exhaustive analysis of the two murderers' characters by experts who, if lacking Freud's stature, at least suffered from no lack of imagination. Charles A. Bonniwell, variously described as a "nationally known psychoanalyst" and a "psychologist and character analyst," studied the features of the accused and presented his conclusions in several articles for the *Herald and Examiner.* He described Leopold as passionate, jealous, uncannily shrewd, selfish, and brilliant. The narrow space between his eyes indicated he lacked a fighting instinct, while the length of his face revealed a dominance of feminine characteristics.[19]

He considered Loeb highly suggestible, smart, combative, selfish, and determined though lacking in tenacity of purpose. His nose was "well shaped with his animal qualities subdued." The curve of his jaw from chin to ear was "distinctly feminine."

Belle Bart, "a scientific astrologist," cast the two murderers' horoscopes for the *Herald and Examiner.* She found that the moon, in the zodiacal sign Gemini, ruled Loeb and made him a split personality, a Dr. Jekyll and Mr. Hyde, with a "seething restlessness, a keen desire for knowledge, but rather of the superficial type than of the profound." Saturn made him precocious, calculating, scientific, and unfeeling.[20]

Miss Bart said Leopold had an innate desire for surgical work and a taste for strife and warfare. Had he been born of humble parents, he would have been trained as a butcher to "quiet the urge that seethed within him." He could have been a brilliant surgeon if his energies had been properly channeled. "With a horoscope such as he possesses," she stated, "he would brook no interference, would be hasty and virulent."

The *Tribune,* not to be outdone, ran two large pictures of Leopold and Loeb with an analysis of their features by James N. Fitzgerald, a phrenologist who had studied twelve photographs of the defendants. According to Fitzgerald, Leopold's forehead indicated lack of reason and of moral and benevolent power. His nose demonstrated his aggressiveness, his lips his sensuousness, and his left ear revealed a dynamic personality. The back of his head indicated a sex drive weaker than Loeb's, while the top of his head showed self-esteem.

Occasionally the focus of the press shifted to include the bereaved Franks family. The *Herald and Examiner,* on the day of the arraignment, ran an interview with fifteen-year-old Jack Franks. Jack referred to his dead brother as Buddy and remembered him as a good tennis player and a debater who believed capital punishment should be abolished. "He had a lot of fun in him," said Jack Franks, "always ready to laugh and kid you along. He couldn't stay mad to save his life."[21]

The dead boy's father, Jacob Franks, also remembered his son: "He was the flower of the family, the idol of my wife's heart. We built so many hopes on him—and now he's gone and nothing we can do or say will bring him back."

Neither Loeb nor Leopold, however, seemed to feel any remorse or grief. Loeb commented after spending several weeks in jail, "I know I should feel sorry I killed that young boy and all that, but I just don't feel it. I didn't have much feeling about this from the first. That's why I could do it. There was nothing inside of me to stop me. Of course, I'm sorry about my family, but not as much as I ought to be."

Leopold believed he and Loeb would be hanged. He intended to do two things before he died. First, to determine once and for all whether an afterlife existed, he would compose ten riddles and commission a group of scientists to try to communicate with him after his death to see if he had solved the riddles. He assumed they would fail to reach him. Secondly, he would write a book setting down his philosophy. Because of the interest in the case, he felt it would be an excellent opportunity to publicize his views. He figured he could write the book in two months or so, the time he figured to have between his sentencing and the execution of that sentence.

14 Examinations

They had achieved immortality by committing the perfect crime: a crime so perfectly without motive or justification that their names would never be forgotten. From the expressions on their bright, shining faces Darrow saw that they were neither displeased nor unhappy over their bargain with immortality.

—IRVING STONE[1]

Chicago vibrated with excitement during June and early July: bombings, shootings, Prohibition raids, extortion threats, more kidnap attempts. The Chicago Crime Commission, noting a rise in the murder rate, found the situation "appalling" and a "blot on the reputation of a city whose supreme achievements in civic and commercial endeavor are attracting the admiration of the civilized world."

Thirty employees prepared for the reopening of the Moulin Rouge, a Loop café which had been closed a year for serving liquor. Suddenly a bomb rolled across the floor and exploded, injuring several persons and causing $30,000 in damage. Another bomb explosion at a "soft drink saloon" on South Dearborn killed one man and injured several others. Still another bomb blew up in a rooming house on West Madison. A bomb also shattered the Sawyer Gardens café on the West Side, which had been padlocked two months for violation of the Prohibition law.

Pudgy Stand of the Valley gang staggered into Mount Sinai Hospital with four bullet wounds, two in the chest, one in the back, one in the neck. He wouldn't reveal who had shot him. "The Valley takes care of its own," Stand mumbled. "All I want is to get sewed up and get a new gun." One of Johnny Torrio's men, John Trucklett, was dumped at the Jefferson Park Hospital with a bullet wound in the chest. He admitted only to having been shot "in a mixup on Ninth Street in Melrose Park," a western suburb near Cicero. Smuts McFarland, a West Side hoodlum, was shot and killed in an inn on West Madison Street. Six persons were murdered in the Chicago area in one twelve-hour period, setting a new record.

The Chicago Crime Commission, reporting a murder a day in

June and a total of 177 killings in the first half of the year, urged all law enforcement agencies to cooperate to stop the rising tide of homicide. "Complacent toleration of such a condition reveals a dangerous social tendency for which the price must be paid sooner or later," the commission warned.

But the people of Chicago were not concerned with 177 murders; only one interested them.

State's Attorney Robert E. Crowe busied himself with preparations for the trial. One afternoon Max Schrayer, the former member of the Phi chapter of Zeta Beta Tau, received a call from the state's attorney's office asking him to come downtown. Schrayer refused, saying he couldn't leave work. "Just wait where you are," said the caller and hung up.

A short time later a Cadillac appeared before Schrayer's business. Two plainclothes detectives got out and told Schrayer to accompany them. When he arrived downtown, they ushered the former student into the office of Robert E. Crowe. Crowe motioned for him to sit down in a chair, then asked, "Did you belong to a fraternity in Ann Arbor?"

Schrayer admitted he did.

Crowe continued: "Was there a burglary in your house the night of November 11, 1923?"

"That's right," said Schrayer. The reason for Crowe's interest in burglary suddenly dawned on Max Schrayer. Richard Loeb had appeared in Ann Arbor the weekend following the burglary, asking all sorts of questions about what happened. Schrayer had told Loeb about sending the porter to Detroit seeking two black kids seen leaving town with suitcases. Loeb must have been laughing at him all the time. Schrayer also realized that one of the items stolen had been an Underwood typewriter! Leopold had used an Underwood to type the kidnap note.

"What did you lose in the burglary?" Crowe asked.

"Well, I lost my watch," Schrayer responded cautiously.

"What else?"

"I lost a medal."

"Anything else get taken?"

Schrayer began to recite what he could remember of the missing items—pens, pencils, pins, money—carefully omitting any mention of a typewriter because he was scared to death. Finally Crowe asked, "Wasn't there a typewriter taken as well?"

"Now that you mention it, you're right," said Schrayer.

A diver had spent more than a week searching Jackson Park harbor before finding a battered typewriter buried in the muck.

The police traced the typewriter through its serial numbers to Pierce Bitker of Milwaukee, a student at the University of Michigan and a member of Zeta Beta Tau. When reached by telephone, Bitker declined a trip to Chicago but suggested the police contact Max Schrayer. Crowe eventually allowed Schrayer to return to work but said he might call him as a witness.[2]

The typewriter was only one piece of evidence among many accumulated by the state's attorney for use in the trial. It seemed unlikely that the defendants could deny having murdered Bobby Franks. Their only feasible way to avoid the gallows seemed to be a plea of insanity. Crowe understandably wanted to go to trial immediately, but Darrow and the Bachrach brothers were not ready.

They had many people to interview and needed time for their psychiatrists to examine Leopold and Loeb. They had to determine strategy and put together their entire case. It was a frantic period for the defense. "We were routed out of bed at all hours of the night," Mrs. Darrow said. "They would come ringing and bursting in upon us with fresh rumors, with bright ideas to discuss, with strangers to meet and to talk with, not infrequently remaining until daylight."[3]

In addition to Drs. White, Healy, and Glueck, the defense employed several other psychiatrists. Dr. Carl M. Bowman arrived from Boston to join Dr. Harold S. Hulbert, who practiced in Chicago and Aurora, in making a comprehensive medical and psychiatric study of the two murderers. Probably never before in the history of jurisprudence had such attention been devoted to the inner motivations of men who had committed murder. In addition to examining Leopold and Loeb on thirteen separate occasions in jail, the two physicians interviewed members of their families and talked to their governesses.

The physicians began their study of Leopold and Loeb in mid-June, most of the sessions lasting all day. Newsmen, equipped with field glasses, stationed themselves in adjoining buildings to spy on the defendants and their doctors.

Leopold approached each session eagerly, enjoying the "microscopic analysis" of his personality.[4] The sessions gave him a chance to talk incessantly about himself and take tests in which he could demonstrate his skill and intelligence. He often wanted to continue after it came time to stop. The examinations, however, bored Richard Loeb. Sometimes when the doctors questioned both of them together, Loeb fell asleep. The legend of Leopold and Loeb has been colored partly by the attitude each brought to his psychiatric examinations. Psychiatrists are supposed to be coolly objective scientists. But Darrow's alienists came away from their examinations totally enamored of Nathan Leopold, but disliking Richard Loeb.

The defendants also received visits from their families while in jail. The *Tribune* reported that Nathan Leopold, Sr., appeared at jail on Wednesday, July 2, accompanied by his sons Mike and Sam. Richard Loeb's mother had visited him the previous Saturday before taking her still-ailing husband to Charlevoix.[5] The story would grow that the Loebs abandoned their son after his arrest and avoided visiting him in prison. It is not entirely true.

Soon after the confessions Anna Loeb had attempted to see Flora Franks, Bobby's mother, to express her sympathy. In effect, each mother had lost a son. She was told at the front door that Mrs. Franks would see no one. Later Mrs. Loeb tried again to see the mother of the boy her son had killed but again was refused. Finally, on her third try, she was ushered into a room where Mrs. Franks sat staring out the window. Mrs. Loeb attempted an apology, but her message failed to penetrate. "I'm sure Bobby will be coming back pretty soon," said Flora Franks.[6]

As the examinations continued, the *Tribune* announced it had learned that Clarence Darrow would plead his clients *not guilty,* basing his defense on a plea of insanity.[7] Crowe scoffed at the suggestion: "The report that Leopold and Loeb are insane is nothing more than propaganda sent out by the defense to throw dust into the eyes of men who may be called to serve on the jury."

Several weeks later the *Tribune* presented a different prognostication: Darrow would plead his clients *guilty* but attempt to defend them on the grounds that the circumstances of the crime were the result of a malfunction of their mental functions. He would seek merely to avoid their hanging and accept a sentence of life imprisonment. But the newspaper's prediction was overlooked among all the speculation about the approaching trial.[8]

Anticipating Darrow's strategy, Crowe arranged an intensive briefing by local physicians for Joseph Savage, John Sbarbaro, and Milton Smith (his trial assistants) on psychiatric principles.[9] He hoped to present his case in simple, understandable terms that a jury of common men could comprehend. He also wanted them to be able more effectively to cross-examine defense psychiatrists. The thrill killers would not cheat the hangman if he could help it.

Attendance at the Wednesday luncheons of the Phi chapter of Zeta Beta Tau boomed. Everybody had an opinion about the case. Everyone had a different story to relate about his mutual acquaintance, Richard Loeb.

One Wednesday a young attorney named Jim Glassner, known

casually by some of the fraternity brothers, appeared at the luncheon. He explained the purpose of his visit: "Fellows, I'm on the staff of Clarence Darrow, and I'd like some help."

Glassner sought friends of Loeb who would be willing to visit Clarence Darrow and talk to him about the case. Suddenly everybody was busy; they had other things to do. Max Schrayer, however, volunteered. "I didn't want to get involved in the case," Schrayer admitted years later, "but I thought it was a great opportunity to meet Darrow."

Schrayer talked Bernard Kolb into accompanying him and they spent two evenings with Darrow in his mammoth ten-room apartment near the University of Chicago.

Darrow told Schrayer, "I wish you would write down everything you know about Richard Loeb."

"I really don't know anything about him that will do you any good," Schrayer protested. "What can I write: that he read detective stories?"

Darrow smiled condescendingly. "Why don't you let me be the judge?"

Schrayer sat down and began to think about Richard Loeb. He recalled that when Loeb had been proposed for membership in their fraternity, they had heard rumors about him and his friend Nathan Leopold. Someone who caught the pair in bed together had claimed they were homosexuals. The fraternity had called Allan Loeb in Chicago to inquire about the charge, and Richard's older brother showed such concern that he traveled to Ann Arbor to talk to the members. He had told the chapter that the two of them were just kids at the time, that the incident had been exaggerated. The fraternity had accepted Loeb for membership, provided he abandon his friendship with Leopold.

Schrayer also remembered that when Loeb was graduated from Michigan at the age of eighteen, he wanted a teaching job at the University. He applied, but was rejected because of his age. That had infuriated Loeb. Schrayer couldn't recall Loeb's showing any evidence of homosexuality during his stay on the Michigan campus. He displayed as much blustering masculinity as anybody else; in fact, he frequently wanted to go to houses of prostitution.

Max Schrayer offered Darrow his written notes, and the attorney asked him, "Will you testify if I tell you that I won't ask you anything that isn't on this paper?"

"I'm not going to testify unless you tell me everything you know about Dick," Schrayer insisted. "I don't want to get involved in the case and have it come out that this guy is a homo, and he's a fraternity brother of mine. Everybody will think I'm one, too!"

"I'll tell you everything," said Darrow. "What do you want to know?"

"Everything," said Schrayer.

Darrow had a preliminary copy of the Hulbert and Bowman report before him. He explained that the report indicated Loeb had a criminal mind and loved crime. "If he had been arrested a week before he robbed your fraternity house and people had been able to find out what he had been doing, they would have been amazed," said the attorney. "He and Leopold shoplifted. They stole cars. They broke windows. They set fires. They attempted other burglaries besides the one of your fraternity."

Darrow pointed his finger at Schrayer. "I'll tell you another thing. If you had awakened during that robbery, you might have been killed. Your friend had a gun and would have shot you." Darrow added that Loeb was not a homosexual, but Leopold was. He hinted that Leopold was in love with Dick Loeb. That was all he would tell him.

Schrayer agreed to testify, but Bernard Kolb, who had accompanied him to Darrow's apartment, did not. Several fraternity members left town rather than appear as witnesses, including Irv Goldsmith, who had proposed Loeb for membership in Zeta Beta Tau. Max Schrayer called one of his former roommates who lived in Cincinnati, Edwin Meiss, and asked him if he would like a free vacation in Chicago. Meiss also agreed to appear.[10]

The document that Darrow had referred to while asking Schrayer to testify was the Hulbert and Bowman report, probably the most comprehensive psychiatric study ever made of two defendants in a murder case.[11] When introduced eventually into evidence, it would constitute nearly three hundred pages of the official transcript, approximately 50,000 words. It dealt with every aspect in the life of the two killers: their personal and family history, the effect of governesses on their development, their childhood memories and fantasies, their sexual life. But probably the most fascinating revelation of the Hulbert and Bowman report was that the Franks murder was not an isolated incident in the lives of two otherwise innocent thrill seekers, but served as a climax to criminal careers that had been developing over a period of years.

Richard Loeb had begun to embark on a life of crime when only eight or nine. At that early age, the psychiatrists indicated, he stole money from a boy next door, hiding it under the roof of a playhouse in his backyard. "He had absolutely no compunction of guilt or fear connected with this theft," reported Drs. Hulbert and

Bowman. "He got quite a 'kick' out of the feeling that he had stolen this money and knew where it was, and that the rightful owner did not."

About the same time he and another boy opened a lemonade stand. While the other boy went to lunch, Richard took the toy cash register containing the money and buried it. He developed the habit of shoplifting, taking items whether he could use them or not. "He feels that the thrill and excitement of doing it was the cause, and the actual value of the thing taken played a very minor role," wrote the psychiatrists.

At camp each boy received two cookies after swimming. One day Loeb told the cook that one of the counselors had asked him to get his two cookies for him. Later the counselor asked the cook for his two cookies, learned what Loeb had done, and denied him swimming privileges for two weeks. Loeb admitted that he had not wanted the cookies but merely thought it a clever trick. He had no feeling of guilt but felt ashamed that his lack of skill caused him to be caught.

He stole from his relatives, taking a $100 Liberty Bond from his brother Allan's desk. He stole two bottles of liquor from a second cousin at the Loeb summer estate in Charlevoix. He stole three bottles of scotch from his uncle, also at Charlevoix. He once removed a bottle of liquor from a man's coat pocket. A pair of trousers that he wore during one of the examinations were ones he claimed to have stolen from a locker at the country club. He had not planned to do it but found the locker unlocked and unwatched, enabling him to put the pants in his case.

Beginning at the age of five, Loeb played with a boy two years older named Jack Mengel, who lived across the street. Mengel, who also apparently was known as Weaver, did not get along well with others in the neighborhood. He gambled with them but had no money to pay his debts. Loeb and Mengel played strip poker and once wrestled naked on a bed; though Loeb admitted having an erection, he claimed he and Mengel never engaged in any further homosexual activity. Mengel told Loeb stories about houses where prostitutes sat around half naked. Loeb thought the stories ridiculous and refused to believe them.

Loeb committed some minor delinquencies with Jack Mengel. One time, at Loeb's suggestion, they stole a silver flower vase from the window of a neighboring house. After stealing it, Loeb threw the vase away. He and Mengel gradually drifted apart at about the age of fourteen. During Loeb's last year at Michigan he heard his former boyhood friend had run off with a chorus girl and had got into trouble passing bad checks, causing him to be sentenced to the penitentiary. Mengel wrote a letter to Albert Loeb requesting money to pay some debts. Since the elder Loeb was ill, Richard's brother Allan had opened the letter. He and Richard discussed it but decided that they should ignore the request. When last heard from, Jack Mengel was traveling in Canada.

At about the time Jack Mengel dropped out of Richard Loeb's circle of acquaintances, Loeb became a friend of Nathan Leopold. Although both lived in the same neighborhood, they attended different schools and apparently did not know each other, or at least did not know each other well, until the fall of 1920, when Leopold entered the University of Chicago as a freshman. Loeb was a sophomore. The school then contained approximately 6,000 students. Their relative ages, plus the fact that both were Jewish, may have helped bring them together.

Leopold also had been a petty thief as a young boy, although seemingly not as active as Loeb. The psychologists reported: "The first theft which the patient [Leopold] remembers is when he stole some stamps from the album of his friend to add to his own collections. (Supposedly he was encouraged in this theft by his governess.) About this same time he was also collecting cigar bands, and he once took some of his brother's neckties and traded them for cigar bands. He made no effort to conceal this, and when asked if he had done it, he admitted it quite frankly with no trace of embarrassment. He also remembers as a small boy stealing fruit from a Greek restaurant."

In February, 1921, Loeb invited Leopold to spend a weekend with him at the family's summer estate in Charlevoix. On the train the pair discussed and developed a system of cheating at bridge by the use of signals. They also had their first homosexual liaison in a Pullman berth. Leopold was attracted to Loeb as a lover. Loeb saw in Leopold an accomplice for his acts of petty thievery. He went with Leopold to a downtown department store where they stole some pipes. They later stole a tennis trophy from the Chicago Beach Hotel, burying it in the sand and retrieving it the next day. Loeb discovered that the keys to his mother's Milburn Electric car would fit other cars of the same make. One night, while Leopold and Loeb were out drinking, they stole a car from a garage. While they parked, a truck from the garage appeared. They drove away chased by the truck. Finally, they jumped from the car while it was still moving, allowing it to crash into a pole.

The pair escaped by running down an alley. Loeb caught a passing trolley; Leopold hid. They met later and changed clothes to disguise themselves, then walked toward the scene of the wrecked car. Leopold, however, refused to continue with such crimes, saying that the danger was greater than the thrill warranted.

A month later Loeb talked Leopold into stealing another Milburn Electric, even though they had one of their own cars to use that night. They parked the stolen car and walked into a restaurant. While they were eating, the police arrived and asked who owned the Milburn Electric down the street. Like all the other patrons of the restaurant, they denied ownership.

Loeb later would comment to the psychiatrists, "I almost wish I had been caught, that first Electric. Still, I don't know if it would have stopped me." (Drs. Hulbert and Bowman mention only these two car thefts, as though Leopold and Loeb lacked either the skill or the initiative to take other makes of cars.)

The two young criminals also drove around town, and Loeb would throw bricks through windshields of unoccupied cars. Once they broke the window of a car in which a man and woman were making love in the back seat. The man shot at them as they drove rapidly away, their taillights doused to conceal their identity. This greatly increased the thrill of the occasion. They also threw bricks through store windows. Two police watchmen once shot at them after they had broken a drugstore window, setting off a burglar alarm, making that event a "memorable experience."

Loeb had hoped that these early crimes of his would attract some publicity. He would look in the newspapers, hoping for some mention of what he and his partner had done. He was disappointed to see that their crimes were too unimportant to rate press coverage.

Not all their activities involved damage to property. On one occasion Loeb and "his companion" (apparently Leopold) called the Harvard School and asked for a certain instructor. On being told the instructor was in class, Loeb said he had a very important message which had to be given him personally. When the instructor came to the phone, Loeb instructed him, "Take the receiver in your right hand and stick it up your ass."

Ten minutes later he again called the school and asked for the same instructor. Learning he could not come to the phone, Loeb asked that they deliver a very important message to the instructor: "Tell him he can take it out now." (According to the report, Loeb's "companion" in this incident was identified and punished.)

The pair frequently turned in false fire alarms. They once sent the fire department to the Harvard School. Another time, while they were eating lunch with two friends (probably Leon Mandel and Dick Rubel) at the Cooper-Carleton Hotel, Loeb telephoned the fire department that the hotel was on fire. Mandel and Rubel became frightened and left, but Leopold and Loeb remained to see the excitement.

Not content with merely phoning in reports of false fires, they soon began to set real ones. At first Loeb neglected to admit these cases of arson to his questioners. When confronted with information which they had obtained from Leopold, Loeb responded without the least embarrassment, "Oh, didn't I tell about that? It was one of the things I meant to tell."

The psychiatrists wrote: "The patient then went on to relate that he, with his companion, had planned to set fire to a shack on a vacant lot. Accordingly, they drove in their cars to within about five blocks of the shack. The patient then parked his car there and got into his companion's car. They then drove over to the shack, poured some gasoline on the floors and walls and set fire to it.

"They jumped into his companion's car, drove five blocks to where the patient's car was parked, got out and got into the patient's car, and drove back to the scene of the fire in order that the patient might have the thrill of watching it and talking with the crowd, sneering at their ignorant guesses as to the cause of the fire, offering impossible solutions themselves, and getting a great feeling of satisfaction from the fact that he knew the real solution to the mystery and nobody else did."

On at least two other occasions they set fire to buildings. Then, as though arson were not serious enough to satiate their growing criminal appetites, they shifted to burglary. The pattern of their criminal activity shows a steady increase in the seriousness of their crimes—as though success at one level provided them with courage to move up to the next step. Some time after Loeb's eighteenth birthday in June, 1923, they planned to loot the wine cellar of some friends who lived in Hubbard Woods but were away visiting in New York. They purchased a chisel which was wrapped with adhesive tape, a weapon Loeb referred to as his "toy." They took ropes to tie up the maid if she happened to be home. They carried loaded revolvers to shoot the night watchman, if necessary.

Their initial attempt at burglary proved unsuccessful. On their first trip to Hubbard Woods Leopold's car developed engine trouble and made so much noise they merely reconnoitered the area and left. Returning the following evening in Loeb's automobile, they attempted to break in a window but failed and abandoned their burglary. "The pleasurable part in this robbery was the planning cleverly," the psychiatrists reported. "The reward of the liquor was secondary. As the planning had been successful, although the execution was a failure, the patient [Loeb] was not disappointed at the outcome."

In November, 1923, Loeb suggested a trip to Ann Arbor to burglarize the Zeta Beta Tau fraternity house. Since Loeb had lived there two years, he knew the layout of the house, plus the habits of its members. Leopold suggested a second burglary at a fraternity of his choice. "We took everything we could lay our hands on that was of any use," Loeb told the psychiatrists. "We knew we would hear about it and could discuss it with the other boys." Among the items taken during the first burglary was the Underwood typewriter on which the kidnap letters later would be written.

But the second burglary that same night had ended in failure when Loeb, who had been reluctant to press their luck by entering a second, unfamiliar fraternity, heard someone upstairs and panicked. They fled, taking only a camera as their loot, and drove back to Chicago.

"Each was disgusted with the other's work in the robberies," explained Drs. Hulbert and Bowman. "They raised other personal questions about which they were disharmonious. Their friendship threatened to collapse. The argument was very bitter and lasted for several hours. It was suggested that the friendship should dissolve. However, both gained by this friendship in several ways, and therefore they came to an agreement to perpetuate the friendship under certain restrictions. The patient (Loeb) wanted an assistant in the carrying out of his plans in the criminal activities. The other one, with his exaggerated idea of his own mental superiority over all the world, and not wanting to be entirely lonesome, but needing someone who could understand him and who could associate with him as requested, they agreed that the patient could call on the other for assistance in a certain number of times, in certain intervals of time, and the other could call on the patient for companionship.

"This relationship was to last until the associate [Leopold] went to Europe in the summer of 1924. The patient's companion agreed to be absolutely under any orders that the patient might give, except ridiculous commands and things that would cause trouble or friction with his family. In order, however, that his companion should not accede to the patient in every minor request and under all conditions, it was understood that the patient's companion should use his own discretion about accepting the patient's suggestions or commands, except when the patient should say, 'for Robert's sake.' Whenever the patient used this phrase in a request, it meant that it was a part of this contract, and that his companion should do as the patient suggested. The phrase was used in conversation in place of the profane phrase, 'for Christ's sake,' or of the slang phrase, 'for John's sake,' which was more or less current in the conversation of groups to which the boys belonged. This rather cryptic use of language was developed. For instance, if one of the boys telephoned the other that he saw a bargain at 12th and 30th Streets, the listener would know that he was to meet the speaker at 12:30 o'clock that night. Or if one said over the telephone, 'I suppose they have destroyed the Lansing envelopes,' the other one would understand that he was to destroy the Lansing envelopes and that the impersonal 'they' directly related to himself, the listener."

(In Chicago Twelfth Street and Thirtieth Street run parallel, east and west, thus do not intersect. The comment might have seemed curious to any Chicagoan who overheard it. As for the other example given, the University of Michigan was located in Ann Arbor while Michigan State University, then named Michigan Agricultural College, was located in East Lansing. "Destroy the Lansing envelopes" would seem to be a cryptic way of saying, "Dispose of the loot taken in the Ann Arbor burglary." Leopold and Loeb may have considered their code clever, but in retrospect it merely seems childish.)

"The patient was the one who planned and enjoyed planning these subterfuges. Each secretly felt that the other was his superior mentally. Each felt that the continuation of this friendship would be extremely profitable to himself, and each felt that abandonment of this friendship would be very hurtful, and possibly dangerous."

Each, in fact, considered killing the other. "I had always considered him a bad influence upon me," Loeb said in speaking of Leopold, indicating that he never could have carried out his crimes alone. Loeb admitted having considered shooting Leopold but denied that he would hit him with the chisel. "The idea of murdering a fellow, especially alone, I don't think I could have done it. If I could have snapped my fingers and made him pass away in a heart attack, I would have done it."

But at other times Loeb contradicted himself, saying he considered hitting Leopold over the head with the chisel, shooting him, robbing him, and breaking the crystal of his watch to give the impression that Leopold had been robbed and killed during the struggle. He decided against such a plan for fear that he would be the prime suspect.

Each contemplated suicide. Once following a quarrel, Leopold had suggested they play a poker game to see which one should commit suicide. Loeb refused to agree to this, even though Leopold threatened to kill him. Yet Loeb frequently contemplated suicide. The psychiatrists reported: "He feels that if there had been some simple and graceful way of committing suicide, which would not allow people to know he had committed suicide, he would have done it."

During their examinations, the psychiatrists questioned the pair about the planning of the Franks murder. Supposedly Leopold had stalled and attempted to delay the crime. Both killers agreed on this point, although Loeb admitted Leopold had made some very useful suggestions toward the end. But the examining doctors noticed a particularly unusual reaction in Richard Loeb when he came to the part about establishing a fictitious identity for Morton D. Ballard. "When the patient came to this point in the narrative," Drs. Hulbert and Bowman remarked, "he looked decidedly interested, drew up his chair, talked almost in dramatic whispers, with considerable tension, his eyes occasionally roaming the room. In fact, he showed intense emotional reaction here in the repetition of that which he said had been very thrilling for him."

Loeb exhibited a different emotion at the point when he described returning the rental car to the agency at four thirty on Thursday. "At this point he choked up and wiped his nose with his finger," commented the psychiatrists. It is unclear from their report, however, whether Richard Loeb was reacting emotionally to his wanton murder of a young boy or merely the failure of his planned perfect crime.

Their plan had been to strangle their victim with the rope purchased the day before. They would wrap the rope around the victim's neck and each one would take an end and pull, both a symbolic and an actual sharing of guilt. Drs. Hulbert and Bowman's version of Loeb's description, though garbled, probably offers an accurate picture of his state of mind.

"We got him into the car," said Loeb. "He was hit over the head with the chisel, dragged him into the back seat from the front seat, gagged, but he was dead when we got to the culvert, and we didn't need to strangle him.

"At the time I got great excitement, great heart-beating, faster, which was pleasant. I was cool and self-possessed. I had quite a time quieting down [Leopold]. I cooled him down in five minutes after we got him into the back seat, thinking him still alive. I got calmer, while quieting my associate. He was hit on the head several times. He bled. My associate said: 'This is terrible. This is terrible.' I told him it was all right, and joked and laughed, possibly to calm myself too."

When asked, Loeb said he did not have an erection, any discharge, nor any sexual sensation during the killing. He claimed that they took no liberties with the body other than pouring hydrochloric acid on the face, on the genitals, and on the abdomen where there was a surgical scar. That was done only to prevent, or delay, identification.

Loeb told his examiners that during the week preceding the crime, his anticipation of it offered him less pleasure, but he did not want to back out, "because of their extensive plans, because of the time spent, because of the trouble they had gone to, and because of his associate being in it with him, and he was afraid of what the associate would think should he not go ahead."

When the psychiatrists asked if he would go through with his crime again if he felt certain that he would not be discovered, Loeb replied, "I believe I would if I could get the money."

Leopold, however, said, "I wouldn't commit another such crime, because I realize that one can never be sure of escaping detection." Leopold claimed that that would be the only reason that would keep him from another attempt; remorse or guilt would not be a factor.

The psychiatrists wrote: "Leopold denies any feeling of remorse at having committed this crime. He states that he has no feeling of having done anything morally wrong as he doesn't feel that there is any such thing as morals in the ordinary sense of the word. He maintains that anything which gives him pleasure is right, and the only way in which he can do any wrong is to do something which will be unpleasant to himself."

The Hulbert and Bowman report makes no attempt to identify which of the two boys was the one who sat in the back seat and physically assaulted Bobby Franks, causing his death, and which one did the driving. One paragraph in the report, however, hints that the actual murderer may have been Richard Loeb: "When Leopold confessed that the patient [Loeb] had killed Robert Franks, the patient then said that Leopold had killed Robert Franks. The reason for that was that his associate had forgotten, apparently, the time limit during which this alibi was to have been used, and used it on the eighth day after the crime, causing their alibis not to agree. The patient when arrested on Thursday, the eighth day, used the secondary alibi, namely that he could not recall where he had been." That paragraph could be interpreted to mean that Loeb attempted to implicate Leopold more deeply than himself to gain revenge for his having misused their alibi plan. But it still fails to pinpoint the identity of the actual killer. The psychiatrists might not have considered it important, or if they knew, they probably wanted to spare one family the added burden of knowing their son had struck the blow.

In another section of the report where Loeb is described discussing his remorse—not for killing Bobby Franks, but for causing distress to his family—he states, "I would be willing to increase the chance of my hanging to save the family from believing that I was the arch fiend. My folks have probably had the blow softened by my blaming him, and his folks by blaming me." The two psychiatrists leave unclear what Richard Loeb meant by the term "arch fiend." Was he referring to the one who planned the murder or the one who struck the blow?

Drs. Hulbert and Bowman, while failing to solve this riddle, raised an even more cryptic *additional* riddle when they tried to probe the area of other unsolved crimes which the authorities had been seeking to connect with Leopold and Loeb. They wrote about Loeb: "He denied being implicated in the so-called gland robbery of Mr. Ream, and he denied being implicated in the case of the 'Ragged Stranger,' who was found dead with his hands cut off and his face mutilated (which crime is usually attributed to Warren Lincoln), and he denied having participated in any other delinquencies, but later referred to four episodes, for which the letters 'A, B, C, and D' were suggested. It was found forensically inadvisable to question him about these."

The question of these so-called ABCD crimes would remain a riddle for many years.

Life in Chicago continued. Prohibition agents raided the Hoffman Products Company on West Monroe Street and found 17,000 barrels of beer. Another raid turned up four big stills, all new, in a garage behind the Presbyterian Training School on South Michigan Avenue. The raiders also discovered 100 barrels of mash and a large quantity of corn sugar in the garage.

A night watchman for Mrs. Edith Rockefeller McCormick accidentally killed himself in the kitchen of her mansion at 1000 Lake Shore Drive. About to sit down for dinner, he noticed a towel on the floor and leaned over to pick it up. As he did, his revolver fell out of his holster and discharged, shooting him in the stomach.

Several doctors with offices in the Loop received letters threatening their lives unless they paid sums of money. "Place $900 in a tomato can and throw it in an alley," instructed a letter signed "Italy" and decorated with a crudely drawn skull and crossbones. A

Coney Island wax museum added the figures of Leopold and Loeb to its collection.[12]

On June 12, while Republicans met in Cleveland to nominate Calvin Coolidge on the first ballot for President, a band of robbers executed one of the most spectacular train robberies in history thirty miles north of Chicago, stealing more than $2,000,000 in bonds and other securities, and $75,000 in cash.[13]

Two armed gang members smuggled themselves aboard a Chicago, Milwaukee & St. Paul mail train leaving Chicago at about 10 P.M., then slipped into the engine compartment, guns drawn. They ordered the engineer to stop the train at a lonely crossing north of Rondout, Illinois, where the rest of the gang waited in four cars. Using tear gas, the bandits quickly overcame the other guards. Ten minutes later they sped away in their car toward Libertyville, having stripped the mail train of the money.

Following the robbery, postal authorities announced that U.S. Marines would guard all future mail trains with orders to shoot anyone attempting to rob the mail. Eventually police arrested the gang members and identified the master criminal who had planned the heist: Michael J. Fahey, a postal investigator. Fahey had solved several previous train robberies before deciding that with his experience he should be able to plan a much more efficient train robbery and commit a "perfect crime." He was no more successful with his attempt than Leopold and Loeb had been with theirs.

The publicity given the Franks case inspired several other kidnap attempts. Irving H. Hartman received a special delivery letter threatening his son Irving, Jr., the boy who had been walking near Bobby Franks at the time of his kidnapping. The letter demanded $10,000 in preventive ransom.

A second letter instructed Hartman to wrap the ransom money in a box, take it to an alley near the Horatio May School, and "throw the box over the fence by the L tracks." The letter warned again that his son's life would "always be in danger" if he failed to deliver the ransom. Hartman informed the police, who placed a guard around his house, while he sent his son to Baltimore to stay with relatives and refused to pay the ransom. The police arrested one suspect, a young man dressed in women's clothes. They released him, however, after he explained he was on his way to visit his wife's grave. "I always wear my wife's clothes on such occasions," said the young man. Hartman heard no more from the would-be kidnappers.[14]

Jacob Franks received a threatening letter, promising to kill his daughter, Josephine, unless he paid $8,000. The letter warned him not to alert the police—which he did immediately, having learned his lesson—and told him to put the money in a package and leave it in a lot in the "Little Hell" section of the city. As instructed by the police, Franks left a dummy package at the designated spot. Shortly after he departed, three eighteen-year-old boys crossed the street and picked up the package. The police arrested the trio, who admitted their guilt. [15]

State's Attorney Crowe received many letters related to the case. One man volunteered to take the place of Leopold and Loeb on the gallows, provided their parents supported his family. "There is no glory in life ahead for me," he wrote.

A Grand Rapids, Michigan, man offered to pay $100 for the opportunity to hang the pair. "I am sixty-six years old, but I am game," he stated. "I have no use for such fiends." Another individual from Oakland, Nebraska, wanted the same job, stating, "I have an idea that I can give them the far greater thrill of jumping off from this world into the next than that which they received in murdering the Franks boy. I am prepared to give them a picturesque sendoff in real Western style, high hat, boots, and quick service. I like thrills myself, but nothing would give me a greater thrill than a hanging party with me to spring the trap."

A Chicagoan appeared one day with a letter he wanted to deliver personally to Albert Loeb or Nathan Leopold Sr. "We have evidence to the effect that your two sons were drugged some time before Franks was killed," the letter read. "They were given alcoholic drinks by some enemy who thought them too smart and wanted to make a fool out of them. So the drug attacked the nerve and broke the control they had over themselves. So they became emotional and also subject to auto-suggestion. Mr. Loeb, I will not talk to your lawyers, but I will talk to you."

The prisoners apparently were not the only ones who needed psychiatric attention.

As the date for the trial neared, the two prisoners received frequent visits from their attorneys. In their spare time they read. The Chicago *Journal* reported Leopold reading *A Refutation of Darwinism* and *The Last Days of Pompeii.* Loeb read *The Circular Staircase,* a detective novel by Mary Roberts Rinehart. He also had in his cell several books by Jack London.[16]

On July 17 the Chicago *Tribune* launched a campaign to convince the public that the trial, set to begin two weeks after the July 21 hearing, should be broadcast on its new radio station, WGN (the call letters standing for "World's Greatest Newspaper"). The paper printed ballots for the public to clip and mail. "The murder was a superlative crime," claimed the *Tribune.* "It will be a superlative trial. And it is a superlative experiment which the *Tribune* has conceived and has submitted to the tribunal of public opinion. The crime, the trial, and the punishment decided upon for the offenders must affect in some manner the course of life, not of a family, a social group, or a city, but the people of this and all other civilized nations."[17]

The *Evening American*, perhaps because Hearst had no broadcast station in Chicago, called the *Tribune's* proposal "by far the finest and most powerful appeal ever made in this city to the moron vote." An editorialist from the *Evening American* suggested, sarcastically, that the trial instead be conducted in one of the baseball parks or on the lakefront.

Early ballot returns disappointed the *Tribune* editors. They received 805 responses the first day, with 420 opposing the proposal and 385 supporting it. Many of those who voted against the experiment felt that much of the testimony would be sordid and unfit for children. But the *Tribune* tried to reassure its critics:

> Such parents need have no fear. The columns of the *Tribune* are kept clean. The broadcasting of the trial will be kept clean. Sensation there will be. Sensation is a part of life. It is an inseparable part of a trial for life. But there will be no filth. The censor will be as discriminating with his push button as are the editors of the *Tribune* with their copy pencils. The *Tribune* can appear at the breakfast table of any family in the country. The broadcasting of the trial will be as clean as the *Tribune*.

The campaign continued as the day arrived for the trial of Leopold and Loeb.

15 Plea

The murder was a superlative crime. It will be a superlative trial.

—Chicago Tribune[1]

The Criminal Courts Building stood on the northwest corner of Dearborn and Hubbard streets, two blocks north of the Chicago River. A market occupied the site from 1851 until the Chicago fire. In 1872 Chicago erected a structure at that corner to house its criminal courts. Unfortunately the city's fathers underestimated the capacity of its citizens to commit crime. Twenty years later the city tore down the first structure and erected a larger six-story building, built with heavy white stone blocks, massive, fortresslike, designed in the Florentine tradition of the Italian Renaissance with an arch over the entrance.

Immediately behind the Criminal Courts Building to the north stood the Cook County Jail, connected to the Criminal Courts Building by an upper-story corridor dubbed by reporters the "bridge of sighs" after the famous bridge in Venice from which prisoners received their last sight of freedom. In Chicago, however, the bridge offered a view of an alley rather than the Grand Canal.

At 9:30 A.M., Monday, July 21, 1924, Clarence Darrow, wearing a baggy gray suit and a blue tie, strolled into Judge John R. Caverly's courtroom on the sixth floor of the Criminal Courts Building. He had taken the elevator as far as it went, to the fifth floor, then walked up the last flight. With him came Nathan F. Leopold, Sr., and his eldest son, Mike. Darrow guided the two men, solemn and unsmiling, to their seats in the front row, pausing several times en route to shake hands and greet friends. The sixty-seven-year-old attorney already looked weary.

Darrow's co-counsel, Benjamin C. Bachrach, tan and trim, arrived shortly afterward with Jacob and Allan Loeb. Bachrach escorted the Loebs to the front of the courtroom, next to the Leopolds. Jacob Loeb, the uncle of one defendant, bent and spoke briefly with the father of the other, before he took his seat. They would see each other frequently during the next several months, as would Mike Leopold and Allan Loeb.[2]

Puffing a large cigar, State's Attorney Robert E. Crowe, who had decided to prosecute the case himself, walked briskly into the courtroom, wearing a dark suit, a clean white handkerchief folded neatly in his left breast pocket, and a jaunty bow tie. "Fighting Bob" exuded confidence. He had an airtight case, the people solidly backed his plan to seek the death penalty, and his name had constantly occupied the headlines since his capture of the killers. His prospects for reelection in the fall couldn't have been brighter.

Precisely at ten, Chief Justice of the Criminal Court John R. Caverly, a short, scholarly-looking man with gray hair and wearing rimless glasses, entered the courtroom from his chambers. Caverly, then sixty-three years old, had served as a judge for fourteen years.

"Hear ye! Hear ye!" cried the bailiff. "This honorable branch of the Criminal Court is now in session pursuant to adjournment."

Sheriff Peter Hoffman had stationed twelve deputies, under his personal command, in the courtroom. A host of reporters and photographers waited anxiously to relay word and pictures of the hearing to an anxious world.

"The case of The People against Nathan Leopold, Jr., and Richard Loeb," announced the judge. The bailiff called for the two confessed murderers.

Nathan Leopold and Richard Loeb arrived from a nearby lockup room carefully groomed and dressed in dark suits and white shirts. Correspondents reported that Leopold, slight, swarthy, and smiling sardonically, had bulging eyes and thick, bushy eyebrows that formed an unbroken line. They described Loeb as strikingly handsome, with regular features, fair skin, and a slender build—although he appeared somewhat sallow. Both wore their hair slicked back in the popular Valentino sheik style.

Leopold anticipated the courtroom confrontation as eagerly as he earlier had anticipated the examinations by psychiatrists. He could study Clarence Darrow in action. Although unimpressed when he first met the famous attorney—being put off mostly by his unkempt appearance—Leopold had come to admire him as the most intelligent person he ever had met. He would later write Darrow that intelligence was the attribute of a man that appealed to him more strongly than any other. Darrow, he felt, seemed heroic in agreeing at his age to risk his reputation on such an unpopular and impossible case.[3]

The deputies removed their handcuffs, and the two defendants seated themselves in front of their attorneys. Bachrach leaned forward and spoke briefly to Leopold, who turned around, smiled, and shook his head. The courtroom was quiet, the crowd expectant. All eyes focused on Judge Caverly. He cleared his throat.

"You may proceed, gentlemen," he said.

Darrow rose and slowly approached the bench, a hunched figure in gray. He stopped and looked up at the judge, wisps of hair splashing over his forehead.

"Your honor," he began softly, "these cases are set for this morning for any motions we might wish to make. I only want a few minutes' preliminary indulgence on this matter.

"Of course, it is unnecessary to say that this case has given us many perplexities and sleepless nights," he began. "Nobody is more aware than we are of what this means and the responsibility that is upon us. We have sought to consider it from every standpoint. First, of course, from the interests of our clients. But I am sure that no one who knows the families of these defendants—or either Mr. Benjamin Bachrach or his brother Walter Bachrach, who has been with us in this matter, or myself—will doubt for a minute that we have the deepest sympathy for every one of the three families involved.

"Of course, this case has attracted very unusual attention on account of the weird, uncanny, and terrible nature of the homicide. There is in the public mind a feeling that in some manner the lawyers might succeed in getting these two defendants into an asylum and having them released."

The spectators leaned forward in their seats, anxious to learn what the great barrister would do. Some of the reporters, writing frantically to record Darrow's lines, glanced quizzically at each other, uncertain what he planned. Many people, already perspiring, fanned themselves for relief.

Darrow said the defense would not ask that the trial be removed from the city because "the same state of feeling exists in all the other counties of the state." They felt, he admitted, they could get as fair a trial in Chicago as anywhere else. Neither would the defense move to quash the separate murder and kidnapping indictments because "we can find no substantial thing to criticize." About fifteen minutes had elapsed since he began his statement.

"We want to state frankly here that no one in this case believes that these defendants should be released or are competent to be," Darrow continued, taking a handkerchief from his pocket and wiping his forehead. "We believe they should be permanently isolated from society and if we as lawyers thought otherwise their families would not permit us to do otherwise. We know, your honor, the facts in this case are substantially as have been set forth, in what purports to be their confessions, and we can see we have no duty to the defendants or their families or society except to see that they are safely and permanently excluded from the public. Of course, after that is done, we do want to do the best we can for them, within those limits."

It was 10:17 A.M. Darrow stuck his thumbs in his galluses—a pose that had become his trademark. He threw his shoulders back.

"After long reflection and thorough discussion," he added, "we have determined to make a motion in this court for each of the defendants in each of the cases to withdraw our plea of not guilty and enter a plea of guilty."

A plea of *guilty*—the words sent ripples of shock and disbelief through the silent courtroom. The prosecution, the judge, the reporters, the spectators, the general public—no one had anticipated a plea of guilty. Recovering from the surprise, several newsmen bolted for the door. Jacob Loeb, head bowed, quietly began to weep. Neither of the defendants showed any trace of emotion. Nathan Leopold, Sr., stiffly erect, stared straight ahead, lost in his own world.

"Quiet in the courtroom! Quiet in the courtroom!" the bailiff cried. "The courtroom will come to order! Quiet please!"

Only that morning had Leopold and Loeb learned that their attorneys wanted them to change their pleas. Their brothers, Mike and Allan, informed them a few hours before the hearing would begin, explaining that both families had discussed the matter thoroughly. All were agreed that a "guilty" plea was in their best interests, that it was the strategy most likely to permit them to escape death by hanging.[4]

When Darrow arrived, he had apologized for not informing them earlier, but said secrecy had been essential. "Crowe had you indicted both for murder and for kidnapping for ransom," Darrow explained. "He'd try you on one charge, say, the murder. If he got less than a hanging verdict, he could turn around and try you on the other charge. There is only one way to deprive him of that second chance—to plead guilty to both charges before he realizes what's happening and has the opportunity to withdraw one of them. That's why the element of surprise is absolutely necessary."

Darrow had another reason for pleading his clients guilty. By pleading guilty, Leopold and Loeb would avoid a trial by jury. The case would be heard by a single judge who, with the verdict already determined, would hear evidence solely to guide him in imposing sentence. The so-called trial of the century therefore would not be a trial. Technically speaking, it would be a *hearing* to hear evidence in "mitigation and aggravation" of the offense.

This being the case, most of Crowe's carefully gathered evidence theoretically was irrelevant because it sought only to prove what Darrow's clients had admitted: their guilt. Judgment would depend on mitigating circumstances such as their age and the psychiatrists' opinions concerning their mental condition.

Darrow could have pleaded his clients not guilty by reason of insanity, but that would have meant a jury trial. And a trial by jury, Darrow reasoned, most certainly would result in his clients being hanged. Public opinion was so inflamed against them that no jury would dare accept insanity as a defense or show the slightest mercy in imposing sentence, then return home and face their neighbors. It would be easier for a jury to sentence the killers to the gallows. Theirs would be a shared decision, and each one could take solace that he alone did not spring the gallows trap.

But with a trial before a judge, the entire weight of the decision to take two lives must rest on the shoulders of one man. It might have been relatively easy for Leopold and Loeb to kill deliberately. It would not be easy for a man such as John Caverly to kill—after deliberation. Darrow knew Caverly, knew of the previous five jury cases resulting in death sentences over which he had presided, knew that he was taking a chance, but felt that with Caverly he had at least a fair chance of obtaining mercy. Had the individual on the bench been a Bob Crowe, Darrow might have taken a different approach.

Darrow's strategy was quite simple: His clients would plead guilty, and he and the Bachrachs would try to convince the judge to spare their lives because of their mental condition and their youth. It was a novel maneuver. Never before had evidence of a defendant's mental condition been offered to lessen a sentence. Such evidence had heretofore been used exclusively to show that a defendant was insane, not responsible for his actions, and thus not subject to punishment. Crowe would be certain to object to such testimony, and the judge might not admit it as evidence in mitigation. Furthermore, even if Judge Caverly accepted their testimony, new-school psychiatrists such as Drs. White, Healy, and Glueck might not impress him. He might even react adversely to their testimony, particularly because of some of the subject matter Darrow knew would be included. But under the circumstances, the defense attorneys felt they could do little else.

"Your honor," Darrow continued, "we dislike to throw this burden upon this court or any court. We know its seriousness and its gravity, but a court can no more shirk responsibilities than attorneys. And, while we wish it could be otherwise, we feel that it must be as we have chosen."

He noted the law provided that when a defendant pleaded guilty and the judge had discretion as to the sentence to be imposed, as in the present case, it was the "duty of the court to examine the witnesses as to the aggravation or mitigation of the offense." The defense would ask that they be permitted "at such time as the court may direct" to offer evidence of the mental condition of the defendants "to show the degree of responsibility they had," to present evidence of their youth, and to have the pleas of guilty taken into consideration—all as grounds for mitigating the punishment.

"With that, we throw ourselves upon the mercy of this court—and this court alone," Darrow concluded.

The formalities continued. Judge Caverly indicated that the defendants should rise and approach the bench. "Nathan Leopold, Jr.," Caverly began, "if your plea be guilty, and the plea of guilty is entered in this case, 33623, the court may sentence you to death; the court may sentence you to the penitentiary for the term of your natural life; the court may sentence you to the penitentiary for a term of years not less than fourteen. Now, realizing the consequences of your plea, do you still desire to plead guilty?"

"I do," said Leopold. By his answer he assured himself a jail sentence of at least fourteen years and did not remove the possibility of facing death on the gallows.

"Let the plea of guilty be entered, Mr. Clerk, in indictment number 33623, charging Nathan Leopold, Jr., with murder."

The judge repeated the question for Loeb, who gave the same answer. Caverly then questioned the defendants about the kidnapping charge. The minimum sentence for kidnapping was five years in prison. Both youths acknowledged that they also wished to plead guilty to kidnapping, then sat down. The attorneys approached the bench.

Removing his glasses, Crowe, no longer jovial, indicated that he intended to present all the evidence he and his assistants had gathered. Guilty plea or not, he intended to establish the aggravated nature of the case.

Benjamin Bachrach had a proposition. He said the defense psychiatrists were men "well known in the country generally and also well known to the alienists for the state." Bachrach proposed a conference between the defense and prosecution alienists.

Crowe, angered at apparently being outmaneuvered once, didn't want to concede any further points to his opponents. "Is there a plea of guilty entered here by two sane men," he persisted, "or is the defense entering a plea of guilty by two insane men? If there is any contention they are insane, I ask your honor to call a jury of twelve men so that the state may demonstrate beyond all reasonable doubt that these boys are sane."

Bachrach replied that the defense did not contend the defendants were insane, in which case a jury trial would be required, but simply wished to offer evidence of their abnormality as grounds for sparing their lives. It was admittedly a fine line on which to draw a distinction, but Bachrach didn't dwell on the matter. He suggested that the defense psychiatrists wanted to meet with the state alienists to see if they could agree on a joint medical report to avoid the "vaudevillian spectacle" that usually occurred when medical experts clashed at a trial.

"Well," Judge Caverly commented. "The court, of course, as you say, has no power to require the state's attorney to do that and the state's attorney, at his leisure or at any time that is fit, may give you his answer."

Crowe needed no leisure time. He rejected the suggestion at once. "The state's attorney," he snapped, "is in a position to prove by evidence beyond all reasonable doubt that these boys are not only guilty, but that they are absolutely sane under the law and should be hanged."

The judge announced that rather than wait until August 4, as projected, the hearing would begin in two days, at 10 A.M. on Wednesday, July 23.

(Over in Paris, France, Meyer Levin would read that the court had decided to hear the case immediately and curse himself for not having remained at home. He would spend the rest of the summer reading in European newspapers what was happening in a Chicago case he could have been covering himself. Frustrated by this missed opportunity, he nevertheless would have an opportunity later to write about Leopold and Loeb.[5])

The preliminary hearing over, reporters flocked to Crowe to obtain his reaction to the startling development. "There was nothing left for Leopold and Loeb to do but plead guilty," rumbled the state's attorney. "The proof was so overwhelming that no jury could return any verdict except one of guilty. The crime was so cold-blooded, premeditated, and atrocious that no jury could fix any punishment except death.

"The fact that the two murderers have thrown themselves on the mercy of the court does not in any way alleviate the enormity of the crime they committed. As I informed the court, the state is going to prove not only that these boys are guilty, but that they are absolutely sane and should be hanged. Every exhibit will be laid before Judge Caverly. There is but one punishment that will satisfy the prosecution—that they be hanged!"[6]

The *Tribune* reluctantly announced it would not broadcast the trial. The newspaper and its radio station WGN had "no other course," because of the final vote—6,529 had opposed the proposal while only 4,169 had supported it. The public had spoken, with surprising good taste.[7]

The newspaper, however, did urge two reforms "to safeguard American justice": drastic restriction of pretrial publicity, coupled with full publicity during trials, which would include radio coverage. Admitting its "share of blame," the paper observed that pretrial publicity had "become an abomination." Stimulated by public demand, the human craving for excitement, newspapers had for years engaged in an orgy of sensationalism and "journalistic lynch law." The Franks case had been especially bad—"a two months moral pestilence imposed upon our people before trial." It was unclear whether the editorialist was speaking to the public or to reporters in his own woodshed.

Yet no one could deny the people had got what they wanted. They hungered for information about the case because the crime horrified and puzzled them. The fact that it was a crime without motive, a murder committed as a lark, bemused the public. That Leopold and Loeb should select their victim by chance, almost as if by the flip of a coin, frightened many people. And there were many who felt that the murder of Bobby Franks was a new kind of crime, one symptomatic of the times.

Judge Ben B. Lindsey of Denver, an authority on juvenile delinquency, would write: "It is a new kind of murder with a new kind of cause. That cause is to be found in the modern mentality and modern freedom of youth, with the misunderstanding between parenthood and childhood. Thus we have the modern misdirection of youth. Do you not, then, see this is more than the story of murder? It is the story of modern youth, the story of modern parents, the story of modern education, even though it is an extreme and exceptional episode in the stream of modern life. There are lesser offenses that come from the same causes and pass us by almost daily. The indifference to the rights of others in stealing of automobiles, in joy rides, jazz parties, petting parties, freedom in sex relations and the mania for speed on every turn. They do not gain our attention, because they are not so startling, so terrible."[8]

Judge Lindsey wrote those words in 1924.

Spring had turned to summer since Bobby Franks' death. The killers had been caught and their trial now would begin before the eyes of the world. Hidden from those eyes, down the block from the Loeb home, in her own mansion, Mrs. Flora Franks sat by the window for hours, waiting for her son to return. Her lilacs had bloomed and faded. Bobby was dead, but Flora Franks, now a pale and listless recluse in her large, still house, had faith that his abductors would release him. His room had been kept just the way it was the day he disappeared—bright and cheery: The set of Dickens in the bookcase, the baseball with Babe Ruth's autograph, Bobby's prize possession, on the shelf in his closet. Nothing had changed. Spring had turned to summer—but not for Flora Franks.

16 Prosecution

At last the curtain rises and the actors come out upon the stage: Master Mind and Angel Face make their grand entrance. They are immaculately dressed—the class of fashion and the mold of form. Dickie saunters along with all the grace and bearing of a Valentino promenading on the screen. Nathan Jr. smiles more condescendingly and hurries to his seat.

—LEONORE OVITT[1]

Sunlight poured through the twelve-foot-high windows in the sixth-floor courtroom of the Criminal Courts Building early Wednesday morning, July 23. The day was hot and getting hotter. By the 10 A.M. scheduled start of the hearing in mitigation and aggravation of the offense by Nathan Leopold, Jr., and Richard Loeb, the temperature would reach 84 degrees. The freshly varnished courtroom glistened in the sunshine. A bank of telegraph machines, especially equipped to transmit noiselessly and staffed by a dozen telegraph operators, had been installed in the jury box to Judge Caverly's left. The counsel tables were before him.

Seats had been reserved on the left side of the courtroom (as viewed by the judge) for the Leopold, Loeb, and Franks families and other friends of the court. Members of the press would occupy the space on the right and behind a wooden railing in the front of the room. The court accommodatd 300 people. Judge Caverly issued 200 pink tickets to local newsmen and correspondents for news agencies and out-of-town papers. Reporters from all over the United States had traveled to Chicago to cover the hearing, but not all obtained access. "There were six hundred journalists at the Democratic convention in New York," one correspondent reported. "It is apparent they all came here." Only seventy seats had been set aside for the public; eager spectators would contest hotly for them each day.

A number of policemen stood at the entrance to the building and also on the fifth floor, the floor where the elevator stopped. Others guarded the staircase leading to the sixth floor, checking credentials. Additional officers lined the hall on the sixth floor leading from stairway to courtroom. Finally, inside, policemen guarded the courtroom itself.[2]

Although nobody so intended it, the trial of the century—as the "hearing" would be misnamed—was taking on the air of a Roman holiday. The Chicago *Tribune* later would comment in its editorial columns: "The courts are in the Coliseum. The Franks case has been a three months' moral pestilence imposed upon our people." Interest in the case remained high all summer and only on rare occasions would another news story shove Leopold and Loeb aside and earn the main headline atop the front page.

The morning the hearing began the *Tribune* published an interview with Dr. James Whitney Hall, one of the defense alienists, who said he and his colleagues agreed that Leopold and Loeb could distinguish right from wrong but were incapable of choosing. "Within five years Leopold will go crazy," Dr. Hall predicted. "Loeb will follow, though his lack of reaction will buoy him up for a while."

In jail the night before, Leopold had conversed with the *Tribune*'s Ty Krum, admitting he could not make up his mind whether or not he wanted to die. Krum asked Leopold how he might act on the gallows.

"I can't say," Leopold replied. "The alienists asked me time after time what my ideas were on death. I used to love life and everything connected with it. Now, it is different. I ask myself what there is for me. I can't find an answer anywhere. I think sometimes that I would welcome death and other times I feel that life is everything. Right now I am in a quandary."

Early Wednesday morning Judge Caverly left his apartment building in the Edgewater Beach Hotel to drive to the Criminal Courts Building. He arrived at 9 A.M. and worked in his chambers for an hour, clearing his desk of other business. On one occasion, as reporters noted, he walked into the courtroom, obtained a file from his clerk, Fred Scherer, and returned to his chambers.

Caverly, a patient and practical man, had worked hard all his life. Born in London, England, in 1861, he came to Chicago with his family at the age of six. He worked his way through school, carrying water in the steel mills for eighty-seven cents a day. In 1897 he received his law degree from Lake Forest University and obtained a job as assistant city clerk in Chicago, a position he held for five years. He then served as a justice of the peace and police magistrate until appointed corporation counsel in 1906.[3]

While in this job, Caverly uncovered a ring of personal injury lawyers who in eight years had cheated the city out of almost $3,700,000 by obtaining fraudulent judgments. He greatly reduced the size of personal injury judgments collected from the city, saving Chicago almost $1,500,000 in three years. He was elected judge of the municipal court in 1910, and again in 1916, and was elected to the circuit court in 1921 on a coalition ticket that defeated the handpicked slate of Big Bill Thompson. Two years later Caverly became chief justice of the Criminal Court.

On one occasion a woman brought a salesman before him in a breach of promise suit. The salesman claimed he was victim of a blackmail scheme, offering in evidence a letter in which the writer demanded money, threatening trouble "if you *dispoint* me."

Judge Caverly asked the woman for a sample of her handwriting, telling her to write: "If I lose this case it will disappoint me."

"If I lose this case it will *dispoint* me," the woman wrote.

"You may go," the judge instructed the salesman, then turned to the woman. "As for you, you should learn to spell."

Caverly at times could be harsh, once reprimanding a jury for acquitting a defendant whom he thought guilty of molesting a little girl. He sentenced the man to six months in jail anyway for contempt of court. The defendant had made the mistake of shouting an indecent word at a witness during the trial. But Caverly also could show mercy, as when an Army veteran appeared before him to plead guilty of stealing an overcoat. The judge offered him probation, saying, "If the government had treated this man fairly after his service, he wouldn't be forced to steal to get warm clothes."

Judge Caverly, however, was not universally well thought of by his peers. According to Ernst W. Puttkammer, the University of Chicago professor under whom Nathan Leopold had studied criminal law: "Judge Caverly did not enjoy the highest of reputations, frankly, for his legal acumen and ability."[4] In addition, Judge Caverly lunched frequently with Alderman "Hinky Dink" Kenna, boss of the corruption-ridden First Ward. Judge Caverly was a product of the system where seats on the bench were filled with men more noted for their political than their legal knowledge.

At one point in his career, while campaigning for office, Judge Caverly recommended sending every criminal to the penitentiary and hanging every murderer. That helped get him elected. Five times during his stay on the bench he had imposed the death penalty, but in each instance it was punishment fixed by a jury.

As they waited for court to convene, Leopold and Loeb smoked cigarettes and chatted with a group of reporters who clustered around their cell. Both had dressed immaculately, Leopold in a sporty gray tweed suit, Loeb in a black suit and powder blue shirt.

"I hear you fellows had a hard time describing our clothes the other day," Leopold remarked. "I don't want you to make any mistakes this time. Remember, this is an important day. Now look at me. What am I wearing? If I walked away this minute not one of you could tell—accurately. So I'm going to help out. Dick's hat is a soft fedora, as you can see. It's dull gray. Mine is slate gray."

He puffed on his cigarette and laughed, then continued: "Now, did you get that straight?"

"Oh, shut up, Babe," Loeb interrupted, turning away.[5]

Just before ten, six bailiffs arrived, handcuffed the defendants, and escorted them from the jail across the connecting bridge to the Criminal Courts Building. When the pair arrived, Judge Caverly sat waiting on the bench. All the attorneys were present: for the state, Robert E. Crowe and his four assistants, Joseph Savage, John Sbarbaro, Thomas Marshall, and Milton Smith; for the defense, Clarence Darrow and the Bachrach brothers, Benjamin and Walter. Every seat was taken, and a large crowd stood in the corridor outside.

The attorneys for both sides agreed that the murder case would be heard first, with only a short concluding presentation of the kidnapping charges. After the defendants again assured the judge of their desire to plead guilty, State's Attorney Crowe, his jaw thrust forward, rose and approached the bench to make his opening statement. He began:

"The evidence in this case will show that Nathan Leopold, Jr., is a young man nineteen years old, that the other defendant, Richard Loeb, is a young man of nineteen years; that they are both sons of highly respected and prominent citizens of this community; that their parents gave them every advantage wealth and indulgence could give to boys. They have attended the best schools in this community and have, from time to time, had private tutors. These young men behaved as a majority of young men in their social set behaved, with the exception that they developed a desire to gamble, and gambled, for large stakes, the size of the stakes being such that even their wealthy companions could not sit with them."[6]

The state's attorney continued: "The evidence will further show that along in October or November of last year these two defendants entered into a conspiracy, the purpose of which was to gain money, and in order to gain it they were ready and willing to commit a cold-blooded murder."

Crowe paused and wiped his glasses. He would make this unconscious gesture frequently. The *Tribune* correspondent reported him wiping them "fifty times" during his opening statement. The state's attorney walked toward a table covered with the evidence he would use to prove his case: Nathan Leopold's eyeglasses, Pierce Bitker's stolen and badly battered typewriter, the blood stained floorboards from the rented Willys-Knight. Crowe picked up the ransom letter and the note that had been hidden in the train telegraph box for Mr. Franks. After reading them, he related the details surrounding the arrest of the defendants. He told of the interrogations and the resulting confessions. In so doing, he let slip an important fact:

"The state will show unargued to your honor that the motive which prompted Richard Loeb to so suddenly and unexpectedly confess was another evidence of his cautiousness and his craftiness and his desire to protect his own hide. He knew that the man who had beaten the life out of this little boy was his confederate, Leopold—"

Until this point in the trial, the identity of the person wielding the murder weapon had remained an unanswered question, each defendant accusing the other. State's Attorney Crowe, however, seemed ready to believe Loeb in his accusation of Leopold. Crowe's identification of Leopold as the killer, however, got drowned in his oratory, and few reporters emphasized it in their stories published the next day.

Crowe, in fact, confused the issue somewhat when he continued: "Their story is identical in all essential details except each of them—careful of their own skin, much more careful than they were of the body of little Franks—says the scheme originated with the other. Each one says the other is the man who struck and choked out the life of this poor little boy." In identifying Leopold as the killer, Crowe may have been operating on information unknown to others, or he simply may have tripped over his own rhetoric. It would not be the last word spoken on that subject.

Crowe spoke on for almost an hour. The temperature outside had risen to 90 degrees, but it seemed even hotter in the crammed courtroom. Most of the men had removed their jackets. Many in the room fanned themselves. Crowe dripped with sweat, his fresh white shirt soaked. He glanced at the defendants, then returned his gaze to the judge.

"The state will show to your honor by facts and circumstances, by witnesses, by exhibits, by documents, that these men are guilty of the most cruel, cowardly, dastardly murder ever committed in the annals of American jurisprudence. The state will demonstrate their guilt here so conclusively that there is not an avenue for them to escape. And making a virtue of necessity, when they have no escape, they throw themselves on the mercy of this court.

"We will prove that all these matters happened in Cook County,

Illinois, and when the state has concluded, when the defense has concluded, and the final arguments are made, in the name of the people of the State of Illinois, in the name of the womanhood and the fatherhood, and in the name of the children of the State of Illinois, we are going to demand the death penalty for both of these cold-blooded, cruel, and vicious murderers."

Crowe sat down, and Clarence Darrow ambled forward to make a short reply. He stuck his hands in his pockets and leaned back. Wisps of hair hung over his forehead.

"A death in any situation is horrible," he began, "but when it comes to the question of murder, it is doubly horrible. But there are degrees perhaps of atrocity, and instead of this being one of the worst of the atrocious character, it is perhaps one of the least painful and of the smallest inducement. Bad, nevertheless, bad enough of course, but anybody with any experience of criminal trials knows what it is to be branded, as it has been repeatedly, as the greatest, most important and atrocious killing that ever happened in the State of Illinois or in the United States."

Crowe rose from his chair. "Objection, your honor," he shouted. Darrow was being argumentative, the state's attorney insisted. It was improper, and this was not the time to make a speech. He should simply put forth what he expected to prove.

Darrow responded, "Your honor, it comes with poor grace from counsel after for more than an hour he sought to stir up feelings in this community."

Judge Caverly allowed Darrow to continue, instructing him to confine his statements to what the defense intended to prove.

"Very well, your honor." Darrow sighed. "I am aware at this time it isn't a proper statement, but I felt outraged at the whole statement that has been made in this case. That accounts for it. All this evidence that is sought to be introduced in this case is utterly incompetent. All of this is added to statements already made publicly and have no bearing on this case whatever with pleas of guilty in it. No one part of the defense claims there was not a conspiracy, that there was not a murder, that it was not done by these two boys, that it was not done in a way that they have already given to the press.

"We shall insist in this case, your honor, that, terrible as this is, terrible as any killing is, it would be without precedent if two boys of this age should be hanged by the neck until dead, and it would in no way bring back Robert Franks or add to the peace and security of this community. I insist that it would be without precedent, as we learned, if on a plea of guilty this should be done.

"When this case is presented, I know this court will take it, take it calmly and honestly, in consideration of the community and in consideration of the lives of these two boys and that any echo that may come back from this extravagant and unlawful statement and from the lurid painting in this courtroom which was made for nothing excepting that a hoarse cry of angry people may somehow reach these chambers—we know your honor would disregard that and do in this case what is just, fair, and merciful, and a court must always interpret justice and mercy together."

Darrow sat down, having spoken for only five minutes, and the prosecution began.

The state presented fifteen witnesses the first day. The defense cross-examined only one, very briefly. That would be the strategy followed by each side. By presenting its evidence in minute detail, as though before a jury, the prosecution hoped to demonstrate the full horror of the crime. The defense, having admitted Leopold and Loeb's guilt, had decided not to challenge a witness unless necessary, hoping this would minimize the impact of the testimony. Unnecessary cross-examination, Darrow and the Bachrachs reasoned, would merely reinforce the crime's brutality. Their job was not to shatter the state's case, but to show, through later arguments, why the defendants should not be hanged. They need not impress twelve inexperienced jurors. They had only to deal with a judge well versed in courtroom procedure who might be thankful for the elimination of unnecessary delay—particularly in the heat of midsummer Chicago.

Edwin Gresham, Mr. Franks' brother-in-law, who identified Bobby's body in the Hegewisch mortuary the day after the murder, testified first for the state. "The body had absolutely no clothing on," Gresham recalled. "It was lying on its back. It had on the glasses. I removed the glasses to make sure that the body was the boy's. I looked further to see that there were marks on the boy's teeth. When the boy was a child, he had rickets, and that had left marks, or pearls, in the teeth, and I looked at the teeth to make sure that the pearls were there. They were there. It was beyond the question of a doubt in my mind that the boy was Robert."

Following Gresham, Jacob Franks grimly testified that he last had seen his son alive before Robert left for school on May 21, 1924. He told of receiving the kidnap letter, of obtaining the money and wrapping it in a cigar box as instructed, of being called by the kidnapper, and of being informed by Gresham of the body identification. He identified Bobby's shoes and class pin.

His wife, dressed in black mourning, next entered the courtroom escorted by Samuel Ettelson and walked slowly to the witness stand. She spent only seven minutes testifying, then left by a rear door, supported by Ettelson and her husband.[7]

Genevieve Forbes of the *Tribune* described Flora Franks' day in court: "Mrs. Jacob Franks, a figure of listless sorrow, reticent in her grief, terrible in her voice, and hopelessly unmindful of the future, took the stand yesterday before Chief Justice John R. Caverly of the Criminal Court and explained with numb obedience that Wednesday noon, May 21, was the last time she had seen her son Robert—alive. And with the same primitive torture chiseled so carefully in her face, the mother dully told that it was Friday—no, Saturday—that she had next seen him—his body."

The article continued: "When they put the crumpled shoes and the one brown stocking into her lap, she fingered them and identified them. But from out of a mosaic of the most brilliant colors, perhaps that have been painted into a sensational murder trial, an obscure, subdued, and broken segment of the pattern was suddenly lifted to the key position. For with her testimony Mrs. Franks became the real victim of the murder for which Nathan F. Leopold, Jr. and Richard Loeb, the confessed killers of fourteen-year-old Bobby Franks are now awaiting sentence."[8]

Flora Franks' appearance obviously impressed the reporter from the *Tribune.* Certainly it would have shocked and stunned a jury much more. Darrow's decision to avoid a jury trial seemed sound.

Dr. Joseph Springer, the coroner's physician, testified that Bobby Franks died "from an injury to the head, associated with suffocation."[9] He indicated, when questioned by John Sbarbaro, that he examined the boy to determine whether he had been molested. "The genitals were intact," he said, "but the rectum was dilated and would admit easily one middle finger." The doctor claimed he found no evidence of a recent forceable dilation. Loeb chuckled at the doctor's remarks.

In having Dr. Springer so questioned, State's Attorney Crowe apparently hoped to show that in addition to kidnapping Bobby Franks and murdering him, the defendants had sexually molested him. In their confessions they admitted that Bobby Franks had been struck by chisel and gagged shortly after five Wednesday afternoon. Both said that Bobby Franks was dead when they removed him from the car and placed him in the culvert, around nine. They also told how during this four-hour time period they paused once in a deserted prairie in Indiana and removed some of his clothing—including his trousers, stockings, and shoes. ("We did this in order that we might be saved the trouble of too much undressing him later on," Loeb had claimed in his confession.)

But neither of the killers could tell—*or would admit*—at what exact moment Bobby Franks died.

Dr. Springer actually confused this issue by his testimony. The coroner's physician first said that he had found partly digested food in the boy's stomach, indicating he had eaten four or five hours before his death. (Dr. William B. McNally, a chemist connected with the coroner's office, would indicate in separate testimony the following day that death came "five to six hours after a meal.") Since Bobby's mother had testified that she last saw him when he came home for lunch at noon on Wednesday, that placed the time of his death anywhere from 4:30 to 6:30 P.M. (Emotional stress, such as fright, however, can retard digestion.)The two killers had paused for hot dogs and root beers at the Dew Drop Inn near Hammond shortly before sundown. It seems unlikely that Bobby Franks, still alive and unsuspecting his fate, might have joined them in that last meal, but a number of questions remain unanswered to this day because of the medical testimony.

This is because Dr. Springer also introduced into evidence his official coroner's report, made several days after the murder, saying the boy had died *two to five hours before his examination* (see page 54). Rigor mortis had not set in, claimed the doctor. Incredibly he did not include in his report the time of his examination! Nor did Sbarbaro press him for that information, perhaps not wanting to embarrass the coroner's physician by calling attention to what seemed to be an obvious error in his testimony. (Rigor mortis disappears eventually, as soon as nine hours after death in some cases, particularly with the young.) Darrow also did not raise the question, partly because of his strategy to avoid unnecessary cross-examination, but also because it was in his clients' interest that the public believe death occurred instantly and therefore painlessly.

Dr. Springer's apparently contradictory statements concerning the time of death were allowed to stand unchallenged, so a gap of twelve hours remains unexplained. The body had been found by Manke and the four railroad signalmen around 9 A.M. Thursday morning and brought to the funeral parlor (according to the testimony of Stanley Olejniczak) between 10 and 10:15 A.M.[10] Had Dr. Springer been summoned from his downtown office immediately, he could not have arrived at the South Side mortuary much before 11 A.M.

Yet it seems he must have appeared near that time. Assuming he knew the body had been found at 9 A.M., it seems unlikely he would have said "two to five hours" had he arrived much beyond that hour. His testimony places the time of death in the early hours around dawn, long after the time Leopold and Loeb said they abandoned the body in the culvert. Therefore, Dr. Springer must have been mistaken in his attempt to establish the time of death. Or was he? There are still unsolved mysteries in the murder of Bobby Franks.

The coroner's physician raised another curious question through his descriptions of the various wounds and scrapes on the body of Bobby Franks. He described cuts and scratches on the forehead which were antemortem, or before death. These were the blows caused by the chisel. And he talked about cuts on the buttocks and the shoulders which were postmortem, or after death. Presumably these were caused when the two murderers dragged the naked body across the ground prior to stuffing it in the culvert. They could also have been caused when the railroad signalmen removed the body the following morning.

But Dr. Springer also described other scratches on Bobby Franks' back, over his left shoulder, and on his right buttocks, "all of which were antemortem." These scratches could have been caused only after the victim's protective clothing had been removed—and when he was still alive. Whether or not a wound is antemortem or postmortem can be determined by the presence or absence of blood. After circulation has stopped, a body generally stops bleeding.[11] Crowe failed to have Dr. Springer questioned about these antemortem scratches; Darrow did not wish to cross-examine him.

The day after Dr. Springer's testimony a trio of toxicologists and chemists from the state's attorney's office (Drs. William B. McNally, Dr. John A. Wesner, and Dr. Ralph W. Webster) appeared on the witness stand to testify concerning the condition of the body and various tests to which it and various items of clothing and parts of the automobile were subjected. Much of their testimony was cold, almost mechanistic, but the fact that comes through is the large amount of blood that was apparently spilled. Blood was found on the robe with which the body had been covered and in which it had been carried to the culvert. Blood was found on the rug of the car in the rear seat. It even soaked through the floorboards beneath. Blood splattered the trousers worn by both killers, as well as the rubber boots worn by Leopold. Most of Bobby Franks' clothing could not be tested since his killers had incinerated it that night. Bobby's shoes and one stocking had been recovered, however.[12] Dr. McNally testified that he found no evidence of blood on either the shoes or the stocking!

Both killers admitted removing the trousers, stockings, and shoes during the first stop in Indiana. If most of the blood flow had occurred after that stop, it would account for the lack of blood on the shoes and the stocking. It might even mean that Bobby Franks still had been alive at the time his trousers were removed. Could he have been conscious? Maybe. The wounds that caused the greatest flow of blood may have been inflicted at the stop rather than immediately after he got into the car, as the two murderers claimed in their confessions.

The existence of the one stocking found in the swamp, however, raised a most fascinating question, one that went completely unnoticed in 1924.

Why was the stocking not burned with the other clothes which were removed from the murder scene? In his confession Leopold said he thought they had dropped the stocking while carrying the robe containing the clothes back to their automobile; Loeb did not mention the stocking at this point. But why were the stockings with the other clothes at this point? Leopold mentioned removing them at the previous stop; so did Loeb. When questioned about what clothing had been removed in Indiana, Loeb mentioned the stockings a second time. Assuming the stockings indeed had been removed in Indiana, it seems puzzling that they should be carried from the car to the culvert and then back to the car, permitting one to be dropped en route.

Several solutions to the puzzle suggest themselves. One is that after the trousers and stockings were removed in Indiana, they were put back on again, perhaps even by a still-alive Bobby Franks. This would support the theory that an act of perversion was committed in Indiana. Yet it seems unlikely. A second solution might be that despite the killers' statements about removing the stockings at the first stop, the stockings did not come off until they reached the culvert. If so, why was the stocking not smeared with blood like everything else? The third and most intriguing solution might be that one stocking was brought from the car and purposely *thrown* into the swamp to serve as a clue in the scavenger hunt devised by the two thrill killers. But if the stocking were left as a clue, could the eyeglasses also have been left as a clue? Had either Leopold or Loeb—or one of them without the other's knowledge—purposely sown the seed of their own doom as another part of their diabolical game?

In their confessions, each of the murderers said he knew Bobby Franks was dead when they stuffed him in the culvert because rigor mortis had set in. Loeb added the additional detail that there had been no tremor of the body when Leopold poured hydrochloric acid on the face, belly, and genitals. But the coroner's physician, in his report, indicated that rigor mortis had *not* set in at the time of his examination. Maybe Dr. Springer was correct in his belief death had come two to five hours before that time. Is it possible the murderers left Bobby Franks alive but dying when they fled that night? And is it possible that death came to the kidnapped boy, unconscious but medically "alive," shortly before Tony Manke discovered the body? Dr. Springer testified, "he came to his death from an injury to the head, associated with suffocation." He did not say when the blow occurred or when the suffocation occurred. The testimony *suggests* that death came much later than has been supposed. Since neither side seemed interested in exploring the questions raised by the contradictions of fact, they had not been answered. Nevertheless, the hint of sexual perversion would hang like a dark cloud over the courtroom as the hearing continued.

State's Attorney Crowe proceeded with his step-by-step detailing of the conspiracy. Other witnesses testified that Loeb rented a room at the Morrison Hotel on May 7, that Leopold rented a car and opened a bank account at the Hyde Park Bank on the same day, and that Loeb posed as Louis Mason and was called at a restaurant at 1352 Wabash as a reference. Thomas Taylor, the house detective at the Morrison, described finding a card in one of the books left in the hotel room identifying it as having been checked out from the University of Chicago library by Richard A. Loeb.[13] Taylor examined the card two days before the murder. It could have been another planted clue, but neither prosecution nor defense seemed interested in pausing for psychological considerations yet. The defense even seemed irritated by the meticulous way in which Crowe was proving what they already had conceded, the guilt of the defendants.

"If the court pleases," Benjamin Bachrach said when William C. Herndon, the assistant manager of the rental company, followed Walter L. Jacobs, the manager, to the stand. "If this is the same corroborative testimony of the witness who has just testified, I suggest there is no use reporting it. There will be no denial of the testimony from the Rent-A-Car people. There will be no dispute about that."

Crowe rebutted: "I prefer, if your honor pleases, to present my case. Of course, the plea of guilty admits everything. Your honor is going to be asked to fix the punishment here and I want to show by the mountain of evidence we have piled up that, when they pleaded guilty, there was not anything else they could do but plead guilty. I want to show their guilt clearly and conclusively, and the details of it, and ask that they be hanged. I don't think I ought to be limited."

"You are permitted to go into every detail," the judge ruled.

The first session ended shortly after four in the afternoon. Bailiffs led the prisoners back over the bridge to the county jail and locked them in their cells on the sixth and seventh floors. "Say, 614, shoot over that paper and let's see what they have to say about us," Loeb said to his cellmate, Edward Donker, who was reading a newspaper.

Leopold had pork chops for dinner. Ty Krum of the *Tribune,* who had seen them every day since their arrest, said they seemed as lighthearted as before. Leopold went to sleep shortly after seven, but Loeb stayed up for several hours, reading newspapers and a book.

"The hangman's noose dangles in Judge Caverly's courtroom," the *Tribune* reported in summarizing the first day of the hearing. "It is just over the heads of Leopold and Loeb. Most of the time these most talked about of all criminals smile and seem to feel pretty good. Clarence Darrow, chief counsel for the defense, paces here and about like an old lion, giving the noose a swift shove now and again. State's Attorney Crowe is there like a panther, darting out to put the noose where he thinks it belongs, just over the heads of Leopold and Loeb."

The nickname Old Lion would stick to Darrow for the rest of his career.

Before court convened the morning of Thursday, July 23, Richard Loeb told a group of reporters he had an important statement to make. The newsmen eagerly pressed against his cell, clutching their notebooks. "We are united in one great and profound hope for today," Loeb said portentously. "Mr. Leopold and I have gone over the matter and have come to a mutual decision. We have just one hope: that it will be a damned sight cooler than it was yesterday." Loeb burst into laughter.

The reporters asked Leopold if he would like to play tennis that afternoon. "Thank you, no," he said. "It so happens that I have another more pressing engagement. Perhaps another time." Leopold told the group that he had been conducting an experiment and had figured out a way to determine the time by watching the sun move across the bars on his window. It was an infallible method, he assured the reporters. "However, I'm thinking of asking to have the sun shifted a bit. As it stands now, my system is worthless for daylight savings calculations. And that's very important." If the atmosphere in the courtroom was grim, life could be maintained on a civilized level between murderers and reporters backstage.

The parade of prosecution witnesses continued, some testifying for but a few minutes. Crowds continued to flock to the courtroom. Jacob and Allan Loeb, Nathan Leopold, Sr., and Mike Leopold reoccupied the seats that would be theirs for the remainder of the summer. Every night Allan Loeb telephoned his parents in Charlevoix and reported on the day's developments. Sad and silent, Mr. Leopold, consumed by grief, seemed a figure of great compassion.

"Here are the sins of the children visited upon the fathers. In all the earth you would not find agony more intense than in the face of the unfortunate man," said Arthur Brisbane, the distinguished Hearst syndicated columnist, of Nathan Leopold, Sr. "A great painter of old days attended the torture chamber to study muscles working in the faces of men stretched upon the rack. Here such an artist would find his subject in the unfortunate father of the young murderer."

Chin in his hand, carefully taking notes, Judge Caverly intently heard all the testimony: a Pullman employee from New York who retrieved the letter to Mr. Franks left in the train by Richard Loeb, the doctor who prescribed Leopold's glasses, the Leopold family's maid, the family chauffeur and his wife, the members of Leopold's study group, the night watchman who found the chisel, the clerk who sold Loeb a train ticket on May 22, the men from whom Leopold and Loeb bought rope, chisel, acid, and stationery, the worker who found Bobby's body, the railwayman who found Leopold's glasses, the owner of the funeral parlor where the body was taken, the pharmacist who answered one of the telephone calls for Jacob Franks, the porter who answered the other call, police officers, reporters, anyone who Crowe thought could shed light on the murder.

Leon Mandel II, just returned from Europe and described by the United Press as "rosy cheeked and curly haired," testified that he knew both Leopold and Loeb socially and that he often played bridge with them for money. They played for between five and ten cents a point, whereas his other friends played for between one and three cents a point. On cross-examination, Mandel said that Leopold and Loeb always played against each other, and that the biggest loss incurred in any of their games was $80. He admitted that he had lost a total of only $300 or $400 in all the games he played with the defendants. Despite the wealth of other evidence assembled, the state's attorney felt he needed to establish a motive for the kidnapping: that Leopold and Loeb wanted the ransom money to cover their high living and gambling debts.

Mandel also admitted under questioning that he and Leopold had worked on a translation of a book on perversion by Aretino, a sixteenth-century Italian author. "We worked together on the translation," Mandel said.

"Does he know as much about it as you do?" Crowe asked. Mandel answered promptly, "I know more than he does."

Leopold reportedly sneered at this comment by Mandel.[14]

A chauffeur, Carl Ulvigh, said he saw Loeb in a dark car—"a real dark blue or dark green, I don't know which it was, but it was a dark color"—going south on Ellis near Forty-ninth at about 4:30 P.M. on May 21. The window curtains were drawn, but he could see Loeb and another man sitting next to him. He had known Loeb for years and waved at him as their cars passed. Loeb "lifted his hand" and waved back.[15]

Leopold shot forward in his seat and leaned over Darrow's shoulder. "That man is lying or he is badly mistaken," he said and informed his attorney that if he did not cross-examine the witness, he, Leopold, would ask the judge to let him do so. He felt the testimony supported Loeb's story that he, Loeb, was driving when Bobby was murdered and therefore Leopold had been the actual killer. Leopold later would admit that the testimony was trivial and had no bearing on the overall case, but he refused to let it pass.[16] Benjamin Bachrach questioned the chauffeur, who described his reaction on reading in the newspapers that Loeb had confessed the murder. "I don't believe that," he said to a friend. "I saw Dick Loeb driving a car that Wednesday, but it was no Winton." (At that time the public still believed that a Winton, rather than a Willys-Knight, had been the murder vehicle.) If anything, Bachrach's cross-examination of Ulvigh seemed to support the chauffeur's contention that Loeb had been driving the car shortly before the murder occurred.

On Friday, July 25, George Porter Lewis, thin, bespectacled, Leopold's birding companion, took the stand. He said Leopold called him after first being interrogated about the Franks murder case to ask if Lewis had lost his glasses during their Sunday visit to Wolf Lake. "I felt my breast pocket and I told him they were there, that I hadn't lost them," testified Lewis. "He said there was the possibility that the glasses that had been found in the vicinity had something to do with the Franks case, but they didn't think it was certain that they did."[17]

Lewis recalled that Leopold asked him if he owned two pair of glasses, but Lewis replied, only one. Leopold had thought Lewis might be questioned by the police and suggested that he not inform his parents about the situation, because "it might worry them."

Ernst W. Puttkammer, Leopold's criminal law professor, appeared to tell of how Nathan had wanted to discuss the Franks case during class several days after the murder. Puttkammer had demurred, but Leopold popped up in his office shortly afterward with probing legal questions about the situation. Leopold thought he had found a flaw in the law. A penalty for kidnapping was death, as was the penalty for murder. The law, therefore, encouraged the kidnapper to kill his victim.

Puttkammer described Leopold as one of his brightest students and said he was one of the leaders in class discussions. As he stepped down from the stand, Judge Caverly called a short recess, and the professor passed the defendants being led away. Leopold tapped him on the shoulder and said, "Mr. Puttkammer, I really want to thank you for those nice things you said about me."

Puttkammer mumbled something in return, and they parted. Leopold's coolness made a profound impression on the law professor. "My testimony actually worked against his interests," he would say later, "because it showed he was a person in possession of the knowledge of what he was doing."[18]

Later that day Detective James Gortland, a large man with an enormous head, testified that he had a conversation with Leopold on the evening of June 1. Leopold had said he was "not at all" sorry that he killed Bobby Franks, and as far as the Franks family was concerned, he did not "give a damn if they would croak this minute."[19]

Gortland continued: "I asked him how it was that he confessed. He said that it became manifestly impossible to maintain his story. I said the people are probably not satisfied with the motive expressed in this case—of adventure, excitement, and money. And I says, 'Is there any other motive?' And he says, 'Well, adventure and money.' And he says, 'But you don't think I am entirely a fool. Don't you think I am entitled to reserve something for my defense?' I said, 'Well, what do you think your defense will be?' He stated, 'Well, that will depend on the wishes of my father and the lawyers. Of course, if they wish me to hang, I will plead not guilty and the jury will hang me, or I will plead guilty before a friendly judge and get life imprisonment.'"

Darrow wheeled around in his seat, his eyes flashing with anger. "Did you say that, Babe?" he snapped at his client.

"Hell no!" Leopold said.[20]

Gortland's testimony continued on Saturday. When the detective finished his direct testimony, Darrow rose and walked to the witness stand. He questioned the detective in a friendly conversational manner. Gortland said he had been with the police department for twelve years and before that had worked as chief clerk to the trainmaster of the Michigan Central. He claimed he and Leopold had held their discussion in the state's attorney's office.

"Who was with you?" prodded Darrow.

"Nobody but he and I," Gortland replied.

"What room were you in?"

"Room five."

"'And how long did you talk with him?"

"Just a short while."

"Did you make any memoranda on it?"

"Not at that time."

As Darrow's questions continued, the attorney's friendly tone slowly disappeared. Gortland insisted he had mentioned the conversation to Detective Frank Johnson and a reporter from the *Tribune* that same night. Later, he said he had told citizens in the street, relatives, and Assistant State's Attorney Joseph Savage.

"Who else connected with the state's attorney's office did you ever make this statement to?" Darrow demanded.

"I made it to Crowe."

"And there is no memorandum in any of your written reports, is there?"

Gortland admitted there was not.

"And there is nothing in writing anywhere that contains any mention of it except the notes that you refer to made after the conversation with Crowe?"

"No, sir."

"This memorandum in your handwriting—I believe you say you made Thursday?"

"Yes, sir."

"Day before yesterday?" Gortland acknowledged that to be true. Darrow paused, glared at the detective, and in a roar denounced him as a liar. "Don't you know that this story of yours in reference to a friendly judge is a pure fabrication made for the purpose of intimidating this court?"

"It is not," said Gortland.

When Crowe reexamined the detective, Gortland admitted he had not talked to the state's attorney about the case last Thursday when they met to review his testimony. But even though Gortland's recollection of Leopold's arrogant remarks had the ring of truth to them, Darrow had shaken, if not destroyed, his credibility at least about the statements concerning the friendly judge.

Most of the early points in the case, however, were being scored by the prosecution. One out-of-town Hearst journalist, William Anthony McGuire, returned to his hotel room after a court session and, being a baseball fan, asked the desk clerk for today's score. "The state won today," the desk clerk replied.[21]

Another reporter visited the defendants in jail one day and told Leopold he felt sorry for him.

"Now, listen," Leopold replied angrily. "I certainly don't like that. I don't want you to feel sorry for me and, if you do, I wish you'd change your mind. I don't feel sorry for myself for what I did. I did it and that's all. I got myself in this jam and it's up to myself to get out. I have great feeling for my father and brothers. But myself? No. As far as being remorseful, I can't see it. Life is what we make it and I appear to have made mine what it is today. That's my concern and nobody else's."

The reporter also spoke with Richard Loeb and told him he seemed to be getting a kick out of the case, that he appeared to be having a good time.

"I sit in the courtroom and watch the play as it progresses," Loeb responded. "When the crowd laughs, I laugh. When it is time to be serious, I'm serious. I'm a spectator, you know, and like to feel myself as one. You can tell the people on the outside that there is no faking or pretending. I've watched others in the courtroom and they laugh, smile, yawn, look bored, and all the other things. Why should I be any different?"

One nonreporter who attended the hearing was Eleanor Baxter, who later that year would marry State's Attorney Crowe's younger brother William. Her future brother-in-law had given her a ticket of admission that allowed her to sit immediately behind the two accused one day. "They snickered all the way through the hearing," she recalled years later. "The two of them were constantly passing remarks back and forth to each other. They acted very smart-alecky. Whether it was the ignorance of the judge or the attorneys that amused them, I don't know. It was remarkable to see two kids on trial for their life acting like that."[22]

The state approached the end of its case. The crowds outside the courtroom increased as time approached for the defense to start presenting its evidence in mitigation. On July 29 a huge crowd, mostly women, surged up to the sixth floor. Several bailiffs had to link arms in the doorway to stop them from barging into the courtroom. The court stenographer who had recorded the two confessions, E. M. Allen, appeared to enter those documents in evidence as well as other transcripts of the preconfession interrogations. When his voice tired, both defense and prosecution attorneys cooperated in reading the documents into the official record.

Jacob Franks had been watching the defendants, trying to analyze them, and he admitted to being baffled. "I thought I was a pretty good judge of human nature during my long experience," he commented, "but I find I have encountered an unsolvable problem. It's impossible for me to sit there and believe, as I watch those boys, that they are the ones who killed my child. They seem so gentle; they're so refined-looking."

On Wednesday, July 30, Nathan Leopold, Jr., and Richard Loeb, their hair freshly cut, took particular pains to look neat. In the lockup before being brought to court, they adjusted their ties, and Loeb slicked back his hair. Mrs. Darrow, wearing a dotted blue dress, and Mrs. Crowe and Mrs. Savage, both in black suits, were in the courtroom. Nathan Leopold, Sr., carried a cane. Jacob Franks wore a lavender shirt and purple bow tie, as he had the day he testified.[23] It was oppressively hot in court that morning as the reading of the confessions was completed.

At 10:10 A.M., only a week after the trial had begun, State's Attorney Robert E. Crowe rested his case. He had summoned eighty-one witnesses and demonstrated, he thought, the guilt of the defendants beyond a doubt. The attorneys for the defense, of course, already had conceded that point by having their clients plead guilty. The question still to be resolved was whether Clarence Darrow and the Bachrachs could convince Judge Caverly that the lives of Leopold and Loeb should be spared.

17 Mitigation

The history of man's attitude toward wrongdoing, be it in the form of sin, crime, or insanity, makes a very dark picture. It is not so many years ago that the sinner was burned and the insane chained in dungeons as moral criminals, nor so many more that the lawbreaker was broken upon the wheel. I wonder if most of those who are crying out for the hanging of those boys are not actuated by the same impulses that moved medieval inquisitors.

—LEONARD BLUMGART[1]

The first defense witness, Dr. William Alanson White, was a heavyset man with gray hair and bushy black eyebrows. Dr. White served as superintendent of the largest mental institution in the country, St. Elizabeth's Hospital in Washington, D.C., and was president of the American Psychiatric Association. Fifty-four years old, a psychiatrist for thirty-one years, and a proponent of the new Freudian theories, he had written numerous books and articles.[2] Nathan Leopold particularly was pleased that a man of Dr. White's stature had agreed to participate in his defense. In addition to having attracted the world's best-known criminal attorney, Darrow, he could now boast of having the man he later would describe, accurately, as the "dean of American psychiatrists."[3]

As soon as Dr. White took the stand, however, State's Attorney Crowe jumped to his feet. Over the weekend the Hulbert and Bowman report had found its way to the newspapers. This was the report made by two of the psychiatrists who had examined Leopold and Loeb: Dr. H. S. Hulbert of Oak Park, Illinois, and Dr. Karl M. Bowman of Boston. (Darrow had referred to it while trying to convince Max Schrayer to testify.) Its release and subsequent publication on the front pages of several Chicago newspapers caused an immediate sensation because of the intimate details it revealed about the lives of the accused killers.

The method in which this "secret" medical report was released caused a mild controversy. Supposedly it was stolen from a secretary's desk in Clarence Darrow's office by an enterprising *Tribune* reporter. Learning of the theft, Darrow expressed his outrage and gave copies to other members of the press so they would not be scooped. The *Tribune* published a condensed version of the report on Monday, July 26, blaming the theft on "a morning newspaper," without saying *which* morning newspaper. The *Herald and Examiner* published a more complete version of the report that same morning. Considering the fact that the report was "stolen" over the weekend and published on a Monday when ordinarily there would be no news from the hearing (the same Monday before the defense was about to present its case), it seems probable that Darrow permitted the report to be stolen. If he did not, he should have.

Crowe understandably was outraged at what he read in the report. (Darrow had made a copy available to his opponent also.) The state's attorney considered it a weaseling document, one that bobbed and weaved around the question of whether or not the two murderers were insane, without ever producing an answer to that question. Crowe suspected that Darrow would adapt that same approach in the courtroom in introducing testimony by alienists (forensic psychiatrists) who would hint the boys were insane while saying they were not.

The state's attorney pounded his fist on the document table in front of the bar. "What is the defense trying to do here?" he objected. "Are they attempting to avoid a trial upon a plea of not guilty with the defendant before twelve men that would hang them and trying to produce a situation where they can get a trial before one man that they think won't hang them?"

Caverly then voiced his opinion, saying, "I have a right to know whether these boys are competent to plead guilty or not guilty." He went on to say that if he decided at any point that the defendants were insane, he would direct the plea of guilty be withdrawn and call a jury.

Crowe, however, was not satisfied and went on to claim there were no degrees of responsibility. "You do not take a microscope and look into a murderer's head to see what state of mind he was in, because if he is insane he is not responsible, and if he is sane he is responsible. You look not to his mental condition, but you look to the facts surrounding the case—did he kill the man because the man had debauched his wife? If that is so, then there is mitigation here. Did he kill the man because the man had spread slanderous stories about him? Then there is mitigation. Did he kill the man in the heat of passion during a drunken fight? That is mitigation. But here is a cold-blooded murder, without a defense in fact, and the attempt on a plea of guilty to introduce an insanity defense before your honor is unprecedented. The statute says that is a matter that must be tried by a jury."

Walter Bachrach rebutted. "We are not interested, in this inquiry, in the legal question of insanity. That is a question which relates solely to the knowledge of the accused as to right and wrong and the ability to choose between the two. But what we propose to show here is a medical condition, a pathological condition, which has absolutely no relation to the legal question presented on an insanity issue, and I have the authorities here."

Clarence Darrow added, "The statute in this state provides that the court may listen to anything, either in mitigation of the penalty or in aggravation. Of course, it does not follow that a man has to be hanged, simply because he has committed murder. The legislature has given a wide latitude to either court or jury. Now, the condition of mind may mitigate—"

In the back of the courtroom, Jacob Franks was heard to murmur softly to his sister-in-law, Mrs. Edwin Gresham, "There are no mitigating circumstances for my wife."

The argument continued to rage for the rest of the day and on into Thursday. Dr. White, apparently resigned to not being able to testify until the lawyers had completed lengthy arguments over the implications of his appearance, arrived in court on Thursday carrying a portfolio. He drew out a number of typewritten sheets and, still seated in the witness chair, began to work on them with a fountain pen as the arguments raged around him.

The lawyers from both sides buzzed around the bench. Assistant State's Attorney Thomas Marshall, an expert on writs and indictments, did most of the arguing for the prosecution. Walter Bachrach, who had remained in the background during the first week of the hearing, now presented the major legal arguments for the defense.

Precedent for the introduction of psychiatric testimony as a mitigating defense was difficult to find; the decision in the Franks murder case would *establish* precedent. The United States Supreme Court had made no decisions, nor had any court in Illinois. A few related cases had been decided in several states, including Alabama and Colorado, with varying results. The closest precedent came from Nebraska, where a boy had pleaded guilty to auto theft and his attorney had sought to introduce evidence regarding his lack of mental ability. The judge had refused to hear it. On appeal the Nebraska Supreme Court reversed the decision, returning the case to the lower court with instructions to allow the evidence to be introduced.[4]

Lawbook continued to pile upon lawbook as the battle continued all day Thursday. Though the spectators appeared indifferent to the haggling, legal history was being made.

On Thursday afternoon Clarence Darrow (whom the *Tribune* the following morning would describe as a "lumpy figure in gray") began to state his final argument: "Now, I understand that when everything has been said in this case from beginning to end, the position of the state's attorney is that the universe will crumble unless these two boys are hanged. I must say that I have never before seen the same passion and enthusiasm for the death penalty as I have in this case, and there have been thousands of killings before this much more horrible in details, where there was some motive for it. There have been thousands before, and there will probably be thousands again, whether these boys are hanged or go to prison. If I thought that hanging them would prevent any future murders, I would probably be in favor of doing it. In fact, I would consent to have anybody hanged, excepting myself, if I thought it would prevent all future murders. But I have no such feeling. I know the world will go on about the same in the future as it has in the past, at least I think so. My clients are not so important to the economy of things, either in their life or their death, and if this case is like all other cases, it ought to be tried calmly and dispassionately upon the facts in this case."

Judge Caverly tapped his lips with a slender lead pencil as Darrow continued: "We have not invoked any harsh and strained rules of law to save the lives of these defendants, and we protest against any such rules of law being invoked to kill them." He then suggested that the legal opinions read over the last day by the assistant state's attorney were absolutely irrelevant and asked the court, "What is a mitigating circumstance? Is it youth? If so, why?"

Darrow answered his own question: "Simply because the child has not the judgment of life that a grown person has.

"Is youth a mitigating circumstance? Well, we have all been young, and we know that fantasies and vagaries haunt the daily life of a child. We know the dream world we live in. We know that nothing is real. We know the lack of appreciation. We know the condition of the mind of a child. Here are two boys who are minors. The law would forbid them making contracts, forbid them marrying without the consent of their parents, would not permit them to vote. Why? Because they haven't that judgment which only comes with years, because they are not fully responsible."

Darrow turned toward State's Attorney Crowe and pointed at him. "I cannot understand the glib, lighthearted carelessness of lawyers who talk of hanging two boys as if they were talking of a holiday or visiting the races." He rapped his knuckles sharply on the table and said that if he could ever bring himself to ask for hanging, he would do so not boastfully, but with the deepest regret. "That has not been done in this case. I have never seen a more deliberate effort to turn the human beings of a community into ravening wolves as has been made in this case, and to take advantage of anything that they might get every mind that has to do with it into a stage of hatred against these boys."

Darrow's voice fell as he redirected his attention toward Judge Caverly. "I don't believe there is a judge in Cook County that would not take into consideration the mental status of any man before they sentence him to death. If there is one anywhere in the world they ought to get rid of him. Now I am not speaking of this as a matter of law. I am speaking of this as a matter of humanity, as a matter of common justice. I know of no judge in this country who would be responsible for the death of a fellow man. It is hard enough to sentence a man to die, and every humane judge seems to find a reason by which he can save life, instead of a reason for taking it, because after all, life is the greatest and the highest concern, even though the life must be spent behind stone walls."

His argument concluded, Darrow sat down, and Walter Bachrach approached the bench, carrying with him several notebooks and typewritten notes of the testimony. He began by criticizing the prosecution for taking the time to introduce eighty-one witnesses to prove a crime which already had been admitted by the plea of guilty and continued through on Friday morning, analyzing cases and calling on legal precedent.

Crowe eventually rose to respond, sarcasm dripping from his voice as he spoke of the defendants: "If your honor please, they are not cold-blooded murderers, egotistical and secure in their conceit that they are above and beyond the law on account of their wealth and their influence. They have not sat here day after day and mocked the law, and as the details of this murder went in, sneered and smiled and laughed at the representatives of the law. No, they merely committed some little boyish prank and they are sitting here sobbing for mercy, crying their hearts out.

"We have a duty to perform. Mr. Darrow would not hang anybody. I have heard him state in the courts of law that he would not convict anybody of any offense. But your honor and I are not like Mr. Darrow, the paid advocate, who has no oath of office, or no duty to the public to perform. We have sworn that we will execute the laws as we find them. The laws in this case demand the extreme penalty, if the facts as presented by the state and uncontraverted by the defense are true."

It was 11 A.M. when Crowe finally sat down, ending more than two days of arguments. Judge Caverly then voiced his opinion: "Under that section of the statute which gives the court the right, and says it is his duty to hear evidence in mitigation, as well as evidence in aggravation, the court is of the opinion that it is his duty to hear any evidence that the defense may present and it is not for the court to determine in advance what it may be. The court will hear it and give it such weight as he thinks it is entitled to."

Sitting in the courtroom, Mike Leopold smiled in relief. His father seemed to relax. The Loebs—Jacob and Allan—betrayed no emotion. Nathan Leopold, Jr., and Richard Loeb laughed openly and began whispering as Judge Caverly continued. "The motion of the state—" He looked toward the state's attorney. "What is your motion?"

"It is an objection," Crowe responded tersely.

"The objection to the witness is overruled and the witness may proceed."

Judge Caverly's decision permitted Darrow, finally on Friday, to introduce his alienists as witnesses for the defense. It also permitted him to put the Hulbert and Bowman report into the court record, although he did not so introduce it on this particular day. Because of the document's length, as well as its frank sexual content, it was not read aloud at the hearing. In a narrative description of the defense testimony, therefore, it does not conveniently fit at any one point. As they testified, the defense alienists not only covered most of the material in the Hulbert and Bowman report, but also tended to echo each other's testimony. Because this report was the basic document on which these alienists based their examinations, their opinions, and eventually their testimony, it is worth considering at this point.

The Hulbert and Bowman report was made, as stated on the opening page of the two volumes (one devoted to Loeb, the other to Leopold), "in order to determine whether or not insanity was a justifiable plea for defense." With its publication, those Chicagoans who closely followed the progress of the Franks case probably knew more about Nathan F. Leopold, Jr., and Richard A. Loeb than they did about their own children. In addition to probing their personal life and their criminal life, it discussed reasons and motivations and cut right to the core of the question: Why did they kill Bobby Franks? *What compelled them to commit the crime of the century?*

The section of the report on Richard Loeb, after a discussion of the conditions (generally excellent) under which the examinations had been conducted, explored first his family history and noted that his paternal grandfather "was abusive to his children, and beat up the boys." As a result, Richard's father, Albert Loeb, reacted the opposite way, treating his sons, including Dick, very tenderly. "Dick and his brothers loved and worshipped their father," claimed the report, "and did not want to lose their father's love and respect. The father's wish was law."

Almost in deference to the people who, through Clarence Darrow, were paying their fee, the psychiatrists spoke kindly of both families. Neither family, they insisted in a disclaimer at report's end, was responsible for its son's going astray. About the Loeb family they wrote: "The father, Albert H. Loeb, is fair and just. He is opposed to the boys' drinking and often spoke of it; he is not strict, although the boys may have thought he was. He never used corporal punishment. In early childhood he was not a play-fellow with the boys."

They found the mother "a woman in good health, with excellent poise, keen, alert, interested."

As for his siblings, the psychiatrists commented, "Dick wanted to get closer to his older brothers, Allan and Ernest, but as the two older ones were more of an equal age, they naturally associated together. Dick felt that he was unpopular with them at times and made his associates boys of his own age, or of his own school grade."

Richard had been a weakly child until four and a half years, when his tonsils were removed. When a small child, he fell from his bicycle going downhill. At age fifteen at his parent's summer estate in Charlevoix, Michigan, he had an automobile accident, suffering a concussion.

(Stories later would spread that Loeb had killed someone in that accident, that he purposely had caused it by ramming a buggy that blocked his automobile, that his family was able to avoid any publicity about it through bribery.[5] Maureen McKernan offers a different version, however, in her book *The Amazing Crime and Trial of Leopold and Loeb,* which was published after the hearing with the cooperation of the defense attorneys. She wrote about Loeb:

> The summer he was fifteen years old, driving to a dance one evening at dusk, his automobile collided with a horse and buggy at a dark street corner. He had not yet turned on the automobile lights and the accident was said to be unavoidable. A wom-

an was hurt and her grandson slightly injured. "Dick" helped take her to the hospital, but, once there, when he realized she was injured, he wept and fainted. He had to be almost carried home. Every day he visited the woman, taking her flowers and fruit, and the best of food. He persuaded his father, not only to pay all the hospital bills, but to pay off a mortgage on the woman's home, and to send her on a trip that winter to mend her shattered nerves.

McKernan's story seemingly refutes the charge of killing, while documenting that of bribery. She also wrote that the woman injured in the buggy accident later cried when she learned "Dickie" Loeb was quartered in jail.[6])

At eighteen, the report continued, Loeb's voice was still changing and he shaved only every second or third day. He still had three baby teeth. He wore glasses only when reading and stammered occasionally, particularly when in the company of other stammerers. Face tremors, noticable when he became emotional, had been increasing for several years. He was cold-blooded, liked summer better than winter, and drank a lot of water. The psychiatrists noted that he did not have to get up in the middle of the night to urinate. He had once had an operation for hemorrhoids.

Probably the most fascinating aspect of the Hulbert and Bowman reports on both Leopold and Loeb was what they revealed of their relationships, during their formative years, with their governesses. At the age of four and a half years, Richard Loeb came under the care of a Miss Struthers, a Canadian, who was twenty-eight years old when she arrived to live at the Loeb household. Her sister had died insane.

Loeb disliked Miss Struthers at first, locking the door on her during the first week of her stay, but he eventually came to prefer her company to that of his friends. She frequently read him books: *Quo Vadis?, Ben Hur,* the works of Dickens. Sometimes he would turn on his bed light, however, and read when he was supposed to be asleep, mostly detective stories. She was unaware of his secret readings.

Drs. Hulbert and Bowman commented: "She also coached him in his school work, thus enabling him to progress more rapidly than the average boy, and she encouraged him to study history and with the vague idea that some day he might be an ambassador. She accompanied him to and from school daily, and kept in contact with his teachers. Once at the age of seven, when she arrived later and he had not waited, she punished him by sending him to bed. When he became homesick his first summer away at camp, she came to visit him. She avoided any discussions about sex, and it was only at the age of eleven that Loeb learned the difference between the sexes from the chauffeur."

As Richard grew older, his mother assigned Miss Struthers to care for his younger brother, Tommy. She did not like this, clashed with Mrs. Loeb, and was fired, receiving a pension, as was the rule in the Loeb household. She moved to Boston and eventually married.

"Before she left," the psychiatrists explained, "she had encouraged this boy to take her side of the disharmony between herself and Mrs. Loeb and apparently at this time she was becoming paranoid and suspicious, and he uncritically accepted her usual methods of training as normal. However, she did try to make him love his parents more than he loved her. She was not successful at first, but later on to her disappointment, she was overly successful."

The psychiatrists found Miss Struthers almost as fascinating as the patient they were studying. When Loeb was in jail, she arrived from Boston, offering whatever help she could give to save her former charge from hanging. They interviewed her, noting that her eyes were red as though she had been weeping recently. "She denied any imperfection in herself while she was governess," they reported, "and she denied any imperfection with the boy during her stay with the family. She said that he was quite all right at fifteen years of age at which time she left the house, whereupon he was defeminized by others who taught him to drink and to go out with girls."

Miss Struthers admitted she had visited Richard during a trip to Chicago over Christmas in 1922 and noticed a change in his attitude toward her. "She did not say that she still loves him and wants him to love her, nor that she is jealous of the girls, nor jealous of his relations, but it is obvious." The psychiatrists found her attitude definitely paranoid toward men in general. They believed her incapable of insights into child psychology and devoid of understanding necessary to deal properly with children. The psychiatrists did not take kindly to Miss Struthers, but then she was not responsible for paying their fees. It apparently did not occur to them to consider long the question of who had hired Miss Struthers. The parents would be absolved from blame for the gap they had permitted to grow between their child and themselves.

"Some of the mistakes that she made were that she was too anxious to have him become an ideal boy and would not allow him to mix enough with other boys," the report continued. "She would not overlook some of his faults and was too quick in her punishment and therefore he built up the habit of lying without compunction and with increasing skill. She was quite unaware of the fact that he had become a petty thief and a play detective.

"After she left," they concluded, "he reacted like the alleged minister's son and mistook liberty for license."

Nathan Leopold also was influenced early by not one, but by a series of governesses, necessitated by his mother's poor health. She suffered from nephritis (a kidney disease), had experienced numerous miscarriages, and remained in bed during her pregnancy with Nathan to prevent another miscarriage. After his birth she remained an invalid, eventually dying when he was seventeen. Nathan blamed himself for his mother's illness, reasoning that if he had not been born, she would have lived.

According to his baby book, he laughed at four weeks, spoke at four months ("*Nein, nein, Mama*"), walked at fourteen months, and said his first prayer at age three: *Ich bin klein. Mein herz ist rein* ("I am small. My heart is pure"). Weak and sickly as a youngster, he had serious attacks of chicken pox and scarlet fever as a teenager. There was a history of diabetes in his family.The psychiatrists mentioned one grand-uncle as having been "insanely jealous" of his wife at age sixty. Nathan's endocrine gland system malfunctioned; his pituitary gland had calcified at an early age. (He also was bothered by dandruff.) He had obtained eyeglasses the previous year to relieve headaches. The psychiatrists noted with amusement how Leopold remarked ruefully that he wished now he had never bought them. The medical experts, in describing his various deformities, seemed to hope to prove that they affected his behavior and suggest that perhaps he was not entirely responsible for his acts.

Nathan had a nurse until he was six months old; then a governess arrived: Marie Giessler, known as Mimi, an older woman who spoke only German and cared for him until he was around five. She was replaced by an Irish-Catholic girl named Paula, who during a six-month stay taught him the lives of the saints. He began to study various religions and, despite his Jewish origins, became particularly fascinated with the Crucifixion. "The idea of nailing anybody to something appealed to me tremendously," said Leopold. (Later he would fill his college notebooks with sketches which included headless bodies, dissected penises, and crucifixion scenes.) The thought of the Madonna also appealed to him, and he began to think of his mother and his Aunt Birdie (Bertha Schwab) in this way. Aunt Birdie reportedly was a woman with thin legs and an ample bosom who somewhat resembled a bird. Around the age of five Leopold developed an interest in birds and insects and began to build an elaborate ornithological collection.

(After his arrest the Chicago *Daily News* uncovered, and interviewed, his second governess, then married under the name of Pauline Van den Bosch. She remembered him as a mean child: "He had a mania for killing and collecting birds," she would recall. She recalled one time when he shot at a bird in his backyard. The shot narrowly missed hitting a nurse at a neighbor's home. Pauline scolded him. He snapped back, "I should give a damn!" It seems almost unbelievable that he would be playing with guns at this early age—he was six during Paula's employment—but then Nathan Leopold was precocious in many respects.[7])

He began his education at Miss Spade's School, once coeducational, but which then contained only one other boy. Leopold transferred after two years to Douglass School, where students included "Negroes and tough boys." He was the only one living on Michigan Avenue, and his governess would take him to and from school, further setting him apart from the others. His family, moreover, would not permit him to visit the toilet while at the school, resulting in his having at least one "accident" in class. Another time when his governess failed to appear, two older boys walked home with him and accused him of stealing pennies from the teacher and playing with her pussy. The psychiatrists reported: "The patient did not understand the exact significance of this last accusation, but appreciated that it referred to some forbidden pleasure and it made a considerable impression upon him."

His third and final governess, an Alsatian woman named Mathilda Wantz, known as Tillie, also made a considerable impression on him. She spoke only German, but a week after she arrived the family took a trip to Colorado Springs, and Nathan took it upon himself to instruct her in English, telling her that "go to hell" meant "good morning." According to the psychiatrists, she was homely, suspicious, had a violent temper, and may have been feebleminded. Nathan nicknamed her Sweetie.

Sweetie occasionally bathed in the same bathtub with Sam, the second Leopold brother, and played with Sam's penis. The report states: "She also played and was more or less familiar with Nathan Leopold, Jr., the patient, although the patient cannot recall it. She showed the boys her menstrual sanitary napkins. She encouraged and permitted the boys to examine her from head to foot in her undressing closet. She was well built but tall." Tillie referred to her breasts (in German) as "balls" and her nipples as "strawberries." Afraid of having children, she avoided grown men. She encouraged the boys to wrestle with her as reward for their good conduct and reportedly allowed Nathan to use his penis on her, inserting it between her legs while she was lying on her face and he on her back. He soon assumed her abnormal habits were normal. She wore brilliant red ribbon bows all over her dress, told the boys this was beautiful, and caused them once to ask their mother why she didn't dress in the same beautiful manner. "She had a great influence over my brother and myself," Leopold told his examiners. "She displaced my mother." Leopold's father was well into his fifties at this time and apparently too involved with his business dealings to take much notice of the upbringing of his youngest child.

Tillie's employment was terminated—and the era of the governesses ended—one day when Mrs. Leopold caught Mathilda dumping her son, who was ill at the time, out of bed. He then was twelve, so she had been with the family a half dozen years.

About that time the Leopold family moved from their Michigan Avenue residence to a house in Kenwood, on the corner of Forty-eighth and Greenwood. Young Nathan entered the Harvard School, where his classmates teased him about his size, his interest in bugs, and his intelligence. They called him "Flea," and "the crazy Nathan," and "the crazed genius." The school yearbook put these words in his mouth: "Of course, I am the great Nathan. When I open my lips, let no dog bark." The ridicule upset him and made him more insecure.

Leopold was only sixteen when he entered the University of Chicago, where Richard Loeb had been attending school for a year. The following year, when Loeb transferred to the University of Michigan, Leopold did, too, even though the dean of admissions supposedly told him, "Go home to your cradle for five years and then come back and enter college."

Leopold's mother died that fall, and after a period of mourning, he began to travel to Detroit to visit cabarets, get drunk, and run around with women. Although the psychiatrists fail to specify it in their report, his companion on these trips probably was Richard Loeb. Loeb, however, soon began to shun him, joining Zeta Beta Tau and hanging around with the fraternity crowd with whom he fitted easily because of his social poise. Leopold, seemingly rejected, transferred back to Chicago the following fall. In addition to his regular courses, he took a correspondence course in Sanskrit; he had always been fascinated by the study of languages and as a young boy had once attempted to learn how to say yes in as many tongues as possible. He hoped to finish college in three years because he wanted to be different from other people to satisfy his ego. He was graduated from Chicago at the end of the winter quarter in 1923, earning a Phi Beta Kappa key. He enrolled the following fall in law school at Chicago.

Richard Loeb had plotted an even more rapid course through

school. Because of his early tutoring from Miss Struthers, Loeb completed grade school at the age of twelve, spent two years at the University of Chicago high school, then entered the University of Chicago at the age of fourteen. (Loeb had an IQ of about 160; Leopold's was 210.)

Loeb's transfer to the University of Michigan had come from a desire to get away from home and out from under the supervision of his family. Although he proceeded through that institution at a normal pace and with only average grades, his precocity permitted him to graduate in two more years at the age of seventeen, supposedly the youngest graduate in the history of the University of Michigan. "The patient himself states that after high school his education was along the lines of least resistance, that he was lazy and only exerted himself as much as was necessary, and that he never received any honors." Unlike Leopold, Loeb failed to earn a Phi Beta Kappa key, but he lied to others (including Leopold), saying he got good grades when he did not.

Loeb returned to the University of Chicago in the fall of 1923 to study American and European history. His schedule of classes was light, and he had ample free time. He would rationalize to his examiners that had he been occupied more with studies he might not have become involved in the kidnapping of Bobby Franks. The history of the South before the Civil War fascinated him, as did the lives of John Calhoun and Henry Clay, but he planned to abandon his history studies and enter law school in the fall of 1924, remaining at the University of Chicago. (Leopold was planning to transfer that same fall to Harvard Law School, which probably would have removed him permanently from Loeb's orbit.)

According to the psychiatrists, Loeb often had swings of mood, particularly when alone. He made friends easily and dumped them quickly and skillfully. He liked to have one or two close friends who looked up to him, but he felt his popularity had waned during the past several years. He contemplated suicide several times. "On the other hand, these spells of depression are fairly superficial and very easily thrown off," said Drs. Hulbert and Bowman, "so that in the midst of one of these spells of depression if he should make a date with some girl friend or go out with one of his boy friends the depression immediately vanishes."

They found him a coward physically, afraid of being injured in fights, yet reckless in regard to personal safety in other ways, such as going out in a storm in a small boat without a trace of fear.

Nathan Leopold was also considered a physical coward by his examiners, who commented, "He has never been able to stand pain or suffering. He says he has always had some fear of physical pain, but that he has never had any fear of death." At camp Leopold always feigned some injury to avoid playing competitive athletics, yet he boasted he could hike, run, and camp very well.

"The patient does not make friends very easily," Drs. Hulbert and Bowman wrote about Nathan Leopold, "and he has especial difficulty in getting along with the opposite sex. He has but little capacity for leadership in athletics or among boys of his own age. At times the boy has experienced definite difficulty with others of his own age and they have often tended to shun him.

"He is inclined to make cutting and sarcastic remarks and sneer at the lesser ability of others. It is interesting to note that his own estimation of this type of reaction is that he has always felt himself inferior and has always compensated for this marked feeling of inferiority by an assumed attitude of superiority and indifference to the opinions of others." Leopold considered himself inferior to Loeb, but Loeb considered *himself* inferior to Leopold.

Leopold told his examiners that there had been two experiences which completely altered his philosophy of life. One of those was the death of his mother, whom he considered a good and exceptional person. If she had to suffer so much in this world, he decided, God must be cruel, and he refused to worship Him. "After my mother's death," Leopold said, "I realized that if I could kid myself into the belief that there was a life hereafter, I would be happy, but I felt I must be intellectually honest." He also said, "I tried to cut out the emotional. My idea was cold-blooded intellect."

Leopold therefore evolved a purely mechanical and physical theory of the universe. He considered the universe merely a mass of electrons, and the mind nothing but a highly complicated reflex center. He saw no difference between right or wrong and felt that justice had no objective existence. "He feels that the only wrong he can do is to make a mistake," said the report, "and his happiness is the only thing in life that matters at all to him."

Drs. Hulbert and Bowman also considered Nathan Leopold's sex life. They determined he never had been attracted to the opposite sex and looked on women as inferior intellectually. His father once had told him that babies were bought at the store, and he believed this for a while. One of his governesses informed him babies were brought by the stork, but she said it with a sneer, so he did not believe her. He first noticed his genitals at the age of five but thought they were some individual peculiarity—like warts.

At around the age of ten he and two friends named Joe and Henry formed a club which had "mysterious initiation ceremonies," usually performed on Joe, who was two years younger. Henry first taught Nathan how to masturbate at age thirteen, and soon he was doing it two or three times a day and engaging in homosexual behavior with Henry, as well as with Joe. Several years later, he and another close friend (apparently Loeb) practiced "mutual masturbation" a number of times.

When he was fifteen, the report says, he and a friend (again apparently Loeb) would drive around in their automobiles, attempting to pick up girls and have sexual relations. Most girls permitted only petting, but one night, finally, two girls offered sexual intercourse "in the car for three dollars, or at their homes for five dollars."

The psychiatrists reported: "He had an extreme desire to urinate, and got out of the car and urinated. When he returned the girl raised her skirts and said, 'Let's go.' The patient found himself quite impotent and was greatly chagrined at this. He swore his comrade to secrecy." (On one occasion in college, a number of his friends took up a collection to take Nathan to a house of prostitution to see if he could perform. Apparently he satisfied them.[8])

"Later he had numerous sex relations," the report continued about Leopold. "He feels, however, that his desire toward women has always been essentially an intellectual one and that he has merely gone with women because it is the thing to do. He often boasted that he had sex relations with a so-called decent girl when such was not the case."

When questioned about his sex life, Richard Loeb emphatically denied ever having masturbated. His governess Miss Struthers, he also said, had carefully avoided any discussions about sex, and he had no realization of the difference between the sexes until he was fourteen, when the family chauffeur told him. Only when he entered college at fourteen did he learn people had sexual intercourse. He tried it himself the following year with "a woman of easy virtue," contracted gonorrhea, and had to undergo treatment for nine months.

The psychiatrists rated Loeb's sex drive as low. "I could get along easily without it," he told them. "The actual sex act is rather unimportant to me." He felt he was less potent than his friends and thought alcohol had decreased his potency further. Yet at other times during the interview he bragged about the frequency of his sexual relations with women, including three times on three nights with three different girls during the week between the murder and his capture.

Loeb, of course, lied frequently, even habitually. The two psychiatrists noted that he was a very skillful liar and that at times when they knew he was not telling the truth, there was no fluctuation in his appearance at all.

"Sometimes his lies take the form of omitting the facts," they noted, "at times by misleading, and at other times by making false claims. When questioned about lying, his philosophy justifies it. He says he knows it is wrong to lie, and yet his own lies do not bring him any sense of guilt."

Loeb was able to conceal many things from his brothers, which allowed him to assume a degree of superiority over them. Sometimes, however, Allan and Ernest Loeb became aware that he was lying to his governess. They disapproved of that. They also noticed he often lied to their parents, even when it was not necessary. He once told a girl he was a bootlegger. Another time he shot a hole in his shirt and bragged to her he had a fight in a saloon and had been shot at.

He was dishonest even with his closest friend, Nathan Leopold, purchasing a pint of gin, offering him half, then lying about the price, so Leopold paid it all. Leopold frequently knew he was being lied to but said nothing. Both boys cheated at bridge.

As for Leopold's truthfulness, the psychiatrists noticed that although he seemed to be reasonably frank during their examinations, at other times he too lied to them, rather plausibly. They reported: "A number of times he inquired if his story agreed with his companion's and seemed to show a good deal of concern about this matter. The patient makes no effort to shift the blame for the crime to his companion, although he insists that he did not desire to commit the crime and derived no special pleasure from it. He feels that his only reason for going into it was his pact of friendship with his companion, and his companion's desire to do it."

Nathan Leopold's willingness to cooperate with Richard Loeb stemmed, the psychiatrists felt, from his feeling of general inferiority, which also caused him a feeling of sexual inferiority. "Psychologically sex has played an enormous role in his life," they reported. "Since he has a marked sex drive, and has not been able to satisfy it in the normal heterosexual relations, this has undoubtedly been a profound upsetting condition on his whole emotional life."

Leopold was nonathletic. "As the patient felt inferior, physically, to others and could not mingle on equal terms with them physically, he endeavored to compensate for this by a world of fantasy in which his desire for physical perfection could be satisfied. We see him therefore fantasizing himself as a slave, who is the strongest man in the world, and who would often fight as a champion for his side against the strongest man on the other side and always win. In other fantasies he saw himself attacked physically by thousands of men, yet able to overcome them."

Nathan Leopold's fantasies began around the age of five when he saw his oldest brother, Mike, who attended military school, in uniform. He idolized Mike and began to initiate fantasies before going to sleep at night that involved a king and a slave. The psychiatrists claimed he served as slave in 90 percent of his fantasies.

They reported: "In some way or other, and the way frequently varies, he saved the life of the king. The king was grateful and wanted to give him his liberty, but the slave refused. The slave was usually comfortable as regarded his living conditions, but occasionally in some of the fantasies would be in a cell.

"There was [sic] often kings' banquets where each king brought his body slave along to serve him. The slaves were all chained, but the patient was chained only with a tiny gold chain which he could easily have broken.

"When the patient was a slave he was always very good looking and very strong. Oftentimes there would be combats when a champion would be picked from each side to settle a question. The patient would be selected to represent his side and would always win." In one fantasy Leopold found thousands of men armed with guns trying to overpower him, but he killed them all. At the same time his conscious mind rejected the logic of such an occurrence as absurd.

When twelve years old, Leopold attended a summer camp and was attracted to a counselor, an attractive-looking boy six years older than he. Leopold proceeded to fit the counselor into the position of slave, the first time he attempted to fit any actual companions into his fantasy. The psychiatrists concluded: "He brings over certain ideas from this world of fantasy into his world of reality and from his world of reality into this world of fantasy. This resulted in his becoming pathologically suggestible to ideas in the world of reality which would fit in with his world of fantasy and make him uncritical of abnormal ideas."

Richard Loeb had an equally active fantasy life, beginning at the age of ten. He dreamed of himself as a frontiersman shooting at others; he would duck under the bedsheets, which he imagined impregnable to bullets. He also dreamed of himself as an "ideal fellow," extremely good-looking, athletic, rich, owning several automobiles, a member of a college fraternity, a football hero scoring touchdowns. But most of his fantasies related to a definitely more abnormal activity: crime.

"There were several fantasies which occurred with great frequency," Drs. Hulbert and Bowman reported. "Perhaps the earliest of these was that he would picture himself in jail. He would imagine that he was being stripped of his clothing, being shoved around and being whipped." Loeb experienced great feelings of self-pity during this, but not fear.

"I was abused," he told the psychiatrists, "but it was a very pleasant thought. The punishment inflicted upon me in jail was pleasant. I enjoyed being looked at through the bars, because I was a famous criminal."

From the jail fantasy, another fantasy evolved somewhat later: that of being a mastermind, directing others. The psychiatrists reported: "In his fantasies about crime the patient generally commenced to imagine himself doing all sorts of crimes. He derived intense pleasure from such a fantasy, and particularly felt a feeling of being superior to others, in that they did not know he was connected with the crime and he knew the truth about it, while they did not. A number of his actual crimes were the direct result of a great deal of pleasurable fantasy in regard to a particular type of crime.

"One particular point connected with all this fantasy was the idea that he was the 'master mind,' who was so clever at planning crimes that he could escape detection from the greatest detectives of the world, thus he would be in truth the 'master criminal mind' of the century, and could work out a wonderful plan for a crime which would stir the country and which would never be solved." In all of Loeb's criminal fantasies, he always had one or more associates, but he was the leader. He never fantasized committing a crime alone, without anyone to appreciate his skill.

"He did not seriously entertain the idea of assuming and supporting a role in a previously organized gang," the psychiatrists continued, "such as joining up with Tommy O'Connor, or Egan's Rats, or the Fontana gang, nor any group of well-known bootleggers in his community. He did not fantasize extensively on such things as robbing the Federal Reserve Bank in Chicago, nor indulging in mail robberies."

Although Loeb dreamed of becoming a professional criminal, he told his interviewers he did not plan to use his legal training to further a career in crime, nor did he plan his studies at school to help him in his criminal reveries. He planned to commit one perfect crime and then retire with the knowledge of his success.

Richard Loeb's criminal fantasies of being a mastermind and Nathan Leopold's fantasies in which a powerful slave served a mighty king eventually became one. The result was the death of Bobby Franks and the hearing on the sixth floor of the Criminal Courts Building which continued on Friday morning, August 1, with Darrow's alienists at last permitted to testify.

18 Alienists

In my opinion, neither Leopold nor Loeb alone would ever have killed anyone. It was the peculiar combination of their characters which, acting together, produced the murder.

—JOHN BARTLOW MARTIN [1]

Finally Dr. William A. White reached into his portfolio for his notes on the case. He removed the regular pair of glasses that he had been wearing and donned a different pair of rimless half glasses to aid him in reading those notes. The psychiatrist began to speak in a quiet voice and used plain terms, causing one observer, Dr. Ralph Hamill of Chicago, to wonder whether the simplicity of his testimony, the absence of scientific words, might minimize the importance of what he was saying.[2]

Dr. White explained he had been approached by Walter Bachrach, who had visited him in Atlantic City at the American Psychiatric Association's annual meeting and asked him to come and examine the two defendants, a request which the psychiatrist (because of his interest in the causes of mental illness) found impossible to refuse. He had arrived in Chicago on July 1 and spent a week both interviewing and observing Nathan Leopold, Jr., and Richard Loeb. He saw them on several other occasions between that period and the present and also had spoken to them that week in jail. Dr. White referred to Richard Loeb as Dickie and to Nathan Leopold, Jr., by his boyhood nickname, Babe. The other defense alienists would do the same, apparently coached by Darrow to emphasize the youth of the defendants. The prosecution alienists, however, later would refer to the two murderers as Mr. Leopold and Mr. Loeb.

"Dickie told me that he thought his family had more or less neglected him," Dr. White testified, "but he thought that their intentions were perfectly good, and that they had intended to do the right thing by him in every way and that he did not harbor any ill feelings toward them."[3]

Dr. White spoke of Miss Struthers, the governess, whom he described as "an extremely rigid disciplinarian," critical of even the most minor infractions. She had interfered with "Dickie" when he tried to associate with boys his own age, particularly with those whom she considered unworthy of him. He echoed the Hulbert and Bowman report, saying, "She pushed him tremendously in his school work, was very ambitious with regard to him and stimulated and pushed him ahead further than he would have gone without that sort of stimulus." Dr. White suggested that when Richard Loeb finally was thrust out into the world, he had to grow up overnight. He had missed the ordinary developmental experiences of childhood.

(Clarence Darrow later in his closing remarks would try to soften the impression given of Miss Struthers. "I am not criticizing the nurse," Darrow said. "I suggest that some day your honor look at her picture. It explains her fully. Forceful, brooking no interference, she loved the boy, and her ambition was that he should reach the highest perfection. No time to pause, no time to stop from one book to another, no time to have those pleasures which a boy ought to have to create a normal life."[4])

At college, in the company of youths four to eight years older, Richard Loeb began to drink. "His drinking was largely a matter of imitation of older boys," explained Dr. White. Loeb had no one at home to whom he could confide his feelings. The governess had taken the place of his mother, but she was gone.

Dr. White described Loeb's fantasy life, the dream of being in prison that had become a reality. "He thought of himself as being confined behind the bars. The men and women that surrounded him were naked. He himself was often being abused or beaten. He would see people peering at him through the bars and commenting upon the fact that he was a great criminal, looking upon him with curiosity. These people were oftentimes young girls."

(Fantasy became reality for Richard Loeb as a result of the celebrity he and his partner achieved by their crime. The two thrill killers, but particularly Loeb, fascinated young women who wept at their plight, used every ruse to gain entrance to the courtroom, and, once inside, often attempted to reach them or pass them notes. Maureen McKernan wrote: "Pretty girls by the dozen pouted and rolled their eyes at the doormen. They were either sweethearts of 'Dick' or 'Babe,' or they 'just once wanted to see those dear boys,' they said. The gruesomeness of the crime seemed to have no effect upon the feeling of the giddy little flappers, who begged to get in."[5])

Richard Loeb seemed to relish his celebrity role in court. Jail for Loeb thus may have been more reward then punishment. He finally was living the life he had fantasized as a boy. He preferred to wear ragged clothes in his cell rather than the fine clothes his money could buy. "He felt comfortable in jail," suggested Dr. White, "felt as if he sort of belonged there."

Loeb's fantasies had not ceased; they continued even in jail. Dr. White described how whenever Dickie began to wander off into his fantasy life, even today, he would use an expression from his childhood: "And, do you know, Teddy—" Then the fantasy would unfold, as though it were a drama being played for the benefit of the Teddy bear that he had taken to bed and talked to as a boy.

Dr. White described pictures of Dickie as a child dressed in a cowboy costume holding a pistol, and again dressed as a policeman. The earnestness of the boy's expression convinced the psychiatrist that he took great interest in playing these roles. "There is a tendency," the psychiatrist summed up, "for the fantasy life, an abnormal fantasy life, to realize itself in reality."

The alienist had been speaking for several hours when Judge Caverly called a recess for lunch.

Some of those covering the trial found Dr. White's testimony difficult to swallow. William Anthony McGuire, a young playwright assigned by the Hearst newspapers to cover the "dramatic" aspects of the hearing, wrote: "An idea strikes me—a great idea, and one that may eliminate murder forever. If childhood pictures are indications of our future deeds, there need never be another murder. A law should be passed at once compelling parents to have photographs taken of their children annually between the ages of three and nine—then if a child should pose in the costume of an Indian, or is snapped while aiming a pop gun at any object whatever, hang the child at once and thus prevent murder for all time."[6]

(Curiously, while boyhood photos of Richard Loeb abound, many of them still available today in the *Tribune* photo library, including one picture of him in tennis garb published at the time of his Michigan graduation, no boyhood photos of Nathan Leopold exist. Apparently his family never photographed him as a child or at least did not photograph him in poses which could be interpreted by the psychiatrists to explain his personality. The only individual photograph of Leopold, other than those taken after his crime, were some prints made of the MacGillivray movie showing him feeding a Kirtland's warbler.)

The Chicago *Herald and Examiner* editorialized: "If the fathers and mothers in general were not gifted with common sense, there would be a lot of worrying in Chicago over the Teddy bear revelations in the Loeb-Leopold case. Thousands of youngsters with healthy imaginations whisper their childish fancies to a toyland companion and grow up to a clean-minded law-abiding manhood. What healthy boy has not set his five-year-old ambition on the captaincy of a pirate ship?"[7]

At two o'clock court reconvened with Dr. White still in the witness chair. He completed his discussion of "Dickie" and turned his attention to "Babe." Dr. White said of Nathan Leopold, Jr., "He developed in early life a feeling that he himself was more or less set apart from others and that he differed from others in the direction of superiority." Babe also developed a feeling of antagonism toward tender sentiments and the emotions, the sympathies which ordinarily animate average people. "He resented them," said the alienist, "because they made him suffer."

Leopold developed a hedonistic philosophy, one devoted to complete and absolute selfishness. "In such a philosophy, without any place for emotions or feelings, the intelligence reigns supreme. The only crime that he can commit is a crime of intelligence, a mistake of intelligence, and for that he is fully responsible. He and Dickie, he refers to as relative supermen, and despite the fact that he knew Dickie lied to him about his marks at school, was boastful and untruthful, he nevertheless says that Dickie not only approached perfection, but far surpassed it. In a scheme of the perfect man which he drew up, he gave Dickie a scoring of 90, himself a scoring of 63, and various other of their mutual acquaintances various marks ranging from 30 to 40."

Young Nathan, the doctor said, used his intellectual ability as a shield for his fragile personality. He adopted a supercilious attitude, a superior pose, and seemed wary about making friends for fear they might wound him if they turned against him. Most of those who disliked Leopold found him arrogant and conceited; those friends he did develop were attracted mostly by his intelligence and sharp analytical powers.

Leopold's problems in his relationships with others were the result of forces similar to those that also had worked on Loeb. Both boys had governesses. Both boys advanced rapidly in school. Both found themselves constantly thrust into the company of boys several years older. Dr. White testified how Nathan began to drink and smoke early in life largely to ape his elders. He felt he had to excel in what the other students in college did. Yet while feeling inferior to them at one level, he felt superior to them on others. Dr. White felt one reason why Leopold in learning languages picked out obscure tongues such as Russian, Greek and Sanskrit, was that he had a desire to be different.

Leopold had been impressed with the German philosopher

Friedrich Nietzsche's Superman theories, the idea of an *Übermensch* not bound by the rules that govern ordinary people. "With reference to the idea of Superman," Dr. White explained, "he at one time discussed with one of the professors in the law school the abstract question of whether Supermen should be held responsible or not for their acts. Babe's view was that they were not." (Leopold had misinterpreted Nietzsche's philosophy, as would another famous criminal, Adolf Hitler. Under the Nietzschean philosophy the true Superman would be such a superior individual that he would not be tempted to acts of evil, more like the comic book character that appeared in the late thirties. Both Leopold and Hitler took from Nietzsche that which suited their own purpose, and discarded what did not.[8])

According to the psychiatrist, Leopold was enjoying the trial because he felt that he was unique and unusual and the trial gave the world an opportunity to see and appreciate this. He thought of himself as standing on a stage from which he could speak to the world and tell it his philosophy. Dr. White said that Leopold had admitted on questioning, however, that his philosophy was one of utter and absolute selfishness that would be destructive if adopted by the world.

After giving a description of Leopold's king-slave fantasy, similar to that which appeared in the Hulbert and Bowman report, Dr. White turned his attention to the personalities of the two murderers and how they interweaved. Loeb he identified as harboring antisocial tendencies, which had gradually increased in strength through the years. "There is no evidence that there was any adequate defense organism at work to protect him. He became increasingly the host of a growing, and more malignant, antisocial disposition." As for Leopold, his emphasis on his uniqueness was merely a defense mechanism to compensate for an inferiority complex growing out of his small stature and physical unattractiveness. "He developed a feeling of life, a compromise for his physical and emotional inferiorities, which makes him feel better satisfied with himself."

The alienist felt the Franks homicide could be understood only by examining the interplay of these two personalities as they related to each other. "Dickie needed an audience. In his fantasies the criminalistic gang was his audience. In reality, Babe was his audience."

He claimed, however, that Leopold had no criminal tendencies. "Babe's tendencies could be expressed—as they were in the king-slave fantasy—as a constant swing between a feeling of inferiority and one of superiority." Dr. White suggested that Leopold needed Loeb to complement him and serve as his alter ego.

In detailing this alter ego relationship, however, the alienist gave an interpretation of Leopold's king-slave fantasy that would later be overlooked by those who wanted to believe Richard Loeb the motivating personality behind the Franks murder: "Now as Dickie sometimes plays the part of the superior and sometimes the inferior, no understanding of this relationship can be complete without understanding this fantasy of Babe's," Dr. White explained. "Babe is generally the slave in the situation." But though Leopold preferred the slave's position, it was that of a *powerful* slave. "He is the slave who makes Dickie the king, maintains him in his kingdom, like the premier who occupies the principal state office over a weakly king. He maintains the kingdom for the king and he is really the strong man. He occupies the position of either king or slave, and he gets the expression of both components of his makeup with a desire for subjection on the one part and a desire for supremacy on the other."

Dr. White continued: "In several joint experiences, whenever Dickie fell down in the role of leader, Babe always stepped into the breach and picked up the situation. In the Franks case, it was Babe who stepped in and insisted upon the alibi arrangement after Dickie would have let it go by. It was Babe who insisted upon sending the last phone message to bring the whole thing to a successful conclusion, after Dickie had insisted that they were fighting a losing cause and there was no sense in subjecting themselves to further danger. So Babe comes in and takes the reins whenever the other boy falls down."

Dr. White summarized his opinion of both boys: "All of Dickie's life, from the beginning of his antisocial activities, has been in the direction of his own self-destruction. He himself has definitely and seriously considered suicide. He told me that he was satisfied with his life and that so far as he could see, life had nothing more to offer, because he had run the gamut. He was at the end of the situation. He had lived his life out."

Leopold, however, had more constructive capacities which might have been realized had he not become infatuated with Loeb. "I cannot see how Babe would have entered into it at all alone because he had no criminalistic tendencies in any sense as Dickie did, and I don't think Dickie would have ever functioned to this extent all by himself. So these two boys, with their peculiarly inter-digited personalities, came into this emotional compact with the Franks homicide as a result."

The testimony would continue for weeks, and debate about it would continue for years, but those words remain one of the most poignant explanations of how the crime of the century came to occur.

Defense attorney Walter Bachrach questioned Dr. White and attempted to obtain his opinion on the boys' mental condition the day of the murder. The alienist said he considered that Loeb's outstanding feature was his infantilism. "He is still a little child emotionally, still talking to his Teddy bear." Leopold also was infantile in his emotions. "His emotional age is very similar to Dickie's, anywhere from five to seven, perhaps." Intellectually, of course, Leopold measured very high. Dr. White concluded by defining how new psychiatrists, the disciples of Freud, differed from the old ones. The old psychiatrists regarded items such as will, intelligence, and emotional feelings as separate entities. New psychiatrists believed that the will, intelligence, and emotions are only different aspects of one unity. "They all function together, and the harmonious function of that unity depends upon their revelations."

State's Attorney Robert Crowe now rose to cross-examine the witness. "Have you any opinion as to who actually committed this murder?" he asked. "Which one of the two?"

"I think so," responded Dr. White.

"Which one in your judgment?"

"I think it was Dickie. He probably did not say so to the authorities because I presume he wanted to lessen his responsibility." The defense alienist thus pinned the actual murder on Richard Loeb for the first time. From a legal point it made no difference which of the pair wielded the chisel, since both stood equally guilty under the law. Yet Dr. White sounded indefinite. Under further cross-examination, the alienist admitted that he did not ask who did the actual killing. "No, I didn't have to ask," he said. "I knew when I got through with the examination—or thought I did. I was interested, but I wasn't curious."

The defense alienist's response to the question of the state's attorney says almost as much about him as it does about the two murderers he was hired to analyze. During the more than a month between the capture of Leopold and Loeb and their hearing, the alienists developed a close relationship with their two "patients," as they often would refer to them in reports and in court. They became friendly with the two boys; they probably grew to like them, Leopold perhaps more than Loeb. Following the hearing Dr. White would return to his Washington hospital. One psychiatric intern would recall his telling the staff, "The boys were perfectly charming." He quoted Leopold as remarking: "I am so glad to meet you, Dr. White. I know the exact number of lines you take up in *Who's Who*."[9]

Years later in an autobiography published posthumously, Dr.

White wrote briefly about his involvement in the Franks case, deploring the Roman holiday aspects of the hearing and his inability to get the prosecution and the defense alienists to confer. He wrote, "We finally tried to get the three families, each of which had in reality lost a son, to come together in friendly conference and try to reach some constructive conclusion for what otherwise seemed to be a total loss in any direction we could look. The suggestion was made that together they found an institution for the special study and understanding of problem children, and that over the entrance to this institution the profiles of these three boys be carved." The man described as the dean of American psychiatrists seemed disappointed that the Franks family apparently was unwilling to have their son's likeness joined with those of his killers.[10]

The questioning continued Saturday morning. When Dr. White finally completed his testimony, court adjourned for the weekend. There were many, however, who did not share the alienist's fascination with the two murderers. Judge Lewis L. Manson, who presided over the Criminal Court of Covington, Kentucky, had attended the hearing as Judge Caverly's guest during Dr. White's testimony. "I fear that if this case were submitted to me," he told reporters, "I would find it very difficult not to give these defendants the rope. This is a brutal case, premeditated. I have followed it closely and if the facts are true, as presented by the prosecution, I believe it would not be right to give them a sentence which would in time allow them to be freed and permit their spawn to be thrown to society."[11]

On Monday morning, August 4, Dr. William Healy took the witness stand.[12] A tall, slender man with sandy hair, Dr. Healy headed the psychopathic institute of the juvenile court in Boston until 1917, then became director of the Judge Baker Foundation, established for the study of behavior problems for the courts, particularly the juvenile court. He carried a portfolio of papers with him and spread them across his knees. The *Daily News* would describe Dr. Healy as looking "less like a witness than a school man turned loose on a subject."[13]

Dr. Healy's testimony was hardly of the sort that would be approved for discussion in most schools, however. As he began to delve into the relationship between Leopold and Loeb, he seemed reluctant that the material be heard in open court, particularly before the large number of reporters who could be trusted to repeat his words to the waiting world. So during certain portions of Dr. Healy's testimony—as well as at other times when testimony became sexually frank—the attorneys would approach the bench and the discussion would proceed in whispers. On some occasions Judge Caverly would order the court cleared. Rumors concerning the secret testimony and hints of perversion circulated through the city.

During the first of the whispered conferences Dr. Healy described a compact between Leopold and Loeb which had been mentioned in the Hulbert and Bowman report, but not explained. (This was the compact, or "contract," agreed upon on the way from the Ann Arbor burglaries.) "This compact," he began, "as was told to me separately by each of the boys on different occasions, and verified over and over, consisted of an agreement between them that Leopold, who has very definite homosexual tendencies, which have been part of his makeup for many years, was to have the privilege of—" Dr. Healy paused, uncertain whether he should proceed. "Do you want me to be very specific?"

"Absolutely," State's Attorney Crowe insisted, "because this is important."

Dr. Healy continued: "Leopold was to have the privilege of inserting his penis between Loeb's legs at special dates. At one time it was to be three times in two months—if they continued their criminalistic activities together. Then they had some of their quarrels, and then it was once for each criminalistic deed. Now their other so-called perverse tendencies seemed to amount to very little. They only engaged in anything else, so far as I can ascertain, very seldom, but this particular thing was very definite and explicit."

"So that it need not be repeated," suggested Benjamin Bachrach, "make it clear what the compact was."

Clarence Darrow looked uneasily over his shoulder at the newspaper reporters, who had been edging closer toward the bench. "I do not suppose this should be taken in the presence of newspapermen, your honor."

Judge Caverly banged his gavel. "Gentlemen, will you go and sit down, you newspapermen. Take your seats. This should not be published!"

Dr. Healy continued: "They experimented once or twice with each other. They experimented with mouth perversions, but they did not keep it up at all. They did not get anything out of it. Leopold has had for many years a great deal of fantasy life surrounding sexual activity. That is part of the whole story and has been for many years. He has fantasies of being with a man, and usually with Loeb himself, even when he has connections with girls, and the whole thing is an absurd situation, because there is nothing but just putting his penis between this fellow's legs and getting that sort of a thrill. He says he gets a thrill out of anticipating it. Loeb would pretend to be drunk, then this fellow would undress him and then he would almost rape him and would be furiously passionate at the time, whereas with women he does not get that same thrill and passion." Dr. Healy had learned details of their homosexual conduct from Leopold. Loeb admitted them but claimed he submitted in order to have Leopold's aid in carrying out his criminal ideas.

"When in connection with the compact, in point of time, did they start?" asked Bachrach.

"Their criminalistic ideas began on the same day when they began their cheating at bridge," explained the alienist. (It had been in February, 1921, when Loeb invited Leopold to accompany him to his family's estate near Charlevoix. They had traveled by train.) "It was the first time in a berth, and it was when Leopold had this first experience with his penis between Loeb's legs. Then he found it gave him more pleasure than anything else he had ever done. To go on further with this, even in jail here, a look at Loeb's body or his touch upon his shoulder thrills him, so he says, immeasurably."

The testimony shifted to other areas, and the attorneys returned to their places. So did the reporters and spectators who had been straining to hear. Dr. Healy had administered most of the intelligence tests given to Leopold and Loeb. On the Monroe silent reading test, Leopold had scored higher than anyone Healy had known to take the test. (Chicago newspapers would soon be publishing versions of the tests given the defendants, challenging their readers to better their scores.) Leopold also demonstrated several feats of memory. Dr. Healy found he could make a list of twenty words, allow Leopold to read them, and Leopold could recite the exact order of words, backward and forward. When told one word, he could tell the word preceding or following it in order. He could do this not only the day he saw such a list, but also the following day. Dr. Healy testified that while Leopold scored high in intelligence tests, he fared not so well on tests involving practical judgment. "He did very poorly indeed, much to my surprise," admitted the psychiatrist. "He made a score of 56.5 out of a possible 100 and that is just the average for twelve years. Stated another way, 25 per cent of the ten year old boys do better than that."

In addition, Dr. Healy found Leopold extremely critical of other people, supercilious about his own mental attainments, and very stubborn in his opinions. "He is right. The world is wrong. His father says that since years ago, Leopold has argued repeatedly with him about the nonsense of ethical ideas, about the nonsense of having a conscience and doing as other people do in regard to right and wrong. As far as I can judge from my numerous interviews, he has extremely little sympathy or feelings or conceptions of gratitude except in some very narrow fields with regard to his family life in particular.

"I am immensely struck too," the psychiatrist added, "by the fact that notwithstanding his opportunities in life for culture and comfort and ease, that he shows so little disgust at jail surroundings. His main concern seems to be whether or not the reporters say the right thing about him." In jail Leopold identified himself with Napoleon exiled on St. Helena. The one thing he considered more important than preserving his life was the preservation of his dignity.

When asked what hardships he had met in the world, Leopold replied he never had any. "I never had any disappointments," he told Dr. Healy. "I was not allowed to have any."

Testimony continued that afternoon, and Dr. Healy began to summarize his thoughts about Leopold, who had said, "Making up my mind whether or not to commit murder was practically the same as making up my mind whether or not I should eat pie for supper, whether it would give me pleasure or not." Healy concluded that Leopold was thoroughly unbalanced mentally, or to use another term, "mentally diseased."

During cross-examination, Crowe pounced on this point. "Is he insane?"

"He has a paranoid personality," the psychiatrist admitted. "Anything he wanted to do was right, even kidnapping and murder. There is nothing in the feelings of sympathy which would prevent him because of his disintegrated personality. There is no place for sympathy and feeling to play any part. In other words, he had an established pathological personality before he met Loeb, but probably his activities would have taken another direction except for this chance association."

Dr. Healy had a lower opinion of Richard Loeb. He described Loeb's facial twitchings and how he stammered slightly and failed to do as well as his partner on mental tests. Despite Loeb's supposed IQ of 160, Dr. Healy actually considered Loeb to be of no more than average intelligence. He found his language ability poor, in both tests and ordinary conversation. "He is not at all interested in mental tasks," testified the alienist. "He forces himself to, and can work with fair attention and persistence, but it is a good deal of a grind for him." Dr. Healy considered Loeb lazy, a person without deep interests who never finished anything and exhibited no ambition. Yet he also noted Loeb's outgoing, well-mannered personality which extended even to seeing that the psychiatrists ordered what they wanted for lunch during interviews in jail before ordering himself.

The testimony continued on into the next day, when Dr. Healy stated that Loeb's mental condition was decidedly abnormal. He responded to a question from the state's attorney, "To my mind the crime itself is the direct result of diseased motivation of Loeb's mental life. The planning and commission was only possible because he was abnormal mentally, with a pathological split personality."

Cross-examination continued into the afternoon until State's Attorney Crowe finally directed a plea to the judge: "We have now got to the point in this hearing where it appears to the court if the defense here is insanity, there is only one thing to do under the law and this is to call a jury."

"The motion is denied," replied Judge Caverly, and the hearing continued on Wednesday morning with the third defense alienist, Dr. Bernard Glueck, taking the witness stand.

Dr. Glueck was a man with a large head and neck and a mane of tousled hair. The *Daily News* described him as impressive in appearance with his gray hair and gray suit. "He conveyed the impression of a scholarly person, self-conscious that he was out of his native pool in a criminal court." A specialist in the treatment of mental disease, Dr. Glueck supervised the psychiatric clinic at Sing Sing Prison. He spoke, slowly and exactly, from sheets of memoranda he carried with him to the stand.[14]

He described the way Richard Loeb had told him about the crime: "As his recital proceeded, I was amazed at the absolute absence of any signs of normal feelings, such as one would expect under the circumstances. He showed no remorse, no regret, no compassion for the people involved in this situation, and as he kept talking on, it became very evident to me that there was a profound disparity between the things that he was talking about, the things that he was thinking about, and the things that he claimed he had carried out. There became evident the absolute lack of normal human emotional response that would fit these situations and the whole thing became incomprehensible to me except on the basis of a disordered personality."[15]

Then Dr. Glueck provided what would be one of the more revealing bits of information to emerge from the hearing: "He told me the details of the crime, including the fact that he struck the blow." Among the alienists who would testify at the hearing, Dr.

Glueck would be the most conclusive in pinning the physical act of murder on Richard Loeb.

The psychiatrist went on to describe his reactions to the two murderers, both in prison and in the courtroom. "I have been sitting here in the courtroom watching the two boys," he said, "and as I watched them, it seemed to me that they absolutely did not take in emotionally the meaning of this whole situation." Loeb, the doctor said, had considered taking his life by hanging himself in jail and only regretted that if he did, he would not be able to read about it in the newspapers. Loeb wondered if he would be able to get a complete file of the newspapers of this period when he came out of prison, with no realization that he might *never* come out of prison. "I have examined a lot of hardened criminals, men awaiting execution," Dr. Glueck admitted. "The hardened criminal shows in every response a kind of crudity. Loeb is affable, polite, and shows an habitual kind of refinement, and yet seems to be incapable of responding to this situation with an adequate emotional response."

On the other hand, the doctor found Nathan Leopold eager to defend his purely hedonistic philosophy. Leopold claimed that any action was justified if it gave pleasure, that it was his ambition to become a perfect Nietzschean. Leopold attempted to justify the murder itself on the basis of Nietzsche's philosophy. The alienist felt that Leopold got a great sense of pleasure in describing his philosophy since it permitted him to enlarge his ego.

Dr. Glueck also stressed the merging of the two. "I think the Franks crime was perhaps the inevitable outcome of this curious coming together of two pathologically disordered personalities, each one of whom brought into the relationship a phase of their personality which made their contemplation and the execution of this crime possible.

"Loeb in my estimation is suffering from such a profound discord between his intellectual and emotional life as to be incapable of appreciating the meaning, the feeling of this situation. Leopold is governed to such a large extent by his delusional thinking and the force that his fantasy life has exercised upon him, plus his aberrant instinctiveness trend, that he too could not have done otherwise than has been carried out in connection with this crime."

The two defendants were not the only ones at the trial unbalanced emotionally. As court recessed for lunch, a woman who identified herself as Mrs. Anna Lurie of Houston (apparently no relation to Susan Lurie; the woman may not have given her right name) attempted to gain admittance to the courtroom. When refused entry, she waited outside the judge's chambers until after he returned from lunch, then followed him inside. "I have been sent by God to see that justice is done!" she claimed. Police took her to the hospital.[16]

The cross-examination by the state's attorney began at one forty-five that afternoon. Crowe asked Dr. Glueck to find the point in his notes where Loeb said he struck Bobby Franks. The psychiatrist responded by locating a passage: "The Franks Murder, profound lack of adequate emotional response in presence of intact intelligence." "Now, I am certain that this was sufficient notation for me," claimed Dr. Glueck, but the seemingly meaningless notation cast another cloud over the absolute identification of the killer.

"What was the motive for the crime?" asked Crowe.

"I don't know that there was a direct motive for this crime," responded the defense alienist. "I do feel that Loeb had in his mind probably the motive of complete power, potency, the realization of the fantasy of a perfect crime."

"How about Leopold," probed Crowe. "What was his motive?"

"I don't know that he had any."

The state's attorney's own motive for the question became apparent when he next asked, "Don't you think the desire to get the ten thousand dollars is a motive here?"

"I don't know whether it is the motive for the crime as you put it."

"Well, do you think it is part of the motive?"

"It may well have been."

Crowe pressed on with his cross-examination, trying to show that Leopold's motivation, at least in part, was to get money so that he could gamble and live high and fast. Dr. Glueck eventually ended his testimony with a statement reminiscent of those of his colleagues: "In my contacts with Leopold, I have found an element of positive interest and responsiveness in connection with certain situations that I was not aware of in my contact with Loeb." Throughout their examinations, the alienists for the defense found themselves drawn more toward Babe than toward Dickie. Leopold's superior "intellect" and his fascination with the act of psychoanalysis appealed to the egos of these eminent doctors, whose profession was not yet considered quite that respectable by the general public. Loeb, on the other hand, had seemed uninterested, had even fallen asleep during some of the tests. At times during the hearing it almost would appear that the experts spent twice as much time dissecting Leopold as Loeb. The result has been a distorted and oversimplified picture of Richard Loeb. In the legend that would grow, Loeb is pictured as little more than a crude criminal, Leopold the evil genius. There was genius and criminality in both.

On Thursday, August 7, Max Schrayer had his day in court. He identified his fraternity brother as a very nervous person. Schrayer had seen Loeb faint on three occasions; he smoked a great deal. "He was known as a reader of dime novels and detective stories," testified Schrayer. In cross-examination by Crowe, he admitted that the executive committee of the fraternity had once censured Loeb for drinking.[17]

Schrayer later would opine that his appearance had been a farce. He felt he had little to contribute, as he had warned Clarence Darrow in advance. Darrow would ask him a question, and Crowe would object; then both attorneys would approach the bench and spend several minutes talking. Later Crowe would ask a question, and Darrow would object, and another long discussion on points of law would occur while he waited uncomfortably on the witness stand. And since he was in the courtroom only during the time he testified, he saw little of the actual hearing. He would have been better off standing in line with the crowds, trying to get in. He did recall that while the attorneys were arguing some minor point before Judge Caverly, he looked at Dick Loeb, who was sitting only about twenty feet in front of him. Loeb cupped his hands over his mouth and said in a stage whisper, "Horseshit!"

Leopold and Loeb had come to court that day especially prepared because of the expected appearance of two of Loeb's girlfriends, Lorraine Nathan and Germaine Reinhardt. "Their black hair glistened and every lock was in place," the *Daily News* described the two killers. Lorraine Nathan appeared dressed in a black and white outfit. She testified that she had noticed a complete change in Richard Loeb recently.[18] He drove recklessly and would not slow down for pedestrians, making them jump out of the way. She had pleaded with him to be careful, but he ignored her. He had had several automobile accidents, and had damaged his father's limousine in an accident in Lincoln Park only a few months before the Franks murder.

Lorraine Nathan also described one evening when Loeb came to her home and was introduced to some friends of her parents. She hardly could believe his reaction, it seemed so bizarre. "He started dancing down the middle of the room," she testified. "We were passing some chocolates around, so he put his thumb into each one of them to find a hard center. He did this in all seriousness. Then he went out in the reception hall and tried on all the hats of the guests." She claimed he had not been drinking either. On other occasions he would steal some item and return it just as he was about to leave.

She spoke of him as irrational, boyish, infantile. "We had quarrels. I told him I found such a change in him that our friendship could not be anything else but sister and brother, and he resented that." She claimed that she once had been fond of Dick, but not since last summer.

Returning to her seat, she passed Loeb's chair. "Thanks, Lorraine," he said, "but I'm sorry you said that about me."

"I'm sorry I had to," she replied.

At the noon recess she attempted to see Loeb, but Crowe blocked her path. Loeb, being led away to jail, was pictured by the press as having tears come to his eyes for the first time.[19]

Newspaper reporters swarmed around the girl, and Darrow reportedly decided that day against calling Germaine Reinhardt because of the harsh treatment given to Lorraine Nathan by the press. (An unusual joke involving Germaine Reinhardt apparently was overlooked by most members of the press. At the bottom of the first kidnap letter delivered to Jacob Franks, beneath the signature of "George Johnson," were the initials "GKR," as though to identify the secretary who typed it. Germaine Reinhardt's middle initial was "K." There is no evidence to suggest she had any prior knowledge of the crime.)

Darrow was unhappy with the way State's Attorney Crowe badgered his witnesses, showing no respect for their professional stature. While the hearing continued, Ruby Darrow wrote Dr. White, who had returned to Washington following his testimony, "You are being constantly remembered as by far the most fortunate of those subjected to Crowe's crude tactics. Your brief whirl with Crowe's miserable method and manner was gentlemanly compared with the incisive, insulting attacks upon Healy, Glueck, Hulbert, Hall—prolonged days and days beyond all intentions. The end [is] not in sight, nor any sign of weariness in Crowe's corner, however little that third-degree trickster accomplishes."

Dr. White also sympathized more with the two murderers than with the man charged with prosecuting them. In a previous letter to Clarence Darrow he had written: "To me it is an infinitely more discouraging and disheartening spectacle to see a public official, presumably an adult of experience and judicial mind, sworn to look after the public interest—presumably with an eye to doing the best that can be done for the public good, now and hereafter—exhibit apparently nothing but a lust for blood than it is to see two adolescent youths stumble and fall when they try to pass the threshold that separates childhood from manhood."[20]

In the eyes of the members of the defense, Crowe had become the villain, Leopold and Loeb mere victims of his wrath.

Edwin Meiss, another member of Zeta Beta Tau, appeared to testify about Loeb's fainting spells and his arguing over irrelevant matters. "He would always walk hastily. He would pop into the room. In coming upstairs he would take two or three steps at a time and run. He very seldom walked in the manner which is customarily done. Even when he lounged he would flop down in a seat and all of a sudden he would jump up." Meiss found Loeb's zeal annoying. As president of the fraternity he did not appoint him a monitor because his actions were not the kind which would incur the respect of freshmen.[21]

Next to testify was John Abt, a law student at the University of Chicago who later would achieve considerable fame as a defender of radical causes. (Lee Harvey Oswald would ask for Abt as his attorney after being arrested for the assassination of President Kennedy.) Abt had known Leopold for four years. "His main thesis was that pleasure was the sole emblem of all conduct," testified Abt. "Whenever he contemplated an act he would weigh the amount of pleasure and balance it against the amount of pain which he thought he would get out of it. If the pleasure was greater than the pain he would do the act." Leopold considered his friends as means to ends, to be used for pleasure and discarded when they ceased giving him pleasure. "He would have no remorse in throwing a friend over, no gratitude in friendship with the one exception of a boy he regarded in the light of a Superman, a boy who could do anything until he got caught. As soon as he made a mistake and was caught he would cease to be a Superman and would return to the level of ordinary mortals, on the same status as with other friends." The boy Leopold regarded as a superman, of course, was Richard Loeb. Abt said that on several occasions Loeb, whom he also knew, would state that he planned to pick someone's pocket—then do it.[22]

Arnold Maremont, who later in life would become a distributor of automotive parts and (whether inspired by his experience in the Franks case or not) a proponent of planned parenthood, testified about Nathan Leopold, with whom he frequently argued philosophy: "He felt that the Superman should be the law giver, because after all he had the super intellect. He knew more than the other men. Therefore, he would be the one logical man to be in a position to make laws and therefore he *should* make laws to suit himself, to satisfy his own needs regardless of man-made laws."[23]

Maremont recalled Leopold once asking a question in a torts class as to whether or not it would be wrong for a superman to commit a supercrime, whether or not his attitude toward right and wrong should not be taken cognizance of in fixing his punishment or guilt for committing a certain offense. Maremont also spoke about Leopold's hedonistic feeling that anything was all right as long as it gave him pleasure. "In fact," said Maremont, "he made the statement one afternoon that if it gave him pleasure to go out and murder someone it would be perfectly all right in his philosophy to go out and murder a person, provided, of course, he were not apprehended for the murder and forced to suffer punishment."

Leopold felt that when you found out what gave you the greatest happiness, you went and did it. He talked about being in Hawaii and seeing a sport that Maremont described as "surf flying, something like getting in a high wave and trying to ride with it or against it on a board." Maremont also recalled hearing about Leopold and Loeb getting drunk one night and sitting down on the corner of Sixty-third and Cottage Grove, where they begged for pennies. (Leopold later would insist that Loeb had done that, but not himself.[24])

More witnesses appeared the next day, Friday, August 8. Dr. Robert Bruce Armstrong, a general practitioner from Charlevoix, described treating the then fifteen-year-old Loeb in the hospital after his auto accident. Loeb suffered no serious injuries but had a half dozen fainting spells after returning home. Dr. Armstrong believed the spells were the result of the accident.

Another Michigan fraternity brother, Leonard Lewy, told of being with Loeb at the Edgewater Beach Hotel one New Year's Eve. Loeb, who had been drinking, fainted in the lobby, frothing at the mouth. When he awakened he wanted to beat up a couple of waiters. Theodore Schimberg, a student at the University of Chicago, testified about Loeb: "It seemed that his actions most of the time were so childish, and we were in the habit of seeing him drunk a good deal, that there were many times we could not tell whether the boy was drunk or sober."[25]

Harry Booth, a law student at the University of Chicago, testified about Nietzsche, commenting that the German philosopher had been insane a good portion of his life. This allowed Crowe to get a dig in at Darrow during his cross-examination: "Don't you know it is improper for a witness for the defense to use the word 'insane'?"

That afternoon Dr. Harold S. Hulbert began his testimony. Dr. Hulbert lived in Oak Park and practiced in that suburb to the west of Chicago, as well as in Aurora. He had coauthored with Dr. Carl M. Bowman the report which had become the base for Darrow's mitigating defense.[26]

In Dr. Hulbert's testimony Richard Loeb emerged as a person without emotion, one who happened to accidentally pass by the Franks house when the coffin was being taken to the hearse, yet felt no remorse. He never had nightmares about the crime afterward; his sleep remained undisturbed. He felt the crime clever, knew it would make a "thrill in the newspapers." Previously he had been disappointed because some of his minor delinquencies, such as throwing bricks through car windshields, had gone unreported. He had no hatred for the Franks boy, who was merely incidental to the scheme.

Loeb, said Dr. Hulbert, had an abnormally low basal metabolism, which indicated a disorder of the endocrine glands and the sympathetic nervous system. Physically he still had not matured, as Dr. White had testified earlier. "My opinion," Dr. Hulbert said, "is that the man is not normal physically or mentally, and there is a close relation between his physical abnormalities, largely of the endocrine system, and his mental condition; that intellectually he far excels the average boy of his age; that in matters of emotion he is much inferior to the average boy of his age, his emotional reactions being those—I estimate, because I cannot measure—of a boy of about nine or ten, certainly less than a boy of puberty, and in matters of judgment he is childish. The discrepancy between his judgment and his emotions on the one hand, and his intellectual attainments on the other hand, is a greater discrepancy than we find in normal persons and therefore I am forced to conclude that he is mentally diseased."

Dr. Hulbert next addressed himself to Leopold, who as was true with Loeb, displayed no emotion. Dr. Hulbert explained: "In jail, in discussing this crime, he took particular pains to be accurate. There was no other emotion of any other kind—neither chagrin, remorse, nor discomfort at being in jail and no apprehension as to his future." He believed his family should disown him if he were hanged. Leopold had told the story of the murder, describing how it upset him so that he had cried out, "My God, this is awful," and it had taken Loeb several minutes to calm him. But Dr. Hulbert pointed out that in telling the story, Leopold showed no emotion and seemed only interested in getting the details right.

As to who struck the blow, Dr. Hulbert indicated that Leopold said he could not have done it, which Dr. Hulbert interpreted as an indirect admission that Loeb had struck the blow.

"He appears to have the intellect of a man thirty years of age who has been a student all his life," the alienist continued on Leopold. "One is next impressed by the disparity between his intellectual development and his emotional life, because there is an emotional poverty, compared with an intellectual wealth. The discrepancy between these two is extreme. One is greatly impressed by the vividness, the intensity, the duration, and the characteristics of his fantasies. The effect of these fantasies was obvious. His judgment is that of a child, a rather nice, obedient child who will do what he is told when he is directed to. His sense of inferiority, which dates back to his physical inferiority as a child when he was so frail, has persisted ever since. The duel between that and the satisfying sense of superiority, which he acquired from his intellectual development, showed an inner mental conflict of monumental importance."

Dr. Hulbert had said earlier, when asked about the motive of the crime, that it was a desire on the part of Richard Loeb to commit a perfect crime and a desire on Leopold's part to do whatever Richard Loeb wanted him to do. Now he expanded on that idea: "Each boy felt inadequate to carry out the life he most desired unless he had someone else in his life to complement him, to complete him. Leopold, on the one hand, wanted a superior for a companion. Loeb, on the other hand, wanted someone to adulate him for a companion. Unless these two boys had the same constitution, which they had, unless those boys had their own individual experiences in life, the present crime could never have been committed. The psychiatric cause for this is not to be found in either boy alone, but in the interplay or interweaving of their two personalities, their two desires caused by their two constitutions and experiences. This friendship between the two boys was not altogether a pleasant one to either of them. The ideas that each proposed to the other were revulsive. Their friendship was not based so much on desire as on need, they being what they were. Loeb did not crave the companionship of Leopold, nor did he respect him thoroughly. But he did feel the need of someone else in his life. Leopold did not like the faults, the criminalism of Loeb, but he did need someone in his life to carry out this king-slave compulsion. Their judgment in both cases was not mature enough to show them the importance of trying to live their own lives."

During his cross-examination of Dr. Hulbert, State's Attorney Crowe remarked that it was a pretty convenient theory of medicine which makes it a sign of a disease for one defendant to have one thing and the other the opposite. Leopold and Loeb glanced at each other and, as they had often during the hearing, began to snicker.

The following day Leopold (who by now admired Darrow almost to the point of idolatry, referring to him as "the greatest attorney and, in so many ways, one of the greatest men it has ever been my privilege to meet"[27]) expressed the contempt he had for Robert E. Crowe: "Crowe is just seeking reelection. He is not moved by any sense of justice in trying to have us hanged. He just realizes if he gets a hanging verdict it will be a big feather in his cap. He strikes me as being a lawyer with political ambitions who is using Dick and me as stepping stones in his career. What are the lives of two people to the ambitions of a rising state's attorney?"[28]

Incredibly, in the three weeks since the beginning of the hearing, Leopold and Loeb, so despised following their confessions of the murder of a fourteen-year-old boy, had begun to emerge almost as folk heroes. The testimony of the defense alienists had produced a picture of them not so much as brutal killers as victims of their overpampered environment and endocrine glands. Their governesses, Miss Struthers and Mathilda Wantz, seemed as much on trial as they. In addition, Clarence Darrow had waged a subtle, but effective, public relations campaign to rebuild their tarnished images. His first act on taking command of their defense had been to make them completely accessible to the press. While being held in the county jail, they often saw half a dozen newspaper reporters daily, sometimes twice daily, in effect holding court for the press. Darrow felt that, bad as much of the publicity had been, his clients could not afford to antagonize the press by remaining inaccessible and receiving even worse publicity.[29] Leopold believed Darrow's policy may have been a mistake; nevertheless, as the trial progressed it is possible to detect a subtle undertone of sympathy for the defendants running through the stories of those covering the hearing every day. At the same time the editorial writers back in the newspaper offices, who had not the opportunity to lunch in the cells of two celebrity killers, continued to scream for blood.

Leopold and Loeb soon realized that they possessed the ability to manipulate the press. Leopold later would boast how they gave interviews only to those reporters who treated them "fairly." He and Loeb avidly read the reports of their hearing carried daily in the Chicago newspapers; journalists who wrote stories that displeased the pair soon found themselves no longer welcome members of the murderers' inner circle. Eventually Leopold and Loeb would decide to cease granting interviews to out-of-town reporters since they had no convenient means of monitoring results.[30]

Clarence Darrow had proved earlier in the case his ability to sway public opinion. For one thing his mere appearance, as champion of the underdog, on their side marshaled a degree of sympathy toward the defense. Irving Stone, author of *Clarence Darrow for the Defense,* described how the attorney had moved early to quiet the outcry of the public against Leopold and Loeb: "He sent men to mingle in the crowds in the Loop and ask people whether they thought Loeb and Leopold should hang. Sixty percent of those questioned said, 'Yes.' He then had the fathers of Loeb and Leopold issue a letter to the press saying that there would be no attempt to free the boys, only to prove them insane, and that they would agree to have Darrow's fee set by the Bar Association. After the newspapers had printed this letter the men went back to the Loop to ask the same question and found that sixty per cent of the people were now willing to accept life imprisonment for the culprits."[31]

Bob Crowe felt he had no time to waste on public relations since he had public opinion already solidly on his side. Yet he had the liability (as a public figure and a very visible Republican politician) of already having made numerous enemies. When he met reporters with the signed confessions in his hands the morning of May 31, Crowe had appeared a winner. But as the summer wore on, as the case continued day after interminably hot day, Crowe's heroic image wilted in the high temperatures of the courtroom. He seemed now merely a picky man haggling over petty details in his cross-examinations. Darrow and Leopold both blamed the state's attorney for prolonging the hearing unnecessarily.[32] "Of Mr. Crowe, the state's attorney," wrote *The New Statesman,* "perhaps the most charitable thing to say is that he provided the psychiatrists with a subject of study not much less interesting than Leopold and Loeb."[33] (The magazine espoused the views of the Labor Party, so could be expected to be antagonistic toward Darrow's enemies.) Bob Crowe was becoming another of the victims of the Franks murder.

Clarence Darrow called his last witness on Tuesday afternoon, August 12. Albert Loeb's secretary, Mrs. Katherine Fitzgerald, testified that she signed checks for as much as $250 for Dickie whenever he wanted them, without even checking with his father.[34]

"Maybe that is one of the things that helped to spoil him?" suggested Crowe during cross-examination.

Mrs. Fitzgerald began to explain how she was not in a position to say that, but Darrow interrupted her. "We will admit it," he said.

Mike Leopold testified that his younger brother received an allowance of $125 a month, plus additional money whenever he wanted it. His father had planned to give him $3,000 for his planned trip to Europe that summer.[35] Darrow sought to suggest with this closing testimony that whatever the motive for the murder, it was not the need for money. He then rested his case.

State's Attorney Crowe in rebuttal offered several witnesses who previously had testified, then summoned the prosecution's alienists. Dr. Hugh T. Patrick, a Chicago physician who specialized in nervous and mental diseases, had been hired, along with the others, almost immediately after the identity of the murderers had been established to observe them and to attest to their sanity.[36] He testified that he had listened to their conversation all that afternoon of June 1, talking with Leopold even about the psychology of birds. Dr. Patrick expressed an opinion that Loeb showed no evidence of mental disease. He explained, "Unless we assume that every man who commits a deliberate, cold-blooded, planned murder must, by that fact, be mentally diseased, there was no evidence of mental disease." The *Daily News* described Patrick as "a chipper little doctor," who "chatted rather than testified." He seemed pleased that he was listened to with interest. Leopold and Loeb, however, slumped down in their chairs and watched with grim faces. The other side had the ball, and they had lost interest in the game.[37]

The following morning in response to a question by John Sbarbaro, Dr. Patrick commented: "If a man is thinking of crime or planning crime or reading about crime, he naturally has fantasies relating to criminal deeds."

Dr. Archibald Church, a specialist in nervous and mental diseases and head of that department at Northwestern University Medical School, next took the stand. He also had observed the defendants on June 1. John Sbarbaro asked about the presence of mental disease in Loeb. "The young man was entirely oriented," replied Dr. Church. "He knew who he was and where he was and the time of day and everything about it. His memory was extraordinarily good. His logical powers, as manifested during the interview, were normal and I saw no evidence of any mental disease." Dr. Church indicated the same to be true of Leopold.[38]

"Do you want to hang these boys?" Darrow asked when he questioned the physician. Crowe leaped to his feet to protest angrily, and the two opposing attorneys raged at each other until Judge Caverly recessed the court for lunch to cool tempers.

"It was another day of romping in psychiatric playgrounds, the personalities of Messrs. Loeb and Leopold," said the *Daily News.*

"These are familiar grounds by now to newspaper readers, quite as well as judge and counsel and alienists. The calcified Loeb pineal gland is a landmark as well known as the Wrigley Building, and numerous Chicagoans know the course of the Leopold slave fantasy as exactly as they know the route of the number twenty-two cars."[39]

Indeed, interest in the case had begun to wane as the prosecution's medical examiners continued to testify. Dr. Patrick returned to the stand Wednesday afternoon, August 13, and remained there until recess the next day. It was the battle of experts—ours vs. theirs—that Clarence Darrow and Dr. William A. White had sought to avoid. (Dr. White had approached Crowe through a mutual friend about allowing the defense and prosecution alienists to consult each other. The friend was told by the state's attorney that Leopold and Loeb were degenerates and deserved to hang and that he, Crowe, refused Dr. White's request.[40])

After the hearing, one influential legal publication would editorialize against the legal practice which permits and requires each of the opposing parties in a case to summon their own expert witnesses. "This vicious method naturally makes the witness himself a partisan," stated the *Journal of the American Institute of Criminal Law and Criminology*. "In the Loeb-Leopold case, where the experts devoted long hours to the study of the defense's case, consulted only with the defense's counsel, made preliminary reports to those counsel, cut down those original reports in their testimony and answered only the questions that were asked by counsel, it was natural and inevitable that their testimony should take on a partisan color. Partly this would be unconscious, in that they came to sympathize with the only side of the case known to them, and in that they committed themselves to conclusions which it was hard to modify when grilled by hostile counsel."[41]

The *Journal* recommended that expert witnesses be summoned by the court, rather than by either side.

Darrow cross-examined Dr. Church Thursday afternoon, eliciting from him the information that others had been present in the room when he had observed the pair and that he did not ask any questions. Darrow tried to show that the doctor did not make an adequate examination and did not even follow the rules for such an examination laid out in his own textbook. At the end Darrow, who probably would have engaged Dr. Church had Crowe not done so first, seemed to admit failure in discrediting the witness's credibility: "Well, I slipped a cog in not calling you first, Doctor. That is all."[42]

Dr. Rollin Turner Woodyatt spent Friday morning testifying

about the endocrine system and related medical information.[43] Dr. Harold Douglas Singer appeared that afternoon. He commented on the defendants' courtroom manner: "I have observed that the defendants have been free and easy in their movements, which were natural, easy and smooth. I have observed them especially during the early part of the trial, laughing and conversing with one another. I have observed them both consulting on frequent occasions with their attorneys, they taking the initiative in those conversations by calling the attorneys back to speak to them. I have noticed that during the last two weeks since the alienists for the state started to testify, their demeanor has been distinctly different. There has been much less laughing, although occasionally they do laugh now, particularly Leopold. I have noticed that they smile and nod to persons in the courtroom and to witnesses on the witness stand. That they have occasionally, particularly Leopold, shaken their heads as if in dissent from various things that have been said. The laughing on the part of Loeb has changed frequently and quite abruptly to a very serious expression. I have observed him show signs of feeling." Dr. Singer summarized his testimony by saying: "There is nothing in those observations that would indicate mental disease."[44]

In cross-examining Dr. Singer Saturday morning, Clarence Darrow asked if the physician had been with the two confessed murderers at the time he, Darrow, was trying to get a writ of habeas corpus so that he might see them, an allusion to the fact that the state's attorney's staff possibly had violated the boys' civil rights by grilling them for so long before allowing them access to an attorney.[45]

"It is too bad you didn't get them before I got them and they would not have talked about it at all," growled Crowe, "and this murder would have been unavenged."

"Strike it out," Judge Caverly ordered.

"It is not the enforcement of law to capture people and compel them to talk," suggested Darrow.

"We didn't compel them to talk," countered Crowe.

"No?"

"When they were talking we couldn't stop them—"

"I know all about that too," mumbled Darrow.

"—and wanted to show how really smart they were in their perfect crime."

After the weekend recess, another comment by Dr. Singer prompted additional complaints by Darrow about his inability to see his clients in time. "I will confess that I violated a number of constitutional rights," argued State's Attorney Crowe, jumping to his feet, "and I intend to continue that as long as I am state's attorney. When a man is charged with a crime I am not going to telephone him and ask him to hire a lawyer before I talk to him."

Darrow reacted angrily. "Well, I don't think in a well-organized, intelligent community, a man could be elected state's attorney under the statement that when a man is charged with a crime, the state's attorney would violate his constitutional rights. Now, maybe Judge Crowe can get away with it, but it doesn't speak well for this community, if he can."

(Ironically in the 1960s the Supreme Court of the United States would rule in the Miranda case that a suspect must be informed of his right to remain silent and obtain an attorney. William T. Crowe, a Chicago attorney and nephew of Bob Crowe, admits today that Clarence Darrow was far ahead of his time in his thinking.[46]

(According to one legend that has grown up around the Leopold and Loeb case, Clarence Darrow had the opportunity to prevent the murderers from confessing and did not choose to take it. James Doherty, who covered the case for the *Tribune,* recalled years later that on the afternoon that Leopold and Loeb were taken to the state's attorney's office and prior to their confessions, Darrow had walked in to inquire about his clients. "Aren't you going to get a writ of habeas corpus for them, Clarence?" Doherty asked. "Oh, no," Darrow reportedly replied. "The state's attorney can have them in custody as long as he wants them." Doherty used this story to prove his point that Darrow was overrated, but almost certainly the reporter was mistaken concerning the day; the Loebs did not employ Darrow until after their son and Nathan Leopold, Jr., had confessed.[47])

At the next session during the cross-examination of prosecution witness Dr. William C. Krohn, Crowe sought to correct what he considered to be a false impression of what he had meant by his words: "The state's attorney of this county in no event intends ever to violate the constitutional rights of any person. His contention in this case is that he has at no time violated any constitutional rights of these defendants. The argument that has been going on between Mr. Darrow and myself has been to the proposition that while the Constitution says you cannot compel a defendant to talk, the state's attorney contends that if he wants to talk voluntarily that it is not the duty of the state's attorney to close his mouth."[48]

The state called no more witnesses and, on the afternoon of August 19 at 2:36 P.M., rested its case.

19 Showdown

Ninety unfortunate human beings have been hanged by the neck until dead in Chicago in history. We would not have any civilization except for those ninety being hanged, and if we cannot make it ninety-two we will have to shut up shop.

—Clarence Darrow[1]

Assistant State's Attorney Thomas Marshall made the opening argument for the prosecution. Reading from a prepared statement in a high-pitched voice, he began: "The position of the state is that there is but one penalty that is proportionate to the turpitude of this crime, only one penalty that applies to this crime, and that is the extreme penalty, death." Marshall felt it necessary to define "turpitude" as "the depravity, the viciousness, the facts and circumstances of the crime."[2] Leopold and Loeb thought that funny.

Marshall continued to speak until the following afternoon, citing case after case as precedents for a sentence of hanging. When he finished, another assistant state's attorney, Joseph Savage, rose to restate in a booming voice the case for the prosecution. Savage minced no words: "You have before you one of the most cold-blooded, cruel, cowardly, dastardly murders that was ever tried in the history of any court!"[3]

Savage continued as the two defendants, no longer laughing, looked down at the floor. He accused them of not giving Bobby Franks even a fighting chance. "The blow was struck from behind, that cowardly blow." He sneered at the defense pleas for mercy. "What mercy did they show to him? Why, after striking the four blows, they pulled him to the rear of the car and gouged his life out. Mercy! Why, your honor, it is an insult in a case of this kind to come before the bar of justice and beg for mercy! I know your honor will be just as merciful to these two defendants sitting here as they were to Bobby Franks."

Many in the court had begun to weep. Finally, after forty minutes of Savage's haranguing, Jacob Franks could take it no longer.

He got out of his seat and walked out of the courtroom. The previous weekend Franks had received still another letter threatening the lives of his wife and daughter and demanding $8,000. Police arrested an eleven-year-old boy who admitted writing the letter, prompted by an older brother. "I read a lot about the case of Loeb and Leopold," confessed the brother, "and decided I could be smarter than they."[4]

Only a few evenings after that arrest, a grisly warning appeared on a porch across the street from the Franks home: a human head, a pair of withered arms, and a single discolored leg arranged in the form of a pirate's skull and crossbones. An envelope lay between the elbows of the two arms addressed to "Chicago, City of Crime." Inside, a note stated: "If the court don't hang them, we will." It was signed KKK, the Ku Klux Klan.[5]

Joseph Savage continued to speak the next day, a hot and muggy one on which Judge Caverly appeared in court wearing a light suitcoat instead of his usual judicial robes. Savage sweated profusely as he demanded the lives of the two defendants: "Hang them! Hang these heartless supermen!" Perspiration ran down his face in rivulets soaking his collar. Leopold and Loeb also had begun to sweat as Savage continued to summarize the facts in the case, dwelling on all the sordid details. "If we do not hang these two most brutal murderers, we might just as well abolish capital punishment, because it will mean nothing in the law. And I want to say to your honor that the men who have reached the gallows prior to this time have been unjustly treated if these two do not follow!"

Of course, that was exactly the point that Clarence Darrow had sought to make. It would be nearly another half century before the Supreme Court of the United States would declare capital punishment unconstitutional in the way it was being applied.

Savage's remarks shattered the smug façade Nathan Leopold, Jr., had shown to the world for the past month. During recess he spoke with his brother Mike and began crying. "My God, Mike, do you think we'll swing after that?"[6]

Walter Bachrach spoke first for the defense. He attempted to educate the court concerning mental disease. "Mental disease is primarily the inability on the part of the person suffering from such disease to make a successful adjustment to the environment in which he lives." He then charged Savage of seeking only to arouse prejudice and passion in connection with a problem that required intelligence and understanding. He accused the state alienists of making superficial examinations that might "just as well have been carried on over at State and Madison Streets on a busy Saturday afternoon as it was up in the state's attorney's office."[7]

The climax of the hearing would come next.

On Friday afternoon, August 22, a mob greater than any that had appeared during the previous month rushed the doors of Judge Caverly's court. They had come to hear Clarence Darrow speak. "The tidal wave of men and women swept over and flattened a skirmish line of bailiffs at the main entrance and poured up the stairs and the elevators, sweeping all obstacles away," wrote the *Daily News*.[8]

When Judge Caverly arrived, he seemed astonished by the scene. Hundreds had pushed and shoved their way up to the sixth floor. The judge had to battle his way through the mob before he could enter his own courtroom. Once inside he angrily ordered its doors barred.

At 2:12 the man everyone had come to hear, Clarence Darrow, wearing an alpaca suit and a white tie, began to talk, although the sound of scuffling still came from outside. Bailiffs and deputy sheriffs continued to battle the crowds; two women were knocked down and trampled. Darrow had not spoken more than a hundred words before he raised his hands in a gesture of helplessness and sat down. "I think we had better wait, if you don't mind," he said. Crowe agreed.

Judge Caverly spoke sharply to a police officer: "Sergeant, I want the whole building cleared out." The judge also telephoned a complaint to Police Chief Collins: "It's disgraceful. The worst riot I ever saw in a courtroom. Somebody may be killed."

At 2:22 Darrow began again. He still could not continue. "I don't know what we can do, your honor," said the attorney.

"Officers, clean out the hall!" shouted Caverly. "Clean it out, and if you haven't got enough men, get fifty more. Put everybody out of the building except those in this room now." The judge mumbled to those near him that he might as well have twenty wooden soldiers out there if they failed to do what they were told.

The sound of scuffling continued, but added to it now was the sound of wooden clubs being applied against human flesh. Then a police sergeant entered the courtroom again to say that the crowd had been dispersed, all but the press.

"All but what?" asked Caverly.

"The press. The newspapermen. I can't make them understand you want them out of the halls."

"All right, let the press in."

The door opened and several reporters entered, accompanied by two small freckle-faced copyboys dressed in short pants and blue shirts. This caused the courtroom to rock with laughter. Finally, it was quiet enough to begin. Nearly twenty-eight minutes had been consumed by the delay as Clarence Darrow rose for the third time and began to speak. He talked first about his anxiety over the almost-unprecedented publicity which had been given the case by newspapers all over the United States. "When the public are interested and want a punishment, no matter what the offense is, great or small, they only think of one punishment and that is death," he said.

The newspapers would describe Darrow's summation that day as brilliant and bearing marks of careful preparation. Lawyers who had followed his career would consider it his finest speech. The attorney had hinted to friends that he planned to make this the last speech of his career as a trial lawyer. He presented a picturesque figure, this old warrior of the courtroom, his coat hung shapelessly over his bent shoulders, folding and unfolding his arms, sticking his thumbs into his vest pockets, wagging a forefinger to emphasize certain points, moving back and forth in the small arena between spectators and judge, turning now and then toward the former, then pivoting swiftly to address his audience of one, Judge Caverly. Leopold and Loeb would not giggle this day; they sat soberly through the speech. The judge, hand propped beneath his chin, followed every word.

Darrow dealt with the rumors that this had been a million-dollar defense. "We announced to the public that no excessive use of money would be made in this case, neither for lawyers, for psychiatrists or in any other way. We have faithfully kept that promise." He insisted that the defense alienists had received the same per diem payments as had those for the prosecution. "If we fail in this defense, it will not be for lack of money; it will be on account of money," he said, adding that had the boys been poor and unconnected not a state's attorney in the state would have refused to consent to a life sentence on a plea of guilty.

Darrow previously had claimed that no minor had been sentenced to death on a plea of guilty in Illinois. He now said that never had a human being under twenty-eight or thirty been so sentenced. "Yet I have heard in the last six months nothing but the cry for blood. I have heard raised from the office of the state's attorney nothing but the breath of hate. I have heard precedents quoted which would be a disgrace to a savage race. I have seen a court urged almost to the point of threats to hang two boys, in the face of evidence, in the face of experience, in the face of all the better and humane thought of the age."

Darrow turned his attention to the closing arguments offered by Assistant State's Attorney Savage. ("Did you pick him for his name or his learning?" snorted Darrow.) Savage had suggested that if these two did not hang, nobody would hang in Illinois anymore. "Well, I can imagine something worse than that," suggested Darrow. "So long as this terrible tool is to be used for a plaything, without thought or consideration, in seeking to inflame the mob with the thought that a boy must be hanged or civilization will be hanged, we ought to get rid of it and get rid of it altogether for the protection of human life!"

Darrow stood still and gazed directly at Judge Caverly. "I am aware that a court has more experience, more judgment, and more kindliness than a jury. And then, your honor, it may not be hardly fair to the court, because I am aware that I have helped to place a serious burden upon your shoulders. And at that I have always meant to be your friend. But this was not an act of friendship. I know perfectly well that where responsibility is divided by twelve it is easy to say, 'Away with him.' But, your honor, if these boys hang, you must do it. There can be no division of responsibility here. You must do it. You can never explain that the rest overpowered you. It must be your deliberate, cool, premeditated act, without a chance to shift responsibility." Judge Caverly's sister sat near the bench, tears streaming down her face.

Darrow turned to statistics, citing the ninety individuals previously hanged in Chicago. Of that ninety, only three had been hanged on a plea of guilty, and only one in the last thirty years. "Three hundred and fifty have been indicted for murder in Chicago and pleaded guilty and only one hanged," claimed Darrow. "And my friend who is prosecuting this case deserves the honor of that hanging while he was on the bench. But his victim was forty years old." Crowe glared at his rival.

"I have never yet tried a case where the state's attorney did not say it was the most cold-blooded, inexcusable, premeditated case that ever occurred," continued Darrow. "If it was murder, there never was such a murder. If it was robbery, there never was such a robbery. If it was a conspiracy, it was the most terrible conspiracy that ever happened." Darrow claimed he considered the Franks murder one of the least cruel. "Poor little Bobby Franks suffered very little," he said. "It was all over in fifteen minutes after he got into the car." While admitting it was a senseless, useless, purposeless, and motiveless act of two boys, Darrow said it was not cruel, except as death is cruel. He dismissed the prosecution's claim that the motive was the $10,000 ransom. "These two boys, neither one of whom needed a cent, scions of wealthy people, killed this little inoffensive boy to get ten thousand dollars?" Darrow shook his head. He wiped his hands with a handkerchief, then tossed it onto the defense table. "It was not money. It was the senseless act of immature and diseased children."

Clarence Darrow spoke for two hours; then Judge Caverly adjourned the court until the following day. Later Nathan Leopold, Jr., gave his opinion of the speech: "That address came through Clarence Darrow's mouth straight from his heart. Into it he distilled a half century's penetrating observation and a half century's profound reflection. Mr. Darrow was pleading not so much for Dick and me as he was pleading for the human race. For love, for charity, for understanding. Especially for understanding."[9]

The crowds appeared again on Saturday morning, but the police contained them on the fifth floor and outside on the sidewalks. Mrs. Charlotte Caverly, the judge's wife, appeared in court for the first time. "I have carefully avoided the courtroom for fear of giving the impression that I was morbidly curious about it," she told a reporter from the *Herald and Examiner.* "I appreciate the awful responsibility that rests on the judge's shoulders and I try to be a help to him by remaining away."[10]

Darrow continued his recital of the crime, the wandering of the two murderers around the Harvard School in their attempt to select a victim, their picking Bobby Franks up within sight of their homes, "where eyes might be at every window as they pass by." He spoke of their twenty-mile drive along thickly populated streets. "The slightest accident, the slightest misfortune, a bit of curiosity, and arrest for speeding, anything, would bring destruction. They go down the Midway, through the park, meeting hundreds of machines, in sight of thousands of eyes with this dead boy. For what? For nothing! The mad acts of the fool in *King Lear* is the only thing I know of that compares with it." Darrow threw his arms upward in a gesture of hopelessness.

And always he continued his crusade against the death penalty. "The law can be vindicated without killing anyone else. It might shock the fine sensibilities of the state's counsel that this boy was put into a culvert and left after he was dead, but your honor, I can think, and only think, your honor, of taking two boys, one eighteen and the other nineteen, irresponsible, weak, diseased, penning them in a cell, checking off the days and the hours and the minutes, until they will be taken out and hanged." (Darrow was mistaken in his assertion that his clients were eighteen and nineteen; they had been at the time of the murder, but while waiting in jail, Loeb had turned nineteen. Both were that age.)

That, Darrow commented sarcastically, would be a glorious triumph for justice. "I can picture them, wakened in the gray light of morning, furnished a suit of clothes by the state, led to the scaffold, their feet tied, black caps drawn over their heads, stood on a trap door, the hangman pressing a spring, so that it gives way under them; I can see them fall through space and stopped by the rope around their necks."

He continued: "You can trace the burnings, the boilings, the drawings, and quarterings, the hanging of people in England at the crossroads, carving them up and hanging them as examples for all to see. We can come down to the last century when nearly two hundred crimes were punishable by death. You can read the stories of the hangings on a high hill, and the populace for miles around coming out to the scene, that everybody might be awed into goodness. Hanging for picking pockets—and more pockets were picked in the crowd that went to the hanging than had been known before. Hangings for murder—and men were murdered on the way there and on the way home. Hangings for poaching, hangings for everything and hanging in public, not shut up cruelly and brutally in a jail, out of the light of day, wakened in the nighttime and led down and killed, but taken to the shire town on a high hill, in the presence of a multitude, so that all might see that the wages of sin were death.

"What happened?" asked Darrow. He shook his head sadly and answered his own question: "Nothing!"

When court reconvened Monday morning, Darrow turned his attention to the testimony of the prosecution's alienists. He talked about Loeb: "I do not know what remote ancestor may have sent down the seed that corrupted him, and I do not know through how many ancestors it may have passed until it reached Dickie Loeb." He continued: "There is not an act in all this horrible tragedy that was not the act of a child, the act of a child wandering around in the morning of life."

The defense attorney then turned to the philosophy of Friedrich Nietzsche. "The Superman was a creation of Nietzsche," said Darrow, "but it has permeated every college and university in the civilized world." He went on to describe Leopold's reaction to this German philosopher: "Here is a boy at sixteen or seventeen becoming obsessed with these doctrines. It was not a casual bit of philosophy with him; it was his life. He believed in a Superman. He and Dickie Loeb were the Supermen. There might have been others, but they were two, and two chums. The ordinary commands of society were not for him."

The defense attorney admitted that many read that philosophy and knew it had no application in life. The error of Leopold and Loeb was in believing it, and Darrow indicated that they could not have believed it except for their diseased minds. "Boys are largely what their ideas make them," he said. "Here is a boy who by day and by night, in season and out, was talking of the Superman, owing no obligations to anyone; whatever gave him pleasure he should do, believing it just as another man might believe a religion or any philosophical theory."

Darrow also stressed the chance aspects of the case. "These boys, neither one of them, could possibly have committed this act excepting by coming together. It was not the act for one; it was the act of two. It was the act of their planning, their conniving, their believing in each other, their thinking themselves Supermen. Without this they could not have done it. It would not have happened. Their parents happened to meet; these boys happened to meet; some sort of chemical alchemy operated so that they cared for each other; and poor Bobby Franks' dead body was found in the culvert as a result. Neither one of them could have done it alone.

"Crime has its cause. Perhaps all crimes do not have the same cause, but they all have some cause. And people today are seeking to find out the cause. We lawyers never try to find out. Scientists are studying it; criminologists are investigating it; but we lawyers go on, and on, and on, punishing and hanging and thinking that by general terror we can stamp out crime.

"It never occurs to the lawyer that crime has a cause as certainly as disease, and that the way to rationally treat any abnormal condition is to remove the cause.

"If a doctor were called on to treat typhoid fever, he would probably try to find out what kind of milk or water the patient drank, and perhaps clean out the well so that no one else could get typhoid from the same source. But, if a lawyer was called on to treat a typhoid patient, he would give him thirty days in jail, and then he would think that nobody else would ever dare to catch it. If the patient got well in fifteen days, he would be kept until his time was up. If the disease was worse at the end of thirty days, the patient would be released because his time was up.

"Lawyers are not scientists," admitted Darrow. "They act unmindful of history and science, and all the experience of the past." Still, Darrow suggested that they were making some progress and that courts had become more humane.

"I do not know how much savage there is in these two boys," Darrow confessed. "I hate to say it in their presence, but what is there to look forward to? I do not know but what your honor would be merciful if you tied a rope around their necks and let them die; merciful to them, but not merciful to civilization, and not merciful to those who would be left behind. To spend the balance of their days in prison is mighty little to look forward to, if anything. Is it anything? They may have the hope that as the years roll around they might be released. I do not know. I do not know. I will be honest with this court as I have tried to be from the beginning. I know that these boys are not fit to be at large. I believe they will not be until they pass through the next stage of life, at forty-five or fifty. Whether they will be then, I cannot tell. I am sure of this: that I will not be there to help them. So far as I am concerned it is over."

A veteran of the Chautauqua circuit, Darrow liked to pepper his lectures and courtroom speeches with literary quotations in the style of many lecturers of the era. He could not resist the opportunity to offer a quotation from his favorite poet, A. E. Housman, author of *A Shropshire Lad:*

> Now hollow fires burn out to black,
>   And lights are fluttering low:
> Square your shoulders, lift your pack
>   And leave your friends and go.
> O never fear, lads, naught's to dread,
>   Look not left nor right:
> In all the endless road you tread
>   There's nothing but the night.

Darrow added: "I care not, your honor, whether the march begins at the gallows or when the gates of Joliet close upon them, there is nothing but the night, and that is little for any human being to expect."

Darrow neared the conclusion of his address, which had held those fortunate enough to gain entry to the courtroom fascinated for three days. He had begun on a note of bedlam caused by the clamor of the crowds shoving noisily to get in. Now the only sound in the courtroom was that of his voice. From outside, six stories below, could be heard the rumble of passing streetcars, the dull roar of automobile engines.

"I have stood here for three months as one might stand at the ocean trying to sweep back the tide. I hope the seas are subsiding and the wind is falling, and I believe they are, but I wish to make no false pretense to this court. The easy thing and the popular thing to do is hang my clients. I know it. Men and women who do not think will applaud. The cruel and the thoughtless will approve. It will be easy today, but in Chicago, and reaching out over the length and breadth of the land, more and more fathers, the humane, the kind and the hopeful, who are gaining an understanding and asking questions not only about these poor boys, but about their own—these will join in no acclaim at the death of my clients. These would ask that the shedding of blood be stopped, and that the normal feelings of man resume their sway.

"I know that the future is on my side. Your honor stands between the past and the future. You may hang these boys. You may hang them by the neck until they are dead. But in doing it you will turn your face toward the past. In doing it you are making it harder for every other boy who in ignorance and darkness must grope his way through the mazes which only childhood knows. In doing it you will make it harder for unborn children. You may save them and make it easier for every child that some time may stand where these boys stand. You will make it easier for every human being with an aspiration and a vision and a hope and a fate. I am pleading for the future. I am pleading for a time when hatred and cruelty will not control the hearts of men. When we can learn by reason and judgment and understanding and faith that all life is worth saving, and that mercy is the highest attribute of man."

Darrow apologized for taking so long to speak, pleaded for Judge Caverly to temper justice with mercy, read one last verse from the poet Omar Khayyám, and then the great attorney was done. He gathered up his notes. Someone offered him a chair. He sat down. As he did, there were tears on Judge Caverly's cheeks.

On the final day of Darrow's courtroom plea the *Tribune* offered its opinion of that which had most concerned the attorney in undertaking the defense of Leopold and Loeb: "Mr. Darrow does not believe that capital punishment is a proper social remedy. We doubt that he believes in punishment as a cure for anything. Capital punishment is provided as a punishment for murder because people thus far in most states believe that it does deter the light taking of life. Possibly in the upward progress of the human race a life will not be taken for a life, but it is our opinion that the whole race then will be up a peg or two and that the individual will not be so quick in taking what society in general has resolved not to destroy."[11]

Benjamin Bachrach had planned a two-day summation on behalf of the defense to begin on Tuesday, August 26. Perhaps in anticipation of what promised to be a long, dry journey over familiar ground, many spectators stayed home that morning. Seats were available in the courtroom. But rather than risk an anticlimax, and being unable to top his colleague, Bachrach wisely chose to speak briefly. "You are listening for the last time in this case to anybody on the part of the defense," he concluded. "Humbly may it please your honor, frankly begging and pleading your honor, to let these boys live and not bring upon the suffering that death upon the gallows to these boys must necessarily bring."[12]

Then all that remained was for one final orator to speak: State's Attorney Robert E. Crowe. "Crowe gave the courtroom a mad day of it," the *Daily News* would report. "He spoke in a frenzy. He shouted and stamped and waved his arms. Now he thrust his face, purple with the strain of his apoplectic speech, into the faces of Loeb and Leopold; now he strode before Judge Caverly, shaking his fist as he put all his lung power into some climax or other. It was all climax, for that matter. There were no valleys in the speech, just peaks. And Crowe's nasal voice accentuated the severity of the sentences it uttered. Into the faces of the two young defendants he hurled epithet after epithet, his eyes blazing and his voice screaming anger."[13]

Crowe had begun: "Before going into a discussion on the merits of the case, there is a matter that I would like to refer to. The distinguished gentleman whose profession it is to protect murder in Cook County—and concerning whose health thieves inquire before they go to commit a crime—has seen fit to abuse the state's attorney's office and particularly my assistants, Mr. Marshall and Mr. Savage, for their conduct in this case. He has even objected to the state's attorney referring to two self-confessed murderers who have pleaded guilty to two capital offenses as criminals.[14]

"Your honor ought not to shock their ears by such a cruel reference to the laws of this state, to the penalty of death. Why, don't you know that one of them has to shave every day of the week, and that is a bad sign? The other one only has to shave twice a week, and that is a bad sign. One is short and one is tall, and it is equally a bad sign in both of them. When they were children they played with Teddy bears. One of them has three moles on his back. One is over-developed sexually and the other not quite so good. My God, if one of them had a harelip, I suppose Darrow would want me to apologize for having had them indicted.

"I have a right to forgive those who trespass against me as I do, in the hopes that I in the hereafter will be forgiven my trespasses. As a private citizen I have that right, and as a private citizen I live that religion. But, as a public official selected by the people, charged with the duty of enforcing the laws of my country, I have no right to forgive those who violate their country's laws.

"It is my duty to prosecute. Your honor has no right to forgive those who trespass against the State of Illinois. And I want to say to you, your honor, in this case, with the mass of evidence presented by the state, if a jury were sitting in that box and they returned a verdict and did not fix the punishment at death, every person in this community, including your honor and myself, would feel that that verdict was founded in corruption!

"And I will tell you why: I have taken quite a trip during the last four or five weeks. I thought I was going to be kept in Chicago all summer trying this case and that most of my time would be spent in the Criminal Court Building. And I find I have been mistaken. I did come up to your honor's courtroom five weeks ago and after I was there a little while, Old Doc Yak—is that his name: the man from Washington? Oh, Dr. White. Dr. White took me by the hand and led me into the nursery of two poor rich young boys and he introduced me to a Teddy bear. Then he told me some bedtime stories and after I got through listening to them, he took me into the kindergarten and he presented me to little Dickie and Babe. And after we had wandered between the nursery and kindergarten for quite a while, I was taken into hand by the Bachrach brothers and taken to a psychopathic laboratory and there I received quite a liberal education in mental diseases, and particularly what certain doctors did not know about them.

"The three wise men from the east came on to tell your honor about these two little babes, and being three wise men brought on from the east, they wanted to make the picture a little more perfect. One of them was sacrilegious enough to say this pervert, this murderer, this kidnapper, thought he was the Christ child and that he thought his mother was the Madonna, without a syllable of evidence any place to support the blasphemous and sacrilegious statement. Who said this young pervert thought he was the Christ child? He has proclaimed since he was eleven years of age that there is no God!"

Crowe turned toward Leopold and marched at him to shake a finger in the defendant's face. "I wonder now, Nathan, whether you think there is a God or not?" Leopold steadfastly met Crowe's eyes and smiled faintly as the state's attorney continued his attack. "I wonder whether you think it is a pure accident that this disciple of Nietzschean philosophy dropped his glasses, or whether it was an act of Divine Providence to visit upon your miserable carcasses the wrath of God in the enforcement of the law of the State of Illinois?"

Crowe paused to allow the weight of his words to sink in, then continued: "Well, if your honor please, after the Bachrachs had completed my education in the psychopathical laboratories, then my good friend Clarence Darrow took me on a Chautauqua trip with him, and, visiting various towns, we would go to social settlements such as the Hull House, and Clarence would expound his peculiar philosophy of life, and we would meet with Communists and anarchists, and Clarence would regale them with his philosophy of the law, which means there ought not to be any law, and there ought not to be any enforcement of the law!"

Crowe had been speaking barely a half hour but was already soaked with perspiration. Breathing hard, he removed his glasses and wiped his forehead. While doing so, he glanced up at the clock and noticed that it was past twelve. "May we have a recess?" he asked.

Word passed swiftly that Crowe had begun his summation, and when court convened at two, the courtroom filled again with spectators eager to see the last battle in the state's attorney's showdown with Clarence Darrow. Crowe continued explosively, hammering home his points by pounding his fist into his hand. Toward the end of the day he shifted the direction of his attack. "I want to tell your honor, bearing in mind the testimony that was whispered in your ear, one of the motives in this case was a desire to satisfy unnatural lust." Crowe mentioned Leopold's early intentions to rape a girl in connection with the kidnap plot, then said that he and Loeb had removed Bobby Franks' trousers long before taking off the rest of his clothes and stuffing him into the culvert. "You have before you the coroner's report, and the coroner's physician says that when little Robert Franks was examined, his rectum was distended that much." Crowe held his hand up making a shape with his fingers almost the size of a half dollar.

Bachrach objected, claiming that the accusation of a sexual assault was merely the state's attorney's mistaken interpretation and not a fair inference from the report. He asked the report be examined.

Judge Caverly asked women to leave the courtroom. Some of them, prompted by bailiffs, began to move slowly toward the exit. Many seemed unhappy over being excluded.

"The coroner's report says that he had a distended rectum," argued Bob Crowe, "and from that fact and the fact that the pants were taken off and the fact that they are perverts, I have a right to argue that they committed an act of perversion."

Judge Caverly, however, seemed less interested in the state's attorney's contentions than in those women who lingered behind pillars to avoid detection by bailiffs. "I have asked the ladies to leave the room," snapped the judge. "Now I want you to leave. If you do not, I will have the bailiffs escort you into the hallway. There is nothing left here but a lot of stuff that is not fit for you to hear!" The remaining women left, complaining as they went.

While the level of hallway noise outside increased in pitch, Walter Bachrach read the part of the coroner's report referring to the genitals being intact and the rectum dilated, but with no evidence of recent forcible dilation.

"This is the evidence of the coroner," Caverly finally ruled, somewhat ambiguously, "and certainly conclusive and we will let it rest with what the coroner says." The question of sexual perversion in the killing seemed to have been left unresolved by Caverly's ruling; nevertheless, court adjourned for the day.

On Wednesday morning Crowe resumed his argument. "If the state only had half of the evidence that it did have, or a quarter of the evidence that it had, we would have had a jury in the box and a plea of not guilty. But trapped like a couple of rats, with no place to escape except through an insanity defense, they proceeded to build it up. A weird, uncanny crime? The crime is not half as weird or uncanny as the defense that is put in here." In mentioning that the sheer weight of incriminating evidence had forced the defense to plead guilty before a judge rather than not guilty before a jury, Crowe had touched on one of the great ironies of the Franks case.

The state's attorney spent the rest of the morning analyzing the Hulbert and Bowman report, point by point. He came eventually to what the doctors had to say about Leopold and Loeb's emotions, or rather their lack of them. "And if it is the fate of these two perverts that they must pay the penalty of this crime upon the gallows, when they realize it, you will find that they have got emotion and you will find they have got fear and you will find these cowardly perverts will have to be carried to the gallows."

Crowe paused when he came to the part of the report where the defendants hinted at "other crimes" they had committed without admitting what those crimes might be. The psychiatrists had made no attempt to probe but had labeled the supposed other crimes as A, B, C, and D. "These four crimes were known to Leopold," theorized Crowe, "and he blackmailed Loeb. He threatened Loeb with exposure if he did not submit to him, and Loeb had to go along with Leopold. And Leopold was willing to go along with Loeb, because he could use his body for vile and unnatural practices."

As Crowe continued, he referred repeatedly to these ABCD crimes, suggesting even that part of the reason for the planned method of murdering the victim (with Leopold and Loeb each holding one end of a rope around his neck) was that Loeb wished to implicate Leopold fully. "He was going to make Leopold pull the rope so he would have something equal on Leopold." No evidence, however, had been introduced to indicate what these ABCD crimes might be. In referring to them, the state's attorney could only hint at additional gruesome murders, just as he had similarly hinted at more perverted actions in the slaying of Bobby Franks.

Eventually court recessed for lunch. Despite the continued references to their evil deeds and character, Leopold and Loeb still remained celebrities to many young Chicago flappers, who clamored to see the two famous killers as they similarly clamored to see movie idols such as Rudolph Valentino. At the noon recess one girl attempted to pass a note to Loeb, only to have it fall to the floor. A member of the state's attorney's staff retrieved the note, which said, "Dear Dick and Babe: Good luck. Alice."[15]

That afternoon Crowe completed his point-by-point dissection of the Hulbert and Bowman report. The following morning he concluded his remarks. But the fire that had marked his attack the first day had begun to flicker. The state's attorney's voice now came out in hoarse rasps. Yet the impact of his words remained strong: "I submit your honor please, if we can take the power of American manhood, take boys at eighteen years of age and send them to their death in the front line of trenches of France in defense of our laws, we have an equal right to take men nineteen years of age and take their lives for violating those laws that these boys gave their lives to defend. Many a boy eighteen years of age lies buried beneath the poppies in Flanders Field, who died to defend the laws of this country. We had no compunction when we did that; why should we have any compunction when we take the lives of men nineteen years of age who want to tear down and destroy the laws that these brave boys died to preserve?"

After having spoken for barely more than a half hour, Crowe had to request a brief recess to allow his failing voice to recover. Ten minutes later he tried again. "When I was listening to Mr. Darrow plead for sympathy for these two men who showed no sympathy, it reminded me of the story of Abraham Lincoln." The state's attorney retold one of Lincoln's stories about a young boy who murdered his wealthy parents. Discovered in his crime, he went to trial. The judge asked him if there was any reason why he should not be sentenced to death. "I hope the court will be lenient to a poor orphan," pleaded the boy.

"I want to tell you the real defense in this case, your honor," Crowe rasped on. "It is Clarence Darrow's dangerous philosophy of life. He said to your honor that he was not pleading alone for these two young men. He said he was looking to the future, that he was thinking of the ten thousand young boys who in the future would fill the chairs his clients filled and he wants to soften the law. He wants them treated not with the severity that the law of this state prescribes, but he wants them repaid with kindness and consideration. I want to tell your honor that it would be much better if God had not caused this crime to be disclosed. It would have been much better if it went unsolved and these men went unwhipped of justice. If would not have done near the harm to this community as will be done if your honor, as chief justice of this great court, puts your official seal of approval upon the doctrines of anarchy preached by Clarence Darrow as a defense in this case. Society can endure, the law can endure, and criminals can escape, but if a court such as this court should say that he believes in the doctrine of Darrow, that you ought not to hang when the laws say you should, a greater blow has been struck to our institutions than by a hundred, yes, a thousand murders."

Crowe had been eloquent, but now he made a serious error in judgment. He thought it necessary to counter Darrow's attack on prosecution witness James Gortland, who had testified to Leopold's desire to plead guilty before a "friendly judge" so as to receive life imprisonment. "I don't know whether your honor believes that officer or not, but I want to tell you, if you have observed these two defendants during the trial, if you have observed the conduct of their attorneys and their families with one honorable exception, and that is the old man who sits in sackcloth and ashes and who is entitled to the sympathy of everybody, old Mr. Leopold. With that one honorable exception, everybody connected with the case have laughed and sneered and jeered, and if the defendant, Leopold, did not say that he would plead guilty before a friendly judge, his actions demonstrated that he thinks he has got one."

Darrow immediately jumped to his feet and objected.

"Let the reporter write up that statement," said Judge Caverly, overruling the objection by Darrow. "Have that statement written up!" But Caverly glared angrily at the state's attorney, and Crowe seemed stunned by the impact his remarks had had on the jurist.

He concluded soon after, then directed the court's attention to the charge of kidnapping. He called only two witnesses: Jacob Franks and Captain William Shoemacher. Then Judge Caverly had something to say: "Before the state rests in the other case, the court will order stricken from the record the closing remarks of the state's attorney as being a cowardly and dastardly assault upon the integrity of this court."

Crowe apologized. "It was not so intended, your honor."

"And it could not be used for any other purpose," continued the judge, "except to incite a mob and to try and intimidate this court. It will be stricken from the record." Crowe tried to placate the judge, but Caverly was seething. "This court will not be intimidated by anybody at any time or place as long as he occupies this position." Caverly then announced that he would rule on September 10 at 9:30 A.M., and that no one would be allowed in court that day but the press, members of the family, and official staff.

On its thirty-second day the hearing in mitigation and aggravation of the guilty plea of Nathan Leopold, Jr., and Richard Loeb for the murder of Bobby Franks stood adjourned.

20 ABCD

He denied having participated in any other delinquencies, but later referred to four episodes for which the letters 'A, B, C, and D' were suggested. It was found forensically inadvisable to question him about these.

—DRS. HULBERT AND BOWMAN[1]

While the world awaited judgment in the Franks murder case, the Chicago newspapers, with no more daily testimony crowding their columns, had time to concern themselves with innovative journalism. They speculated on whether Leopold and Loeb might have committed other even more ghastly murders, centering their attention on a brief one-paragraph reference buried in the middle of the section of the Hulbert and Bowman report devoted to Richard Loeb. These were the so-called ABCD crimes that State's Attorney Crowe hammered on time after time in the closing hours of the hearing.

Hulbert and Bowman, after having documented the criminal activities preceding the Franks murder, said Loeb denied at first any more delinquencies other than those detailed in the report, but later referred to "four episodes, for which the letters 'A, B, C, and D' were suggested." The alienists found it "forensically inadvisable to question him about these." Later, when Dr. Hulbert appeared in court, he was asked under cross-examination about his analysis of the defendants regarding this matter. Dr. Hulbert replied that "he knew that both defendants were lying to him at times, and when he attempted to pry into certain things, he was told that their counsel advised him not to go into it, and they did not go into it."[2]

Why? Because these episodes were crimes equally as terrifying as the murder of Bobby Franks? Were Leopold and Loeb guilty of not one murder but five?

The *Tribune* seemed to think so and in its September 1, 1924, editions attempted to unravel the riddle posed by ABCD. In a front-page story, the newspaper suggested four unsolved crimes that might have been the work of Bobby Franks' murderers:

A. The murder on November 25, 1923, of Freeman Louis Tracy, a part-time University of Chicago student whose body was thrown from an automobile at Woodlawn and Fifty-eighth Street. He had been either kidnapped or lured into a machine while returning from a dance. There was evidence of a struggle which ended when a bullet smashed into Tracy's head.

B. The kidnapping and subsequent mutilation of Charles Ream, a taxi driver. Several hours after being dragged into an automobile and slugged on the morning of November 20, 1923, he regained consciousness on a deserted section of prairie on the far South Side. It is held significant that Ream positively identified Loeb and Leopold, following the latter's arrest for the Franks murder, as the youths responsible for his present condition.

C. The murder of Melvin T. Wolf, a young man who lived at 4553 Ellis Avenue, a few blocks north of the Franks and Loeb residences. Last April he set out to mail a letter. Although a strenuous search was made for him, no trace was found until his body was taken from the lake at the foot of Sixty-fourth Street last May.

D. The murder about two years ago of the "Handless Stranger." The nude body of this man, never identified, was found in the snow near Geneva. His hands had been hacked off.[3]

The *Tribune* seemed uncertain about its identification of the four episodes, however, and at the end of its article suggested that the state's attorney considered this last murder unlikely to have been committed by the defendants. Arson might have been the fourth crime, the newspaper theorized.

The following day, the *Tribune* had an entirely new theory to offer its readers. Citing the state's attorney's office again as its source, the newspaper now stated its belief that Loeb had committed a number of chisel-connected crimes several years before in the Hyde Park and Woodlawn area (two neighborhoods immediately south of Kenwood). An unidentified alienist believed the two had worked up to their murder of Bobby Franks by assaulting a number of people on the streets and stealing watches, pocketknives, fountain pens, matchboxes, cigarette cases, and other such items. "In their rooms a bushel of such pocket pieces was found," claimed the *Tribune*'s source, who added, "They did then as they had done on other occasions—threw the chisel away. When the Hyde Park police found the particular chisel used on Bobby Franks, they recalled the finding of the others. Each time one had been picked up after a holdup had occurred in the vicinity."[4]

An attorney named Ephraim London, whose path much later crossed that of Nathan Leopold, would question Leopold about the *Tribune* 's solution to the ABCD crimes. Loeb's partner denied any knowledge of what happened to Tracy, Wolf, and the "Handless Stranger." He did respond to a question related to Charles Ream's identification of him:

"I remember Mr. Ream being placed by his attorneys, whom he had hired, in a corner of a corridor in the Criminal Court Building, which Loeb and I had to pass on our way to or from the court, and we passed this certain corner—the newspaper reporters and photographers all ready with their cameras—somebody pointed or gave him a signal and he pointed his finger and said, 'That's them,' and the flash bulbs all flashed."

The two defendants were handcuffed to guards at the time, so the identification was not difficult for Ream to make. Leopold said he and Loeb discussed this incident but did not know what it was about at the time. Later he decided it was an attempt at blackmail. "I had nothing to do with it, and from the tenor of the conversation, I'm practically sure that Loeb had nothing to do with it."

Later during London's questioning, however, Leopold seemed to contradict himself, indicating that a newspaper reporter, not one of Ream's attorneys had been responsible for the identification. "A newspaper reporter later told our attorneys and us that he had given Ream five or ten dollars to stand in this place, and when he, the newspaper reporter, signalled, to point his finger and say, 'It's them.'" London asked Leopold if he could recalled what newspaper the reporter was affiliated with, but he could not. "It's another one of those things that's gone," Leopold responded.[5]

London also questioned Leopold about the so-called chisel crimes. Leopold branded the *Tribune*'s second article as false. (It does have the ring of fiction. Information concerning the use of a chisel as a weapon in robberies would certainly have been mentioned earlier than this, particularly since a bloodstained chisel was found the same night Bobby Franks died.)

In responding to this line of inquiry, Nathan Leopold did admit he carried a revolver when he was with Loeb on at least six or eight occasions. (The *Tribune* article had mentioned Leopold's use of a gun.) One such occasion was the burglary of Zeta Beta Tau. London asked him on what occasions he carried the pistol, which Leopold identified as an automatic .32 caliber Smith and Wesson.

"They were all on occasions when we were together on either an actual criminal adventure or a would-be criminal adventure," said Leopold. "One, specifically, was the robbery of the Zeta Beta Tau house in Ann Arbor. Another was the time—the two times—that we attempted to break into the house at Hubbard Woods to steal some liquor. In each case I was armed. And on at least one occasion—perhaps two or even three—when we went out on trips to steal Electrics, to break plate glass windows, I was carrying a gun. Now whether on that occasion I took it out of my pocket and Dick saw it, I'm not prepared to swear."

London asked if Leopold could recall any other such criminal excursions when he carried the pistol. Leopold said he could not.

During his interview with Ephraim London Nathan Leopold would often exhibit almost total recall when it came to remembering minute details of his life. He had been known for doing memory tricks, of course, reciting lists of names backward and such. His memory failed, however, in several matters related to his criminal activities. He refused to admit burglarizing a second fraternity house in Ann Arbor until London reminded him that such an admission had been made before Drs. Hulbert and Bowman. Leopold then admitted it must be true, if the record so indicated. He claimed he and Loeb had set only one small fire, and it had been a shack. London corrected him, indicating that the record claimed that arson had been committed on at least *three* buildings. Leopold then acknowledged that the number of arsons may have been three—"but one of them was a shack." Leopold's denial of any knowledge on the assaults on Tracy, Ream, Wolf, and the Handless Stranger—or the chisel robberies—can hardly be accepted as proof of his, or Loeb's, innocence in those affairs. He was at that time projecting an image as having fallen victim to a single boyhood mistake; he did not desire corroboration of any further crimes, which would have marred that image.

The riddle of ABCD thus continued to defy solution, although an unpublished memo from the files of the Chicago *Sun-Times* would later shed some light on the question. The memo was written (dated May 19, 1953) by Ray Brennan, who apparently had interviewed State's Attorney Crowe on that date.[6] His memo states:

> Robert E. Crowe recalls that Nathan Leopold and Richard Loeb were reputed to have mutilated two men about two months or more before the murder of Bobby Franks.
>
> He said that he and Clarence Darrow, defense lawyer, had an agreement not to bring out at the trial any filthy testimony not needed to convict.
>
> Along that line, since the defendants had confessed and there was plenty of supporting evidence to convict, the testimony was sharply limited.

> He and Darrow had an agreement not to hold back information or developments from each other, Crowe said.
>
> During the trial, Crowe continued, Darrow came to him with a written report and recommendation made for the defense by two alienists.
>
> The alienists, in their report, urged Darrow to refrain from bringing up any references to homosexuality and to dodge any mention of sex crimes—including emasculation or mutilation offenses, according to Crowe.
>
> Crowe said he read the report, handed it back to Darrow, and never used any of the material at the trial. One of the emasculation victims was reported at the time to have been a taxi driver.
>
> Crowe said no reference ever was made to the matter at the trial and he feels certain there is no official record of it anywhere.

Crowe's comments thirty years after the fact would seem curious, since he alluded continuously to the ABCD crimes during his summation. Of course, he made little attempt to explore this uncharted channel in any depth. In what he considered to be a "hanging case," he probably felt no need to. The report of the alienists mentioned in the Brennan memo probably was the one by Drs. Hulbert and Bowman, but that contains only a brief mention of the two mutilations involved, along with a denial: "He denied being implicated in the so-called gland robbery of Mr. Ream, and he denied being at Geneva in the case of the 'Ragged Stranger,' who was found dead with his hands cut off and his face mutilated (which crime is usually attributed to Warren Lincoln)." The Brennan memo would merely add to the confusion surrounding the riddle of ABCD.

In attempting to solve this riddle the first problem is determining the likelihood of Leopold and Loeb's having been involved in the four motiveless and unsolved crimes generally assigned to them: Tracy, Ream, Wolf, and the Handless (or "Ragged") Stranger. Consider these crimes one by one:

A. *Freeman Louis Tracy.* Apparently few persons attempting to connect the murder of Tracy, an electrician and former part-time student at the University of Chicago, with Leopold and Loeb have bothered to study the facts surrounding his death. On Saturday, November 25, 1923, Freeman Louis Tracy, age twenty-three, who wore an artificial leg, the result of a crane accident several years before, left his room at 1317 East Fifty-third Street at about 9 P.M. to attend a dance at a United Craftsman Bazaar. His foreman,

Daniel Murphy, drove him from the dance and left him near Sixtieth and Cottage Grove in front of Midway Gardens at 12:30 A.M. Between 1 and 1:30 Sunday morning, Tracy reportedly went to make a telephone call at a club above the Frolic Theater, a place where a group known as the Kenwood gang often hung out.

According to one newspaper report, members of the gang frequently would slip up to the clubhouse during late hours by a back fire escape. Police later found drops of blood on the floor and bloody splotches in the washroom of the clubhouse. A taxicab driver named Elmer Rudy said he noticed a wounded man being led along Kenwood Street by several other men. Police received a call from a woman saying there was a fight in front of Swan's Restaurant at Fifty-eighth and Kenwood. Shortly afterward, at around 3 A.m., a student named Dudley Lundon discovered the body of Freeman Louis Tracy on Fifty-eighth Street near Woodlawn Avenue. A fedora hat, supposedly belonging to the victim, was found in front of 5734 Kenwood Avenue. A block-long trail of blood on Fifty-eighth Street was apparently caused by Tracy's head hanging out over the running board of an automobile before his body had been dumped out onto the street. Police eventually found a Cadillac smeared with blood abandoned in La Grange, a suburb southwest of Chicago. Three men were seen vanishing into the nearby forest preserve as the police approached. The Cadillac had been stolen the previous day from in front of a home on Chicago's West Side.[7]

Very few details in the murder of Freeman Louis Tracy fit Leopold and Loeb's known criminal patterns. Tracy's murder remains clouded in mystery, but it seems extremely unlikely that he could have been the victim of Leopold and Loeb. More likely he was victim of a gang slaying.

Tracy might never have been connected with the ABCD crimes had not police at the time he was slain speculated that he might have been killed by the same persons who assaulted Charles Ream in the same neighborhood only five nights before. Six months later, when Ream pointed at Leopold and Loeb, he provided a tenuous link between them and Freeman Louis Tracy.

B. *Charles Ream.* Early the morning of November 20, 1923, Ream took a streetcar home from his job as Yellow Cab driver and alighted at Fifty-fifth and Dorchester. The time was 3 A.M. Suddenly two men jumped from an automobile and commanded him to get inside. When they reached an area near Ninety-second Street (according to newspaper reports immediately after the event), one thrust a cloth soaked with chloroform against Ream's nose.[8] He remembered nothing until he awoke lying in the grass nearly three hours later, having been castrated.

Six months later, when Ream made his identification in the corridors of the Criminal Court Building, he claimed the crime had been committed near 108th Street and Avenue G ("that is within a mile of where Robert Franks' body was found and it is near a culvert and a railroad track," said Ream).[9] The fact that he changed his story concerning the place where the assault occurred has been overlooked by chroniclers of his case.

At the time of Ream's mutilation in the fall of 1923 police originally suspected the motive had been revenge. One early suspect was Earl English, Ream's cousin, a nineteen-year-old student at the University of Chicago and a member of Delta Upsilon fraternity. Police arrested him two hours after Ream was taken to the hospital. An automobile similar in description to the one Ream had been kidnapped in had been seen in front of English's home on recent evenings. According to one newspaper report, English had walked into the room of his younger sister several days before and found her partially disrobed in the company of Ream.

Ream, however, made no attempt to implicate his cousin, instead telling reporters, "Find Red Carrigan. He threatened that he'd get me and I'm sure he knows a lot about this business." Red Carrigan reportedly was another taxicab driver with whom Ream had argued three weeks before over a fare at a roadhouse. Police eventually arrested a chauffeur named *James* Kerrigan, but he was the wrong man. On November 24, 1923, the *Tribune* announced that English had been arraigned before Judge J. Fred Gilster and would be tried on December 21 in municipal court. If any such trial occurred, it escaped the attention of the Chicago press. Earl English eventually was graduated from the University of Chicago, had a distinguished career as a stockbroker, and died in 1966.

Apart from Ream's own identification of the Franks defendants (which could have been financially motivated), the one aspect of his mutilation, other than geographic, which seemingly might link him with them was the use of chloroform to render him unconscious. Nathan Leopold frequently used ether to anesthetize birds; he and Loeb had originally planned to do the same with Bobby Franks. But they were hardly the only ones with knowledge in this area. In February police arrested Robert Philson, known as the "ether bandit," who sneaked into South Side homes and subdued residents with ether before burglarizing their apartments. Did Philson assault Ream? That hardly seems likely either.[10]

One other coincidence is worth noting. Ream's mutilation occurred in the early-morning hours after Leopold's nineteenth birthday, November 19, 1923, and within a week of the establishment of his compact with Loeb. The defendants used their attendance at Leopold's birthday party as an element of their defense, claiming to have gone home to bed immediately after the party. Perhaps, but the two frequently sneaked out of their rooms for other crimes without anyone's knowledge and might have done so in this case too.

The most convincing argument in favor of their innocence in the Ream affair is the behavior patterns Leopold and Loeb established in other, known criminal activities. Leopold and Loeb feared face-to-face encounters. Hulbert and Bowman branded them as physical cowards in their report. They were sneaky, rather than bold. They had fled two attempted burglaries of a friend's home in Hubbard Woods when faced with failure; they had done the same in the second of the fraternity house burglaries in Ann Arbor. They began their criminal careers as shoplifters and continued a pattern of furtive, rather than aggressive, acts. Despite having guns, no evidence exists that they ever fired them—except when Leopold hunted birds. In the Franks case they had selected a small boy to kidnap mainly because he would be easy to overpower. The scope of their criminal activities had escalated gradually over a period of years, culminating finally in the Franks murder, but it seems unlikely that they would have been ready as early as November, 1923, to assault a victim near their own age and size. They may have been responsible for the mutilation of Charles Ream, but theoretical evidence argues strongly against it.

C. *Melvin T. Wolf.* Of the supposed crimes connected with Leopold and Loeb, the least is known about Wolf, who approximately a month before the Franks murder apparently walked from his home one evening never to be seen alive again. A month later, his body washed up on the beach. At the time the incident seemed so minor that the Chicago newspapers showed no interest in it. Apparently nobody suspected in April, or early May, that Wolf might have been assaulted. But was he assaulted? Nobody apparently knows. He could have gone walking to the lake, or he could have jumped into the water, or he possibly might have been pushed into the water.

As with the two previous crimes, the strongest connection between Melvin T. Wolf and the defendants in the Franks case is geographic. He lived near them. But at the time of his death—even assuming he were murdered—Leopold and Loeb most likely were too preoccupied with plans for their kidnap plot to waste time on such an adventure. And they feared physical conflicts. The chances of their having been involved in the death of Wolf seem extremely remote.

D. *The Handless Stranger.* The link between this murder and Leopold and Loeb is weaker still. The crime occurred two years before the Franks murder and appears to have been included in early ABCD lists only to round out the number of motiveless crimes to four.

But if Tracy, Ream, Wolf, and the Handless Stranger cannot be connected with the ABCD crimes, who, or *what,* can?

A partial solution to the riddle may be found in the pages of a newspaper that apparently escaped the attention of most inquirers into ABCD, including the state's attorney's office, because it is not circulated to the general public. The *Daily Maroon* is the student newspaper of the University of Chicago, and while during 1924 it was inconsistent in its approach to the news (devoting a full page to an earthquake in Japan while devoting not one single word to the sensational crime committed by two students at the university), it does provide several important clues related, perhaps, to ABCD.

On November 22, 1923, the *Maroon* described the arrest of a man named I. W. Allen, who attempted entering the Beta Theta Pi fraternity. Allen, alias Anderson, alias Rutledge, was a paroled convict. Police who took him into custody speculated that he might have been involved in previous burglaries from the Chi Psi lodge and the Sigma Chi house.[11]

Allen merely was suspected of those crimes, and unfortunately the *Maroon* failed to report further on the arrest, which was not newsworthy enough to rate mention in the downtown newspapers. The Chi Psi and Sigma Chi burglaries apparently never were solved—if they even occurred. Fifty years later, when contacted, several residents of Sigma Chi from that era could not recall any such burglary. One resident of Chi Psi recalled a burglary one spring but claimed it was the work of a black houseboy. Though the loot was found in his apartment, he never was prosecuted because the Union League insisted he had been persecuted and framed.[12]

Five days after the Allen arrest (and coincidentally about the same time that Freeman Louis Tracy was about to be killed), two masked burglars were surprised rifling rooms in the Sigma Nu house. They escaped by brandishing .32 and .45 caliber pistols.[13]

On Sunday night, February 3, 1924, members of Delta Sigma Phi fraternity left their house vacant to attend a banquet following a formal initiation. When they returned later that evening, they discovered that their rooms had been burglarized by persons who apparently knew enough about university functions to realize that the house would be standing vacant at that time. The burglars stole two tuxedos, a full-dress coat, a number of dressing gowns, and five or six suits, and three grips. "The burglars showed great fastidiousness," reported the *Maroon,* "choosing only the newest garments, leaving a slightly worn tuxedo."[14]

Several hours later a curious incident occurred. About 1 A.M. a five-passenger automobile stopped across the street from the Delta Sigma Phi house, its motor idling, its lights turned off. Members of the fraternity turned out their lights and waited. They could see the occupants of the car looking at the house.

One member of the fraternity, Paul Fredericks, left the house by the front door causing the automobile to speed away. When it reached Fifty-seventh Street, it turned east. Several members of the fraternity rushed through the backyard to the next street, Woodlawn Avenue, but arrived only in time to see the car speeding by. They could not see the license plate. One can almost visualize Leopold and Loeb sitting in the front seat of that speeding car laughing at the members of Delta Sigma Phi, whose fraternity they had burglarized earlier that evening. The scene seems reminiscent of Loeb's return to Ann Arbor to see the reactions of his friends in Zeta Beta Tau.

Yet did they commit this crime? Were it and the other three fraternity burglaries (Sigma Chi, Chi Psi, Sigma Nu, Delta Sigma Phi) reported on campus by the *Maroon* during 1923 and 1924 the ABCD crimes later alluded to by Drs. Hulbert and Bowman? Unfortunately these four fraternity burglaries were so insignificant that information on them is difficult to obtain fifty years later.

One of the fraternity house burglaries even appeared to have been solved. The *Maroon* reported the arrest of a man named Charles Conley, found wandering in the Delta Sigma Phi house several days after the burglary. The police found stolen goods in his room, although apparently none of the loot reported taken from the fraternity.

Had Leopold and Loeb been guilty, instead of Conley, of the burglary of Delta Sigma Phi (and three other similar crimes) they might have been ready to move on to bigger things. No more fraternity house burglaries were reported on campus that year. And it is interesting to note that one of the items of evidence in the Franks case was a suitcase left by Richard Loeb (alias Morton D. Ballard) in a room in the Morrison Hotel. The suitcase seemed a bit ragged for someone who dressed as carefully as Loeb. Three suitcases were stolen in the burglary of Delta Sigma Phi. If any members of that fraternity saw that suitcase and recognized it, nothing was ever said.

In confessing the Franks murder, Leopold said they had begun planning the crime six months before in November, following the Ann Arbor burglary. Loeb, however, contradicted this statement, saying that they had begun planning the crime only *two* months before it occurred, two and a half months at the most. He seemed insistent on this detail. Perhaps Leopold meant they had begun discussing a kidnapping in November, while Loeb referred to the planning as being when they started the actual reconnaissance work. By Loeb's account, the planning would have begun shortly after the last fraternity house burglary on the University of Chicago campus.

Did Leopold and Loeb commit four burglaries on the University of Chicago campus, and were those the ABCD crimes? They may have been the two masked intruders at Sigma Nu. (Leopold did own a .32.) They seem even more likely to have been the two who fled in the car at Delta Sigma Phi. Connecting them to burglaries at Chi Psi and Sigma Chi, however, is like trying to connect them to the drowning of Melvin T. Wolf or the death of the Handless Stranger. It rounds the number out to four, but there is little evidence.

One additional clue to the identity of the ABCD crimes, however, can be found in the Hulbert and Bowman report itself, not the original version that became part of the official court record, but instead the expurgated version that was included in *The Amazing Crime and Trial of Leopold and Loeb* by Maureen McKernan. In her foreword to this book, reproducing many of the documents and reports connected with the 1924 hearing, the author acknowledged her indebtedness to State's Attorney Robert E. Crowe, Clarence Darrow, Benjamin C. Bachrach, and Walter Bachrach "for their valuable cooperation and material embodied in this volume."[15] The introduction to her book, in fact, would be written by Darrow and Walter Bachrach, and the defense attorneys seem to have exercised some control over what appeared in it.

Whether they ordered it or not, the paragraph relating the "four episodes for which the letters 'A, B, C, and D' were suggested" was eliminated from McKernan's book. It seems improbable that the reference, considering the sensation it had caused at the hearing and afterward, would be overlooked by any responsible journalist. It must have been censored! McKernan did condense and edit the Hulbert and Bowman report either to conserve space or to make it more readable, or both, but in the case of the section that previously had contained information on the ABCD crimes, she not only eliminated, but added a new reference that was not part of the original record. It appears to have been fabricated especially for the book. It reads: "At various times the patient had sent in false telephone messages, false fire alarms, and has committed arson. He has sent in several false riot calls to the police. *As far as is known the patient has never set any large fires, but has confined himself to small shacks or out-buildings.*"[16]

The statement would resemble an exchange between Ephraim London and Nathan Leopold in their later meeting where the latter claimed only to have set fire to one shack. London corrected him saying, according to (the original) Hulbert and Bowman report, it had been *three* buildings. "Maybe the number was three," Leopold admitted, "but one of them was a shack." One from three leaves two. Echoes of ABCD.

Could arson committed to two buildings have been crimes A and B? Could the burglaries of two University of Chicago fraternity houses have been C and D? We probably never will know for certain, but it seems likely.

As to why it was "forensically inadvisable" to question Leopold and Loeb about crimes so relatively insignificant, these were crimes for which restitution might have been expected had they been identified. All other crimes mentioned in the Hulbert and Bowman report were either minor (shoplifting, broken windows, thefts of autos long since recovered) or ones already known to the police (the Ann Arbor burglaries, the Franks murder). Leopold and Loeb apparently did not care at the time how much more incriminating evidence was put in the record; their attorneys did.

21 Judgment

This was virtually the trial, as well as the crime, of the century.

—ELMER GERTZ[1]

With the hearing ended, the focus of attention shifted to Judge John R. Caverly, but the chief judge of the Criminal Court would have no truck with those seeking clues to his position on the question of life or death for the two killers. "If anyone molests me during the next few days while I am deliberating on this case," he said, "they will be arrested and sent to jail instantly."[2]

All during the hearing Judge Caverly had received letters: suggestions that skulls and crossbones be tattooed across the heads of Leopold and Loeb or that they be tied to anthills to allow ants to devour them; warnings that a plague would overtake the world if he failed to grant mercy.[3] One writer said he would bomb the courthouse if Caverly failed to impose the death penalty. Another promised to shoot Caverly and hang him from a telephone pole if he ordered execution for the two. "I am not afraid of these insane threats," said the judge, "but I do not want to endanger the lives of any of the lawyers, the defendants, or any members of the Leopold, Loeb, or Franks families." In response to the numerous threats, Sheriff Peter Hoffman assigned fifty additional motorcycle policemen to reinforce the deputies already protecting the Criminal Courts Building. Further precautions were planned to protect against mob action. Hoffman revealed that he would close the building to all visitors during the sentencing and keep citizens from approaching within a block of the building.

Before rendering judgment, Judge Caverly had to go over in his mind the issues raised by prosecution and defense during half a summer of testimony and argument. By parading as many witnesses to the stand as he had, State's Attorney Crowe had attempted to show by the sheer mass of evidence that the two murderers had no choice other than to plead guilty; therefore, their having entered that plea should not sway the judge to mercy. The state's attorney portrayed their crime as a sadistic, perverted act done for money. Leopold and Loeb were the personification of evil. They were conscienceless beings who, sneering and laughing their way through the hearing, reveled in the attention brought to them by their criminal acts. As for the testimony of the defense alienists, it was merely an attempt to cloud the main issue with bogus pseudoscientific theories that had no place in a court of law. No mitigating circumstances existed, nor could they exist in such a brutal crime. Crowe saw but one issue: vengeance! Did they commit murder, or did they not? Since no doubt existed concerning that question, the judge had no alternative but to apply the maximum sentence prescribed by law. The pair caused death; they deserved death. The defendants' youth should no more sway justice's sword than Bobby Franks' youth had swayed the hand that held the chisel.

Darrow had sought to portray the case differently. His defense attempted to ignore the facts of the crime (as documented so fully by the prosecution) and concentrate instead on the motivations for it. The defendants had murdered not for any normal motive, but because they were mentally ill—though not insane. Darrow, by introducing so much psychiatric testimony, sought to develop sympathy for two misguided youths more the products of their upbringing than their own free will. Certainly there were mitigating circumstances here. But in approaching the case from a scientific point of view, Darrow hoped to allow time for the heat of indignation caused by the brutal act of slaying to cool. The case should be decided intellectually, not emotionally. Darrow regarded capital punishment as more cruel than the act of murder, because it was done not in passion but deliberately, in courts of law by men who should know better. The single issue for Darrow was mercy, and he pleaded for it. Particularly he pleaded that the judge consider the youth of the killers and not send two more to die unnecessarily.

After the cases of the prosecution and defense were stripped of rhetoric, the issue came down to a balance that had to be struck between two points of view: vengeance vs. mercy.

Judge Caverly, accompanied by a bodyguard, worked mornings and evenings in the study of his apartment at the Edgewater Beach Hotel on the North Side of Chicago. On several afternoons he visited Hawthorne Race Track. Sunday he attended mass at St. Ita's Roman Catholic Church. One afternoon, with the judge away attending a funeral, the telephone rang in his apartment.

His wife answered. A person identifying himself as Captain Roberts of the police department announced, "Your husband, the judge, has been shot to death as he was entering the gate of Calvary Cemetery. Come quick!" Mrs. Caverly rushed by taxicab to the cemetery and found her husband unharmed. The judge, enraged, ordered his telephone disconnected and had an additional policeman stationed at the hotel entrance to keep out anyone looking for him.[4]

On Saturday Genevieve Forbes and John Herrick, two reporters who had covered the hearing all summer, got married. Years later (while reviewing *Compulsion* for the *Tribune*'s *Book World*) Genevieve Forbes Herrick would write that Judge Caverly had originally planned to announce his verdict that weekend, but that she talked him into postponing it until the following Wednesday so as not to interfere with her wedding plans![5]

Meanwhile, Leopold and Loeb waited. Reporters eventually informed Richard Loeb that the judge had made his decision. "Why worry?" said Loeb, trying to seem nonchalant. "Judge Caverly has made up his mind and worrying isn't going to change it." He continued to chain-smoke cigarettes.[6]

On Wednesday, September 10, Judge Caverly rose at 5:30 A.M. and finished his breakfast before 6. Accompanied by two policemen, he went for a brief walk, then returned to his apartment for about an hour. At eight a number of cars arrived before the Edgewater Beach Hotel. Caverly left the hotel at eight fifteen accompanied by Chief of Detectives Michael Hughes, two officers with shotguns, and a reporter for the *Daily News.* One police car preceded the judge's car; another followed it. The *Daily News* man reported that the judge seemed in good spirits; he did not mention the case during the trip downtown. As his car approached the Criminal Courts Building, Caverly looked warily out at the crowds, then strode to the elevator with Chief Hughes at his side.[7] A *Tribune* reporter noted that as he stepped from the car, the judge looked pale, worn, and weary.[8]

One by one the principals in the hearing arrived. Nathan F. Leopold, Sr., and his son Mike came, as always, together. They took a seat in the courtroom near Jacob and Allan Loeb. Clarence Darrow appeared and commented in response to a question, "Well, I'm always a little nervous on these occasions." The state's attorney's staff appeared—Crowe, Marshall, Savage, Sbarbaro, Smith, and Fairbank. Jacob Franks chose to stay home.

Judge Caverly entered the courtroom promptly at nine thirty, carrying copies of his opinion under one arm. The bailiff gave three raps with his gavel on the bar. "Everybody must be seated," said the judge. "If you cannot find seats, leave the room." The judge adjusted his steel-rimmed glasses and unfolded a typewritten document. He nodded toward his clerk, Ferdinand Scherer, who called for the two defendants.

Nathan F. Leopold, Jr., and Richard Loeb were led in from the right rear of the courtroom. Leopold walked to his seat, eyes down, glancing up only once or twice. Loeb gazed around the court and smiled briefly as he caught the eyes of his relatives.

Judge Caverly asked if the two defendants had anything to say before he passed sentence. Benjamin Bachrach said no. Loeb shook his head. Leopold said no, shaking his head. His father, seated behind him, gripped the arm of his seat and looked down at the floor. The judge began to read: "In view of the profound interest that this case—" A clatter of cameras began, and the judge looked up, annoyed.

"Go ahead now," he said to the photographers. "Take your pictures. I'll wait until you get through." After a minute the judge announced that no more pictures would be taken until he completed his statement. Then he began again, reading in a low, almost-shaking voice: "In view of the profound interest that this case has aroused, not only in this community, but in the entire country and even beyond its boundaries, the court feels it his duty to state the reasons which have led him to the determination he has reached."[9]

Caverly then began a discussion of the plea of guilty, which was usually made by agreement between the defendant and the state's attorney, agreement that did not exist here. Normally, the judge said, a guilty plea made the state's task easier, "by substituting admission of guilt for a possible difficult and uncertain chain of proof."

Caverly glanced up briefly. "Here the state was in possession not only of the essential, substantiating facts, but also of voluntary confessions on the part of the defendants. The plea of guilty, therefore, does not make a special case in favor of the defendants." Leopold would admit later that when the judge reached this point in his reading, he became convinced the sentence would be death by hanging.[10]

Caverly discussed his duty in hearing the case, both for murder and kidnapping. "The testimony introduced, both by the prosecution and the defense," the judge continued, "has been detailed and elaborate as though the case had been tried before a jury. It has been given the widest publicity and the public is so fully familiar with all its phases that it would serve no useful purpose to restate or analyze the evidence."

Caverly stated his satisfaction that a case for insanity could not be made, then moved to the question of the testimony offered as to the physical, mental, and moral conditions of Leopold and Loeb. "They have been shown in essential respects to be abnormal; had they been normal they would not have committed the crime. It is beyond the province of this court, as it is beyond the province of human science in its present state of development, to predicate ultimate responsibility for human acts.

"At the same time the court is willing to recognize that the careful analysis made of the life history of the defendants and of their present mental, emotional, and ethical condition has been of extreme interest and is a valuable contribution to criminology; and yet, the court feels strongly that similar analysis made of other persons accused of crime would reveal similar or different abnormalities."

Leopold showed no sign of emotion. Loeb stared at the base of the dais where the judge sat. Caverly continued: "The value of such tests seems to lie in their applicability to crime and criminals in general. Since they concern the broad questions of human responsibility and legal punishment, and are in no ways peculiar to these individual defendants, they may be deserving of legislative, but not of judicial consideration. For this reason the court is satisfied that his judgment in the present case cannot be affected thereby.

"The testimony in this case reveals a crime of singular atrocity. It is, in a sense, inexplicable; but it is not thereby rendered less inhuman or repulsive. It was deliberately planned and prepared for during a considerable period of time. It was executed with every feature of callousness and cruelty.

"And here the court will say—not for the purpose of extenuating guilt, but merely with the object of dispelling a misapprehension that appears to have found lodgment in the public mind—that he is convinced by conclusive evidence that there was no abuse offered to the body of the victim."

That was the first statement favorable to the defendants. Leopold later would express his gratefulness that sex perversion as a motive for the crime appeared to have been discarded by the judge, while regretting that much of the public seemed not to have noticed that. Caverly, however, quickly seemed to shift against the defendants' case once more. "But it did not need that element to make the crime abhorrent to every instinct of humanity, and the court is satisfied that neither in the act itself, nor in its motive or lack of motive, nor in the antecedents of the offenders, can he find any mitigating circumstances!"

A cloud of gloom hovered over the defense table. Mitigation was what they had spent an entire month seeking. Some of the spectators in the court began to whisper knowingly to each other, "It's hanging."

Judge Caverly then briefly summarized the law which held that persons found guilty of murder could be punished by death, or imprisoned for life, or for a term not less than fourteen years. The crime of kidnapping, he explained, was similarly punishable, except the penitentiary term could not be less than five years. Caverly added that on a plea of guilty the term must be fixed by the court. He then said—perhaps wistfully—that in some states, legislatures had provided for a bench of three judges to determine penalties. "Nevertheless," he stated, "the court is willing to meet his responsibilities. It would have been the path of least resistance to impose the extreme penalty of the law."

Leopold's head jerked upward. Did he mean that death would not be the sentence? Caverly quickly confirmed it. "In choosing imprisonment instead of death, the court is moved chiefly by the consideration of the age of the defendants, boys of eighteen and nineteen years. It is not for the court to say that he will not in any case enforce capital punishment as an alternative, but the court believes that it is within his province to decline to impose the sentence of death on persons who are not of full age."

Judge Caverly looked unsmilingly into the faces of the two young men as he read on: "This determination appears to be in accordance with the progress of criminal law all over the world and with the dictates of enlightened humanity. More than that, it seems to be in accordance with the precedents hitherto observed in this state. The records of Illinois show only two cases of minors who were put to death by legal process—to which number the court does not feel inclined to make an addition."

Leopold later would comment on the judge's verdict, "If Judge Caverly meant literally what he said in his opinion, the whole elaborate psychiatric defense presented in our behalf and the herculean efforts of our brilliant counsel were of no avail. The only thing that influenced him to choose imprisonment instead of death was our youth; we need only have introduced our birth certificates in evidence!"[11]

The judge continued: "Life imprisonment may not, at the moment, strike the public imagination as forcibly as would death by hanging; but to the offenders, particularly of the type they are, the prolonged suffering of years of confinement may well be the severer form of retribution and expiation.

"The court feels it proper to add a final word concerning the effect of the parole law upon these defendants. In the case of such atrocious crimes, it is entirely within the discretion of the department of public welfare never to admit these defendants to parole. To such a policy the court urges them strictly to adhere. If this course is preserved in the punishment of these defendants it will both satisfy the ends of justice and safeguard the interests of society."

Judge Caverly's words would haunt the two convicted killers, particularly Nathan Leopold, in later years. The judge next announced his sentence:

"For the crime of murder, confinement at the penitentiary at Joliet for the term of their natural lives.

"For the crime of kidnapping for ransom, similar confinement for the term of ninety-nine years."

The judge rose and returned to his chambers as Leopold and Loeb exchanged handshakes with their attorneys. Many in the audience pressed forward to offer them congratulations, but the bailiffs pushed the prisoners away toward the door from which they had arrived. Neither looked back as they left the courtroom. State's Attorney Crowe rose and grimly offered his hand to Clarence Darrow, who appeared boyishly happy, then left the room to dictate an official statement which he presented later to the press. "The state's attorney's duty was performed," announced Crowe. "He is in no measure responsible for the decision of the court. He must be content with the decision of the court, because in this case it is final. I don't intend, and have no desire, to criticize the decision of the court, but I still believe the death penalty is the only penalty feared by murderers."[12]

One newspaper the following day, almost as though mocking the state's attorney, headlined its story containing his remarks: CROWE CONTENT WITH DECISION.

Clarence Darrow commented, "I have always hated capital punishment. This decision at once caps my career as a criminal lawyer and starts my path in another direction." He thought that the pair might be eligible for parole within thirty-seven years. "Perhaps the sentence is worse than a death penalty for the two boys, but not for their families."[13]

Jacob Franks (who three months previous had said he would be willing to spring the trapdoor hanging them)[14] announced afterward that he was satisfied with the verdict, saying, "My wife and I never believed Nathan, Jr., and Richard should be hanged."[15]

Eventually a rumor would spread that he set up a trust fund to fight, after his death, any attempts to parole the killers.[16] The rumor was false.

Jacob Loeb issued a statement for both the Leopold and Loeb families: "There is little to say. We have been spared the death penalty, but what have these families to look forward to? Here are two families whose names have stood for everything that was good and reputable in the community. Their unfortunate boys, aged nineteen years, must spend the rest of their lives in prison. What is there in the future but grief and sorrow, darkness and despair?"

Max Schrayer was skeptical when he heard the decision, since he thought his fraternity brother probably deserved to hang. He suspected, although he had no proof, that rumors that the Loeb family had bribed the judge might be true. Schrayer called Allan Loeb some months later to ask if he could get back his watch and the medal he had received for being editor of the yearbook.[17] Some of the loot from the Ann Arbor burglary had been buried behind the Loeb mansion. Allan Loeb refused to return the items, although several years later, when another fraternity brother persisted, he finally did.

Ernst W. Puttkammer was also skeptical when he heard the decision, not because of the judge's choice but because he had been able to voice his opinion so aptly. Judge Caverly was not known as a learned man or one especially skilled at putting his thoughts into words. Later Puttkammer learned that Ernst Freund, a law professor at Northwestern University, had written the opinion over the weekend, working at the Morraine Hotel in Highland Park, apparently in consultation with Judge Caverly.[18]

Still further light on Judge Caverly's opinion was shed nearly four decades later while attorneys Robert Bergstrom and Leon Despres were trying to find a judge to hear a motion on a law suit involving *Compulsion,* the novel based on the Leopold and Loeb case. One old judge disqualified himself because he had been Caverly's master of chancery and was prejudiced against Nathan Leopold. During the brief discussion that ensued, the judge said that Clarence Darrow's final oration, no matter how stunning it had seemed to spectators, had been no factor in Judge Caverly's decision. He did not indicate, unfortunately, what the major factor had been.[19]

Another story concerning Caverly related to how Chicago newspapers where able to reach the streets so quickly with news of the verdict. They appeared on newsstands within minutes of the announcement, supposedly because alternate front pages saying

LIFE as well as DEATH were kept in readiness for the word to be released.

According to George Murray, author of *The Madhouse on Madison Street,* Frank Carson, managing editor of the *Herald and Examiner,* asked Caverly to dine with him at the Edgewater Beach Hotel the night before the verdict. Toward the end of a sumptuous meal Carson indicated it would be a great advantage to him to know the verdict in advance. "I know you cannot utter a single revealing word and I would not ask you to do so," said the newspaperman. "But if I should guess correctly at the sentence, I wonder if you would simply look out that window at the blue waters of the lake?"

Caverly reportedly smiled. Carson said, "Life?" And Caverly's head turned until he was gazing toward the lake.[20] The story is probably apocryphal.

Reaction in newspapers across the country was varied. "The sentence shakes the faith of the people in the blind equality of justice," announced the New York *Evening Sun.* "They will not believe that any poor man who committed the crime to which Loeb and Leopold pleaded guilty—or any crime approaching its diabolical brutality—would have escaped death."

The Washington *Post* commented: "The best feature of the decision is that it has been finally rendered. Judge Caverly contributed too much to the notoriety and sensationalism that marred the administration of justice in this case. The long drawn out hearing was unnecessary."

The Kansas City *Star* wrote: "Responsible murderers are subject to the death penalty not as Judge Caverly seems to suppose for 'retribution and expiation,' but to restrain other persons. Society looks to the courts for protection. Under the development of technicalities and sentimentalism, the courts are failing in their duty."

The Chicago *Herald and Examiner* commented: "These young men should, and probably will, stay in jail for life. The governor who extended any clemency to them, even twenty years from now, would be inviting his own oblivion. The public forgets many things, but a murder like this is not one of them; and the public will insist on full atonement."[21]

"Already the sneering is heard in many quarters," wrote the Chicago *Daily Journal,* "that 'no rich man is hanged.' It is not that money is used to corrupt courts or juries in capital cases. Probably no one whose mind and character make him worth considering harbors such an idea. The fact rather seems to be that the prejudice in this community against capital punishment is so great that any determined defense is sufficient to prevent execution."[22]

Finally, the Chicago *Tribune* editorialized: "It seems to us that the next person about whose neck an Illinois sheriff knots a rope has a case against the people of Illinois, which eternal justice would uphold. A life sentence is not a final decision of justice. We hope in this case the life sentences mean imprisonment for life. But no one knows."

The prison doors would soon close behind Leopold and Loeb, the most publicized murderers of the decade. Within a few days their names would disappear from the front-page headlines, then even from the back pages, to reappear only sporadically again. It would be nearly fifty years before their story would reach its conclusion.

PART THREE:

Nothing But the Night

22 Joliet

Three months ago, if their friends and the friends of the family had been asked to pick out the most promising lads of their acquaintance, they probably would have picked these two boys. With every opportunity, with plenty of wealth, they would have said that these two would succeed. In a day, by an act of madness, all this is destroyed, until the best they can hope for now is a life of silence and pain, continuing to the end of their years.

—CLARENCE DARROW[1]

Following Judge Caverly's verdict, bailiffs returned Leopold and Loeb to jail to await transport to the state prison in Joliet, thirty miles southwest of Chicago. Their lives would never be the same. The lives of others involved in the case had also changed.

Clarence Darrow received more national attention for his defense of Leopold and Loeb than for any of his previous cases. The following year, however, he played a principal role in another almost equally fascinating event: the so-called Monkey Trial, involving a Tennessee schoolteacher named John T. Scopes, arrested for teaching Darwin's theories of evolution. Darrow's connection first with Leopold and Loeb and then with Scopes assured his reputation as America's most famous attorney.

Darrow did little trial work after 1925, contenting himself mostly with writing and lecturing. In the thirties, seeking an office to hang his hat, he joined a law partnership recently founded by three of State's Attorney Crowe's assistants, all of whom had worked on the Franks case: Bert Cronson and the two Smiths. They immediately put the Darrow name in front of theirs on their firm.[2]

Although Darrow served in the Monkey Trial without fee, the sum paid him for defending Leopold and Loeb became a point of controversy. To counter newspaper charges of a "million-dollar defense," the families in June had issued a statement that the Bar Association would assign a fee. The promise was never fulfilled.

In the months after the verdict Darrow sent several letters asking for a settlement, but a year went by without payment. Finally, several members of the families arrived at his office, including Jacob Loeb, Richard's uncle. Darrow mentioned $200,000 as a reasonable fee. "You know, Clarence," Jacob Loeb supposedly said, "the world is full of eminent lawyers who would have paid a fortune for the chance to distinguish themselves in this case." He may have been piqued because Darrow spent so much money hiring the battery of defense alienists who all testified to the same things.

The following day, according to Darrow, the families made him an offer of $75,000, which he accepted. When the check arrived, however, it only was for $70,000.[3] Darrow kept $35,000 of that sum, under an agreement that his law firm receive half his fees in return for clerical support and other expenses. "The fee was about a quarter of the amount I should have received," Darrow complained later, "but there's no use rowing about it now."[4] Actually it was probably a larger fee than he had received for any of his previous cases.

(The amount paid Darrow is still a subject of controversy. Irving Stone in *Clarence Darrow for the Defense* suggested that the attorneys in the case received a $100,000 fee, of which $10,000 had been paid in advance to Darrow for expenses. The remainder supposedly was divided with the Bachrachs, resulting in $30,000 for each attorney.)

Judge John R. Caverly disappeared from sight immediately following the trial. Only several weeks later did the public learn that he and his wife had checked in as patients at Mercy Hospital. Caverly supposedly was suffering from nervous fatigue, caused not only by the tremendous strain of the trial, but also from having spent eight years on the bench without vacation. He remained hospitalized until late October. When he returned to duty, he resigned as chief of the Criminal Courts and accepted assignment with the Chancery Court hearing divorce cases. Two years later he requested another transfer to even less strenuous duties on the bench. "In the past six years I have heard six trials in which three men have been sentenced to death and two sentenced to prison for life," he said. "My health has been sapped."[5] He died at the age of seventy-eight on August 4, 1939, while on a cruise to Bermuda.

Robert E. Crowe was reelected to the state's attorney's office in November, but his political career soon turned downward. In 1928 John A. Swanson defeated him in the Republican primary, and Crowe resumed the practice of law. Ten years later one of his law partners (and former assistant), Joseph Savage, sued him for misuse of funds. Judge Caverly ironically heard the suit in which Crowe finally agreed to a $37,500 settlement. Crowe switched parties in the thirties and in 1942 obtained a judicial appointment as a Democrat.[6]

Within a few weeks after the end of the trial, the Franks family sold their Kenwood home and moved to the Drake Hotel. During the transfer of deeds, it was learned that Albert Loeb had sold Jacob Franks the lot on which he had built his home fifteen years previously.[7] In 1928 Jacob Franks, then aged sixty-seven, died of a heart attack. The newspaper accounts attributed his death partly to "grief over the murder of his son."[8] Flora Franks later remarried, indicating that newspaper reports related to her almost total collapse and lack of comprehension concerning her son's death may have been greatly exaggerated.

Albert Loeb had remained in Charlevoix during the entire summer of the court case, still ill from the heart attack he had suffered only a few days before the murder. Journalists would use his absence from Chicago during the hearing as evidence that he had disowned his son. Toward the end of the summer Albert Loeb recovered enough to walk around the grounds of his estate. In September he even played golf on his private course. He returned to Chicago the following month but on October 27 suffered a final fatal heart attack. He was fifty-six years old. He had not seen Richard since May 29, the day detectives arrived at his home to arrest his son.

The Leopold family moved from their home in Kenwood shortly after the trial. Several years later Nathan Leopold, Sr., whose first wife had died several years before the Franks murder, married Mrs. Daisy K. Kahn of Los Angeles. In 1929 he died at age sixty-eight.[9] His two other sons, Mike and Sam, changed their last names in an attempt to achieve some anonymity and forget the family crime.[10]

In December, 1924, State's Attorney Crowe, Chief of Police Collins, and Henry Barrett Chamberlin, director of the Chicago Crime Commission, announced the distribution of reward money in the case. Although thousands of dollars had been offered during the days immediately following the commission of the crime, nobody would get rich for his part in solving it. Most of the reward total consisted of "contingency" money offered by newspapers for *exclusive* information leading to the killers. The newspapers obtained the publicity from having offered the reward, yet never had to pay it. All that remained after the hoopla passed was $5,000 offered by Jacob Franks and another $1,000 offered by Chief Collins.[11]

Of this $6,000 total, the two *Daily News* reporters Jim Mulroy and Alvin Goldstein (who had helped identify the body and also had located the typewritten notes linking Leopold with the kidnap letter) received $1,500 each. They also received a Pulitzer Prize for their journalistic efforts.

Tony Mankowski, the Polish laborer who discovered the body while walking in Hegewisch, received $850. Paul Korff, the leader of the railroad signal crew who found Leopold's glasses, received $750. Coming as it did so near to Christmas, the money was very welcome. He bought his wife a new washing machine and also purchased gifts for his two sons. Billy got a punching bag; Claude received an electric drill.[12]

The other signalmen—John Kaleczka, Walter and George Knitter—received $300 each. Bernard Hunt, the night watchman who picked up the chisel after Richard Loeb hurled it from the window of his car, received $500.

Fifteen policemen who worked on the case received honorable mentions, as did Frank Blair, the diver who recovered Leopold's typewriter from the Jackson Park lagoon. Jacob Weinstein, manager of the Almer Coe & Company store at 105 North Wabash Avenue, also received an honorable mention.

This angered Coe himself, and he wrote a letter to the Chicago *Tribune* complaining about distribution of the reward. He claimed that Weinstein spent thirty-six hours going through 54,000 prescriptions to identify the owner of the glasses, and his employee deserved more recognition and credit. "No other case has been solved on so slender a clue," wrote Coe, "and I want to say, if it were not for the systematic method, the efficient way in which Almer Coe & Company keep their records, Leopold and Loeb would be walking the streets, free men, today."[13]

Coe had a point, and Weinstein probably deserved more than a token handshake from the police, yet one wonders how absolutely necessary were those dropped eyeglasses to the eventual apprehension of the culprits. The dropped eyeglasses have become part of the legend of the murder case. Yet despite their genius—or maybe because of it—Leopold and Loeb had stumbled through their amateurish murder/kidnap plot leaving clues everywhere—a bloodstained rental car, a suitcase abandoned in a hotel room, kidnap notes that could be traced to one of their typewriters, bank withdrawals and deposits under assumed names—that sooner or later might have led the police to them. Years later Meyer Levin would write that Leopold and Loeb had a *compulsion* to kill, but it also seems that they had a compulsion to be caught!

Immediately after Judge Caverly's verdict, jail authorities placed Nathan Leopold and Richard Loeb in the death cells. (Warden Westbrook had decided in advance, for security purposes, to shift them to solitary confinement cells: permanently if the verdict was death, temporarily if the verdict was life.) They seemed happy. "Go out and order us a big meal," Leopold instructed his jailer. "Get us two steaks this thick." With thumb and finger he indicated three inches.

"Be sure they are smothered in onions," suggested Loeb, "and bring every side dish that you can find. This may be our last good meal."

"And bring chocolate éclairs for dessert," added Leopold.[14]

Loeb wanted to ask their attorneys to delay their departure to Joliet another week to allow them to say good-bye to friends and families; Leopold desired to leave immediately. The pair had no choice. Sheriff Hoffman planned to transfer the prisoners to Joliet as quickly as possible. The newspapers announced that they would depart for the state prison at 9 A.M. the next day.

While the state had gone to extreme lengths to obtain the death penalty for Leopold and Loeb, now it took equal measures to safeguard their lives. The sheriff doubled the number of guards surrounding the Cook County Jail in response to bomb threats. Cars full of shotgun-toting policemen patrolled the nearby streets and alleys. Motorcycle policemen stood in doorways, their mounts by the curb. Other armed guards took positions at upper windows within the jail. Leopold and Loeb slept in cells with the lights blazing watched by four special guards to foil any suicide attempts. Leopold later would admit that immediately following the verdict he had given little consideration to his future. He had no idea what Joliet Prison would be like, although he did learn that the best prison job was chauffeur to the warden. He would never hold that job.[15]

As the two slept, the police outside noticed a man walking suspiciously back and forth near the jail. His name was Samuel Gistensen, age forty, and he claimed he had found two pennies on the sidewalk and was looking for more. The police detained him for further questioning, and so another name was added to the official record of the Franks case.[16]

Leopold and Loeb awoke early in the morning, but the scheduled time for their departure came and passed. They ordered another "good last meal," a double order of peaches, scrambled eggs, port sausages, fried potatoes, toast, cookies, and coffee.[17]

A *Daily News* reporter visited them in their cells that day and in his story quoted Loeb as telling his companion, "I do regret saying it was you who struck the blow, Babe." (The dialogue, as used in the newspaper, sounded artificial. In addition, the two supposedly were being held separate, in solitary cells.)[18]

Their departure was postponed until noon, but that hour came and went. State's Attorney Crowe had refused to release his prisoners until he completed the documents which would accompany them. In a ten-page "statement of facts," he characterized Leopold and Loeb as degenerate murderers. "We want to make the record clear and clean," he told United Press reporter Edward C. Derr, "so that no efforts of the defense will succeed in setting these murderers free. The state's attorney presented an air-tight case that should have resulted in hangings. The court decided otherwise, and now the responsibility lies in other hands than mine. Since they cannot be hanged, I trust they shall never be freed from prison."[19] Crowe added later, "It is unfortunate for the welfare of this community that they were not sentenced to death."[20] Crowe would go to his grave thirty-four years later never wavering from that opinion.

At four thirty that afternoon, Crowe finally sent the documents to John Passmire, clerk of the Criminal Court. Passmire spent nearly two hours studying the papers, then summoned Sheriff Hoffman and handed them to him. Hoffman told Captain Westbrook, the prison warden, to prepare the prisoners for transport to Joliet. Westbrook went to the jail cell and found them playing cards, eating sandwiches, and talking with their guards.[21] Their belongings long had been packed, but when six o'clock had passed, the pair assumed they would be remaining in Chicago at least one more night. Now Hank Thompson, first assistant jailer, fastened one handcuff on Leopold's right wrist and another on Loeb's left wrist, the two cuffs being joined by a three-foot chain which Thompson grasped in the middle.[22] Sheriff Hoffman then marched them between double rows of guards carrying shotguns toward four automobiles parked in the prison courtyard below.

Thompson climbed into the rear of a Packard with Leopold and Loeb, still in chains, on each side. Harold Reese, a banker's son and the owner of the Packard, sat behind the wheel of the car. (Why a banker's son and not a law official received this assignment was never made clear.) The prison yard gate swung open, and the four automobiles headed south. Immediately more cars filled with reporters and photographers, who had been parked outside, joined in line. Sirens screaming, the cavalcade headed south across the Loop and turned west on Jackson Boulevard, traveling at speeds up to 40 mph. Just before reaching Sacramento Avenue, in a scene like from a latter-day Hollywood chase movie, the lead Cadillac sideswiped a roadster, shoving it into a car parked at the curb and breaking both the parked car's wheels. The cavalcade did not even pause. "Hey, where's the fire?" shouted Loeb. "We've got a long time ahead of us."

The cars continued southwest, but the brakes of the lead car soon began to smoke. Outside the suburb of Argo, the Cadillac was pulled off the road for adjustments. The guards leaped out, shotguns poised. After a brief repair stop, the cars continued along Archer Avenue at speeds of 50 mph until near Willow Springs the brakes in the Cadillac locked. It slid to an abrupt halt.

Harold Reese, the driver of the Packard containing Leopold and Loeb, swung quickly to the right to avoid crashing into the rear of the lead car. The Packard slid off the road, crossed a ditch, and bounced onto some railroad tracks paralleling the highway. With Reese fighting the wheel, the car careened along the bumpy railroad ties for several hundred feet before coming safely to a halt. "God, that's clever driving," said Loeb.

Leopold looked over his shoulder through the back window where he saw an interurban train approaching at high speed. For a moment he thought Judge Caverly's carefully considered opinion might be reversed.[23] The train ground to a safe halt. (Most newspapers the following day failed to mention the approach of the train, so its threat may have been more imagined than real.)

Following further repairs, the cavalcade resumed its journey, arriving outside the Illinois State Penitentiary in Joliet at eight fifty that evening. The prison was an ancient and ugly stone fortress. "Well, boys," said Loeb, as the Packard approached the prison. "Let it be written that we came through here on the eleventh of September, 1924." It would be so written and for many years afterward the Chicago newspapers would celebrate the anniversary of Leopold and Loeb's confinement with a small news story mentioning their current status.

They pushed through a large waiting crowd. Inside the prison jail officials ordered the two prisoners to face the wall. Sheriff Hoffman handed their record folders to Warden John L. Whitman. Guards stripped the cuffs from the hands of the two prisoners and led them toward another door. Before they exited, Leopold had time for one last remark to Ty Krum of the *Tribune:* "It's 1924. It will probably be 1957 when we get out and I'll have a beard so long." Leopold made a motion with his hand from his chin down to his waist.

The prison officials hustled the pair through a steel door. It clanged shut behind them. Edward C. Derr of the United Press would describe the two sentenced murderers as having lost their nonchalant attitude. "They tried to muster a cheery smile of goodbye to newspapermen," he wrote, "but the best they could do was a wan smile." He described them as appearing almost frightened.[24] He apparently saw them from a different point of view than had Ty Krum, but the view of the public toward the two murderers would never be unanimous.

Warden Whitman later explained to newsmen that the two prisoners—who received the numbers 9305-D (Loeb) and 9306-D (Leopold)—would spend their first night in solitary confinement, what was known as court solitary. Court solitary was a remnant of an old Illinois statute providing that each prisoner must spend his first day, and one day of each year, in solitary confinement.[25] "Our plan is to separate Nathan from Richard," explained the warden. "They will be assigned to separate shops and their cells will be on opposite wings of the building." The warden said Loeb would work in the chair factory, Leopold in the rattan factory.[26]

At six the next morning, the two arose along with the 1,100 other inmates of the Illinois State Penitentiary. They ate a breakfast of beef stew, coffee, bread, and butter. Wearing denim shirts and khaki pants which had been issued the night before, they had their photographs taken and their fingerprints recorded. At the prison barbershop, a convict barber trimmed their Valentino-style hair to prison length. Finally, they marched with other prisoners to an auditorium to hear an address by the chaplain, the Reverend Mr. Hamilton, in honor of Defense Day.

Leopold would note later that never before had Defense Day been celebrated at Joliet, nor would it again. Defense Day became a holiday in 1924 apparently for the convenience of the several dozen reporters still hovering around Joliet, trying to find words with which to write the final chapter on Leopold and Loeb. These reporters sat on a raised platform and craned their necks, trying to locate the celebrity murderers among the mass of prisoners before them. Finally, someone spotted the pair in the ninth row, their faces ashen gray, trembling and shifting uneasily at first, but finally relaxing, their old nonchalance returned, whispering to each other as they had during their month in Criminal Court.

The chaplain's address seemed more directed to the two celebrity prisoners and the visiting newspapermen than to the other 1,100. "I met a pacifist the other day," lectured the Reverend Mr. Hamilton. "We got to talking about capital punishment. I argued that he was guilty of taking a life every time a prisoner was electrocuted, because he paid the taxes that made it possible for the executioner to push the button. Speaking of the electric chair, of course, we're getting past that now. Men aren't electrocuted any more provided they are friends of politicians."[27]

The prisoners, including the pair at whom the jibe was aimed, reportedly roared with laughter. Led to the platform, Leopold and Loeb winked at reporters. The Chicago *Tribune* later quoted Leopold as saying that the guards gave him the creeps. He said they did not have a drop of friendliness in them. "I suppose this wouldn't be so hard for some dull fellow with not much intelligence, and no imagination, and no real life behind him. That's what makes it hard for me and Dick, I suppose."[28]

It was the last interview Nathan Leopold would grant reporters for twenty years.

23 Life

Murder is very rare, and the people who commit it, as a rule, are of a much higher type than others. You may go to any penitentiary and those who have been convicted of murder become the trustees.

—CLARENCE DARROW[1]

As a year passed, only small bits of information escaped Joliet prison concerning the killers of Bobby Franks. Stories about them appeared in newspapers, but on the back pages. They joined the other Jewish prisoners at Joliet for a Passover celebration. Leopold was working in the rattan shop. Loeb bored holes for chair rungs. Leopold had appendicitis. Loeb got the measles. At the end of the year both received promotions. Leopold now was doing clerical work in the shoe department. Loeb had been named "straw boss" over other prisoners cleaning the prison yard. The pair were being kept apart as much as possible.[2]

During the first year of their imprisonment the press focused some of its attention on Bernard Grant, who became a sidebar to the main story of Leopold and Loeb and added to their legend. The theme was poverty vs. wealth. Grant and a friend, Walter Krauser, had been convicted of the murder of policeman Ralph Souders. Though Grant was in his early twenties, his hair turned white while he awaited his hanging, which was scheduled for October 17, 1924. Grant did not hang: Governor Len Small delayed the hanging ninety days, then granted several further extensions. Krauser, meanwhile, was granted a new trial.

In June, however, Krauser and Grant got into a fight in prison. Krauser plunged a pocket knife into Grant's neck and chest, shouting that Grant had plotted to kill him. Grant lingered for several days, complaining that he wanted to avoid blood transfusions. "Why save me?" he asked with a certain grim logic. "You'll only hang me sooner or later anyway." Finally he died.[3]

As for Loeb's bout with the measles, suffered in June, 1925, so much had been said about his emotional and physical immaturity during the hearing, it seemed ironic he should get a childhood disease. However, it nearly killed him. He seemed to be recovering in the prison hospital when suddenly he became feverish and began arguing with guards, throwing objects at them. He tried to jump out the window before Warden Whitman ordered him strapped to his bed, where he mumbled incoherently for his mother. The physicians called to examine Loeb suspected he might be malingering but later diagnosed his problem as a mental disorder. One doctor, after observing him for three days, declared, "Loeb is insane." Speculation rose that Loeb might have to be transferred to the state mental institution.[4] Eventually, however, he recovered; perhaps he had indeed been malingering. Most newspapers, however, failed to publicize his recovery, leaving the general public with the impression that Loeb had indeed gone mad. On the first anniversary of the pair's imprisonment, reporters gathered at the penitentiary for an update on the story that had mesmerized newspaper readers all over the United States the previous summer. Included among members of the press was James Mulroy of the *Daily News,* who wrote: "One year behind the walls of the state penitentiary here has wrought great changes in Richard Loeb and Nathan Leopold, who, as convicts 9305 and 9306, today ended their first twelve months of life sentences behind prison bars for the murder of Robert Franks."[5]

Mulroy's report featured scorched nerves, drawn faces, twitching lips, brooding expressions. The prison guards told him the pair had suffered tremendously. Loeb now was working in the yard of the old prison within the city of Joliet. Leopold had been transferred to the newly constructed prison facility at Stateville, west of the city, where he served as a checker in the shoe factory. Warden John L. Whitman predicted the pair would not live more than fifteen years. He thought Loeb would be lucky to last five.

Leopold refused to be interviewed, but Loeb came to the prison door and shook hands with several reporters. "I can't talk to you, boys," he said. "I'd like to say something, but I'm afraid I'll get in bad. I bear no grudges against any of you and I'm trying to do my best down here to make good."

Mulroy thought he "presented a particularly pitiable figure, compared with the dapper Loeb of old." *Daily News* readers undoubtedly were relieved to hear that the prisoners were suffering as they were expected to do.

On Loeb's twenty-first birthday on June 11, 1926, his mother visited him in prison accompanied by one other son, Ernest. Many newspapers described it as Mrs. Loeb's "first visit" of her son, but she had visited him on at least one other occasion: October 9,

1924, accompanied by her son Allan. (She also had visited him before the hearing in Cook County Jail.) On at least one occasion Will Gehr, who had spent the summer of 1924 traveling in Europe with Meyer Levin, also traveled to Joliet with Mrs. Loeb. Undoubtedly other visits by her and other members of the family would go unreported, and the story would grow that Richard Loeb had been abandoned by his family.[6]

Leopold had beeen transferred to the new prison facility at Stateville during his appendicitis attack in May, 1925. He found his new home "clean and airy" and was able to look over the wall and see rolling farmland—and birds. He had hoped Loeb might join him at Stateville but discovered it had apparently become prison policy to separate the two partners with Leopold in one prison, Loeb in the other.[7]

This caused Richard Loeb effectively to disappear from the public's sight. While Leopold eventually wrote about his prison experiences, Loeb did not. The outside world received only brief hints of Loeb's activities in prison during the next decade (such as his enrolling in a correspondence course in Latin during 1927).[8] Much more is available about Leopold's activities, although the account given in his autobiography, *Life Plus 99 Years,* cannot be trusted entirely. Leopold wrote the book at a time when he hoped to obtain a parole and included little which reflected unfavorably on him.

He does admit being sent to solitary confinement in May, 1926. Prisoners referred to solitary confinement as the hole. He claimed his offense had been illegally raising pigeons; newspapers at the time reported he had been caught stealing sugar. In what would be considered cruel and unusual punishment today, guards manacled solitary prisoners to the bars of their cells during the day, a metal door only inches from their faces. At the end of the day prisoners were unmanacled and given bread and water. Cells in the hole contained only a single window, a concrete bench for a bed, a single electric light bulb that remained on all night, and a bucket for toilet facilities. To amuse himself, Leopold tried humming songs, reciting poetry, doing multiplication tables, and naming Presidents. He also daydreamed.[9] His father traveled to Joliet on the regular Tuesday visiting day but was turned away.

Then on Wednesday the peephole through which food was passed opened. One of the convict clerks in solitary stared at him. "What's happening?" Leopold asked, but the clerk refused to say. A few minutes later the peephole opened again and Leopold saw Bernardo Roa and Gregorio Rizzo, two inmates he had been helping with English lessons. (In keeping with his policy of using fictitious names, Leopold identified Gregorio Rizzo in his autobiography as "Juan Rizo.") They and five other inmates had overpowered the guards, killing Deputy Warden Peter M. Klein. They asked Leopold if he wished to escape with them. He said no, asking only that they remove his handcuffs, give him some water, and a cigarette.

The seven escaped from prison, but the police recaptured five almost immediately, wounding Bernardo Roa. One escapee, Charles Duschowsky, eluded his pursuers for several days, then was captured. The seventh convict, James Price, vanished. Many years later he was arrested after a New York robbery. Returned to Illinois, he pleaded guilty to murder and received a 150-year sentence. His companions, in the meantime, had been executed. Had Leopold gone with them, he might have met the same fate.[10]

The police suspected Leopold of directing the escape, particularly because of a note found in his cell, which seemed to indicate a willingness to join them:

> DEAR FATHER,
>
> As I am about to go away, I want you to know that in my last hours I acknowledge that had I followed your teaching I would have avoided trouble.
>
> I am sorry, dear Father, for the trouble I have caused you and realize that I did not do the right thing.
>
> Lovingly, your son,
>
> NATHAN[11]

Leopold contended he had written the note while in fear for his life at the hands of the convicts who had slain the deputy warden, a strange alibi considering the fact that several had been his students. Perhaps he planned to join them, hoping he might be shot escaping, then chickened out—or was left. Supposedly the jail break had been planned by the seven during a prison baseball game the previous week. At the trial of the escapees, one of their defense attorneys called Leopold as a witness, but he refused to testify.[12]

During the aftermath of the Franks case a number of people filed (or threatened) suits against Leopold and Loeb or their families. One litigant was Walter T. Wilson, the former Harvard school teacher and early suspect in the kidnapping. His attorneys asked for $100,000 from a list of defendants which also included Jacob Franks, Samuel Ettelson, and several members of the Chicago police department.[13] Another litigant was a woman who charged Leopold and Loeb had picked her up one night in front of the Uptown Theater and forced iron rods into the orifices of her body. She also wanted $100,000. The woman's attorney, according to Leopold, spoke to his father and brother Mike, offering to settle for a smaller sum. Mr. Leopold and Mike explained that the boys, being in jail, technically were paupers, suggested the attorney sue, told him to leave, and promised to throw him out a thirty-third-story window if he returned. Leopold claimed that eventually all but one person dropped their suits.[14]

That person was Charles Ream, the former taxi driver who charged that Leopold and Loeb drugged him and mutilated him during the early morning hours of November 20, 1923. Many people, including the *Tribune,* suspected that the mutilation of Ream might have been one of the so-called ABCD crimes alluded to in the Hulbert and Bowman report. Ream's attorney was also asking for $100,000.[15] The case finally came to trial in Will County Court in Joliet, January 5, 1927.

The reporters who came down from Chicago to cover the case did not seem to take Ream's claims too seriously. Ream had been arrested only recently for stealing a car. Instead of reporting the testimony related to the case, they fastened their attention on Leopold and Loeb, treating them as they might a couple of popular movie stars who had just come out of retirement. They described the pair as enjoying the opportunity to visit again with their friends and with each other. Leopold appeared jaunty and mirthful while on the stand. Loeb sat in the courtroom in front of Leopold and "tilted back his chair and talked animatedly with his former close companion, paying little attention to the questioning of witnesses." Their attorneys (one of whose names coincidentally was Bert *Crowe,* no relative) finally warned them not to appear as though the case were too much of a picnic.[16]

After three days of testimony the jury retired to vote. On the first ballot, seven jurors sided with Charles Ream, five with the defense. During twenty-three hours and thirty-one minutes of deliberation, the jury took thirty ballots, but only one more juror shifted position. He joined those favoring Ream. The case ended in a hung jury.[17] That four people could be found to side with the two defendants in this era of intense prejudice against them says something about the weakness of Ream's case. In later years, when Nathan Leopold attempted to obtain parole from prison, one of those who wrote a letter to Governor Stratton favoring the parole was Ream's former attorney.

Rather than see the case retried with more unfavorable publicity for the families, the parents of the two boys made a cash settlement with Charles Ream out of court. (Leopold later would admit this, although not in his autobiography.)[18] Their sons returned to their respective cells at Stateville and Joliet, saying, as they left, that they had had a "fine vacation." They faded once more from public scrutiny.

Nathan Leopold learned that prison life could be cruel. In April, 1929, one of the deputy wardens called him over and asked, "Did you hear anything about your old man?"

"No," Leopold replied.

"Well, I hear he kicked the bucket."

A half hour later Leopold obtained a copy of that morning's *Tribune,* carrying his father's picture and details of his death the previous night. That afternoon a telegram from home officially informed him. "His passing came as a great shock to me," Leopold wrote, "and my grief at losing him was intensified by my bitter knowledge of how unhappy I had made the last five years of his life. It sobered me."[19]

Leopold believed his father's death finally caused him to mature, but soon afterward he had four fights, three of them with an inmate who made homosexual advances to him—advances he reportedly resisted. Leopold lost the first two fights but claimed he won the third. For his victory in his third fight Leopold got five days in the hole.[20] The fourth fight, with another inmate, which Leopold also lost, was about the division of some eggs from a brood of canaries that he and a cellmate were raising.

As Nathan Leopold developed seniority at Stateville, he was able to obtain better jobs. As one of his tasks he reorganized the prison library. Loeb remained in the old prison within the city of Joliet. During the summer of 1930, however, Leopold learned through the prison grapevine that Loeb was attempting to obtain a transfer to Stateville. Leopold, then working in the chaplain's office, looked forward to their reunion with some delight. Then in October prison authorities caught him signing the chaplain's name to slips which permitted prisoners to come to his office.

Leopold received seven days in solitary confinement. On his release from the hole Warden Hill informed him of his impending transfer back to the old prison within the city of Joliet, which Leopold abhorred. This would permit Loeb to come to Stateville while maintaining their separation. Leopold became so despondent at the news that he vowed to commit suicide. But when he told his older brother his plans on visiting day, Mike talked him out of it.[21] Although Leopold would claim in his autobiography that it was the dreariness of the old prison that depressed him the most, more likely his greatest disappointment was his continued separation from Richard Loeb, whom he still loved.

Leopold pleaded with Warden Hill to allow him a transfer back to Stateville. The warden, Leopold protested, should not permit the Chicago newspapers to dictate policy. This challenge seemed to anger the warden, who promised Leopold that if he served six months without any further disciplinary problems he would be returned. In March, 1931, officials finally informed Leopold of his impending transfer. He was jubilant. He boarded a prison bus. The bus traveled the twenty miles separating the two institutions. The bus driver blew his horn as signal for the gate to open, but the gate remained shut. Inside, prisoners were rioting, the aftermath of an incident where guards machine-gunned three inmates to death. Several weeks later, after Stateville had returned to normal, Leopold made the bus ride once more. He was appalled at the damage—a half million dollars' worth—particularly because the library, which he had helped organize, had gone up in flames. His canaries had also perished during the riot.

Leopold was given the job of reorganizing the library, a task he undertook with relish because he could do it without supervision and because it permitted him many privileges, including freedom to travel within the prison. Loeb worked in the greenhouse nearby, and they visited each other during work hours. "We spent a lot of time together," Nathan Leopold later would write. "The next four years from 1932 to 1936 were, in many ways, the best I have known in prison."[22]

24 Death

All of Dickie's life, from the beginning of his anti-social activities, have been in the direction of his own destruction.

—Dr. William A. White[1]

In November, 1932, Richard Loeb suggested to Nathan Leopold that they attempt to improve educational facilities within the prison. Stateville had a school supervised by a civilian superintendent, but it went no further than eighth grade. Prisoners could take commercial correspondence courses, but this cost money. Loeb once enrolled in a correspondence course in Latin at Columbia University but apparently never completed the course. Leopold constantly expanded his knowledge through reading and self-study, examining such subjects as calculus, logic, and Egyptian hieroglyphics, but no program existed within the walls for those of lesser means.

That January, with the warden's blessing, Leopold and Loeb opened a correspondence school for the prisoners at Stateville. They enrolled twenty-two students and had applications from sixty-four others. Loeb acted as registrar and director of the school and also taught classes in English composition, history, and Spanish. Other faculty members (according to newpaper reports) included Edward "Toddy" Dillon, known as the society bandit, a teacher of English literature; Joseph Pursifull, a former Peoria attorney, schoolteacher, and kidnapper, who would teach Latin; and Mark Oettinger of Chicago, a forger and teacher of mathematics. Curiously, early newspaper accounts failed to credit Nathan Leopold for his role in the enterprise. Maybe, as had been the case with the Franks murder, he was giving Loeb all the credit. Perhaps prison authorities feared enflaming public opinion by giving out press releases of any joint activity, no matter for what worthy purposes, connecting Leopold again with Loeb.[2]

The motivation for Leopold and Loeb in establishing the school is difficult to determine, just as determining motivation in the

Franks slaying had proved an elusive quest for a phalanx of psychiatrists. Beginning soon after his father's death, Nathan Leopold had begun to show signs of what later would be classified as rehabilitation. He involved himself in constructive projects, beginning with his work in the prison library, in which his intelligence and college education could be put to some use. His motives may not have been entirely altruistic. Working in a library was undoubtedly more pleasant for him than working in a shop. Such conduct also would be more likely to impress a future parole board—although it seems unlikely that Leopold, or Loeb for that matter, should yet look that far in the future. But both were smart enough to realize that by cooperating with the system, they could obtain more privileges, a break from prison monotony, and freedom of movement within the walls.

The correspondence school also provided them a measure of privacy, the opportunity to sequester themselves in a section of the prison where they could not be interrupted by the guards. For their classrooms the warden assigned them a suite of rooms near the mess hall which had once been used by guards as a private dining area. Included in this suite was a washroom with a shower that could be locked from the inside. There is no evidence to indicate that Leopold and Loeb used the correspondence school as a cover for homosexual activity, either with each other or with others, but the opportunity was there.

They did see each other frequently. They played handball together; they played bridge. Each morning after breakfast they would sit around for twenty minues and talk.[3] They also drank together. In October, 1933, Loeb stopped by the cell of Robert Scott, sentenced to life for murder, to deliver some correspondence school examination papers. He found Scott, Leopold, and another prisoner, Lefty Sullivan, sharing a bottle of bonded liquor. Some time later Captain Oscar Nelson heard laughter coming from one of the cells and found the four merrymakers, who fearlessly gave him a Bronx cheer. He placed all four in solitary confinement, but Leopold and Loeb managed to obtain a release within an hour.[4] They had apparently become men of privilege. The offense apparently did not even result in a disciplinary notice being placed in their prison records, since Leopold later would claim that Loeb never received such a notice during his entire time in prison. Leopold himself received many such disciplinary notices.

But life in prison also had its deadly aspects. One day a prisoner asked Leopold, who had been on his way to the powerhouse, to stop and talk to him. Leopold would identify the man as Jay Craig in his autobiography, although that was a fictitious name. They moved to one side, whereupon Craig pulled a knife from his pocket and thrust it against Leopold's chest. He motioned for Leopold to move with him to a more private corner of the yard. The prisoner insisted that Leopold had seduced his sister and had promised him $50,000 for not prosecuting. Recognizing the other prisoner's unbalanced mentality, Leopold attempted to stall him. "I don't have fifty thousand dollars with me," he said. "I'll talk to you later."

That night Leopold told Richard Loeb and several other friends what had happened. They arranged a meeting with Jay Craig and his friends. Craig apologized, admitting he had made a mistake, and said it would not happen again. Yet after the meeting ended, he called Leopold over and asked, "Where's the fifty thousand dollars?"

Leopold might have informed the guards, but he believed strongly in prison ethics. He didn't like stool pigeons. His friends afterward saw that whenever he traveled within the prison, someone accompanied him. Later the assistant warden separately called Leopold and Loeb into his office to ask what they knew about Craig. True to the prison ethic, they said nothing. Jay Craig was discharged. Three weeks after his release, Craig rang a doorbell and without saying a word, shot dead the person who answered. That person, in effect, fell victim to prison ethics. The state sent Craig without trial to the state hospital for the criminally insane.[5]

In 1932 James E. Day, a transplanted Virginia hillbilly with a long record of offenses as a juvenile, held up a Chicago gas station. He obtained $9.75, not a lot of money even during the Depression. He split half that sum with his companion, a boy named Morris, who Day claimed provided the gun. The police nabbed the pair the next day. Day pleaded guilty (supposedly on the advice of Morris' lawyers). Morris also pleaded guilty but succeeded in blaming the crime on Day, so Day claimed, and received a sentence of probation.[6] Day received a one- to ten-year sentence, probably because of his extensive previous police record. Before this offense he had served terms in the St. Charles School for Boys, one term in Cook County jail, and had been given another probationary sentence—all for thefts.[7]

Day, only eighteen years old at the time of his arrest, served three years in the Illinois State Reformatory at Pontiac. As a twenty-first birthday present he received a transfer to Stateville. Day stood 5 feet 6-1/2 inches tall, weighed 135 pounds, and had a pockmarked complexion. Chicago *Daily News* reporter Edwin Lahey described him as possessing "the frightened eyes of the street corner youth, always on the lookout for a squad car."[8] Joseph Ragen, who became warden at Stateville in 1935, considered Day a "bad actor, erratic, given to wild temper tantrums."[9]

When Ragen arrived at the prison, he found discipline extremely lax. Privileged convicts had their own huts within the walls and could stay at any one of four or five cell houses. Considerable cash was in the possession of prisoners, and nearly every prisoner had a knife or other form of weapon. In one shakedown, guards recovered twenty-seven straight razors—although as events would prove, they missed finding at least one.

Not only because of the ample funds provided by their families, but also because of their positions as heads of the prison correspondence school, Leopold and Loeb ranked as Stateville's princes of privilege. They kept themselves supplied with tobacco and other commissary items and also supplied their cellmates and friends.[10]

One recipient of their largesse was James Day, who celled with Loeb. According to Leopold, Loeb at this time received an allowance from his family of $50 a month. Since Day had no income, Loeb supplied him with cigarettes, candy, and food. Day, however, frequently argued with Loeb over division of these gratuities, jealous perhaps because of Loeb's gifts to other inmates. When Ragen arrived, he limited each prisoner's commissary allowance to $3 a week, cutting Loeb's buying power by more than three-quarters. He now barely had enough to supply himself. Arguments between Day and Loeb increased until in December, 1935, Ragen moved Day to another cell two doors away. The two continued to argue, however, including one time around the second week of January.[11]

Day, however, told a different story about his relationship with Richard Loeb, one that would contribute considerable spice to the legend of Leopold and Loeb. In fact, Day told *several* different stories, depending on when he was questioned about the matter. The most imaginative one appeared in the May, 1960, issue of *True Detective,* where in an article ghosted for him by Ray Brennan of the Chicago *Sun-Times* Day described plans of a prison break for which Loeb needed assistance. Day claimed Loeb (who Day also claimed wore a perfectly fitting uniform specially made for him in the prison tailor shop) asked him to help him smuggle four .45 caliber guns into the prison for an escape to include someone Loeb cryptically referred to as R.T. Day assumed Loeb meant Roger Touhy, the celebrated gangster, then a resident of Stateville. "Loeb hinted," Day wrote, "that he and his tough guys would grab the warden at gunpoint and force him to give them safe conduct to the outside, where getaway cars would be waiting. He would go to a level farm field not far away from Stateville, Loeb said, and an airplane would start him on his way to a remote part of South America. A million dollars would be waiting at his destination." For his part in the plot, Day supposedly would receive $5,000 plus a $35-a-week job in a downtown Chicago store upon his release. If he failed to cooperate, he might be framed for a crime that would keep him in prison for life.[12]

In 1936, however, Day told a different story to prison authorities. He said that the previous June, Loeb (who had got him his job in the prison office) had wanted to talk to him. The Chicago *Daily News,* which published portions of the report, said that it included "unprintable details." Loeb supposedly offered Day $20 a week to engage in homosexual activities. Loeb, described as the "cock of the walk," had such influence with prison guards that they would look the other way.[13] Day, however, said he had too much integrity to accept such a liaison. "You're a double-crosser and not a friend!" Day said he shouted at Loeb.

"Don't fly off the handle that way," responded Loeb. Supposedly the relationship between Loeb and Day deteriorated after that.

Leopold later would comment: "The story Day told—that Dick had made sexual proposals—was so ridiculous in the minds of anyone who knew the two men as to be laughable."[14]

Father Eligius Weir, Catholic chaplain at the prison, later would say, "Day was after Loeb because he would *not* engage in homosexual relations with him."[15]

On January 28, 1936, Richard Loeb spent the morning with Nathan Leopold. Rather than go to the dining room for breakfast, they had sweet rolls brought to them from the commissary and, as they often did, ate breakfast in one of their cells with their cell partners. Leopold would remember Jimmie Day passing by en route to work and stopping to talk to Loeb. Day had a black eye, the result of a recent fight with another convict. Day told Loeb he would see him around noon. Leopold paid little attention to the remark at the time. For the rest of the morning Leopold and Loeb corrected examination papers and discussed an algebra course they planned to add to the curriculum of their correspondence school. Between eleven fifteen and eleven forty-five the correspondence school group went to lunch.[16] Leopold and Loeb either did not go with them or ate fast and returned early. About eleven thirty Loeb grabbed a towel and some clean clothes and said he planned to take a shower in the school's private washroom, whose outer door was about forty feet from the mess hall door. Leopold returned to his cell.[17]

James Day worked in the business office of the administration building along with about sixty other men. They left for lunch at noon. Day made certain he was last in line to enter the mess hall. As he passed the school washroom, he ducked inside. Day later told prison authorities he suddenly was seized with the necessity to go to the toilet.[18] In his 1960 *True Detective* article, Day said Loeb had asked to meet him at the shower at noon and claimed that he had to wait shivering outside in the cold until Loeb appeared to unlock the door. But judging fom other accounts, the door to the washroom was on a corridor rather than leading to the outdoors. Despite varying stories as to how they got there and *why* they got there, the fact is that at around noontime on January 28, 1936, James E. Day and Richard A. Loeb were alone together in the shower for an unspecified amount of time with the door locked from the inside.

A short time afterward the door opened again. Richard Loeb staggered through it into the corridor naked and covered with blood. He collapsed into the arms of the first inmate he saw. Captain Austin Humphrey of the penitentiary guards rushed to the scene in time to see Day emerging from the washroom clad only in a pair of trousers. "Ever since I've been in here, Loeb's been trying to bother me," Day mumbled to the officer. He handed Humphrey a straight razor.[19]

The guards rushed Loeb to the prison hospital. A few minutes later one of the convict workers in the dining room came to Leopold's cell to tell him that his friend had been taken to the hospital. "He's hurt," said the convict. Leopold remembered that the time was twelve twenty, less than an hour since he had seen Loeb, towel in hand, head for the shower. Worried about his friend, Leopold tried to obtain permission to go to the hospital. Nobody seemed to have the authority. He tried calling Warden Ragen but learned the warden had rushed to the yard in time to see Loeb being placed on a stretcher. "I'm all right, Warden," Loeb whispered. "I'll pull through." Reportedly Loeb also asked to see Father Weir.

Leopold, meanwhile, convinced a prison official to escort him as far as the hospital gate where he saw Father Weir arrive. The Catholic chaplain finally escorted him in. He found Richard Loeb on the operating table, an ether mask over his face, four doctors laboring over him. His throat had been cut. "His trunk, his arms, his legs were one mass of knife cuts," wrote Leopold. "Nowhere on his entire body could you go six inches without encountering a cut." A tube had been inserted into his windpipe through a hole in his throat so that he could breathe.[20]

Loeb had between fifty-six and fifty-eight razor wounds on his body.[21]

Leopold rushed from the operating room to the laboratory to offer his blood for a transfusion but discovered that three donors already had contributed their blood. He returned and took a place at the foot of the operating table. The doctors—seven now, three more physicians having arrived from Joliet—continued to labor over Richard Loeb's still-bleeding body, attempting to suture the cuts and halt the blood loss. Leopold noticed his friend getting noticeably whiter, his breathing shallow and rapid, his blood pressure dropping alarmingly. When the doctors attempted a transfusion, a geyser of blood rose from the wound in Loeb's throat.[22]

Loeb's temperature began to drop. Prison physician Frank J. Chmelik asked Leopold to cover his feet with a blanket and obtain several hot-water bottles. The same doctor in the next minute asked Leopold to get a priest. By now the time was two twenty. Leopold was puzzled but figured that perhaps the doctor had spoken from force of habit without thinking. In the corridor outside he spoke to Father Weir, who said that while he would be willing to give him the last rites, if Leopold so desired, he saw no reason for doing so. Loeb, after all, was Jewish, even though his mother had been Catholic. Leopold thanked him and returned again to the operating room, where he realized that Loeb, still bleeding from his numerous wounds, had no chance to survive.

At two forty-five the Loeb family physicians, Dr. Lester E. Frankenthal and his son, Dr. Lester Frankenthal, Jr., arrived from Chicago. The older doctor had been the obstetrician who had delivered both Leopold and Loeb into the world. Only minutes after the two physicians arrived, Richard A. Loeb died. He was thirty years old.[23]

The physicians left the operating room. Leopold remained to help the surgical nurse wash his dead friend. Each time they moved the body it began to bleed again. Leopold noticed that the deepest cut was the one on the throat, apparently inflicted from behind, beginning under the left ear and circling the throat. He would say later that until that moment he never had fully comprehended the meaning of the phrase "cut to ribbons." He knew now.

In *Life Plus 99 Years,* Nathan Leopold writes, movingly, about the death of his friend. It is perhaps the most poignant section of that otherwise awkwardly written book: "We covered him at last with a sheet, but after a moment I folded the sheet back from his face and sat down on a stool by the table where he lay. I wanted a long last look at him.

"For, strange as it may sound, he had been my best pal.

"In one sense, he was also the greatest enemy I have ever had. For my friendship with him had cost me—my life. It was he who had originated the idea of committing the crime, he who had planned it, he who had largely carried it out. It was he who had insisted on doing what we eventually did. But that doesn't, in my eyes, at least, alter the truth of the first statement. Every human being, I suppose, is an infinitely complex mixture. On some it doesn't show so much; outwardly, at least, they manage to maintain a certain degree of consistency. Whether their inner thoughts and feelings are equally consistent is an open question. But it wasn't that way with Dick: he was, during all the period of his life when I knew him, a living contradiction.

"As I sat now by his cooling, bleeding corpse, the strangeness of that contradiction, that basic, fundamental ambivalence of his character, was borne in on me.

"For Dick possessed more of the truly fine qualities than almost anyone else I have ever known. Not just the superficial social graces. Those, of course, he possessed to the nth degree. Dick could charm the birds out of the trees. He could get along with anyone, make anyone like him. He always knew how to act, what to say. In any company. With older people or those of higher social position he was respectful. Genuinely and effortlessly respectful. With age-fellows and equals he was natural, friendly, lovable. With social inferiors he never condescended. Outside, servants adored him; in prison, the lowliest, most friendless prisoner looked on Dick as a friend. He helped hundreds.

"But the more fundamental, more important qualities of character, too, he possessed in full measure. He was loyal to a fault. He could be sincere; he could be honestly and selflessly dedicated. His devotion to the school proves that. He truly, deeply wanted to help his fellow man.

"How, I mused, could these personality traits coexist with the other side of Dick's character? It didn't make sense! For there was another side. Dick just didn't have the faintest trace of conventional morality. Not just before our incarceration. Afterward too. I don't believe he ever, to the day of his death, felt truly remorseful for what we had done. Sorry that we had been caught, of course. And truly remorseful for the grief he had caused his family. That was as genuine as could be. But remorse for the murder itself? I honestly don't think so.

"And yet he could, and did, make sacrifices for his ideals. He could, and did, face danger courageously. He was true to his lights. And yet there persisted in his make-up, to the very day of his tragic death, an element of the demoniac.

"And my attitude toward Dick was as ambivalent as was its object. Before our arrest I was bedazzled; I couldn't see his faults. But afterward—especially after our seven years of total separation in prison—I surely wasn't bedazzled any longer. I had opportunity enough to think, and think hard about him. To attain some degree of objectivity at a safe distance from the magnetism of his personality. That's where the inexplicable, incomprehensible ambivalence arose. For I could see his bad points all too clearly. I certainly knew Dick better than anyone else in the world. And the blindest person in the world couldn't have overlooked his faults. Certainly not I, who had been carried along to destruction. But with all I knew about that side of his character, there still was no blinking the wonderful traits that were his."[24]

Nathan Leopold's epitaph to his dead friend (written nearly two decades after his murder) itself is a study in contradictions. While praising Loeb for many human qualities, Leopold nevertheless lays the blame for the Franks murder squarely in the coffin with Richard Loeb. *"It was he who had originated the idea of committing the crime,"* insists Leopold, *"he who had planned it out. It was he who had insisted on doing what we eventually did."* Author and columnist Max Lerner has written that "history is written by survivors," and Nathan Leopold had survived.[25] Although he may not have realized it while he stood at the foot of the prison operating table, the biggest obstacle standing between him and freedom had now been removed.

The exact facts of Richard Loeb's death remain somewhat of a puzzle in the same sense that the facts of Bobby Franks' death also remain a puzzle, and for the same reason: No witness survived other than the murderer(s). We only had Leopold and Loeb's word as to the facts of the Franks murder—and they contradicted themselves. We only have James Day's word as to how, and *why*, Richard Loeb died—and he hardly could be considered an unbiased witness. Day, in fact, claimed that Loeb attacked him! He insisted Loeb made homosexual advances, that Loeb possessed the razor. Day confessed only to acting in self-defense—despite the viciousness of the attack, despite the fifty-six wounds on Loeb's body, despite Loeb's throat being slashed from behind.

Many reporters writing about Loeb's death would accept Day's word—at least initially. Edwin A. Lahey of the Chicago *Daily*

News, in writing about the murder, began with what many newspapermen consider the classic lead paragraph of all time: "Richard Loeb, a brilliant college student and master of the English language, today ended a sentence with a proposition."

It was a cute turn of a phrase, but unfortunately one that was untrue. Nevertheless, the idea that Loeb initiated his death because of homosexual advances made to another prisoner has become part of the legend of Leopold and Loeb. Another version of of the story claims that the prisoner who killed Loeb was a black man. The most imaginative version of this story appears in George Murray's *The Madhouse on Madison Street:*

> One day Dickie Loeb caught his loved one alone in the shower. The Negro was apparently defenseless against the youth who still thought himself the embodiment of the Nietzschean superman. Dickie Loeb approached the fearful Negro prisoner with the same smile that had proved so fatally charming to Bobby Franks. When he had the Negro in a corner of the shower stall, Dickie threw himself on his knees before the naked black body and clutched his captive around the legs, determined to satisfy his lust.
>
> All he got for his shower of kisses was a shiv between the shoulders, wielded by the powerful arm of the black man who was revolted by the very touch of Loeb's slavering lips.[26]

There was something about Leopold and Loeb that seemed to move authors to poetry. Murray claims he realized later that the story of the black was in error, but it was too late to make changes in his book. He also claimed that Lahey had written his lead as a joke, and the city editor was about to change it when another reporter named Bob Casey looked over his shoulder and said, "If you kill that lead, I resign." The lead reportedly ran in only one edition before being changed.

Undoubtedly, many people accepted the story that Loeb died making homosexual advances as true because they wanted it to be true. They considered the Franks murder an act of perversion—which was never proved—so it seemed fitting that Loeb die while attempting another perverted act.

While Loeb lay dying on the operating table, James Day was telling his version of the razor slashing incident to prison authorities. "I have been in here about eighteen months," Day said, "and all that time I have been bothered by Loeb."

Day described going to the shower room next to the correspondence school suite. Loeb, he claimed, pulled a razor on him and told him to take his clothes off. "The thought struck me," said Day, "that I should act as if I was giving in and watch for my chance to do something." They began undressing. Then Day claimed he kicked Loeb in the groin. "He grabbed at me with his free hand and slashed at me with the razor as he fell. He missed me by inches. I hit him on the neck with my fist. I'm confused here and can't remember everything as clearly as I should.

"Loeb's hand, the one with the razor in it, hit the sill of the shower as he fell and the razor dropped. He grabbed for it as I jumped over his body and caught him by the wrist and throat, and we fell together. The razor dropped again. I grabbed it this time.

"Loeb swung at me and hit me in the face. I slashed back at him and blood flew all over my face. I slashed at him again and he fell back against the sill of the shower.

"Loeb got the razor away from me then and got on top of me, holding me by the throat. Something told me I was going to die if I didn't get out from under. I got him off me, I don't know how. The razor was in my hand when I got up.

"Loeb swung at me, half laughing, and hollered: 'So you can fight when you have to?'

"I started slashing at him again and he backed into the shower and turned on the hot water. I stepped in after him, but I could hardly see on account of the steam. Anyway, I kept slashing at him.

"I can't remember much more except that after some minutes, he sank into a sitting position. In a funny sort of way, Loeb took two fingers of his right hand and kept pushing in the flesh in his abdomen where it seemed to be cut.

"Then Loeb got up slow. His eyes were big and starry. He put everything he had in a lunge at me. He held his hands up in front like claws. I started slashing some more and kept on until he fell.

"He was mumbling, like. I just stood there. Didn't know what to do. Finally I turned off the hot water and turned on the cold and stepped in the shower to wash the blood off me. I was all red.

"Pretty soon I heard like laughter or a groan and I turned around. Loeb was standing straight up. He lunged and knocked me down. He fell away and fell down at the door. Then he got up and started fumbling with the key.

"I let him go and didn't see him again."[27]

James Day's retelling of the story fourteen years later for *True Detective* also included his claim that the razor changed hands at least three times. "It seems to me that I had the razor in my hand, lost it, then wrenched it away from Loeb again," claimed Day. The *True Detective* version did not explain (nor did Day's earlier version explain) how Loeb could have had the razor several times with intent to harm Day, yet Loeb had at least fifty-six wounds while Day had none. The blood on Day's body, which he described washing off in the shower following the attack, was entirely that of Richard Loeb.

Several questions were posed by the manner in which Loeb died. Many wondered how James Day, who according to some sources was a small man only five feet one inch tall, could overpower a large and well-conditioned athlete like Richard Loeb, who supposedly kept himself in shape by regular handball games. The answer is, Day was not that small and Loeb not that large. Day's prison record when he was transferred to Menard in 1938 lists him as five feet seven inches tall, weighing 145 pounds. When Drs. Hulbert and Bowman examined Loeb in June, 1924, they listed his height as five feet nine inches and his weight as 142 pounds. By the time Loeb arrived in Joliet three months later, fortified by all those meals from Stein's Restaurant, his weight had ballooned to 160. At the time of his death, he supposedly weighed 170 pounds, and it seems dubious that all that weight increase was muscle. Regardless of any difference in their size, a tough little man with a razor is a match for a well-bred big man any time.

The question of where the murder weapon came from has never been satisfactorily answered—at least in public. At first, prison authorities thought that the razor had been stolen from the prison barbership.[28] Loeb's cellmate, a young burglar named Skeplowski, insisted that the razor did not belong to Loeb. He pointed out that Loeb shaved barely once a week. Books crowded their cell because Loeb had been writing a history of the Civil War. They had a radio, but Loeb rarely used it. "He'd get sore at me if I wanted to turn it on at night while he was studying his history," said Skeplowski.[29]

Warden Ragen ordered Leopold placed in solitary confinement—supposedly to protect him from a similar assault. Day also went to solitary confinement and the following June was tried in Will County Court in Joliet for the murder of Richard Loeb. After a brief trial and fifty minutes of deliberation by the jury, James Day was judged not guilty.

The decision angered Warden Ragen, particularly because he had not been allowed to testify freely in the case.[30] By then the warden had discovered the origin of the razor. George Bliss, Day's cellmate, who was in prison for robbery and who worked as assistant to the Protestant chaplain, had stolen it earlier and hidden it in the chaplain's desk. When the prison had been shaken down for weapons soon after Ragen's arrival, the razor had not been discovered. Ragen decided that he did not want publicly to accuse the Protestant minister, so he remained quiet. Though he appeared as a witness, he was asked only a few meaningless questions. (Leopold, in his autobiography, says that Ragen was called to the stand and asked only his name, how long he had been warden and whether or not he had witnessed the attack. Then he was dismissed.[31]) Had he been asked about the razor, presumably Ragen would have been obliged to tell what he knew. That might have been sufficient to convict Day—assuming the twelve members of the jury showed any interest in punishing the murderer of Richard Loeb.

Many years later Joseph G. Schwab, who in 1936 had been twenty-six years old, the youngest member of the jury, as well as its foreman, still remembered the reasons why twelve men had decided that James Day had been justified in his assault on the murderer of Bobby Franks. "Nobody liked a queer, a homo, or a lesbian, which all seems okay today," Schwab would write in 1974, "so it was a good thing to get rid of such people. They were Skum [sic]. Even Clarence Darrow said it was the only verdict we could bring in, which made me feel okay."

Schwab, however, seemed impressed by Day's Chicago lawyers and claimed later to have heard that rich Jews, ashamed of Loeb, paid to defend James Day. Supposedly Day's Jewish friends held a celebration party after the trial featuring liquor and champagne. Schwab remembers that during the trial the jury had fun with the bailiff, hiding the doorstop of the jury room in a safe that one of the jurors was able to open. The first ballot had been eleven voting not guilty and only one opposed. "It did not take us long to convince the holdout, a poor, skinny, little old man, a timid soul," recalls Schwab, now retired from his job with the railroad and admitting to being an old man himself.[32]

Had this jury of Day's peers been more interested in other matters than playing games with the bailiff, they also might have been swayed by the testimony of Father Weir, the Catholic chaplain. He too had learned how Day obtained the murder weapon, but decided it was none of his business.[33] (Father Weir also denied later the persistent rumor that Loeb, before dying, had confessed that he and not Leopold had struck the blow that killed Bobby Franks. "Richard was unconscious when I entered the operating room," said Father Weir. "He was incapable of speech."[34])

The only one who might have sought vengeance for the death of Richard Loeb was his closest friend, Nathan Leopold. Leopold, of course, continued to subscribe to the prison ethic that you do not squeal on your fellow prisoner. "Punishing Day would not help Dick," reasoned Leopold. "It wouldn't bring him back."[35]

Leopold also had suspected that George Bliss had given Day the razor. He thought probably the idea of the murder had been that of Bliss, who had used James Day only as an accomplice. In another one of his many versions of the killing years later, Day would say that Bliss and Loeb had been fighting for control of prison rackets and Bliss merely had used him as a hit man. For some time Leopold suspected Bliss of being in the shower with Day and Loeb. Later he learned Bliss had been elsewhere. But he still suspected that Bliss was the prime mover and Day only his instrument. Bliss later was released from prison. Several years later one of his partners in a holdup shot and killed him.[36]

The body of Richard Loeb went by hearse to Donnellan's funeral home on the South Side of Chicago, carefully guarded by police, who forbade people to pass even on the same side of the street. After a brief funeral service the remains of Richard Loeb were cremated at Oakwoods Cemetery. For some time afterward a rumor circulated that the prisoner killed in the shower fight had been someone other than Richard Loeb.[37] The real Loeb supposedly had escaped from prison and left for South Africa (where presumably he lived to a ripe old age with Adolf Hitler his next-door neighbor). No evidence supports such a story.

If no one else took vengeance on James Day, Warden Ragen did. When Day returned to prison from the trial, Ragen canceled all of Day's time for good behavior. Day served the full ten years of his prison term. During the remainder of his time in prison Day received punishment seven times for breaking the rules. On one occasion he was caught committing an act of sodomy with another prisoner.[38] He was transferred to Menard Penitentiary and eventually released in 1942.

At the time of his release, Day told reporters that he had been abused, beaten, and tormented by prison guards after his acquittal in the murder case. He also claimed to believe the theory that Leob had not been killed and the fight had been engineered as a ruse to free him.[39] (In his 1960 *True Detective* article, however, the erratic Day reversed his field again, stating, "I know the man I killed. He was Loeb and nobody else.") The following year police arrested James Day, who was then working as a bus driver in Joliet, for some offense, apparently minor. Bus officials claimed they did not know he had served time in prison. Day was told to get out of town.[40]

In 1965 he reappeared in the news when he terrorized a babysitter and three children on the North Side of Chicago with a shotgun. The police arrested him while he was talking on the phone to his former wife in Baltimore. Day, who had been trying to put his daughter through nursing school, admitted that he had been drinking and taking pills to ease the pain of an illness.[41] He was sentenced to six months in the house of correction.[42] When last heard from, according to one source, Day was managing an apartment building in Atlanta. (The department of corrections in that city, however, had no record of his being there.)

After Loeb's death, reporters asked Clarence Darrow for his comment. "He's better off than Leopold," said Darrow, then seventy-nine years old. "He's better off dead."

The reporters asked Darrow why then had he battled so hard to save them from hanging. "I had no right to trifle with the lives of those boys," said the attorney. "They wanted to live. My duty was to help them do so."[43] (Darrow died at the age of eighty-one on March 13, 1938, after a painful year-long illness.)

Nathan Leopold remained in solitary confinement for several months, lodged in the same area with the murderer of his best friend. One day Day would be allowed out of his cell in the morning and Leopold in the afternoon. The next day they would switch. Leopold protested his confinement, but not until six months after Loeb's death could he return to his regular work assignment. He no longer had a cell partner. For an additional six months, whenever he left the cellhouse, he received an escort. Though this was supposedly for his own protection, he resented it. He also had time to think about his departed friend. "The realization that Dick was dead took some time to become vivid and real to me. It just didn't seem possible. I missed him terribly—all the more so since all the years in prison we had shared everything and planned everything together. I was very lonely."[44]

25 Light

He was in darkness when he came here, but he has made a magnificent struggle toward the light.

CARL SANDBURG[1]

In 1957, prior to publication of his autobiography, *Life Plus 99 Years,* Nathan Leopold addressed a letter to Timothy Seldes, a senior editor with Doubleday & Company, in response to a request that he list his achievements since entering prison. "I take it for granted that, since this is for business purposes in connection with the promotion of the book," Leopold wrote, "you will not think me conceited or ostentatious if I list every last thing I can think of."

Leopold then proceeded to fill four pages, single-spaced, recording his accomplishments, which included the study of fifteen languages before incarceration (Greek, Sanskrit, Russian, Umbrian, etc.) and twelve more afterward (Portuguese, Swedish, Arabic, Japanese, etc.). He also took many university courses, including integral calculus, Egyptian hieroglyphics, and the comedies of Plautus and Terence. He reclassified the prison library, spent three years gathering statistics on parole prediction, helped found the Stateville Correspondence School (with Richard Loeb), and became an X ray technician. He raised canaries, registered inmates for the World War II draft, translated "portions of books (usually obscene) for other inmates," gave blood, wrote a parole booklet titled "A New Day and How to Make It," collected case histories of psychotic patients, once conducted Protestant Sunday school services in the absence of the chaplain, and served as a volunteer victim in a prison medical project designed to find a cure for malaria.[2]

Nathan Leopold, as he passed into middle age, indeed became a singular individual, one who might be described as a Renaissance man. He also found himself torn between two emotions: *hope* that he some day might become eligible for parole and *despair* that the prejudice against him in the outside community was so great that he never would obtain it.

In 1948 Gene Lovitz, a twenty-one-year-old bright, handsome ex-Marine, who later would write a biography of Carl Sandburg, arrived at Stateville, having been convicted for armed robbery. After several months in prison Lovitz went one day to the medical clinic where Leopold worked as an X ray technician. Leopold walked over and introduced himself, mentioning a mutual acquaintance.

Lovitz knew Leopold by reputation but had previously seen him only from a distance. Leopold was a loner, particularly now that Loeb was gone, who never hung out in a group but walked in the prison yard alone. Lovitz soon became a good friend of Nathan Leopold, and during recreation hours they would walk together or sit on the grass against a cyclone fence and talk.

Lovitz recalls Leopold as incessantly smoking Camels cigarettes, hating the Chicago *Tribune,* displaying a prejudice toward blacks, showing intense pride in his high IQ, and disliking the prison system which put inferior men in charge of his life. "Why should we have to be told what to do by a bunch of illiterate farmers?" Leopold raged, referring to the guards. "They're nothing but little Hitlers."

This talk eventually led into a discussion on the theories of Friedrich Nietzsche. Lovitz was surprised to learn that Leopold first had learned about Nietzsche in the pages of *The Sea-Wolf,* Jack London's novel about a villainous captain named Wolf Larsen. (London mentioned Nietzsche in the first paragraph of that book.)

Wolf Larsen possessed both fantastic strength and a superb intellect. In the end, however, he goes blind, suffers ferocious headaches, and dies slowly and painfully as paralysis sets in. The narrator of the story is a wealthy, but weak, castaway named Humphrey Van Weyden, who gains strength as Wolf Larsen loses his and eventually emerges the victor, winning the love of the heroine in the process.[3]

Leopold and Loeb had apparently read *The Sea-Wolf* early in life and, rather than being repelled by the bestiality of Wolf Larsen, had been impressed by it. Indeed, Leopold identified more closely with the vanquished Larsen than with the triumphant Van Weyden. At one point in the book Wolf Larsen snatches a raw potato from the narrator, who is peeling it, and crushes it in one hand, the potato squirting out between his fingers in mushy streams. He drops the pulpy remains into the pan and turns away. After having read that passage, Leopold and Loeb had attempted similarly to squeeze a potato, without success.

"I might be able to squeeze a baked potato," suggested Lovitz.

"I'm talking about a *raw* potato, idiot," snapped Leopold. "It would take *phenomenal* strength to do that!" Lovitz later would recall that it was almost like a kid talking about Superman.

Lovitz saw *The Sea-Wolf* as more than a mere adventure story and felt that Leopold had misinterpreted London's message. London, Lovitz believed, was a Marxist who used Wolf Larsen as an example of the evils of capitalism. His death in the end was symbolic that the Nietzschean superman philosophy was self-destructive and collectivism would win out in the end. Leopold disagreed, thinking it merely an adventure story. He did recall Wolf Larsen quoting Milton's *Paradise Lost* at one point in the book: "It is better to reign in hell than serve in heaven." Lovitz thought that was a fairly good description of what Leopold was doing in Stateville.

The two men argued over Nietzsche. "His precious superman theories would have put you in the ovens," claimed Lovitz, who was one-quarter Jewish. "Nietzsche never gave an answer to anything in his life. He only asked questions."

Leopold treated that comment with scorn. "Nietzsche's questions were the answers, smart alec!"

Later, however, Leopold considered some of Lovitz's comments about Jack London's political philosophy and decided Lovitz might be correct. He also told Lovitz that he reminded him of Loeb. "He was argumentative like you. His mind worked a lot like yours does."

Lovitz did not take that as much of a compliment. He always had thought of Richard Loeb as queer.

Leopold perhaps sensed Lovitz's feelings and defended his dead friend. "He was a real man. He wasn't afraid of anything."

Lovitz noticed that Leopold frequently switched from one speech pattern to another. During their early discussions Lovitz spoke prison slang, whereas Leopold carefully used good grammar. So Lovitz began watching his grammar more carefully only to discover that Leopold shifted his talk again to the prison vernacular. "He would constantly switch back and forth," recalls Lovitz. "At no time were we using the same language."

Occasionally they discussed sex. "He never spoke about women," Lovitz recalls. "He would just talk about sex as sex." One time during a discussion on masturbation, Leopold claimed to have developed a superior way to masturbate. Prior to ejaculation he would tighten his sphincter muscles and delay orgasm, which would permit him to start all over again a few minutes later. Lovitz, following his release from prison several years later, tried this technique during sexual intercourse with his wife and discovered it worked. "This could be Nathan Leopold's greatest contribution to mankind," suggests Lovitz, "the perpetual orgasm."

Lovitz claims that Leopold obtained no extraordinary privileges while in prison, and that he had no more freedom than other prisoners with equal time in grade who had learned to cooperate and use the system to their advantage. He thought Leopold and Warden Ragen did not get along well; Leopold seemed to stay as far away from the warden as possible. Lovitz, however, also thought Leopold's contributions to society in prison were overrated: that he and Loeb had established the prison school for the opportunity it offered them of getting together, that Leopold's much-publicized participation in the malaria project had been no more than that of hundreds of other convict volunteers, that he had wasted his intellect through learning all those languages.

Lovitz had been arrested with another individual named Dave. They discussed that arrest, and Leopold commented that Lovitz and Dave were alter egos and that they would not individually have committed those robberies. Two alter egos are a mob, Leopold explained, and compared this to his own relationship with Loeb. "The danger with alter egos," explained Leopold, "is that talk can become action."

This led Leopold into a discussion on sex in which he claimed that no matter how heterosexual a person was, some place in the world there was another person of the same sex with whom, under the right conditions and circumstances, he could make love. One seldom found his counterpart, or true alter ego, in real life. "Leopold said Loeb was his alter ego," recalls Lovitz, "and that I was an alter ego. That he had only met one other alter ego besides me and Loeb."

Lovitz had a disability pension from the Marines because of asthma, but it had been canceled during his stay in prison. Leopold suggested that they take some X rays. By fogging them, Leopold thought he might be able to fool the government into renewing Lovitz's pension. Leopold had a key to the X ray room and the two went there one afternoon. While taking the X rays, Leopold suggested they become more friendly, repeating his comment that Lovitz reminded him of Loeb, and finally made what Lovitz interpreted as a homosexual proposition. Lovitz declined and left the X ray room. He never did get his Marine pension renewed, and afterward Leopold stayed clear of him in the yard.

The remark Lovitz interpreted as a homosexual pitch had

been: "Why don't you let the *anopheles* bite you?" referring to the female mosquito. Of all the activities Nathan Leopold participated in during his prison years, probably the most valuable—both to mankind and himself—was the malaria research project, begun in September, 1945.[4] A group of research scientists, directed by Dr. Alf S. Alving of the University of Chicago, were seeking a cure for malaria, the tropical disease which afflicted many American soldiers fighting the Japanese during World War II.

Dr. Alving planned to use prisoner volunteers, who would submit themselves to bites from infected mosquitoes, then have various drugs used on them in an effort to discover a cure. Leopold, then attached to the medical section of the prison, enthusiastically embraced the program and devoted long hours to it as he had earlier with the prison correspondence school. He served as one of the test supervisors and eventually offered himself as a bite victim. The scientists identified SN-13276, or pentaquine, as an effective malarial cure. Leopold, therefore, became one of the first humans ever cured of malaria by a safe, usable drug. The discovery came too late for utilization in the Pacific during World War II, but another and less toxic version of the drug (SN-13272, or primaquine) became an important remedy during the Korean War. Leopold later called the malaria project "the finest thing that happened since I was in prison."[5] (Malaria has not been cured entirely, however, and research on the disease continues.)

In 1961 free-lance writer Charles Remsberg would interview Dr. Alving and his assistant, Willie Bennett, for an article he was writing for *The Kiwanis Magazine* of convict contributions to medical research.[6] Remsberg had obtained the impression from reading *Life Plus 99 Years* that Leopold had made an important contribution to the project and said so. Alving and Bennett looked at each other and chuckled. "I cannot recall the exact words used," says Remsberg, "but apparently Leopold interfered with the smooth running of the research program by engaging the prisoner guinea pigs in homosexual acts. He capitalized on his access to the prison hospital that his malaria work gave him for that purpose. Alving gave the distinct impression that Leopold was more interested in what he could get out of the experiment homosexually than in any 'contribution to mankind' as Leopold's press agentry suggested. By manner and comment, Alving's assistant made clear that he agreed with this assessment."

(Later, Elmer Gertz would approach Dr. Alving to get him to appear in Leopold's behalf at a parole hearing. Gertz found the physician unwilling to do so. He deprecated Leopold's contribution to the malaria project and said others had contributed more. "Something disturbs him!" Gertz wrote Leopold about his meeting with Dr. Alving, apparently not knowing what.[7])

Gene Lovitz spoke with other prisoners about Nathan Leopold's reputation as a homosexual. Lovitz never located anyone willing to confess carnal knowledge of Leopold, but several convicts supposedly knew *others* who had been involved intimately with him. One told of how Leopold had committed homosexual acts with his cellmate. Lovitz learned Leopold's *modus operandi:* As an X ray technician, Leopold had access to the prison medical records. At his leisure he could thumb through the photographs of new inmates. Any who appealed to him could be called in for X ray examinations. X rays were taken behind two doors which could be locked for complete privacy. Lovitz emphasized that Leopold was not promiscuous, that he was very selective whom he chose.

A legend had built up around Nathan Leopold among the prisoners just as it had on the outside. Lovitz heard from other convicts that Leopold had ghost-written Warden Ragen's book for him—he had not. He heard that the shower where Loeb died had been welded shut—it was not. Supposedly money for the defense of James Day came from a trust fund established by Jacob Franks—it did not. Rumors concerning Leopold's homosexual activity may similarly have been false, as Lovitz is quick to point out. On the other hand, the Hulbert and Bowman report had documented Leopold's early homosexual activity as well as an enormous sex drive; a state penitentiary does not offer an atmosphere in which a previous homosexual would be likely to change. Nathan Leopold's official prison file shows no record of homosexuality, which means either that Gene Lovitz's suspicions of him were unfounded or that Leopold was never caught.

Although prison officials had promised no favors, many of those who had volunteered for the malaria project did so expecting it might result in time cut from their sentences. Leopold hoped that might be the case with him, too, despite the insistence by so many in 1924 (including Judge Caverly) that he *never* be released from prison. Leopold had assiduously avoided the press for nearly a quarter century, feeling they would do nothing more than exploit his crime; now he began a conscious, calculated, but subtle upgrading of his public image. When *Life* magazine arrived to photograph the malaria project, he posed for pictures. He did the same in 1946, when the newspapers became interested in the nearly 400 convicts who voluntarily signed contracts donating their eyes on death to an eye bank. (There was a catch: The convicts would have to die in prison for the eye bank to obtain the eyes. Very few did.)

"Every bit of the enormous amount of publicity I had received over a period of twenty years had been bad," wrote Leopold. "The one thing I was known for was being a kidnapper and murderer. That I was, all right, but I was more than that. I was a human being too."[8]

In February, 1947, Governor Dwight Green asked the Illinois Parole Board to review the cases of the malaria project volunteers, a total of 441 men. Nearly half this number already were eligible for parole. Many received immediate releases. Others received reduction in their sentence. The remaining volunteers, including Nathan Leopold, had not yet served their minimum time. They needed to apply for commutation of their sentences which required further interviews and examinations by psychiatrists, sociologists, and criminologists. Leopold remarked that the average psychiatric interview of those involved lasted only six or eight minutes. In his case, however, the psychiatrists spent six hours, in three sessions, on the interview. Leopold, even in later years, continued to fascinate the headshrinkers.[9]

Leopold hoped that the parole board might act during the regime of Governor Green, a Republican up for reelection in the fall of 1948. The parole board, however, postponed his hearing until April, 1949. Everyone had expected Presidential candidate Thomas Dewey to defeat Harry Truman and sweep other Republican candidates into office with him, but Truman upset Dewey. The Democratic candidate, Adlai Stevenson, replaced Green as governor of Illinois.

Sentiment a quarter century earlier had run strongly against any possible parole for Leopold or Loeb. "If at any time in the next twenty years, young Loeb and Leopold are released on any pretext whatsoever," editorialized the Chicago *Daily Journal,* "the theory of equality before the law will get a jolt that will make criminal administration in this community all but impossible."[10] The *Journal,* however, no longer stood guard, having ceased publication. Clarence Darrow also had died, although his words during the 1924 hearing were remembered: "We have said to the public, and to this court, that neither the parents nor the friends, nor the attorneys would want these boys released. They should be permanently isolated from society."[11] And in the records folder of Nathan Leopold, the statement of State's Attorney Robert E. Crowe, no longer in office but still living, remained: "In malice, premeditation, and deliberation, the crime of these defendants is unequalled in the criminal history of the state. I desire to emphasize most emphatically the absolute necessity from the standpoint of the safety of society that these degenerate murderers be imprisoned for the entire period of their natural lives."[12]

The parole board held a public hearing in Springfield on April 12, 1949. Cook County State's Attorney John Boyle opposed Leopold's parole application. Ten days later the board met in Stateville but did not announce its decision until September 22. That day, figuring that the press might receive the news before he heard through official channels, Leopold returned to his cell and turned on the radio. On the six o'clock news the announcer said that Leopold's sentence had been commuted from ninety-nine to eighty-five years. Governor Stevenson said, "The commutation in this case was recommended and is being made pursuant to a program to reward prisoners who voluntarily risked their lives in malaria experiments for the armed services."

The reduction of Leopold's sentence from ninety-nine to eighty-five years may have seemed trivial to those unfamiliar with parole law. Actually, it was anything but that. Leopold had received a sentence of life plus ninety-nine years, but life did not necessarily mean life, nor ninety-nine years mean a full ninety-nine years. In Illinois at that time all prison sentences were subject to reduction depending on a prisoner's behavior. A prisoner sentenced to prison for life actually becomes eligible for parole in twenty years. Leopold technically had become parolable under his life term, but he still had the ninety-nine-year sentence to serve.

He need not serve all that time either. A person sentenced to prison for a specified length of time becomes eligible for parole when one-third of that sentence has been served. In Leopold's case this would have meant thirty-three years, or in 1957. Fortunately, when Judge Caverly sentenced Leopold to prison, he made no stipulation that the sentences be served consecutively—that is, one after another. Instead, Leopold was able to serve them concurrently. While saying publicly that Leopold should *never* get out of prison, the judge, consciously or unconsciously, permitted an early parole. Judge Caverly's true intentions would be subject to interpretation long after his death.

Thus, the reduction from ninety-nine to eighty-five years was anything but arbitrary. It permitted Leopold to become eligible for parole in January, 1953, at a time when Governor Stevenson would be either out of office or safely beginning his second term with four more years to serve. As it turned out, since Stevenson sought the Presidency rather than a second term as governor, the former was the case. As Leopold himself would note, all matters involving his parole would be determined on political, not humanistic, grounds.

On January 8, 1953, a three-man committee of the five-man parole board met in Stateville to review Nathan Leopold's case. Joseph D. Lohman, a Northwestern University professor and an enlightened criminologist, served as chairman. Albert Manus and Samuel Arndt accompanied him. Attorney William Friedman represented Leopold at the parole hearing. He had known his client and Loeb prior to their imprisonment and often played tennis on Loeb's court. Nine witnesses spoke in favor of Leopold, including Professor W. F. Byron of the Northwestern University criminology department, who said, "In my opinion Leopold is a good risk and society would gain from his freedom."[13]

Leopold also had significant opposition. John Gutknecht, now state's attorney for Cook County, became the latest in a succession of those to take up Crowe's burden. Gutknecht admitted both Leopold's rehabilitation and the fact that his release posed no danger to society. He considered that irrelevant, since he had become a "symbol." If Leopold were released, reasoned the state's attorney, judges would be afraid to sentence defendants to life when faced with similar cases and would have to resort to capital punishment. "A parole for Leopold would be a terrible mistake," he claimed, "and one with harmful social effects that would far outweigh any individual gains to one particular criminal. Society owes Leopold nothing."

Gutknecht's assistant, Richard Austin (who had been a classmate of Leopold at the University of Chicago), asked that the parole board not aggravate two mistakes made at the hearing in 1924: (1) that the death penalty was not inflicted, and (2) that the sentences were not made consecutive instead of concurrent. "You can understand the motive of a man who kills a policeman to escape arrest," he said. "But this is a case of murder for murder's sake alone. This is a murder committed for mental stimulation by one of the highest IQ's ever to occupy a cell in this prison."

Leopold spoke for thirty minutes and was asked the motive for his crime. "I couldn't give a motive which makes sense to me," he responded. "It was the act of a child—a simpleton kid. A very bizarre act. I don't know why I did it. I'm a different man now."

Robert E. Crowe did not attend the hearing. "I said all I could say at the time they both pleaded guilty," Crowe, now retired, commented to reporters. "I thought at the time they ought to hang. I still think the same way. There were no extenuating circumstances; it was a brutal murder."

Republican William Stratton replaced Adlai Stevenson as governor of Illinois only four days after the parole hearing. Governor Stratton probably could have quietly permitted the already-convened parole board to complete its action on the Leopold case without fear of undue criticism. He chose not to assume a passive role, however. Within two hours after assuming office, he removed Lohman and Arndt from the parole board, thereby eliminating two of the three committeemen who had heard Leopold's plea.[14]

The complete five-man board heard Leopold again in May. State's Attorney Gutknecht continued actively to oppose Leopold's release. Apparently not satisfied with the testimony already given, Gutknecht sent a telegram to the chairman of the parole board repeating his contention that Leopold had become a symbol and a legend. "Too many have been punished too much more for doing much less to make any additional mercy for Leopold other than a mistake in its effect on the public and their attitude toward law enforcement."[15]

The Stratton parole board apparently agreed. It met a few days later and not only rejected Leopold's parole request, but continued his case until May, 1965, a period of twelve years! This was the longest continuance in Illinois history and proved that the impact of Nathan Leopold and Richard Loeb's crime had not been forgotten.

Victor I. Knowles, the new chairman, presented the majority opinion of the five-man Illinois Parole Board. He said the board did not think Leopold had sufficiently rehabilitated himself, stating that Leopold had been a "con man" in the penitentiary, meaning a person who got things for himself without going beyond the rules. He also said that the circumstances of the crime weighed against a parole. Judge Caverly was remembered as saying the two murderers of Bobby Franks should never be permitted to return to society. Clarence Darrow had said the same. Of course, both Darrow and Caverly had indicated by their actions, and by words at other times, that they thought otherwise.[16]

Leopold accepted the verdict as might a defeated political candidate, who knows he will face the voters again. "I am naturally somewhat disappointed," he said. "I had hoped the board would see fit to parole me, but since it hasn't, I can accept its decision as gracefully as possible and hope that some time a board will feel my debt is paid."

Six months after the parole hearing Nathan Leopold's brother Mike died. Nathan's father had visited him in prison until his death in 1929, and afterward Mike assumed that duty. Leopold had a visitor every visiting period. His brother Sam remained distant but did visit and write on occasion.

Nathan Leopold, however, would have many visitors in prison during the next few years. Through his attempts to obtain freedom, he had reestablished himself as a celebrity in the eyes of the general public. His efforts to rehabilitate his image were bearing fruit. Once the brutal murderer of a defenseless boy, he now had become a remorseful political victim in the classic Dreyfusian mold. During the years he had served in prison a new generation had grown to maturity, having heard of his crime only second hand.

One visitor who appeared at Stateville during this period was Meyer Levin, now an author and living in New York. For years since his apprenticeship with the Chicago *Daily News,* Levin had wanted to write something about the Franks murder. It was, he would state, "one of those subjects I had for years carried in back of my mind, as something that would one day come ripe. The Leopold-Loeb case. A crime without reason, a Nietzschean superman exercise, the harbinger of our entire murderous era." In 1954 he obtained a contract from McGraw-Hill to write a novel based on the Franks murder case.[17]

Levin began his novel by researching it as he might a work of nonfiction. He traveled to Chicago, where in the morgue files of his old newspaper he found, among a mountain of clippings about the case, a feature story he had written about the courtroom arraignment, centering on Nathan Leopold's father. Gossip columnist Tony Weitzel spotted Levin at work, inquired about his mission, and included an item in his column the next day.

Ralph Newman, proprietor of the Abraham Lincoln Bookstore in Chicago, read the item. Newman, a close friend of his brother Mike's, was encouraging Leopold at the time to write his autobiography, which Leopold had begun at the suggestion of Father Weir and Rabbi Louis Binstock. Leopold had two purposes in mind: to occupy his time and serve as therapy, and to attract public attention to his case and gain sympathy for his attempt to gain parole.

According to Levin, Newman called the *Daily News* and spoke with Levin, suggesting that some sort of collaboration be arranged. (Newman, however, believes Levin initiated the contact.) Levin soon received word that Newman had arranged for him to visit the prison. He rode to Stateville in a chauffeured limousine, the Leopold family car, which was regularly supplied for visits to the penitentiary. Driving the car (although Levin did not realize it at the time) was Sven Englund, still in the employ of the family.

Levin would describe the visit to Stateville later in an autobiographical book of his own called *The Obsession:* "Nathan Leopold appeared, almost as in a stage entrance, in the raised doorway. In his neat prison-gray shirt and trousers, a distinguished-looking man who might have stepped out of a laboratory. He was exactly my age; both of us had been college precocities. Though there had been reports of serious illness, he looked plump and well. Entirely self-possessed, he had in his bearing an air of breeding that was also noticeable in his manner of speech."[18]

Leopold and Levin entered into a discussion that the former would later insist took less than an hour and the latter claimed actually lasted much longer. They spoke mostly about the business aspects of publication. "Whenever I tried to turn to anything related to the crime," Levin would recall, "he smoothly changed back to questions about percentages, film rights, and syndication." Leopold seemed interested in having Levin collaborate with him on the book he had begun, but one problem got in the way. Leopold did not want to write about the crime itself.

"I had no desire for any sensational retelling of the story," Levin would insist afterward, "but was interested in the psychological approach. With him alone there rested an opportunity to probe this area. Just as he had during the war volunteered his body for anti-malaria experiments, here was a case where he could volunteer his inner knowledge to humanity. Others, as well as he, had undergone the anti-malaria experiment, but in this, he alone could provide a body of material that would enlarge our understanding of human behavior. That was where my interest lay. If he would collaborate on such a book, I would drop my novel and concentrate all I had to offer as a writer in his project."

Leopold, however, felt that a retelling of the crime would have a negative effect on his parole situation, and, indeed, told from his point of view, this might have been the case. Thus, their discussion and further negotiations with the Leopold family resulted in an agreement that Levin would help Leopold write a book about his prison experiences. It was also agreed that if the book did not include details on the crime, Levin would be free later to write his novel. But Levin secretly hoped that as he gained Leopold's confidence, he would convince him to change his mind and discuss the crime.

Nathan Leopold eventually did change his mind, but not the way Meyer Levin hoped. Levin received a letter from Ralph Newman explaining that Leopold had decided to handle the prison book in another way. The *Saturday Evening Post* was interested in Leopold, although not in his first-person account. They wanted him to cooperate with their premiere contributor, John Bartlow Martin, who would do a series of articles based on Leopold's reminiscences. The magazine understandably desired exclusive access to Leopold.

When he learned of the *Post* project, Levin considered abandoning his own but later talked with Martin and came to an agreement. "In effect, we divided Leopold up," recalls Levin. "He was going to write mostly about Leopold in prison, and I planned to write about what happened before he got there."

In April, 1955, a four-part series about Nathan Leopold appeared in the *Post,* written by Martin, attracting considerable attention to, and sympathy for, the prisoner. The articles presented a straightforward account of Leopold in prison and were similar in many respects to Leopold's own book, which came out three years later—although Martin claims he never saw a manuscript of that book.[19] Levin, who thought the *Post* articles pictured Leopold as a "saintly savant," continued work on his novel, originally titled *Compulsion and Free Will,* but later simply *Compulsion.*

Levin's book was rejected by McGraw-Hill, which may have believed that Leopold's own impending book would kill demand for a fictional re-creation of the crime. Levin approached several other publishers with his manuscript only to be rebuffed until finally Simon & Schuster agreed to publish *Compulsion,* which appeared in 1956 and became an immediate best-seller, selling 130,000 copies in hard cover.

Leopold, meanwhile, was doing his best to suppress publication. In his autobiography he admits that his attorney wrote one publisher who was considering the manuscript (Leopold does not specify which one), saying that if it published Levin's book, it would do so at its own peril, since Leopold would sue for any libelous statements. "That publisher did not bring out the book," wrote Leopold, "whether because of the warning, I do not, of course, know."[20]

Pocket Books later published a paperback edition that sold more than 1,000,000 copies. Still later the book became a Broadway play and a Hollywood movie and enabled Meyer Levin, who had published a number of previous books without becoming either rich or famous, to free himself from salaried jobs and devote himself to writing.

Whether because of some sense of obligation or not, Meyer Levin campaigned actively for Leopold's release as he went on radio and television talk shows promoting his book. He also published an article in the May, 1957, issue of *Coronet* titled "Leopold Should Be Freed!" In it he suggested that if Nathan Leopold had committed the crime of the century, releasing him could be the correction of the century.[21]

Later Levin would appear at one of Leopold's clemency hearings and say: "I didn't make this a crusade, a novel for his release. I made it an objective study and withheld my opinion, and people couldn't tell from the book how I felt about his release." In *Compulsion* Levin had renamed Richard Loeb Artie Straus. Nathan Leopold became Judd Steiner. Bobby Franks was Paulie Kessler. The plot of the book followed true-life events closely, and Levin even reprinted the kidnap letters and used dialogue from the transcript of the hearing. But Levin went beyond even the Hulbert and Bowman report in attempting to look into the minds of the murderers and determine what compulsion had made them commit the crime. After the book was published, Levin lectured one night in Highland Park and afterward a young niece from the Franks family approached him. She said, "In our family we have always hated these boys. After I read your book, I felt also that this man should be paroled."[22]

Leopold continued work on his autobiography, to be titled *Life Plus 99 Years.* He and Ralph Newman had asked Elmer Gertz, a Civil War buff as well as an accomplished Chicago attorney, to handle any legal matters that arose from the book. Gertz had met Leopold's brother Mike at meetings of the Civil War Round Table, to which he and Newman belonged, but he had never met Nathan Leopold. Nonetheless, he soon found himself involved in Leopold's efforts to win release. Gertz, who later in his career also would defend *Tropic of Cancer* author Henry Miller, and Jack Ruby, the murderer of Lee Harvey Oswald, knew the Franks case well. He was of the same generation as Leopold and Levin and had also attended the University of Chicago. While many boys of his generation had taken Babe Ruth or Red Grange as their idols, Gertz most admired Clarence Darrow. He admits he became fascinated with the thought that he might bring to conclusion what he considered to be "Darrow's most famous case."[23]

"Mike and I discussed the matter of an attorney when it came time for the parole hearing," recalls Ralph Newman. "We both agreed that we didn't want any 'name' lawyer involved. The family had done that more than two decades before, and this time it had to be a low-key representation. Elmer was a University of Chicago student, and although he had not known Babe as a student, it would sound better to have one of his university contemporaries represent him."

Gertz visited Leopold in prison for the first time on May 16, 1957, and later said, "He was soft-spoken, smiling most of the time, humorous, highly articulate, polite, and friendly." Gertz found it difficult to believe that this was the monster who had murdered Bobby Franks. The attorney had previously thought Leopold had lead Loeb, but now he decided it must have been the other way around.

In 1957 Leopold attempted once more to obtain his release. Petitions for parole rehearings in 1955 and 1956 had resulted in rejection, so a new approach was attempted. "We thought we would change the tactics by asking for some form of clemency from the Governor," Gertz explains. The parole board met in the state capital on July 9, 1957, to hear petitions for executive clemency. Gertz appeared as attorney along with a number of other Leopold allies, including his foster brother Bal, Abel Brown, and Arnold Maremont. (Leopold stayed in Stateville.) Also present was Meyer Levin. Although the success of Levin's book *Compulsion* had contributed to a reawakening of interest in Nathan Leopold, Gertz felt Levin should not testify, and told him so. Levin testified anyway, and Gertz later acknowledged he made a good witness.

The board postponed its decision until the fall, and in the interim Governor Stratton received numerous letters about the case, most (according to Gertz) urging Leopold's release. One came from Thomas F. Eagleton, then circuit attorney of St. Louis, who at the 1972 Democratic national convention would be selected by presidential candidate George McGovern as his running mate (only to have the nomination yanked away from him when word leaked out about his having undergone treatment in a mental institution). Finally, in November, Governor Stratton made an announcement, denying executive clemency, but suggesting they file a petition for a rehearing on the question of pardon. Despite the twelve-year continuance, the parole board (by a split vote) granted the rehearing. In February, 1958, Leopold appeared once more before the board. Elmer Gertz believed that Leopold's inability, or unwillingness, to express a motive for his crime in his previous hearing had hurt his case. This time Leopold came up with an answer: "The question of what motive impelled me to take part in the crime has arisen frequently. At my last appearance before the board, May 1, 1953, Mr. Bookwalter asked me, why I had done what I did? I couldn't answer him then; I can't do much better now, though I have spent the four years since reflecting upon it. I committed my crime because I admired Loeb extravagantly, because I didn't want to be a quitter, and because I wanted to show that I had the nerve to do what he insisted on doing. They are, admittedly, not very reasonable motives. They don't, now, make sense even to me. It is not an easy thing, even with my liberty possibly at stake, to throw blame on the dead. And it is, perhaps what you would expect when the surviving one of the two defendants throws the major part of the blame on the one who is dead. But I cannot answer Mr. Bookwalter's question honestly in any other way—and answer, I feel I must. This horrible crime was not a thing I had the least desire to commit. But I was a boy of nineteen, not old enough to vote, not old enough to make a legal contract. And I was completely carried away by my admiration for Loeb. I had not then learned to control the fierce emotions of adolescence; I did what he wanted. It is fortunate that these statements do not rest upon my unsupported word, but are attested by Mr. Darrow in a book written four years before Loeb's death, when he could not know which of us would survive the other."[24]

(Darrow had written in his *The Story of My Life:* "It seemed that Loeb had gotten it into his head that he could commit a perfect crime, which should involve kidnapping, murder, and ransom. He had unfolded his scheme to Leopold because he needed someone to help him plan and carry it out. For this plot Leopold had no liking whatever, but he had an exalted opinion of Loeb." Darrow also identified Loeb as the wielder of the chisel.[25])

During the hearing Elmer Gertz and board member Robert J. Branson would argue as to where the actual blame lay in the Franks murder case. "How do you justify the fact that Leopold and Loeb differ in who struck the boy?" Branson asked.

"But in the trial, it was testified that Loeb committed the actual act," Gertz replied.

"And Loeb died saying that Leopold hit him," insisted Branson. "Now he is dead and no one can speak for him."[26]

Actually Branson was mistaken. Loeb died saying nothing about the matter. He had made no public comment between the completion of the hearing in 1924 and his death in 1936. The question of who struck the fatal blow remains unanswered today. The weight of circumstantial evidence, including testimony by Carl Ulvigh, who supposedly saw Loeb driving, supports the contention that Leopold wielded the chisel. All of Darrow's alienists, however, seemed to believe Loeb the one. Unless some unsuspected document should appear wherein either one of the two confessed his true involvement, no one can be completely sure. It appears, however, to have been Richard Loeb.

Leopold's petition for rehearing, prepared by himself and Goetz, had contained 9,000 words. In it he denied that Judge Caverly had believed he should forever be denied parole, explaining that Caverly could have imposed a nonparolable sentence, but instead selected the parolable one of life plus ninety-nine years.

"Who could say with any degree of assurance that Judge Caverly's opinion would still be the same if he were alive and had at his disposal all the facts concerning me in the last thirty years?"

Leopold also spoke about a Catholic nun who several years before had communicated with his brother Mike, identifying herself as having taken care of Judge Caverly during one of his illnesses. She had claimed the judge had discussed the sentence with her and had believed the major guilt to have been Loeb's. Gertz was able to introduce the nun's supposed comment into the record because the rules of a parole hearing do not prohibit what in a court of law would be judged hearsay evidence. The nun's superior had forbidden her from testifying in person.

Leopold claimed Darrow had hoped for his release, quoting a letter from the attorney dated October 3, 1928. "I don't know how anybody else feels about it," Darrow had written, "but I shall always cling to the idea that sometime you will be out."[27] He said Nathan Leopold, Sr., hoped the same, having promised only not to use improper methods to obtain the release. Bobby Franks' sister, Josephine, married now, had been asked if she were in favor of the release and while offering no support said at least she would not attempt to block it.

The hearing was a repetition of the two previous occasions with Leopold's friends (with poet Carl Sandburg now added) and his enemies (including a new state's attorney, Benjamin Adamowski) appearing to restate their views. Sandburg had become interested in the case partly through the intercession of Gene Lovitz, who had written a biography of the poet after being released from prison.[28] Sandburg said, "I never thought it would get to the time I would make a winter morning journey to Joliet to face the Board of Paroles, to plead for a Chicago Jewish boy who at nineteen was out of his mind." Elmer Gertz commented afterward that Carl Sandburg rambled a bit, "but in the swell of words one could sense something magnificent."[29] Nathan Leopold also testified at his own hearing and returned to his cell to await the decision.

It came in two weeks: After thirty-three years in prison, Nathan Leopold had been granted a parole.

26 Compulsion

Ultimately, Leopold's life had to be seen as triumphant. He overcame everything—himself, first of all, and then thirty-three years in prison, and then the ongoing contempt of his fellows.

—M. W. NEWMAN[1]

On the morning of March 13, 1958, a group of several dozen people met at the bridge over the lagoon in Jackson Park from which Clarence Darrow's ashes had been scattered exactly twenty years before. A cold wind blew off Lake Michigan, and the group huddled together for warmth. Darrow had promised that if there were an afterlife, he would try to give some sign, but none of the people gathered expected any, and if he gave one, they failed to recognize it. They came only to pay their respects to the memory of the famous attorney.

Arthur Weinberg, editor of a book of Darrow's speeches, *Attorney for the Damned,* threw a wreath into the lagoon's quiet waters. The Reverend David Cole, pastor of the First Universalist Church, offered a prayer, admitting that it seemed presumptuous to pray for a professed atheist. (Actually, Darrow had claimed to be an agnostic rather than an atheist.) "We should pray, however, that he lived among us," said the Reverend Mr. Cole. "Let ours be a prayer of thanksgiving that he stood for what he did—the right of every man to be free from fear."

That same morning Nathan F. Leopold, Jr., stepped through the front gate of Stateville, free for the first time since the day Sergeants William Crot and Frank A. Johnson appeared at his door to ask him to accompany them to the LaSalle Hotel where State's Attorney Robert E. Crowe wanted to question him about a pair of glasses. *Time* magazine had noted in a recent issue that 33 years, 275 days, and 18 hours had passed between the time the chisel smashed Bobby Franks' skull and the official notice of Leopold's parole.[2] Robert E. Crowe had not survived that long. The state's attorney had died in a convalescent home on the North Side of

Chicago in January, at age seventy-eight, never having publicly abandoned his position that Judge Caverly had erred.[3]

(Elmer Gertz, however, contends that Crowe did soften his position toward the end and considered writing a letter to the parole board favoring Leopold's release. He finally decided against it, feeling it would look as though he had sold out, but reportedly told Mike Leopold that such a letter would be available after his death. No such letter ever was found.[4])

Leopold wore a blue suit, a tweed topcoat, and a smile. The suit and topcoat had been made in the prison tailor shop. The smile was his own. Ralph Newman, Elmer Gertz, Warden Joseph Ragen, and two assistant wardens accompanied Leopold, who had in his pockets $1 given him as bus fare to Chicago, $25 as the going-away stipend that each departing prisoner received, and $613 from the fund in his prison account.

The smile faded as he saw more than a hundred people awaiting him, most of them photographers and reporters. The photographers began thrusting their cameras at him. The reporters began throwing questions. "No, I'm not jittery. Not at all," he responded to one questioner. Someone else asked him if he felt like a free man. "No, I feel hemmed in," said Leopold, and everybody laughed. He walked toward a waiting battery of microphones and began to read a statement he had prepared in advance, asking for compassion so he could live the remainder of his life in peace. "I appeal as solemnly as I know how to you, and to your editors, and to your publishers, and to society at large, to agree that the only piece of news about me is that I have ceased to be news," he said. One of the conditions of the parole had been that he avoid undue publicity.

But it seemed as though those standing before him had not heard or, if they heard, had not understood or, if they understood, still chose to ignore his plea. As members of the press they had come to get a story, and they would get it whether or not Leopold wanted them to.

The questions began again as soon as he stopped talking. "Do you think prison does a man any good?" asked one reporter. "Are you happy to go to Puerto Rico?" asked another, referring to where Leopold had obtained a job. "What will you do after completing your five-year parole period?"

Leopold responded calmly; then Gertz pressed closer to him, whispering something in his ear. "I simply can't answer any more questions," pleaded Leopold. "I cannot violate my agreement with the parole board."

Then he climbed into the front seat of a white 1958 Oldsmobile, a rented car driven by Ralph Newman. Leopold had spent thirty-three years in prison for what happened in a rented car, and he would leave prison in one. Gertz climbed in beside him, and the car sped off toward Route 66 and Chicago.

Leopold's return drive to Chicago proved almost as harrowing as his ride to Joliet thirty-three years previous. Nearly a dozen cars full of reporters and photographers relentlessly pursued the white Oldsmobile even though Newman drove as fast as 80 mph in an effort to lose them. Then a blue Cadillac pulled alongside the car containing Leopold, its driver making gestures of some sort to the passengers within. The Cadillac slowed, then attempted to cut off the following cars, including one driven by Ted Gertz, the twenty-one-year-old son of Leopold's attorney. The two cars scraped fenders. The Cadillac eventually stopped. Joseph Egelhof, reporter for the *Tribune,* spoke with the Cadillac's driver, who admitted to being a former prison friend of Leopold's trying to prevent reporters from harassing him.

Whether because of the excitement or because of the motion of the car, Leopold became ill. Newman halted the Oldsmobile while Leopold vomited in a ditch beside the highway. Again they stopped. And again. Each time Newman's car paused to allow his passenger to retch in the gutter, the entire caravan pulled to the side of the road to witness the act. Photographers took pictures which when later published would outrage Leopold's friends.[5]

The reporters also recorded Leopold's weak stomach, failing to agree, however, on how often he became sick. Gladys Erickson of Chicago's *American* described Leopold as vomiting three times. The *Tribune* said four. John Justin Smith of the *Daily News* counted four times. Hugh Hough of the *Sun-Times* agreed with Smith's count, but in a story several years later that same newspaper changed its count to six. Elmer Gertz in *A Handful of Clients* seemed to corroborate this last count, while being understandably miffed over the invasion of privacy.

Thus, regurgitating, did Nathan F. Leopold, Jr., return to the world.

The Oldsmobile paused at Ralph Newman's Oak Park home, where Leopold changed into a better suit than his prison attire. They drove then to the Lake Shore Drive apartment of Leopold's former University of Chicago classmate Abel Brown, who had once planned to spend the summer of 1924 traveling in Europe with him. Brown had not turned his back on his friend and had maintained contact with him in prison, testifying at his commutation hearing. Now he offered his home as Leopold's first refuge. His wife served sukiyaki that night, a food she knew he had not got in prison. Leopold had not dined sumptuously since those days in the Cook County Jail when he and Loeb had sent out to Stein's Restaurant for all their meals, a luxury not allowed at Stateville.

The reporters maintained their vigil in the lobby and even in the hallway outside Brown's apartment, asking neighbors to permit them the use of their telephones to call stories in to their newspapers. In the morning they trailed Leopold and Gertz as they walked in the park. Leopold had hoped to visit the graves of his parents and his brother Mike, but he abandoned the idea because of the press.

That night he boarded a plane with W. Harold Row, executive secretary of the Brethren Service Commission, a church group with headquarters in Elgin, Illinois. The Church of the Brethren, a small Protestant sect, sponsored a hospital in Castaner, a tiny community up in the hills of Puerto Rico, about three hours' drive from San Juan. Leopold planned to work at the hospital as an X ray technician for the nominal sum of $10 a week plus room and board. As he checked his bags in at the counter, a stranger approached him and said, "I hope you enjoy your trip and I wish you happiness."[6]

Leopold supposedly had selected the small distant village to avoid as much as possible of the glare of publicity. Certainly he could not remain in Chicago and do so. One of the unusual conditions of his parole was that he not grant any interviews. As it was, he had granted very few since 1924, and only when it suited his purpose. It was not that Nathan Leopold disliked publicity; he, like many other celebrities, disliked *unfavorable* publicity. He may have sensed that the mere fact of his inaccessibility would make him even more interesting to the general public.

He also knew he had become a legend in his time, and he hoped that he could continue to shape that legend in his favor. He knew he never could escape the shadow of Bobby Franks, but he felt he might be able to soften its edges. A garrulous Nathan Leopold openly courting the limelight would have been intolerable, particularly to his own generation. A Nathan Leopold fleeing the spotlight somehow seemed tolerable, human, almost likeable. Yet despite his supposed attempts to avoid publicity, Nathan Leopold would see his name almost continuously in the news for the remainder of his life.

A year and a half after his release from prison, Leopold sued

Meyer Levin. Through his attorney Elmer Gertz, Leopold filed suit against the book *Compulsion,* its author, its publishers, and the producers and distributors of the movie based on the book. He sought $2,970,000. Meyer Levin reacted angrily, considering the suit an outrageous attempt a third of a century after the deed to collect the ransom money for Bobby Franks.[7]

Leopold disliked *Compulsion* intensely—or so he claimed. (According to Gertz, he read it four times while still in prison, even though it had been against prison regulations for him to obtain a copy.[8]) He particularly disliked Levin's characterization of his mother, who he felt had been slightingly handled. And he claimed to have been horrified that the book had been published on the thirty-fifth anniversary of his mother's death, causing him a double sorrow. Levin, to simplify the structure of his novel, had combined Leopold's two brothers, Mike and Sam, into a single character named Max. Since Leopold liked the one brother and disliked the other, this too displeased him. He also objected to Levin's fictional treatment of his father, of his Aunt Birdie, and of the Susan Lurie character, whom Levin named Ruth.

Leopold complained, "The insidious, devastating thing about the book, as I see it, is Mr. Levin's consummate artistry. He has taken a large amount of fact, and to it he has added an even larger amount of fiction—or pure balderdash. And he has done it in such superbly artistic fashion that the seams don't show. No general reader can possibly know what is true and what contrived. I confess that I, on several occasions, had to stop and think hard to be sure whether certain details were true or imaginary."[9]

But one suspects that Nathan Leopold was most angered that Meyer Levin had got into his brain, deeper even than had Darrow's alienists, uncovering motives that Leopold himself was not aware existed. At the end of *Compulsion* a student named Willie Weiss (who bears some superficial resemblance to Dick Rubel) becomes a psychiatrist and goes to Vienna to study with Sigmund Freud. He meets the narrator, Sid Silver (a composite of Alvin Goldstein, Howard Mayer, and even Meyer Levin himself), and spells out his version of the meaning of the crime. Weiss saw the chisel as a phallic symbol, a substitute penis. He saw the culvert into which the body of "Paulie Kessler" had been stuffed as a symbol of the womb. The hydrochloric acid poured on the body was not merely to make that body hard to identify, but to obliterate the evidence of a circumcised penis and thus his identity as a Jew and to allow "Judd Steiner" (Nathan Leopold) to kill the girl within himself. "If he wished he had never been born—wished he had never been born as a girl kind of boy—then the gesture was complete: he had exorcised the curse on himself. He had become unborn, in the womb of the mother who was in the earth." So wrote Meyer Levin.[10]

"Another overwhelming thought came to me, changing the conception I had had until then of the crime," wrote Levin through his narrator Sid Silver. "'Then Judd was not merely Artie's accomplice. He wasn't there only because he was in love with Artie. He had to do the murder because of some compulsion in himself. Just the way Artie did.'"

It was probably this one paragraph, with its summation of Meyer Levin's view of Nathan Leopold's role in the killing of Bobby Franks, that disturbed Leopold the most. Over the years Leopold had carefully constructed a new image for himself. The public now believed—or at least Leopold wanted it to believe—that Loeb had wielded the actual blow, that he, Leopold, had gone along more or less for the thrill, to maintain his status with his partner, that he had actually attempted to stall Loeb and had taken part only reluctantly, and then with revulsion. This had become part of the legend of Leopold and Loeb. But Meyer Levin portrayed Leopold as equally guilty not only under the law for the murder of Bobby Franks, but under a higher justice.

And what of Richard Loeb? Had he merely not lived long enough to allow his public image to soften? Had James Day struck down Nathan Leopold instead, would Loeb have one day emerged from prison a symbol of rehabilitation?

Yet another factor may have motivated Leopold's suit: envy. The Chicago newspapers in 1924 had profited greatly from public interest in the Franks murder. Clarence Darrow had earned more than $30,000 for his defense. Crowe gained reelection as state's attorney after his stance as avenging angel. The horde of psychiatrists received fees of $250 a day for their efforts for or against him. Goldstein, Mulroy, Mankowski, and others responsible for the culprits' arrest shared a $6,000 reward. Meyer Levin's book had earned him more than $250,000 over a dozen years plus a measure of literary fame while Leopold's own autobiography sold fewer than 20,000 copies and was childish in its style. True, it had helped get him released from prison, but Nathan Leopold seemed obsessed with the notion that everyone had made money off his crime but himself.

Leopold, through his attorney Elmer Gertz, sought redress not because Levin had libeled him, as Leopold had warned publishers in his prepublication attempts to suppress the book, or embarrassed him (it hardly seems possible that one stripped so bare in public as Leopold had been by Darrow's alienists could ever be so embarrassed again), but because Levin had appropriated his literary property.

There was also the question of appropriation of his name. The publishers had identified *Compulsion* on its jacket as based on the famous Leopold and Loeb case. Meyer Levin admitted this also in his introduction to the book although not mentioning Leopold and Loeb by name. (He did name Darrow.) Twentieth Century-Fox, in advertising their film based on the book, had blatantly identified it with Leopold and Loeb.

Levin thought it monstrous that Leopold should expect to collect. "What a justification for himself and his dead friend Dickie Loeb!" he cried in anguish. "Wasn't he by this action making the very same boast that he and Dickie Loeb had made as a rationale for their murder: We are above the common laws as we are above the common run of mankind? It was an attitude that was to become the plague of our time."[11]

Elmer Gertz took a more reasoned approach to the matter. "We recognized that anyone had the right to write a biography, a history, or a purely factual account of newsworthy events and personalities," he wrote. "I had doubts, though, whether even a factual treatment of stale events should be protected, if done in bad faith. However, for the purpose of this proceeding we assumed that if Meyer Levin or anyone else had written a straight history, without sensationalism or fictionalizing or commercialization, he would be fully protected."[12]

During the legal jousting that occurred before the suit was presented to a judge, the attorneys on Levin's side (who included Ephraim London and Leon Despres for Simon & Schuster and Robert Bergstrom for Twentieth Century-Fox) obtained the right to depose Nathan Leopold. Hoping they could compel Leopold to come to them in Chicago, they were told by the court that they would have to travel to Puerto Rico at their own expense to question him. They also had to obtain a court order to get the family to release the transcript of the 1924 hearing, which had belonged to Clarence Darrow. Then they had to lug the bulky transcript—it filled a file drawer—all the way to San Juan. Beginning on November 15, 1960, and for almost a week, London and Bergstrom met with Leopold and Gertz in that city in a government office building. Also present were Gertz's associate, Harold R. Gordon, and court reporter Seymour Spanier.[13]

Leopold impressed London during the first three days of the deposition as arrogant and contemptuous of everybody, even his own attorney. While being questioned, Leopold made secret notes—in Sanskrit!

London went through *Compulsion* page by page, reading a section, then asking Leopold if it was factually accurate. Whenever Leopold denied the accuracy of a statement, London read him the appropriate section from the McKernan digest of the 1924 hearing to prove the novel's accuracy. Leopold claimed he and Loeb had burned down a shack, not a building. London quoted the record to show not only that it had been a building, but that there had been three of them. Leopold admitted there had been three—but added, "One of them was a shack." Leopold could not recall the fraternity house burglaries but granted they may have happened if the record so stated. He pleaded the passage of thirty-six years to explain his lapses of memory as to past crimes, yet seemed to have a photographic memory when it came to certain details, such as why he once had a laughing fit at the hearing.

When Bergstrom took over the examination, he produced a file drawer contained Darrow's transcript. Meticulously he questioned Leopold on the truth of different items of testimony. "Leopold seemed fascinated by his first opportunity to see the trial record," remarked Bergstrom later. "He would retire to a corner of the room to study portions of the testimony before returning to confirm them."

Levin's attorneys then produced copies of an even 100 newspaper stories on the case dating back to 1924 and again asked Leopold to verify their accuracy. One by one, Leopold branded them as inaccurate (as London and Bergstrom already knew).

During one of the recesses, Leopold approached Ephraim London and said, "You know, Mr. London, I'm beginning to see what you are trying to get at, and it's very interesting."

London thought that a patronizing statement, but at least it showed that Leopold had begun to understand the purpose of the cross-examination.

London and Bergstrom sought to combat a theory in law that you did not violate the right of privacy if you reported facts about an important event even though you revealed the name of a person, but if you wrote a fictional report and revealed the same facts, you could be held guilty of violating the right of privacy.

Leopold began to treat the opposition lawyers more as equals and warmed sufficiently to Ephraim London to invite him to dinner. London also attended one of his classes. London found him to be a dry, somewhat humorless teacher who had little empathy with his students despite their obvious desire to learn. "He was almost half-disinterested," said London, "which was curious because I would have imagined that was a role he would have enjoyed very much."

London was even more fascinated by Leopold after their dinner conversation. Their talk covered many subjects, including Leopold's former partner. "He was obviously still madly in love with Loeb," London recalls. "That was strange, because Loeb was clearly a criminal psychopath and Leopold was certainly not that. This was certainly a man of intelligence. He knew Loeb's limitations. And he still did not accept any of them. He was still deeply in love with him, yet from what I have read of Loeb I don't think he had the capacity to return that kind of affection."

During the examination Leopold agreed on most of the facts in the transcript of the 1924 hearing. There was one significant exception. London asked Leopold if it was not true that he had the king-slave fantasies described in *Compulsion.* Leopold agreed that he had. But when asked if it was not true that he had been the slave 90 percent of the time and the king 10 percent of the time, Leopold became visibly angry. "That's not true!" he snapped.

London quoted a passage from the transcript in which Darrow had said he was the slave 90 percent of the time, a figure the lawyer obtained from the Hulbert and Bowman report. "Drs. Bowman and Hulbert were mistaken," insisted Leopold, adding that he had fantasized himself as king 90 percent of the time and as slave only 10 percent of the time.

In seeking to correct the record, however, Nathan Leopold had unwittingly done damage to the legend that had its roots in these very psychiatric reports. According to the delicately woven tapestry constructed by Darrow's alienists, Richard Loeb had lived his fantasies by becoming the master criminal mind who planned the Franks kidnapping. Nathan Leopold had lived his fantasy by becoming a slave to Loeb and obeying his wishes to create a perfect crime. But if Leopold fantasized himself as a king, that upset the popular image of him as being the one led astray by his more evil companion.

Many who had sought to understand the relationship between Leopold and Loeb also overlooked the fact (documented by Hulbert and Bowman but not published) that Leopold was the aggressor in their homosexual acts, while Loeb played mainly a passive role. This was again put on the record during the Puerto Rico deposition:

> Q. You were aware that there was some kind of talk about that that the two of you had homosexual relations.
>
> A. Yes sir.
>
> Q. And you were aware of the fact that you were thought of as the aggressor in that relationship.

A. Yes sir.
Q. And as a matter of fact, that was true.
A. Yes.

Ephraim London considered it revealing that during the week-long cross-examination Leopold was willing to stand corrected on facts related to the crime but would not yield an inch on the interpretation of his fantasies. "The only thing that had any real importance to him was his fantasies, and not the terrible events of his life."

Later, after London returned to New York, he received a letter from Leopold. Leopold recalled London's mentioning he had a son seven or eight years old and wondered if he still had any old toys that he might be willing to donate to the children of Puerto Rico. One of the hospitals was holding a Christmas pageant, and Leopold wanted some gifts to give the children. *Nathan Leopold was playing the part of one of the three kings!*

On April 15, 1964, Judge Thomas Kluczynski handed down a summary judgment in favor of Nathan Leopold, citing as a precedent a case in which a blind girl had been awarded damages for the unauthorized use of her photograph in a dog food commercial. Elmer Gertz indicates in *A Handful of Clients* that he felt the case was a landmark decision. He quoted extensively from the judge's opinion that "freedom of speech and of the press does not encompass freedom to exploit commercially or 'make merchandise' of one's name or likeness in an advertisement."

But alas, Leopold was not awarded $2,970,000 in damages or even a fraction of that sum. The decision decided the merits of the case with the question of damages reserved for another hearing. Gertz suggested a settlement. The attorneys for the defendants voted and came within one vote of accepting the suggestion before finally deciding to continue as a matter of principle.

The case dragged on through the courts, with Levin becoming increasingly irate at what he considered a blatant attempt to suppress his work. When the stock of the paperback version of *Compulsion* was exhausted, Pocket Books declined to reprint it. Levin eventually arranged for a different paperback publisher (New American Library) to bring out another edition. But when professional and amateur acting groups desired to produce the play version of *Compulsion,* they found scripts difficult to obtain. On several occasions Levin supplied his own copies, urging groups to perform the play without royalty to him, insisting that the play was not involved in the suit. Twentieth Century-Fox, meanwhile, declined to pay Levin the last two installments on the movie rights until the case was settled.

Eventually the suit was placed on the docket of the Illinois Supreme Court, where it stalled because two of the seven judges had been asked to retire, after having been charged with bribery. A third, Judge Kluczynski, recently appointed from the lower court, excused himself. Eventually three more judges were appointed, and the court ruled against Nathan Leopold, deciding his right of privacy had not been violated by *Compulsion.* "Having encouraged public attention," wrote Justice Daniel P. Ward, "he cannot at his whim withdraw the events of his life from public scrutiny."[14]

Nathan Leopold had lost, but while doing so, he had extracted his pound of flesh from those he had accused of exploiting his property. Simon & Schuster, Twentieth Century-Fox, and Meyer Levin had to spend nearly $40,000 defending their position. Elmer Gertz was disappointed at the final verdict but consoled himself that the suit had prevented further sensationalization of Nathan Leopold's life for nearly ten years. "It brought him some peace," said Gertz.

27 Atonement

All I want is to find some quiet place where I can sink from sight and live quietly, and serve others to atone for my crime.

—NATHAN LEOPOLD[1]

On the tenth anniversary of his release from prison Nathan Leopold wrote Elmer Gertz and Abel Brown, his friend from college days, describing the decade as "just about perfect." At the time Leopold was married and living in Santurce, Puerto Rico.

"Merely to have my freedom restored was, in itself, the greatest single thing that could have happened in my life," wrote Leopold. "Nothing has ever been more important to me. Sometimes in prison and a number of times since my release I have tried to figure out at just what point in time the whole business has become worthwhile. If I had died the day after my release, obviously it would not have been worth-while to serve the thirty-three years. What about a week then? A month? A year? By certain esoteric calculations of my own, that wouldn't make sense to anyone else, I came to the conclusion that on September 15, 1963, I reached the point where it all became worthwhile: that the joy of being a free man again equalled the grief of those thirty-three years. Look at the nearly five years of pure profit I've accumulated since that date. I am now very happy that I did not avoid serving the thirty-three years by suicide."

Leopold then summarized the events and accomplishments of ten years of freedom. He had worked two years at the Church of the Brethren Hospital. He attended graduate school at the University of Puerto Rico, obtaining a master's degree. He taught at that university, did research in the social service program of Puerto Rico's department of health, worked for an urban renewal and housing agency, and did research in leprosy at the University of Puerto Rico's School of Medicine. He also published a book on ornithology titled *The Birds of Puerto Rico.*

"Well, how about society?" Leopold asked. "Negatively, at least I have not committed another felony nor [sic] otherwise got into trouble. From the point of view of the statistics of parole violation, I qualify as a 'success.' But honestly, I think it has gone a bit farther than just that. I've done a few things that I think needed doing in the professional field.

"My reputation, locally, is good; people here, in general, not only tolerate me but positively like me! In a word, even if it sounds very immodest, I believe that society has not been the loser in granting me, at long last, my liberty."[2]

After his release from prison Leopold would write frequently to his friends back on the mainland—Ralph and Mary Lynn Newman, Elmer and Mamie Gertz, Abel and Kathy Brown, to name a few. For one who, except for Richard Loeb, had seemed so friendless during the summer of 1924, Nathan Leopold had become strangely companionable and very socially acceptable forty years later. His letters have the tone of those one might receive from an old retired uncle whom everybody loved and who, moreover, knew that everybody loved him.

Though not wealthy, Leopold had a modest inheritance from his family and had earned some money from book royalties and the rights to a never-completed documentary film on his life after leaving prison as well as from various jobs. Many years previous, in the summer of 1924, he had planned a trip to Europe with Abel Brown, a trip he never took. In 1963, finally off parole and free to travel, Leopold burst from his cocoon ready to fly. "He went to Europe two or three times," writes Elmer Gertz in his autobiography, *To Life,* "to Latin America, to the South Pacific, and around the world as well as on many trips to the States. He had an almost uncontrollable urge to be up and around. He dared to do all sorts of venturesome things. When he was in Singapore, a journalist mentioned that he was going to Saigon in the midst of the carnage of Vietnam. Without a moment's hesitation, he accompanied the journalist and saw our involvement at first hand."[3]

Whenever Leopold traveled, he had a coterie of friends with whom he stayed. These were not just ordinary people—to them he still could be cold, arrogant, aloof—but usually people who would be labeled "pillars of the community." They lived in the proper suburbs and had the right addresses. On his frequent visits to Chicago he rationed himself among his friends, becoming the guest on one trip of Ralph Newman, the next Elmer Gertz, then Abel Brown—at the same time apologizing to others, saying they would get their chance at him in turn. "I've got to distribute my favors," he said. Leopold, in always staying with others, seemed to reflect a desire to be with people, to be wanted, to be loved, and to prove to the world that he was human.

While in Chicago, he would have Elmer Gertz drive him back to the old neighborhood and often to the cemetery to visit the graves of his family. "He was very nostalgic," Gertz recalls. On one occasion they traveled to the area where his family had lived before moving to Kenwood. As a boy Leopold had removed a brick from a neighbor's garage and hidden some coins and postage stamps behind it. Leopold removed the brick, but nothing was there. As far as Gertz knows, Leopold never revisited the scene of his crime during any visit to Chicago.[4]

Leopold had polished his image well, although there still were many who never could forgive him. One was his only remaining brother, Sam, who had even changed his name to escape the shadow of his brother's crime. Sam was unhappy with Elmer Gertz's attempts to obtain Nathan's parole because they caused a renewal of publicity about the Franks case. Before one parole hearing Gertz, Sam, and Abel Brown traveled to Stateville together, and Sam blurted out belligerently, "Remember, I never hired you to handle this matter!"

Nathan Leopold resented his brother's attitude and the fact that Sam never invited him to dinner at his residence. They met only in restaurants or in other homes. Finally, in 1968, Sam softened and asked Nathan to become his houseguest, causing Nathan to confide to his friend Abel Brown, "Maybe this betokens a change in relations between Sam and me." He also added almost pathetically, "This is the first time I've seen Mother's portrait since 1924!"[5]

During his first years out of prison Leopold seemed to be trying to build himself an image as another Dr. Schweitzer. He worked at a twenty-nine-bed community hospital in Castaner, Puerto Rico, run by the Church of the Brethren. He received only room and board, plus $10 weekly, serving as a hospital technician. He also helped raise money to build a clinic. He did many thoughtful things such as obtaining a motorized chair so a crippled child could get around, obtaining surgery to correct a harelip on a girl, arranging for a boy to go to school in San Juan.[6] He seemed sincerely bent on atonement. According to Abel Brown: "The people in Castaner seemed to revere him."[7] Leopold himself said in a strangely revealing quote, "Helping others has become my chief hobby. It is how I get my kicks."[8]

He soon tired of the Dr. Schweitzer routine, however. After a few years, perhaps sensing that Castaner was yet another form of prison, he began to strike out, to mold an even newer life. He moved to San Juan and began a year of study in social medicine at the University of Puerto Rico. He earned his master's degree, graduated first in his class, and was elected president of the student body. He also joined the faculty, teaching mathematics in Spanish.

The fact that there were others on the faculty with more advanced degrees irritated the former child prodigy. A teacher with a PhD earned more money than he did with his master's degree, and this bothered Leopold. He made inquiries at several universities back in the United States about obtaining an advanced degree, but partly because of the restrictions it would have imposed on his life—time in residence on campus, another form of imprisonment—he abandoned the idea. He also abandoned his job as a teacher. Later, working for Puerto Rico's department of health, he did research on the intestinal diseases that plagued the lives of the island's poor. Still later he would do similar research on a cure for leprosy. In prison Leopold had moved from one task to another, as though he had to have variety to stifle boredom. In his years outside the walls, he continued this pattern of jumping from one challenge to another. He seemed to sense he was running out of time, yet he had so many things to do.[9]

Leopold also, for the first time in many years, had the opportunity to meet members of the opposite sex. He wrote to Ralph Newman and Elmer Gertz about the number of women, many of them young, who were attracted to him. At one point shortly after his arrival in Puerto Rico, Leopold seemed on the verge of marrying a nurse from Indiana, who worked with the Church of the Brethren. He described her in one letter as his "number one choice to push my wheelchair," but she eventually returned home.[10] Several of Leopold's friends, however, suspected that he might have been lying about his conquests of women, that he actually had become impotent.[11] Ralph Newman suspected he never completely outgrew the homosexuality of his early life. He also never outgrew his early fascination with Susan Lurie, who had become a symbol to him of what might have been, even though she had married another. Shortly after arriving in Puerto Rico, he wrote Newman asking if he could obtain a photograph of her.[12]

Leopold also never overcame his love for Loeb and kept a photograph of him prominently displayed in his apartment. When Elmer Gertz visited him in Puerto Rico, the attorney Gertz was disconcerted to see that the Loeb photo was coupled with one of himself. When Leopold moved later, he coupled the Gertz photograph with one of Clarence Darrow, much to Gertz's relief.[13]

Soon after his arrival in Puerto Rico, Leopold attended Passover services at the home of a rabbi where he met Mrs. Gertrude Feldman Garcia de Queveda, a widow. A former social worker from Baltimore, Trudi (as she was called) had met a Puerto Rican doctor on a trip to San Juan and married him. Older than she, the doctor soon died, but she remained in Puerto Rico, opening a flower shop and sharing an apartment with her sister Anita. She became attracted to Nathan Leopold, the social worker in her apparently resurfacing. "He looked like he needed a friend more than anyone I had ever known," she said.[14] They were married on February 5, 1961.[15]

It irritated Nathan Leopold that he had to obtain permission to marry from his parole board. Other terms of his parole included: a ten thirty curfew, not owning or driving a car, not leaving Puerto Rico without special permission, and reporting to his parole officer regularly.

Now and then Leopold's anger over these restrictions would spill out in letters to his friends, particularly one he sent Elmer Gertz in 1962 complaining about the patronizing attitude that many had toward him: "Of course, I'm hypersensitive to this type of thing, precisely because I had to put up with thirty-three years of it, not only from ignorant, bigoted, sadistic motherfuckers in the employ of the State, but also from my own brother. Like you, he always patronized me only out of the purest motives—for my own good. (And that's the worst kind.) He was perfectly honest; he acted, I am sure, always for the right, as God gave him to see the right. That's one reason that your advent and that of Ralph on the scene was a God-given breath of fresh air in a stagnant dungeon. Here were two guys, not my social or intellectual inferiors, nor yet people who were trying to get something out of me, who appeared perfectly willing to treat me as an adult and not as a Mongoloid idiot, who didn't know how to wipe his own ass or blow his own nose. What a shot in the arm that was for my psyche (to mix metaphors a bit). Don't, for Christ's sake, become a Sam, even when you're out of sorts."[16]

Leopold's comments, more forthright than any of the carefully chosen ones that appear in his autobiography, tell much about his attitude toward life—and himself. While in Puerto Rico, he began work on another book, tentatively titled *Reach for a Halo,* but he found himself unable to complete it. Maybe he sensed that despite what he did later in life, the halo would never fit comfortably on his head.

Even though he had created it, Leopold sometimes had difficulty believing his own image. In some of his public appearances, occasional flashes of insight into his own culpability would appear, as at his parole hearing when committee member John M. Bookwalter asked whether he shared equally with Richard Loeb in the responsibility for the crime, including the premeditation. Nathan Leopold had not hesitated. "Very definitely," he responded.[17] Later when the tide of publicity had turned in his favor and he was being held up to the world as an example of the effectiveness of prison rehabilitation, Leopold would admit to Chicago *Daily News* reporter M. W. Newman, "I don't think prison has ever really rehabilitated anybody."[18] Leopold believed that if he was rehabilitated, it was despite prison, not because of it.

Such moments of public introspection came rarely. Even private moments of introspection are rare, although he did unburden himself in a letter to Elmer Gertz, complaining about the terms of his parole, and relating how, with almost Nietzschean zeal, he craftily violated it. "Now, almost from day one," he confessed to Gertz, "I have not abided by the parole regulations." He drank. He stayed out past the curfew hour. He communicated with prisoners and ex-prisoners (he cannily mentioned Harry Golden as one). He went to places of questionable reputation. "I have visited most of the better whore-houses, cheap bars, and gambling casinos in Greater San Juan and like 'em fine," he bragged. He possessed weapons, including a shotgun and a rifle used for ornithological activities. He frequently traveled outside the county without asking permission. He changed addresses and employment without notifying his parole agent. "And that ain't all, Butch," Leopold ended. "I intend to continue violating these provisions whenever the occasion arises."

The restrictions imposed by his parole do indeed seem ludicrous, as Leopold was attempting to point out, and one almost wants to congratulate him in his ability to confound the parole board. Leopold was a human; perhaps laws need be more human, too. But then one remembers that one reason Leopold and Loeb felt free to murder Bobby Franks was their belief that laws did not concern them.[19]

An interview Leopold granted in March, 1965, to Chicago *Daily News* reporter M. W. Newman also offers insight into his character. "When I went to prison, I was nineteen years old," Leopold told Newman, "rebellious, defiant, smart-alecky. I knew more about everything than anybody else in the world. I grew up eventually, I think I would have grown up as rapidly in a different environment. I don't think there was any element in prison which caused me to grow up, to mature emotionally. I think this is something that happened from within. Just as at a certain age I grew a beard, so, at a certain age, my rebelliousness declined. Perhaps I just became middle-aged."

Leopold even admitted he had been given too much credit for his prison activities, telling Newman that he had become involved in most of his so-called good works to relieve monotony. "I didn't do it because I wanted to pay my debt to society particularly," he confessed. "I did it because it was a challenge and an interesting thing to do."[20]

Leopold admitted he felt no remorse for his crime until many years after he had been imprisoned but said, "I would not, I think, ever have committed another crime. I was all through. I think had I not been apprehended, I would have led a very normal life. I was a student in law school and intended to become a corporation attorney. I think that's just what would have happened."

Nevertheless, Leopold could not entirely escape the effect of what he had done; he would continue to brood about his public image. In 1964 he wrote Abel Brown with details of the negotiations then under way for a documentary film about his life. He reminded his friend how, back in 1958, Brown had hoped only to get Leopold out of prison and allow him to slip into obscurity. "You advanced the idea," he reminded Brown, "which I'll admit sounded crazy to me at the time, that I might some day succeed in making my name something to be proud of rather than a symbol of the ultimate in evil. All the rest of the folks involved agreed that this was Utopian—impossible. I certainly was convinced that was how it was.

"But, Abe, even now, after six years, my 'public image'—at least down here in Puerto Rico—has begun to change. I am respected by many people, liked, I think, by many people. And this picture, if it is really well done, and if it is not hooted down by such publications as *Time* Magazine, could just give that change in the public image a big, big boost."[21]

In another letter written in 1970, Leopold wrote about doing research in leprosy and possibly developing a vaccine. "Wouldn't THAT be a note to go out on," he wrote, "ridding the world of the scourge of leprosy?"[22]

Leopold claimed that nothing gave him greater pleasure than being introduced to someone to whom his name meant nothing. At the same time he thrived on his notoriety, the fact that people *did* recognize him, that he did have celebrity status—even if for distasteful reasons. His desire to escape the memory of his one great misdeed and his yearning for the public attention he achieved from his ability to rise above it would tear at him during the last decade of his life. One of those who visited Leopold in Puerto Rico was Dr. Bernard Glueck, one of Darrow's alienists who was then in his upper seventies. Dr. Glueck had a long conversation with Leopold, then returned home and told his son that his original assumption in 1924 that Leopold was a paranoid schizophrenic was still correct despite all the good work he had done in prison and afterward.[23]

Another visitor was Ernst W. Puttkammer, Leopold's old law professor, who had maintained contact with him during the prison years. Professor Puttkammer and his wife spent a day with Leopold, who guided them around San Juan. They found him bitter, particularly about Meyer Levin's portrait of him. "When you saw him, you became aware of the human tragedy," recalls Puttkammer. "Of course, the murder was horrible and inexcusable, but it was the tragedy that surfaced in your feelings. This wasted life!"[24]

Leopold never would rid the world of leprosy. He did not have enough time. Even had he lived another decade, it seems doubtful that his interest could be focused on one activity for a long enough period to achieve anything of that magnitude. He still became bored easily and liked to move on to new sensations.

As long ago as the 1924 hearing, the medical experts had noted Leopold's poor health, predicting in some instances that he had but a few years to live. He had confounded them by surviving, but now his health began to fail. He had had several heart attacks, even as early as the forties in prison. He was a diabetic, but always the epicure, he failed to watch his diet. He began to experience increased heart problems in 1970. During a visit to Chicago in the summer of 1971, he had to be rushed to the hospital by Elmer Gertz. He spent twenty days recovering and every day was visited by his brother Sam.

His friends began to notice that his moods seemed to change, that his previously placid manner often gave way to explosions of temper. He drove his car fast and erratically and became preoccupied with money. Where once he had refused interviews with members of the press, now he gave them, but he wanted to charge. He talked to his Chicago friends of marital problems. "He wasn't ready for marriage," said Ralph Newman. "In fact, he was way past being ready. When I saw the two of them in 1971, it was obvious they were getting on each other's nerves."

In his final months, Nathan Leopold displayed bitterness and anger at the world, but he also showed flashes of insight: "I would say that, on the whole, I have had a good life, a satisfactory life.

Even many parts of the prison years. How many people outside prison have had time to pursue such nonremunerative subjects as Egyptian hieroglyphics and the theory of relativity? I did."[25]

On August 30, 1971, Nathan F. Leopold, Jr., died what was described as a "quiet, natural death" in Mimiya Hospital near San Juan, Puerto Rico, after having been hospitalized for ten days. He was sixty-six. He willed his eyes to the University of Puerto Rico eye bank and his body to that university for research. His wife was with him at the time of his death. She waited until the doctors and nurses left the room, held his hand for a few moments, kissed his lips, left, then waited in the lobby until the ophthalmologist arrived to remove his eyes. The following morning one of his corneas was given to an elderly Puerto Rican widow. The other recipient was a man.

Epilogue

Plaintiff was a public figure in 1924 and never sank back into obscurity. His deed and conduct may be well called a "public legend."

—JUDGE ABRAHAM W. BRUSSELL[1]

On the day following Nathan Leopold's death, the Chicago *Sun-Times* (a newspaper not in existence in 1924) published an editorial that offered a stark contrast with those crying for vengeance nearly a half century before: "Perhaps in the new age of violence that besets us, a Leopold-Loeb case would rate only passing attention. But in 1924 the idea that young men of wealth and genius could coldly set out to commit the perfect crime gripped and horrified the nation. The murder of Bobby Franks by Leopold and his friend Richard Loeb became a classic in the annals of crime. Here, certainly, is a classic case of rehabilitation. And clearly it argues against the death penalty even for heinous crimes, for no one can reasonably say that society would have benefitted more by Leopold's execution. Yet analogies cannot be too widely drawn, for the case and the man were unique. Perhaps it is enough to say that with Leopold's death a multiple and long-drawn tragedy has finally come to an end. Three lives were lost in that long-ago moment of youthful madness. Justice was served. And the only saving feature was that one of the killers was able, in a small way, to prove that redemption is sometimes possible."[2]

One wonders: would the editorialists have written so charitably about Richard Loeb had he lived as long as his partner? Time has a way of healing wounds. In fact, a rather subtle change had occurred in the way people referred to the protagonists in the Franks murder case. At the 1924 hearing they most frequently were referred to as Loeb and Leopold, but with Loeb's early death and as time passed they became Leopold and Loeb. Only by Loeb's death had Leopold been freed of his demon, the person he described as "his best friend and worst enemy." Whether or not he redeemed himself, he certainly succeeded in redeeming his image and shaping the legend of Leopold and Loeb. Had he died on the gallows in 1924, or even in prison in 1936, history would not have remembered him as well.

Fifty years afterward a few landmarks of the crime of the century remained. The Hotel Morrison, where Loeb checked in with a suitcase filled with books to establish an identity for Morton D. Ballard, was razed in 1964 to be replaced by a modern skyscraper belonging to the First National Bank of Chicago. The building that housed the agency where Leopold rented a Willys-Knight serves as a parking lot for the state of Illinois' department of children and family services. The hardware store on Cottage Grove, where Loeb bought thirty-five feet of rope and a chisel, is a vacant lot filled with weeds, glass, and RC Cola cans. The Leopold and Loeb homes are gone from Kenwood, although the Leopold garage survives, converted into a town house at the time of World War II. It was occupied then, coincidentally, by Mrs. Bert A. Cronson, wife of the former assistant state's attorney (then deceased) who had Sven Englund brought downtown. One day while cleaning out a dark area she came across the hubcap from a Willys-Knight automobile—and some homosexual photographs.[3]

The Harvard School for Boys continues to educate the wealthier children of Kenwood, although girls now go there too, and it is called the Harvard-St. George School. The scholastic records of two of its most famous pupils—Nathan F. Leopold, Jr., and Robert Franks—remain in the school files tucked away in a closet. Both boys had attained excellent grades during the separate times they attended the Harvard School. The conduct of one, however, seemed to worry the instructors. They frequently penned negative notations on his record. The other had none on his. The record of the problem child includes statements such as "too self-satisfied to make a good student" and "made strides of progress in scholarship, but still hampered by unpleasant characteristics." There was another notation on the record of this problem child: "Died, May 21, 1924." The record was that of Bobby Franks.

The shell of a building that once had housed the Van de Bogert & Ross drugstore, where Bobby's father never did answer the phone, lasted until the end of the summer of 1974; then the bulldozers pushed it over, smoothing the soil after the rubble had been trucked away. At the same time workmen were leveling the Illinois Central station at Twelfth Street, where Loeb had boarded the four o'clock train to Michigan City long enough to plant a note of instructions on where to throw a bundle. The Champion factory at Seventy-fourth and the IC tracks are gone, too.

On the Southeast Side of Chicago, along the Illinois and Indiana border, the birds still come to Wolf Lake, ducks migrating north in the spring, migrating south in the fall, many other birds which Nathan Leopold catalogued years before. Hunters rent duck blinds by the season. Chicago maintains a forest preserve to the north (Egger Woods), and Illinois has a state park to the south (William W. Powers Conservation Area), but they are mere dots of green in the midst of an industrial slum.

Nevertheless, fishermen crowd the shores of Wolf Lake at all times of the year, even cutting holes through the ice in the winter. Sailboaters, powerboaters, and even iceboaters use the lake, which is bisected now by the Indiana toll road. Hyde Lake, however, has vanished, having been filled in many years ago by Republic Steel, so although the Pennsylvania railroad track remains, there no longer is a culvert beneath it at what would be 118th Street joining one lake to another.

The Army erected a Nike missile base in the fifties just east of the place where Chief of Detectives Michael Hughes, accompanied by other officials, stood staring down into a ditch. The weapons of war quickly change, so in the sixties the government removed its obsolete missiles and its barracks without removing the asphalt and concrete slabs on which they once stood. The slabs remain today as scars on a much-scarred landscape. "Bad Ass 93rd" it says in paint on one of the slabs.

Mammoth power lines cross the tracks right over where Paul Korff found a pair of eyeglasses. You can hear the lines humming as you walk beneath them. Although the executives of the surrounding industrial concerns will tell you they have achieved compliance with government pollution regulations, the air is acrid and gray. West of the tracks, gravel roads crisscross an area of weeds and scrub grass which seems to have become a community garbage dump for old tires, rusted engine blocks, broken television sets, the debris of twentieth-century civilization. It was an ugly place on the night of May 21, 1924, and it is an ugly place today.

Acknowledgments

The Crime of the Century involved research that lasted over a period of several years. The work would have been much more difficult had it not been for the collaboration of James Singer, a reporter with the Chicago *Sun-Times* during the early research stages. He did almost all the preliminary library work, interviewed many of the more than a hundred people whose reminiscences about the case added to the public record, and also contributed some of the actual writing. Finally, after he moved to Washington to join the publication *National Journal Reports,* he provided important technical assistance in preparation of the final manuscript and helped check it for accuracy. At the same time, the direction of this book, including opinions expressed within it, are mine, and I bear ultimate responsibility should any factual errors have gone undetected. Because of contradictions in what passes as fact fifty years after an event, writing history is as much art as science.

The book would not have been possible without the inspiration provided by Walter J. Minton, president of G. P. Putnam's Sons, who first of all provided the idea that grew into *The Crime of the Century.* Shortly after the death of Nathan Leopold in 1971 he suggested that, with the last of the principals in the Franks case now dead, a book finally could be written telling the complete fifty-year story of the crime and its aftermath. Walter Minton later guided me through several revisions and reorganizations of the massive amount of material related to the case. The story is much more difficult to tell than might first be suspected mainly because of the way bits and pieces of the crime became known back in 1924—first in the newspapers, then in the confessions, in the psychological reports, and finally at the hearing. His greatest contribution was in helping me determine what material belonged where, no easy task.

Roy Porter, my agent at Porter, Gould & Dierks of Evanston, Illinois, provided valuable counsel as the work progressed from contract to library to typewriter to galleys. Many others contributed. Valerie Brady, Carolyn Wood, and Ann Gabriele provided important secretarial services. James Singer's wife, Mary S. Singer, assisted him in his early research. My wife, Rose, offered her ear whenever I wanted to talk about aspects of the book and its progress. Our children, Kevin, David, and Laura, sat through many of these discussions. It almost became *our* family crime as a half century earlier it had become the family crime of the Leopolds, the Loebs, and the Franks.

Several out-of-town librarians did research at my request, including: Dietar U. Wagner (Ann Arbor, Michigan); Elizabeth Hilderbrand (Peoria, Illinois); Geraldine Noble (Lebanon, Ohio); and J. A. Monahan (Boston, Massachusetts). In addition, I was assisted by many other librarians, particularly in the Chicago area, whose faces I came to know, but not their names. I received aid and guidance from many others too numerous to mention.

While the base for this book was laid in the library, a great deal of information (much of it not previously published) was uncovered through personal interviews. It was fascinating for me to discover how many people involved in a case that occurred fifty years ago were still around, but then Leopold and Loeb were aged only nineteen and eighteen at the time of their crime. One individual I interviewed had been a law partner of Clarence Darrow back in 1905! Most of those who contributed information to this book are credited in the notes; many others who contributed insights but not necessarily facts unfortunately are not. Several people did not want their participation in this project known. Even after fifty years all the wounds have not healed. Because of the nature of their contribution, a few individuals merit special mention, and these include Abel Brown, Ralph Newman, Howard Mayer, and Max Schrayer.

The single most important document related to the Leopold and Loeb case is the official transcript of the 1924 court hearing, the complete account of all the testimony in the so-called trial of the century. For several decades this fascinating document was unavailable to researchers, and when Meyer Levin wrote *Compulsion* in the fifties, he made public pleas to the Leopold family (who had possession of Darrow's copy) to obtain access to it. He eventually saw the transcript through the intercession of Nathan Leopold's then attorney, William Friedman. This copy is now in the Elmer Gertz collection at Northwestern University, which also includes many other valuable books and documents related to the case and Gertz's successful attempt in obtaining parole for Leopold. Other less important papers are contained in an additional Gertz collection at the Library of Congress in Washington, D.C. Acknowledgment is also due Elmer Gertz for his cooperation in providing information on all aspects of the case and for granting permission, as Nathan Leopold's executor, to quote portions of Leopold's autobiography, *Life Plus 99 Years,* as well as parts of Leopold's letters.

A second copy of the transcript is available in the Chicago law offices of Robert Bergstrom. He and attorneys Ephraim London and Leon Despres obtained the transcript by court order prior to their taking a deposition from Nathan Leopold in Puerto Rico in 1961. Little new information emerged as a result of that deposition, but the document serves as an important cross-check for accuracy and provides a fascinating portrait of Leopold at the end of his career.

Apart from the official record, the most valuable sources of information about the case were the Chicago newspapers, whose coverage of the crime and the hearing was almost encyclopedic. Among the Chicago newspapers, the two most valuable sources are the *Tribune* (because of the completeness of its coverage) and the *Daily News* (because of the color and readability of its reports). Although he can hardly be considered unbiased, Nathan Leopold stated during the Puerto Rican deposition that the *Tribune* and the *Daily News* offered the most accurate accounts. He gave low grades to the Hearst papers, the *Herald and Examiner* and the *Evening American* (the latter available only at the Chicago Historical Society), but they have been consulted during preparation of this book, along with the *Daily Journal* and various out-of-town newspapers, particularly two Indiana ones: the Michigan City *Evening Dispatch* and the South Bend *Tribune.* These were consulted as the two most easily available newspapers that contained, respectively, United Press and Associated Press dispatches, which sometimes included different material from what appeared in the Chicago press. I also used the morgues of the Chicago *Sun-Times* and the Chicago *Tribune* to locate news stories that appeared outside the obvious time periods of the case. In the *Tribune* reference room I was delighted to discover four boxes of glass slides, black-and-white relics from an era of primitive photographic techniques. One final newspaper source was back issues of the *Daily Maroon,* the student newspaper at the University of Chicago, available at its library. While making a routine check for information, I stumbled by accident across a short news item which enabled me eventually to solve the riddle of ABCD.

The Chicago newspapers, in covering the hearing, reprinted large blocks of testimony. For that reason, references to testimony in the notes utilize the dates the person testified rather than the page numbers in the less accessible official transcripts.

The report by Drs. Hulbert and Bowman, who conducted the preliminary psychiatric interviews of Leopold and Loeb while they were awaiting trial, appears as part of the official transcript. The Chicago newspapers published condensed versions of this report on July 28, 1924, after it had been stolen (or had been leaked) from the office of Clarence Darrow. The newspapers published separate editions of the report, a fact which apparently escaped the attention of microfilmers. The section on Richard Loeb appears only on the *Herald and Examiner* microfilm; the section on Nathan Leopold appears only on the *Tribune* microfilm. The Hulbert and Bowman report is also reprinted in *The Amazing Crime and Trial of Leopold and Loeb* by Maureen McKernan, originally published in 1925 and reprinted in paperback in 1957. She excludes much of the sexual material as "unprintable" and reprints only Leopold's confession, excluding that of Loeb, which in many ways is more interesting. The *Tribune* published Leopold's confession on June 6, 1924. The *Daily News* published Loeb's on June 7, 1924. McKernan contented herself mostly with editing documents related to the case while offering no opinions on the material in those documents.

During the course of completing *The Crime of the Century,* people to whom I mentioned my work-in-progress would ask, "Hasn't there been an awful lot written about that already?" The answer is, not really. Several volumes appeared immediately after the summer of 1924, but in the intervening half century most have disappeared from library shelves. The Chicago Public Library contains, incredibly, only one book directly related to the case: Meyer Levin's *Compulsion.* The library does not own a copy of Leopold's own autobiography, *Life Plus 99 Years.* Bits and pieces of the story appear in other books, the most valuable being the account of Loeb's death in Gladys Erickson's *Warden Ragen of Joliet,* but *The Crime of the Century* is the first attempt to present a complete retelling of the Franks murder case up to the death of the last participant.

Life Plus 99 Years offers a fascinating account of Leopold's life in prison, but it must be considered at least partially suspect. Leopold wrote the book as part of his campaign to obtain parole from prison, so he suppressed much material which might have been embarrassing to him, including any discussion of the actual murder. The book begins after the crime has been committed. John

Bartlow Martin's four-part series in the *Saturday Evening Post* ("Murder on His Conscience," April 2, 9, 16, and 23, 1955) covers the same ground, but from a different point of view. When I first read Leopold's book and Martin's articles, I suspected the *Post* author had had access to Leopold's manuscript when he did his series, but Martin claims he did not. Gene Lovitz, currently a prisoner at Illinois State Penitentiary, offered assistance in preparing the chapters of this book related to the prison period.

Anyone interested in the Leopold and Loeb case sooner or later must read *Compulsion,* the best-selling novel Meyer Levin based on that case. Levin researched the book as though it were to be nonfiction, but it sometimes is difficult to tell where fact ends and fiction begins, a point that Leopold himself made in a lawsuit against Levin. Levin's autobiographical book, *The Obsession,* includes material about his writing of *Compulsion.*

Elmer Gertz, who represented Leopold in his parole hearing and in his suit against *Compulsion,* wrote about both in *A Handful of Clients.* Gertz's book was published in 1965, at a time he thought his client had won his suit, which was lost later on appeal. Gertz also included a chapter about Leopold in a later autobiography, *To Life.*

Clarence Darrow included two chapters about the case in his autobiography, *The Story of My Life,* but covers the events only sketchily. Irving Stone wrote about the case in his Darrow biography, *Clarence Darrow for the Defense.*

As of this writing, two additional books related to the case are in progress. Trudi Leopold, Nathan's widow, reportedly is working on a book about her husband's Puerto Rican years in collaboration with New York author Ron Martinetti. James Day, Loeb's killer, has committed eighty hours of his prison recollections to tape for a book to be written by Jean Ratcliffe of Indianapolis, who was kind enough to review the Day chapter for errors.

Nathan Leopold's documents and papers have been collected by the Chicago Historical Society, but they were not available for study in time for publication. At his direction, they are not to be released until five years after his death, meaning September, 1976.

HAL HIGDON

Michigan City, Indiana
February 22, 1975

Notes

Prologue

1. Clarence Darrow spoke at the hearing, August 23–25, 1924.

Chapter 1

1. Leopold made the statement at his 1953 parole hearing, quoted by Elmer Gertz, *A Handful of Clients* (New York: Follett, 1965), p. 104.
2. Chicago *Tribune,* November 11, 1924.
3. The Michigan *Daily* contains information on student activities that evening.
4. Interview with Max Robert Schrayer.
5. Details of the burglary were included in the Hulbert and Bowman report.
6. An item in the Michigan *Daily,* November 15, 1923, seemingly identifies the second fraternity house as Trigon. Max Schrayer, however, insisted in an interview that it was Pi Lamba Phi. Nathan Leopold in his November 15, 1961, deposition suggests the fraternity may have been Delta Kappa Epsilon.

Chapter 2

1. Clarence Darrow spoke at the hearing, August 23–25, 1924.
2. Chicago *Tribune,* November 8, 1923.
3. Ann Arbor (Michigan) *Times News,* November 13, 1923.
4. The University of Michigan is unable to confirm whether Richard Loeb actually was its youngest graduate.
5. Interview with Max Schrayer. The Michigan *Daily,* November 15, 1923, however, said two former students were seen leaving the city in a large truck for their homes in *St. Louis.*
6. Occasionally Leopold is identified by people writing about the Franks case as the youngest graduate of the University of Chicago. Nathan Leopold never made that claim himself.
7. In the Puerto Rico deposition Leopold insisted he had got the permit to shoot in the parks himself and his father, as suggested in some accounts, had nothing to do with it.

8. Bay City (Michigan) *Times,* March 11, 1971.
9. Leopold's paper was published in *Auk,* Vol. 41 (1924), pp. 44–48.
10. Leon Mandel testified at the hearing that they often played bridge for 5 to 10 cents a point (July 24, 1924). During the Puerto Rico deposition, Leopold claimed 5 cents a point was the maximum.
11. Leopold described his plans to make the translation while being questioned at the state's attorney's office, May 30, 1924. The transcription of their conversation was introduced at the hearing by court reporter E. M. Allen, July 28–29, 1929.
12. Interview with Leon Mandel III, who said that it is part of the Mandel family legend that the typewriter on which the kidnap letters were written originally belonged to his father. That, of course, is impossible.
13. Arnold Maremont testified at the hearing, July 24, 1924.
14. Interview with Arnold Maremont.
15. Chicago *Tribune,* January 1, 1924.
16. *Ibid.,* November 25, 1923.
17. *Ibid.,* November 21, 1923.
18. *Ibid.,* November 23, 1923. Also June 3, 1924.
19. *Ibid.,* November 26, 1923.
20. Chicago *Daily Maroon,* November 22, 1923. Despite its name, the *Daily Maroon* did not appear daily. It came out only several times a week and never during the summer.
21. *Ibid.,* November 27, 1923.
22. *Ibid.,* October 3, 1923.
23. *Ibid.,* January 15, 1924.
24. *Ibid.,* February 5, 1924.
25. *Ibid.,* February 7, 1924. Also, February 13, 1924.
26. *Ibid.,* March 11, 1924. Also, March 13, 1924.
27. Chicago *Tribune,* September 2, 1924. See story on ABCD crimes.
28. Interview with Max Schrayer.
29. Clara Vinnedge testified at the hearing, July 23, 1924.
30. Charles E. Ward testified, July 23, 1924.
31. Walter L. Jacobs testified, July 23, 1924.
32. David L. Barish testified, July 23, 1924.
33. Margaret Fitzpatrick testified, July 23, 1924.
34. Interview with Max Schrayer.
35. Interview with Robert Asher.
36. Chicago *Tribune,* April 3, 1924.
37. Chicago *Tribune,* April 9, 1924.
38. *Ibid.,* May 9, 1924.
39. For an interesting (though occasionally embroidered) account of life on the Hearst newspapers in Chicago, see George Murray, *The Madhouse on Madison Street* (Chicago: Follett, 1956).

Chapter 3

1. *The Sea Wolf,* by Jack London. Wolf Larsen is the main character in London's novel about a ruthless sea captain.

2. *This Side of Paradise,* by F. Scott Fitzgerald.
3. Chicago *Tribune,* May 22, 1924, and other local papers.
4. Sven Englund testified, July 24, 1924.
5. Details from confessions of Leopold and Loeb made May 31, 1924. Court reporter E. M. Allen presented the confessions at the hearing, July 28–29, 1924.
6. Walter L. Jacobs testified, July 23, 1924.
7. Interview with Max Schrayer.
8. Sven Englund testified, July 24, 1924.
9. Leopold acknowledged this response in the Puerto Rico deposition.
10. Interview with Robert Asher.
11. Chicago *Daily News,* November 9, 1957.
12. Interview with John Levinson. J. T. Seass testified, July 24, 1924.
13. Chicago *Tribune,* May 29, 1924.
14. *Ibid.,* May 23, 1924.
15. *Ibid.,* May 25, 1924.
16. For information on how graft was involved in the Ogden Gas Company deal, see Lloyd Wendt and Herman Kogan, *Bosses in Lusty Chicago* (Bloomington: Indiana University Press, 1971).
17. Chicago *Tribune,* May 24, 1924. Also, April 24, 1928.
18. Jacob Franks testified, July 23, 1924.
19. Interview with Robert Asher.
20. Chicago *Daily News,* November 7, 1957.
21. Chicago *Tribune,* May 23, 1924.
22. Mrs. Flora Franks testified, July 23, 1924.
23. Chicago *Tribune,* May 23, 1924.
24. Bernard Hunt testified, July 24, 1924.
25. Chicago *Tribune,* May 23, 1924.

Chapter 4

1. Gertz, *op. cit.,* p. 14.
2. George Porter Lewis testified, July 25, 1924.
3. Correspondence with Gerry Gentry of the American Maize Products Company uncovered the information that the Tony *Minke,* as named in most accounts of the crime, was employed under the name Tony *Manke.* His Polish name had been Mankowski.
4. The track, according to K. E. Smith, general manager of the Penn Central Transportation Company's western region, is known as the S.C.&S. Branch. The letters stand for South Chicago and Southern. The track connects two main lines and is still used for passenger and freight trains. Newspaper accounts of the era often referred to the track as belonging to the Panhandle Railway, a nickname applied to the Pennsylvania Railroad west of Pittsburgh.
5. The men who discovered Bobby Franks' body testified, July 23–24, 1924. Chicago newspapers carried stories of the discovery beginning with the afternoon editions of May 22, 1924. Paul Korff's son, Claude Korff, also supplied important details.

6. Jacob Franks testified, July 23, 1924.

7. The kidnap letter was placed in evidence by State's Attorney Crowe at the hearing on July 23, 1924. It had been reprinted in numerous newspapers immediately after news of the murder broke on May 22, 1924.

8. Chicago *Tribune,* May 23, 1924.

9. Tony Shapino testified, July 24, 1924.

10. Jacob Franks testified, July 23, 1924.

11. Chicago *Tribune,* May 23, 1924.

12. Chicago *Daily News,* May 31, 1924.

13. *Ibid.,* May 23, 1924.

14. Chicago *Herald and Examiner,* May 23, 1924.

15. Chicago *Tribune,* May 24, 1924.

16. Charles Robinson testified, July 28, 1924.

17. Chicago *Tribune,* May 23, 1924.

18. James C. Kemp testified, July 25, 1924.

19. Percy Van de Bogert testified, July 25, 1924.

Chapter 5

1. South Bend *Tribune,* May 23, 1924.

2. Leopold and Loeb mentioned their encounter with Mott Kirk Mitchell while being interrogated at the state's attorney's office, May 30, 1924. Court reporter E. M. Allen presented a transcript of this interrogation at the hearing, July 28–29, 1924.

3. Alvin H. Goldstein testified, July 25, 1924.

4. Interview with Elmer Gertz. See also Elmer Gertz, *To Life* (New York: McGraw-Hill, 1974), p. 187.

5. Chicago *Tribune,* June 1, 1924. The newspaper did not reveal the girl's identity.

6. George Porter Lewis testified, July 25, 1924.

7. Chicago *Tribune,* May 23, 1924.

8. Michigan City *Evening Dispatch,* May 23, 1924.

9. Interview with Mrs. Bert A. Cronson.

10. Chicago *Tribune,* May 25, 1924.

11. *Ibid.,* May 24, 1924.

12. South Bend *Tribune,* May 24, 1924.

13. Interview with Howard Mayer. Mayer, James Mulroy, and Alvin Goldstein also testified, July 25, 1924.

14. Chicago *Daily News,* May 31, 1924. The newspaper deleted the expletive.

15. Joseph Springer testified, July 23, 1924.

16. Chicago *Trubune,* May 24, 1924.

17. *Ibid.,* June 2, 1924. During examination by Drs. Hulbert and Bowman, Loeb boasted of having sexual intercourse on the Friday, Sunday, and Tuesday nights after the murder.

Chapter 6

1. Chicago *Herald and Examiner,* May 26, 1924.

2. Chicago *Tribune,* May 24, 1924.
3. *Ibid.,* May 23, 1924.
4. Michigan City *Evening Dispatch,* May 23, 1924.
5. Dayton (Ohio) *Daily News,* January 18, 1953.
6. Chicago *Tribune,* May 25, 1924.
7. *Ibid.,* May 26, 1924.
8. *Ibid.,* May 25, 1924.
9. Interview with Claude Korff.
10. Chicago *Tribune,* May 25, 1924.
11. *Ibid.,* May 27, 1924.
12. South Bend *Tribune,* May 27, 1924.
13. *Ibid.,* May 25, 1924.
14. Loeb later denied to Drs. Hulbert and Bowman that he had sent the flowers.
15. Thomas McWilliams testified, July 24, 1924.
16. Samuel Goldfarb's recollections are in the Gertz collection at Northwestern University.
17. Interview with Mrs. Bert A. Cronson, who was not present when Leopold made the statement (assuming he did), but heard the story from others.
18. Interview with Abel Brown.

Chapter 7

1. Robert E. Crowe in a 1920 campaign brochure when he was running for state's attorney. A copy is in the author's possession.
2. Thomas C. Wolfe testified, July 25, 1924.
3. Leopold described his visit to the police station in his book, *Life Plus 99 Years* (New York: Doubleday, 1958). Page references are from the paperback edition (New York: Popular Library), p. 30.
4. The statement by Leopold was read at the hearing by Wolfe, July 25, 1924.
5. Chicago *Tribune,* June 1, 1924.
6. Interview with William Friedman.
7. The Hulbert and Bowman report contains a medical profile of Nathan Leopold.
8. George Porter Lewis testified, July 25, 1924.
9. Leopold, *op. cit.,* p. 32.
10. Chicago *Herald and Examiner,* May 26, 1924.
11. Chicago *Tribune,* May 26, 1924.
12. Hulbert and Bowman report.
13. Chicago *Herald and Examiner,* May 26, 1924.
14. *Ibid.,* May 30, 1924.
15. Chicago *Tribune,* June 10, 1924.
16. Chicago *Daily News,* June 9, 1924.
17. Michigan City *Evening Dispatch,* May 26, 1924.
18. Chicago *Tribune,* May 29, 1924.
19. *Ibid.,* May 28, 1924.
20. Interview with Max Schrayer, who insists the incident was sepa-

rate from the drugstore tour made by Loeb, Goldstein, Mayer, and Mulroy the previous Friday.

21. Chicago *Tribune,* June 2, 1924. In the Puerto Rico deposition, however, Leopold insisted Susan Lurie's re-creation of their luncheon conversation was incorrect.

22. Ernst W. Puttkammer testified, July 25, 1924. Based also on an interview with him.

23. Chicago *Tribune,* May 29, 1924.

24. Chicago *Daily News,* June 9, 1924. The Harvard School annual for the 1924–25 school year shows that Wilson taught there that year.

25. During the Puerto Rico deposition, Ephraim London mentioned the rumor about the teacher who went to a mental institution. Leopold claimed he never had heard anything about this.

26. Chicago *Tribune,* May 30, 1924.

27. According to newspaper accounts the cat was named Wilson. The name of Walter Wilson's landlady was Mrs. Chase, leading one to suspect that the reporter may have come up with a false story.

28. Chicago *Tribune,* June 1, 1924.

29. *Ibid.,* May 29, 1924.

Chapter 8

1. Chicago *Daily News,* February 2, 1925.

2. Chicago *Tribune,* May 30, 1924. Also, Jacob Weinstein testified, July 26, 1924.

3. Interview with Ephraim London.

4. William Crot and Frank A. Johnson testified, July 25, 1924. Leopold also offers a version of the day's events in Leopold, *op. cit.,* p. 33.

5. Chicago *Sun-Times,* August 20, 1942. A profile of Crowe by Herman Kogan offers details of his career.

6. From a 1920 campaign brochure in the author's possession.

7. Chicago *Daily News,* October 22, 1920.

8. Chicago *Sun-Times,* August 20, 1942.

9. James Gortland testified, July 25, 1924.

10. Court reporter E. M. Allen recorded a large amount of the questioning of Leopold. Much of the information in this chapter related to the interrogation comes from the official transcript. E. M. Allen testified, July 28–29, 1924.

11. Apparently the police confiscated the letter during one of their trips to the Leopold home.

12. Frank B. Tuttle testified, July 24, 1924.

Chapter 9

1. Gertz, *A Handful of Clients, op. cit.,* p. 93.

2. E. M. Allen testified, July 28–29, 1924.

3. Howard Mayer testified, July 25, 1924. Also based on an interview with Mayer.

4. Article by James Doherty, Chicago *Tribune,* June 8, 1952.

5. Chicago *Tribune,* June 6, 1924.

6. *Ibid.*, May 31, 1924.

7. Chicago *Daily News,* May 30, 1924. Also, May 31, 1924.

8. Arnold Maremont testified, July 24, 1924. Also based on an interview with Maremont.

9. Chicago *Daily News,* May 31, 1924.

10. Maurice Shanberg testified, July 24, 1924. Also based on an interview with Shanberg.

11. William Shoemacher testified, July 28, 1924.

12. Interview with Mrs. Bert Cronson.

13. Sven Englund testified, July 24, 1924.

14. Interview with Mrs. Bert Cronson.

15. A detailed description of the events immediately preceding Loeb's confession appeared in the Chicago *Herald and Examiner* on June 1, 1924, and in a slightly different version on June 10, 1924. Crowe gave details about how Leopold confessed during his opening remarks at the hearing, July 23, 1924.

16. E. M. Allen testified, July 28–29, 1924.

17. Interview with Jack McPhaul. See also Chicago *Sun-Times,* January 9, 1953.

Chapter 10

1. Dr. William Healy testified, August 4–5, 1924.

2. E. M. Allen presented the confessions at the hearing, July 28–29, 1924. State's Attorney Crowe had already released them to the newspapers. The Chicago *Tribune* published Leopold's confession on June 6, 1924. The Chicago *Daily News* published Loeb's confession on June 7, 1924. This chapter is based on the confessions, although some other specific details come from different sources, particularly the Hulbert and Bowman report.

3. The identity of many of the potential victims did not become public knowledge until the release of the Hulbert and Bowman report. State's Attorney Crowe also provided information on potential victims in his opening remarks at the hearing, July 23, 1924. In their confessions Leopold and Loeb only mentioned a few of the many people they considered.

4. Wallace Sullivan testified, July 29, 1924.

5. Leopold offered this detail in the Puerto Rico deposition.

6. Hugh T. Patrick testified, August 12, 1924.

7. Peoria (Illinois) *Evening Star,* May 31, June 2, June 4, 1924.

8. George C. Fry testified, July 24, 1924. Some versions of the events of this day offer a slightly different, and often confusing, timetable, but only because of the difference between standard and daylight time. The timetable in this book reflects the latter.

9. Leopold, *op. cit.,* p. 45.

10. Chicago *Daily News,* May 31, 1924.

11. Chicago *Herald and Examiner,* June 1, 1924.

Chapter 11

1. Chicago *Herald and Examiner,* June 1, 1924.

2. Chicago *Tribune,* May 31, 1924.
3. Chicago *Herald and Examiner,* June 3, 1924.
4. Chicago *Evening American.*
5. Meyer Levin, *In Search* (New York: Horizon Press, 1950), p. 27.
6. Chicago *Herald and Examiner,* June 1, 1924.
7. Chicago *Tribune,* June 1, 1924. Additional information on the Loeb family history was obtained at the Chicago Historical Society.
8. Interview with Mrs. Bert Cronson, who heard stories about Mrs. Loeb from a friend, whose mother had belonged to her Catholic church.
9. Interview with Richard Lowenstein.
10. Chicago *Tribune,* June 1, 1924.
11. Captain William Shoemacher testified July 28, 1924, about the events of the May 31 caravan. Sergeant Bernounsky similarly testified, July 25, 1924.
12. Irving Stone, *Clarence Darrow for the Defense* (New York: Doubleday, 1941), p. 242.
13. Ben Hecht, *Gaily, Gaily* (New York: Doubleday, 1963).
14. Clarence Darrow, *The Story of My Life* (New York: Scribner's, 1932).

Chapter 12

1. Chicago *Tribune,* June 2, 1924.
2. *Ibid.,* June 1, 1924.
3. Darrow spoke, August 22–25, 1924.
4. Full descriptions of the June 1 caravan appear in the Chicago newspapers the next day. Several participants also testified at the hearing, particularly: Joseph Bernounsky (July 25, 1924); Wallace Sullivan (July 28, 1924); and William Shoemacher (July 28, 1924).
5. Chicago *Tribune,* June 2, 1924.
6. Leopold, *op. cit.,* p. 49.
7. Each of the prosecution psychiatrists testified regarding their observations at the hearing.
8. James J. Gortland testified, July 25, 1924.
9. Frank A. Johnson testified, July 25, 1924.
10. Stone, *op. cit.,* p. 250.
11. Chicago *Tribune,* June 3, 1924.
12. Leopold, *op. cit.,* p. 54.
13. Chicago *Tribune,* June 3, 1924.
14. Chicago *Herald and Examiner,* June 6, 1924.
15. Leopold, *op. cit.,* p. 53.

Chapter 13

1. Leopold, *op. cit.,* p. 6.
2. Chicago *Tribune,* June 6, 1924.
3. *Ibid.,* June 4, 1924.
4. Hulbert and Brown report.
5. Leopold, *op. cit.,* p. 60.
6. Chicago *Tribune,* June 6, 1924.
7. Chicago *Herald and Examiner,* June 4, 1924.

8. Chicago *Tribune,* June 5, 1924.
9. Chicago *Herald and Examiner,* June 4, 1924.
10. *Ibid.*
11. Stone, *op. cit.,* p. 257.
12. Chicago *Tribune,* June 2, 1924.
13. *Ibid.,* June 7, 1924.
14. Darrow, *op. cit.,* p. 235.
15. Chicago *Tribune,* June 12, 1924.
16. Chicago *Daily News,* June 11, 1924.
17. Meyer Levin, *The Obsession* (New York: Simon & Schuster, 1973), p. 106.
18. Interview with Meyer Levin.
19. Chicago *Herald and Examiner,* June 1, 1924.
20. *Ibid.,* June 9, 1924.
21. *Ibid.,* June 11, 1924.

Chapter 14

1. Stone, *op. cit.,* p. 262.
2. Interview with Max Schrayer.
3. Stone, *op. cit.,* p. 261.
4. Leopold, *op. cit.,* p. 66.
5. Chicago *Tribune,* July 3, 1924.
6. Chicago *Daily News,* August 12, 1924.
7. Chicago *Tribune,* June 16, 1924.
8. *Ibid.,* July 11, 1924.
9. *Ibid.,* July 13, 1924.
10. Interview with Max Schrayer.
11. The Hulbert and Bowman report appears as part of the official transcript of the hearing. See also Chicago *Tribune* and *Herald and Examiner,* July 26, 1924. Another, and different, version appears in Maureen McKernan, *The Amazing Crime and Trial of Leopold and Loeb* (New York: New American Library, 1957), p. 63.
12. Chicago *Herald and Examiner,* June 23, 1924.
13. Chicago *Tribune,* June 13, 1924.
14. Chicago *Daily News,* June 19, 1924. See also Chicago *Tribune,* June 20, 1924.
15. Chicago *Tribune,* June 25, 1924.
16. Chicago *Daily Journal,* July 16, 1924.
17. Chicago *Tribune,* July 17, 1924. See also several days following.

Chapter 15

1. Chicago *Tribune,* July 17, 1924.
2. *Ibid.,* July 22, 1924. See also other Chicago newspapers same and preceding day.
3. Leopold, *op. cit.,* p. 57.
4. *Ibid.,* p. 61.
5. Interview with Meyer Levin.
6. Chicago *Tribune,* July 22, 1924.

7. *Ibid.*
8. Chicago *Daily News.*

Chapter 16

1. Chicago *Herald and Examiner,* August 3, 1924.
2. Chicago *Tribune,* July 23, 1924. Also, July 24, 1924.
3. Chicago *Daily News,* September 3, 1924. See also August 30, 1924.
4. Interview with Ernst W. Puttkammer.
5. Chicago *Daily News,* July 23, 1924.
6. Crowe's opening remarks and further dialogue within the courtroom in this and other chapters come from the official court transcript, available in the Elmer Gertz collection at Northwestern University library. In addition, the Chicago newspapers each day published a great deal of verbatim testimony, apparently taken down by their stenographers.
7. Chicago *Daily News,* July 23, 1924.
8. Chicago *Tribune,* July 24, 1924.
9. Dr. Joseph Springer testified, July 23, 1924.
10. Stanley Obniczak testified, July 24, 1924.
11. Interview with Dr. Milton Bankoff. Also, Dr. Robert E. McBride.
12. Chicago *Tribune,* May 23, 1924.
13. Thomas Taylor testified, July 23, 1924.
14. Michigan City *Evening Dispatch,* July 24, 1924.
15. Carl J. Ulvigh testified, July 24, 1924.
16. Leopold, *op. cit.,* p. 67.
17. George Porter Lewis testified, July 25, 1924.
18. Interview with Ernst W. Puttkammer.
19. James Gortland testified, July 25, 1924.
20. Leopold, *op. cit.,* p. 70.
21. Chicago *Herald and Examiner.*
22. Interview with Mrs. William P. Crowe.
23. Chicago *Daily News,* July 30, 1924.

Chapter 17

1. *The Nation,* September 10, 1924.
2. Dr. White was so identified upon taking the stand, August 1, 1924.
3. Leopold, *op. cit.,* p. 65.
4. *Ibid.,* p. 73.
5. Interview with Ernst W. Puttkammer, who heard the rumors from friends in Charlevoix.
6. McKernan, *op. cit.,* p. 50.
7. Chicago *Daily News,* July 4, 1924.
8. Interview with a person who prefers to remain anonymous.

Chapter 18

1. Quoted by Elmer Gertz in *A Handful of Clients, op. cit.,* p. 64.
2. Dr. Ralph Hamill, quoted in the Chicago *Daily News,* August 1, 1924.
3. Dr. William A. White testified, August 1–2, 1924.

4. Clarence Darrow spoke, August 23–26, 1924.
5. McKernan, *op. cit.*, p. 56.
6. Chicago *Herald and Examiner,* August 12, 1924.
7. *Ibid.,* August 5, 1924.
8. For a book that treats Nietzsche, his life and theories, see Jano Lavrin, *Nietzsche: A Biographical Introduction* (New York: Charles Scribner's Sons, 1971). Nietzsche's best known book, and the one in which he outlines his *Übermensch* philosophy, is *Thus Spake Zarathustra.*
9. John Holland Cassity, *The Quality of Murder* (New York: Julian Press, 1959), p. 56.
10. William A. White, *William Alanson White: The Autobiography of a Purpose,* 1938. From a manuscript (p. 229) in the National Archives.
11. Chicago *Daily Journal,* August 2, 1924.
12. Dr. William Healy testified, August 4–5, 1924.
13. Chicago *Daily News,* August 4, 1924.
14. *Ibid,* August 6, 1924.
15. Dr. Bernard Glueck testified, August 5–6, 1924.
16. Chicago *Tribune,* August 7, 1924.
17. Max Schrayer testified, August 7, 1924. Also, interview with Max Schrayer.
18. Lorraine Nathan testified, August 7, 1924.
19. Chicago *Daily News,* August 7, 1924.
20. Dr. William A. White's papers, National Archives.
21. Edwin Meiss testified, August 7, 1924.
22. John Abt testified, August 7, 1924.
23. Arnold Maremont testified, August 7, 1924.
24. Puerto Rico deposition.
25. Dr. Robert Bruce Armstrong, Leonard Lewy, and Theodore Schimberg testified, August 8, 1924.
26. Dr. Harold S. Hulbert testified, August 8, 1924.
27. Leopold, *op. cit.*, p. 54.
28. Chicago *Daily Journal,* August 12, 1924.
29. Leopold, *op. cit.*, p. 90.
30. Leopold described this policy during the Puerto Rico deposition. See also Chicago *Tribune,* September 1, 1924.
31. Stone, *op. cit.*, p. 261.
32. Darrow, *op. cit.*, p. 238. Also, Leopold, *op. cit.*, p. 67.
33. *The New Statesman,* from the Gertz collection at Northwestern University library.
34. Katherine Fitzgerald testified, August 12, 1924.
35. Foreman M. Leopold testified, August 12, 1924.
36. Dr. Hugh T. Patrick testified, August 12–13, 1924.
37. Chicago *Daily News,* August 13, 1924.
38. Dr. Archibald Church testified, August 13, 1924.
39. Chicago *Daily News,* August 14, 1924.
40. A letter from Tiffany Blake to Dr. William A. White (National Archives) describes her attempts on his behalf to bring the two groups of alienists together.

41. Editorial by John H. Wigmore, *Journal of the American Institute of Criminal Law and Criminology* (November, 1924).
42. Dr. Archibald Church testified, August 14, 1924.
43. Dr. Rollin Turner Woodyatt testified, August 15, 1924.
44. Dr. Harold Douglas Singer testified, August 15, 1924.
45. The exchange occurred August 18, 1924.
46. Interview with William T. Crowe.
47. The article by James Doherty appeared in the Chicago *Tribune*, June 8, 1952.
48. Dr. William C. Krohn testified, August 19, 1924.

Chapter 19

1. Clarence Darrow spoke, August 22–25, 1924.
2. Thomas Marshall spoke, August 20–21, 1924.
3. Joseph Savage spoke, August 20–21, 1924.
4. Chicago *Tribune*, August 21, 1924.
5. *Ibid.*, August 19, 1924.
6. Chicago *Daily News*, August 21, 1924.
7. Walter Bachrach spoke, August 21–22, 1924.
8. Chicago *Daily News*, August 22, 1924.
9. Leopold, *op. cit.*, p. 75.
10. Chicago *Herald and Examiner*, August 23, 1924.
11. Chicago *Tribune*, August 26, 1924.
12. Benjamin C. Bachrach spoke, August 26, 1924.
13. Chicago *Daily News*, August 26, 1924. Also other Chicago newspapers, particularly the *Tribune*. Robert E. Crowe spoke, August 26–28, 1924.
14. Chicago *Daily News*, August 27, 1924.

Chapter 20

1. Hulbert and Bowman report (page 93 in the official transcript of the hearing).
2. Quoted in Defendants-Appellees' Excerpts from Record in the *Compulsion* suit, p. 183.
3. Chicago *Tribune*, September 1, 1924.
4. *Ibid.*, September 2, 1924.
5. The exchange between Leopold and London appears as part of the Puerto Rico deposition.
6. Memo by Ray Brennan in author's possession.
7. Chicago *Tribune*, November 26, 1924. Also, November 27 and 28.
8. *Ibid.*, November 22, 1924. Also, November 23 and 24.
9. New York *Times*, June 3, 1924.
10. Chicago *Tribune*, February 4, 1923.
11. Chicago *Daily Maroon*, November 22, 1923.
12. Interview with Keith Capron.
13. Chicago *Daily Maroon*, November 27, 1923.
14. *Ibid.*, February 5, 1924.
15. McKernan, *op. cit.*, p. vi.
16. *Ibid.*, p. 74.

Chapter 21

1. Gertz, *A Handful of Clients, op. cit.*, p. 4.
2. Chicago *Tribune,* August 29, 1924.
3. Chicago *Herald and Examiner,* July 30, 1924.
4. Chicago *Tribune,* September 3, 1924.
5. *Ibid.*, October 28, 1956.
6. Chicago *Daily News,* September 8, 1924.
7. *Ibid.*, September 10, 1924.
8. Chicago *Tribune,* September 11, 1924.
9. Judge Caverly's opinion is part of the court record. It was reprinted in a 1925 edition of *Chicago Legal News,* as well as in McKernan, *op. cit.*, p. 294.
10. Leopold, *op. cit.*, p. 79.
11. *Ibid.*, p. 82.
12. Chicago *Tribune,* September 11, 1924. The out-of-town editorial quotes in this chapter, unless otherwise noted, are from this same source.
13. Chicago *Daily News,* September 10, 1924.
14. Chicago *Tribune,* June 4, 1924.
15. *Ibid.*, September 14, 1924.
16. *Ibid.*, April 19, 1928.
17. Interview with Max Schrayer.
18. Interview with Ernst W. Puttkammer, who obtained the information from the wife of Ernst Freund.
19. Interview with Robert Bergstrom, who unfortunately does not recall the name of the judge.
20. Murray, *op. cit.*, p. 339.
21. Chicago *Herald and Examiner,* September 11, 1924.
22. Chicago *Daily Journal,* September 11, 1924.

Chapter 22

1. Clarence Darrow spoke at the hearing, August 23–25, 1924.
2. Interview with Mrs. Bert A. Cronson.
3. Arthur Weinberg, *Attorney for the Damned* (New York, Simon & Schuster, 1957), p. 17. See also Stone, op. cit., p. 272.
4. Chicago *Tribune,* December 31, 1927.
5. From unidentified clips from the Chicago *Sun-Times* morgue, dated October 2, 1924, and July 11, 1926.
6. Chicago *Tribune,* April 8, 1938. See also Chicago *Sun-Times,* September 20, 1942.
7. Chicago *Tribune,* September 23, 1924.
8. Chicago *Daily News,* April 19, 1928.
9. Unidentified clipping, Chicago *Sun-Times* morgue, April 4, 1929.
10. Chicago *Daily News,* November 11, 1924.
11. Information on the distribution of the rewards appeared in the Chicago *Tribune,* December 11, 1924.
12. Interview with Claude Korff.
13. Chicago *Tribune,* December 12, 1924.

14. New York *Times*, September 11, 1924.
15. Leopold, *op. cit.*, p. 84.
16. Chicago *Tribune*, September 11, 1924.
17. Michigan City *Evening Dispatch*, September 11, 1924.
18. Chicago *Daily News*, September 12, 1924.
19. Michigan City *Evening Dispatch*, September 12, 1924.
20. New York *Times*, September 12, 1924.
21. *Ibid.*
22. Leopold, *op. cit.*, p. 84. See also Chicago *Tribune*, September 12, 1924.
23. Leopold, *op. cit.*, p. 85. Also Michigan City *Evening Dispatch*, September 12, 1924.
24. Michigan City *Evening Dispatch*, September 12, 1924. See also Chicago *Tribune* and New York *Times*, same day.
25. New York *Times*, September 11, 1924.
26. Michigan City *Evening Dispatch*, September 12, 1924.
27. *Ibid.*
28. Chicago *Tribune*, July 28, 1957.

Chapter 23

1. Weinberg, *op. cit.*, p. 94.
2. See the New York Times *Index* for the years 1924 and 1925.
3. See Chicago newspapers, June 23–25, 1925.
4. New York *Times*, June 7–8, 1925.
5. Chicago *Daily News*, September 12, 1925.
6. New York *Times*, June 12, 1926. Also, interview with Will Geer.
7. Leopold, *op. cit.*, p. 143.
8. New York *Times*, November 4, 1927.
9. Leopold, *op. cit.*, p. 160.
10. *Ibid.*, pp. 160–75.
11. New York *Times*, May 16, 1924.
12. New York *Times*, November 21, 1926. Also, November 23, 1926.
13. New York *Times*, September 1, 1925.
14. Leopold, *op. cit.*, p. 134.
15. Michigan City *Evening Dispatch*, January 5, 1927.
16. New York *Times*, January 6, 1927. See also Chicago *Daily News*, January 8, 1927.
17. Chicago *Daily News*, January 8, 1927.
18. Leopold admitted the settlement during the Puerto Rico deposition.
19. Leopold, *op. cit.*, p. 193.
20. *Saturday Evening Post*, April 9, 1955.
21. Leopold, *op. cit.*, p. 198.
22. *Ibid.*, p. 238.

Chapter 24

1. Dr. William A. White testified, August 1–2, 1975.
2. See Chicago newspapers, January 12, 1933.

3. Leopold, *op. cit.*, p. 263.
4. Chicago *American,* October 3, 1933.
5. Leopold, *op. cit.*, p. 269.
6. Over the years convict James E. Day "authored" three articles for the Official Detective Group, each ghosted by a different writer: (1) "I Killed Dickie Loeb" (*Master Detective,* November, 1936) as told to Harry Spurrier; (2) "Why I Killed Richard Loeb" (*Master Detective,* September, 1942) as told to Barry Stephens (although Tom O'Dwyer was the actual writer!); and (3) "Why I Killed Richard Loeb" (*True Detective,* May, 1960) as told to Ray Brennan.
7. Gladys Erickson documents Day's record, *Warden Ragen of Joliet* (New York: Dutton, 1957).
8. Chicago *Daily News,* January 29, 1936.
9. Interview with Gladys Erickson.
10. Details of prison conditions at Stateville in 1936 were described in a report dated January 24, 1958, which Warden Joseph Ragen submitted to the Illinois Parole and Pardons Board.
11. Leopold, *op. cit.*, p. 302. See also Erickson, *op. cit.*, p. 80.
12. *True Detective,* May, 1960.
13. Chicago *Daily News,* January 29, 1936. See also Chicago *Tribune,* same day and January 30, 1936.
14. Leopold, *op. cit.*, p. 302.
15. Interview with Father Eligius Weir.
16. Erickson, *op. cit.*, p. 78.
17. Leopold, *op. cit.*, p. 291.
18. A memo in the Chicago *Sun-Times* morgue, authored by a reporter named Mooney, contains an interview with Father Weir as well as other information related to the Leopold and Loeb case.
19. Chicago *Daily News,* January 29, 1936.
20. Leopold, *op. cit.*, p. 291.
21. Chicago *Tribune,* January 29, 1956. The *Sun-Times* memo mentions fifty-eight slashes instead of fifty-six. In Erickson *(op. cit.,* p. 77) the number is listed as fifty-seven.
22. Leopold, *op. cit.*, p. 292.
23. Chicago *Tribune,* January 29, 1936.
24. Leopold, *op. cit.*, p. 293.
25. Max Lerner, *It Is Later Than You Think* (New York: Viking, 1938). Lerner used the comment as title to the epilogue of that book.
26. Murray, *op. cit.*, p. 344.
27. Chicago *Daily News,* January 29, 1936.
28. Chicago *Tribune,* January 29, 1936.
29. Chicago *Daily News,* January 31, 1936.
30. Interview with Gladys Erickson.
31. Leopold, *op. cit.*, p. 303.
32. Letter from Joseph G. Schwab, dated November 3, 1974.
33. Interview with Father Eligius Weir.
34. *Chicago Sun-Times memo, op. cit.*

35. Leopold, *op. cit.*, p. 301.
36. *Ibid.*
37. Chicago *Daily News*, January 30, 1936.
38. *Saturday Evening Post*, April 16, 1955.
39. Unidentified newspaper clipping dated February 20, 1942.
40. Joliet *Herald-News*, May 25, 1943.
41. Chicago *Sun-Times*, April 15, 1965.
42. Chicago *Daily News*, April 26, 1965.
43. *Ibid.*, January 29, 1936.
44. Leopold, *op. cit.*, p. 305.

Chapter 25

1. Carl Sandburg testified at Leopold's parole hearing. Chicago *Daily News*, February 5, 1958.
2. Letter to Timothy Seldes, dated July 1, 1957.
3. Interview with Gene Lovitz.
4. Leopold, *op. cit.*, pp. 332–64.
5. *Ibid.*, p. 358.
6. Interview with Charles Remsberg. His article "The Convict and Medical Research" appeared in the April, 1961, issue of *The Kiwanis Magazine.*
7. Gertz, *A Handful of Clients, op. cit.*, p. 43.
8. Leopold, *op. cit.*, p. 363.
9. *Ibid.*, p. 371.
10. Chicago *Daily Journal*, September 11, 1924.
11. Darrow spoke at the hearing, August 22–25, 1924.
12. Chicago *Daily News*, April 13, 1949.
13. Chicago *Tribune*, January 9, 1953.
14. For a good summary of events related to the parole, see Meyer Levin's article in the May, 1957, *Coronet:* "Leopold Should Be Freed!"
15. Chicago *Sun-Times*, May 5, 1953.
16. Chicago *Tribune*, May 15, 1953.
17. Levin, *The Obsession, op. cit.*, p. 103. Also interview with Meyer Levin.
18. *Ibid.*, p. 108.
19. Interview with John Bartlow Martin.
20. Leopold, *op. cit.*, p. 21.
21. *Coronet*, May, 1957.
22. Gertz, *A Handful of Clients, op. cit.*, p. 21.
23. *Ibid.*, p. 9.
24. Leopold made the statement at his parole hearing, February 5, 1958.
25. Darrow, *op. cit.*, p. 228.
26. Gertz, *A Handful of Clients, op. cit.*, p. 61.
27. Quoted in Leopold, *op. cit.*, p. 129.
28. Interview with Gene Lovitz.
29. Gertz, *A Handful of Clients, op. cit.*, p. 71.

Chapter 26

1. Chicago *Daily News,* August 30, 1971.
2. *Time,* March 3, 1958.
3. Chicago *Sun-Times,* January 20, 1958.
4. Interview with Elmer Gertz.
5. Chicago *Daily News,* March 13, 1958. See also: Chicago's *American,* same day, and the Chicago *Tribune* and Chicago *Sun-Times,* March 14, 1958.
6. Chicago *Tribune,* March 15, 1958.
7. Interview with Meyer Levin.
8. Gertz, *A Handful of Clients, op. cit.,* p. 11.
9. Leopold, *op. cit.,* p. 403.
10. Levin, *Compulsion, op. cit.,* p. 529.
11. Levin, *The Obsession, op. cit.,* p. 227.
12. Gertz, *A Handful of Clients, op. cit.,* p. 168.
13. Interviews with Ephraim London, Robert Bergstrom, and Elmer Gertz.
14. Chicago *Daily News,* May 27, 1970.

Chapter 27

1. Chicago *Daily News,* February 6, 1958.
2. Letter to Abel Brown, dated March 10, 1968.
3. Gertz, *To Life, op. cit.,* p. 193.
4. Interview with Elmer Gertz.
5. Letter to Abel Brown, dated November 6, 1968.
6. Interview with Elmer Gertz.
7. Interview with Abel Brown.
8. Chicago *Daily News,* July 11, 1971.
9. Chicago *Daily News,* March 13, 1965. See also Chicago's *American,* March 12, 1963.
10. Letters to Ralph Newman, dated September 5, 1959, and May 31, 1960.
11. Interview with Elmer Gertz.
12. Interview with Ralph Newman.
13. Gertz, *To Life, op. cit.,* p. 192.
14. Chicago *Sun-Times,* August 30, 1971.
15. For information related to Trudi Leopold, see: Chicago *American,* January 10, 1961, and January 19, 1961; Chicago *Sun-Times,* January 12, 1961, and June 22, 1961.
16. Letter to Elmer Gertz, dated May 4, 1962.
17. Gertz, *A Handful of Clients, op. cit.,* p. 102.
18. Chicago *Daily News,* August 30, 1971.
19. Letter to Elmer Gertz, dated May 4, 1962.
20. Taped interview by M. W. Newman, March, 1965.
21. Letter to Abel Brown, dated March 31, 1964.
22. *Ibid.,* dated December 17, 1970.
23. Interview with Dr. Bernard C. Glueck, the son.
24. Interview with Ernst W. Puttkammer.

25. Chicago *Daily News*, August 30, 1924.

Epilogue

1. Opinion filed in the *Compulsion* suit, March 29, 1968.
2. Chicago *Sun-Times*, August 31, 1971.
3. Interview with Mrs. Bert A. Cronson.

Bibliography

CASSITY, JOHN HOLLAND. *The Quality of Murder.* New York: Julian Press, 1959.

DARROW, CLARENCE. *The Story of My Life.* New York: Scribner's, 1932.

ERICKSON, GLADYS A. *Warden Ragen of Joliet.* New York: E. P. Dutton, 1957.

GERTZ, ELMER. *A Handful of Clients.* New York: Follett, 1965.

———. *To Life.* New York: McGraw-Hill, 1974.

LEVIN, MEYER. *Compulsion.* New York: Simon and Schuster, 1956.

———. *The Obsession.* New York: Simon and Schuster, 1973.

LEOPOLD, NATHAN F., JR. *Life Plus 99 Years.* New York: Doubleday, 1958.

MCKERNAN, MAUREEN. *The Amazing Crime and Trial of Leopold and Loeb.* New York: New American Library, 1957.

MURRAY, GEORGE. *The Madhouse on Madison Street.* Chicago: Follett, 1965.

STONE, IRVING. *Clarence Darrow for the Defense.* New York: Doubleday, 1941.

WEINBERG, ARTHUR. *Attorney for the Damned.* New York: Simon & Schuster, 1957. p. 195

Index

Index

ABCD crimes, 21–23, 249–60; "Handless Stranger" murder, 250, 257; Ream castration, 250, 254–56; Tracy murder, 250, 253–54; Wolf murder, 250, 256–57
Abelson, Lester, 19, 90
Abt, John, 222
Adamowski, Benjamin, 320
Adler, Sidney, 118
Allen, E. M., 93–95, 108, 186
Allen, I. W., 257
Almer Coe and Co., 76, 276
Alving, Alf S., 308, 309
Alwood, Fred, 58
Amazing Crime and Trial of Leopold and Loeb, The (McKernan), 194, 259–60
Anderson, Edward F., 46
Anderson, I. W. *See* Allen, I. W.
Anti-Semitism, on campus, 14
Aretino, Pietro, 19
Armstrong, Robert Bruce, 223
Arndt, Samuel, 312, 313
Arson, 151
Asher, Bobby, 26, 31, 34, 67
Associated Jewish Charities, 66
Austin, Richard, 312
Austrian family, 65

Bachrach, Benjamin C., 122–23, 128, 130–31, 137, 144, 160, 162, 166, 172, 175, 180, 183, 187, 242, 244, 259, 264
Bachrach, Walter, 137, 162, 172, 175, 187, 192, 206, 233, 245, 259
Baer, Walter, 96
"Ballard, Morton D." (Leopold alias), 24–25, 30, 62, 85, 98, 120
Ballenberg, Adolph, 67
Balmer, Edwin, 117
Barker, Gertrude, 68–69
Barrett, Michael, 46
Bart, Belle, 140
Baxter, Eleanor, 186
Believe It or Not (Ripley), 58
Bennett, Willie, 308
Bergstrom, Robert, 268, 327, 328
Bernounsky, Sergeant, 127
Beta Theta Pi, 257
Binstock, Louis, 314

Birds of Puerto Rico, The (Leopold), 332
Bitker, Pierce, 15, 173
Blair, Frank, 276
Bliss, George, 300, 302
Block, Philip D., 66
Bohnen, Anna, 118
Bonniwell, Charles A., 140
Bookwalter, Mr., 318–19
Booth, Harry, 223
Borena, Lillian, 71
Bowman, Carl M., 144, 147–48, 151–56, 188, 300
Boyle, John, 311
Branson, Robert J., 319
Brennan, Ray, 252–53
Brisbane, Arthur, 182
Brown, Abel, 63, 121, 323–24, 332–34, 336, 338
Brown, Kathy, 333
Buchman, Hamlin, 96
Burglary, 13–15, 16–17, 151–52
Byron, W. F., 312

Capone, Al, 26–27, 138
Carrigan, Red, 255
Carson, Frank, 269
Casey, Bob, 298
Caverly, John R., 130–31, 138, 161–87, 213, 214, 220, 230, 233–37, 241, 242, 244, 245, 247–48, 261, 262–69, 273, 274–75, 309, 313, 319–20, 322; hospitalization of, 274; judgment, 261–70; sentencing, 267
Caverly, Charlotte, 237, 263
Chamberlin, Henry Barrett, 275
Chase, Mr. and Mrs. George D., 58, 73, 74
Chi Psi Lodge, 257
Chicago Crime Commission, 275
Chicago crime rate, 20–23, 142–43
Chicago *Daily Journal,* 269
Chicago *Daily News,* 48, 52, 53, 78, 84, 89, 90, 94, 138, 139, 197, 213, 217, 220, 228, 242, 263, 276, 277–78, 283, 293, 297–98, 314, 323, 337
Chicago *Evening American,* 50, 52, 55, 86, 115, 116, 139, 159, 323
Chicago gangsterism, 26–28
Chicago *Herald and Examiner,* 50, 68, 94, 112, 115, 126, 128, 134, 139, 141, 189, 208, 237, 269
Chicago journalism, 27–28
Chicago *Sun-Times,* 252, 292, 323
Chicago *Tribune,* 50, 54, 56, 57, 67, 75, 88, 115, 119, 126, 127, 128, 133, 134, 136, 139, 140, 145, 158, 159, 167, 170, 172, 176, 181, 185, 188, 189, 208, 231, 241, 249, 250–51, 255, 263, 270, 276, 279, 281, 305, 323
Chmelik, Frank J., 295
Church, Archibald, 128, 129, 228–29
Clarence Darrow for the Defense (Stone), 227, 274
Coe, Almer, 276
Cohen, Justin, 35
Coleman, Clarence, 96
Collins, Morgan A., 50, 59, 61, 69, 74–75, 234, 275
Compulsion (Levin), 316–17, 325–31; Leopold suit against. 325–31
Confession, 92–112, 160–68
Conley, Charles, 258
Cost, of trial, 137
Courts on Trial (Frank), 77
Craig, Jay, 290–91

Cronson, Bert A., 50, 59, 88, 91–92, 108, 125, 273
Cronson, Ethel, 50
Crot, William, 59, 77, 79, 84, 97, 125, 321
Crowe, Robert E., 50, 58–59, 70, 71, 73, 76, 77, 78–79, 86–87, 88, 90, 91–94, 95, 96, 99, 102, 105, 106, 108, 109, 112, 120, 122, 125, 127, 128, 129, 130, 131, 132, 137, 138, 143–44, 145, 158, 161, 163, 164, 165, 212, 214, 220–31, 236, 242–44, 245–47, 249, 252–53, 259, 267, 273–75, 278, 310, 312, 321; death of, 321–22; and defense, 188–205; and defense summation, 242–47; effect of trial on, 227; opening statement, 172–74; and trial prosecution, 169–87
Crowe, Mrs. Robert E., 187
Crowe, William T., 186, 231
Cuneo, Lawrence, 125

Daily Maroon, 257, 258
Darrow, Clarence, 123, 233, 310, 319, 320 *passim;* defense, 188–231, 234–74; death of, 303; funeral of, 321; income from case, 326; literary quotes used in defense, 238, 240, 241; motives for taking case, 135–37; nickname, 181; opening statement, 174–75; record as defense counsel, 124, 131; and Scopes trial, 124, 273; takes case, 123–24
Darrow, Ruby, 136, 144, 187, 221
Day, James E., 291–94, 297–303, 309, 326; acquittal of, 300–1; and death of Loeb, 294, 298–301
De Young, Frederick, 71, 73
Debs, Eugene V., 123
Defense of Leopold and Loeb, 188–231, 234–74
Delta Sigma Phi, 257–58
Delta Upsilon, 255
Dennis, Eugene, 74
Derr, Edward C., 278, 279–80
Despres, Leon, 268, 327
Deutsch, Billy, 96
Deutsch, Emil, 76
Dillon, Edward "Toddy," 289
Disfigurement of Bobby Franks, 104, 155, 179
Doherty, James, 88, 231
Doherty, Thomas, 133
Donker, Edward, 133, 181

Eagleton, Thomas F., 318
Eckstein, Frederick G., 60
Egan, Charles, 59
Egelhof, Joseph, 323
Elijah Muhammed, 10
English, Earl, 255
Englund, Sven, 30, 31, 37, 91–92, 100, 106, 107, 314
Ennis, James, 71
Erickson, Gladys, 323
Ettelson, Samuel A., 35, 36–38, 42, 44, 45, 46–47, 49–50, 57, 72, 74, 79, 108, 125, 177, 285
Evidence: psychiatric, 206–31; search for, 125–32
Eyeglasses: found at crime scene, 51–52, 59–60, 64, 105; tracing, 76–83

Fahey, Michael J., 157

Farrell, John Joe, 59
Fay, Agnes M., 60
Fitzgerald, James N., 140
Fitzgerald, Katherine, 227
Fitzgerald, Thomas R., 78
Fitzmorris, Charlie, 78
Forbes, Genevieve, 263
Foreman, Celia, 66
Foreman, Edwin, 66
Foreman, Florence, 65–66
Foreman, Helen, 66
Foreman, Oscar, 66
Frank, Jerome, 77
Frank, Mike, 233
Frankenthal, Lester E., 295
Frankenthal, Lester Jr., 295
Franks, Bobby, 32 *passim;* car used in crime, 60–61, 69; disfigurement of body, 104, 155, 179; disposal of body, 104–5; finding of body, 40–41, 42–43; funeral of, 62, 67; identification of body, 46; glasses found at crime scene, 51–52, 59–60, 64, 76–83, 105; kidnap note, 41–42; kidnapping of, 34–40; murder of, 102–4, 109–10, 154–56; personality and character, 141; reaction of Jewish community to crime, 116; selection of as victim, 96–97; theories about crime, 51–55, 59, 68; witness to kidnapping, 52, 60; wounds on body, 54
Franks, Flora, 33, 34–35, 36, 42, 50, 58, 67, 106, 119, 145, 168, 175–76, 275
Franks, Jack, 33, 34, 122, 141
Franks, Jacob, 32–33, 34–37, 41–47, 55–59, 75, 89, 105, 107–8, 119, 141, 157–58, 173, 175, 182, 187, 232, 248, 263, 267–68, 275, 285, 309; crank notes to, 61, 72; offers reward, 50; and ransom, 43–44; receives kidnap note, 41–42
Franks, Josephine, 33, 34, 157, 320
Fredericks, Paul, 258
Freud, Sigmund, 128, 137, 139–40
Freund, Ernst, 268
Friedman, I. K., 135
Friedman, William, 312
Fry, George C., 107

Garcia de Quevada, Gertrude Feldman, 336, 340; marries Leopold, 336
Gehr (Geer), Will, 139, 284
Gertz, Elmer, 49, 308–9, 317–20, 322–31, 332–36, 339
Gertz, Mamie, 333
Gertz, Robert, 49, 323
Gessler, Marie, 196
Gilster, Fred J., 255
Gistensen, Samuel, 277
Glassner, Jim, 145–46
Glenn, Otis F., 71, 72, 73
Glueck, Bernard, 137, 144, 217–20, 339
Goldfarb, Sam, 63
Goldsmith, Irv, 17, 18, 147
Goldstein, Alvin, 44, 45, 48–49, 52, 55, 57, 72, 89–90, 94, 139, 276, 325, 326; awarded Pulitzer Prize, 276
Gordon, Harold R., 327
Gortland, James, 79, 125, 184–85, 247
Grant, Bernard, 282
Greenebaum, Henry Everett, 66

Gresham, Edwin, 175; identifies Franks' body, 45
Gresheimer, Freddie, 74
Guilty plea, 145, 160–68
Gutknecht, John, 312–13

Hall, James Whitney, 170
Hamill, Ralph, 206
Hamilton, Reverend, 280
Handful of Clients, A (Gertz), 323, 330
"Handless Stranger," murder of, 250–53, 257–58
Hartman, Irving H., 157
Hartman, Irving, Jr., 34, 52, 60, 96, 101–2, 157
Harvard School, 33–34, 48, 57, 72, 74, 96, 100, 150, 199, 237
Healy, William, 137, 144, 213–17
Hearst, William Randolph, 139
Heath, Charles, 74–75
Hecht, Ben, 123
Heitler, Mike, 123
Herndon, William G., 25, 180
Herrick, John, 263
Hertz, John, 24
Hill, Warden, 287–88
Hoffman, Peter, 134, 161, 261, 277, 278
Homosexuality, 55, 83–84, 146, 149, 201–2, 214–15, 293–94, 306–7, 329–30
Hough, Hugh, 323
Howard, Joseph L., murder of, 27
Hubinger, Albert, 120
Hughes, Michael, 37, 42, 53, 72, 79, 92, 93, 108, 125, 126, 263
Hulbert, Harold S., 144, 147–48, 151–56, 188, 224–25, 300
Hulbert and Bowman report, 188–89, 193–200, 210, 214, 245, 246, 249, 252, 253, 256, 259, 260, 309
Humphrey, Austin, 294
Hunt, Bernard, 37, 121, 276

Illinois State Bankers' Association, 66
In Search (Levin), 116
Investigation of Franks kidnapping and murder, 56–59, 60–62, 71, 73, 74, 86–132; choice of victim, 96–97; confession of culprits, 92–112; interrogation of suspects, 86–94; leads, 64–75; map of crime scene, 103; planning and execution of crime, 95–112; search for evidence, 125–32; typewriter used in kidnap note, 89–91

Jacobs, Josephine, 61
Jacobs, Walter L., 24–25, 180
Jeffrey, Bert, 69
Johnson, Frank A., 59, 77, 79, 84, 86, 97, 125, 130, 185, 321
Johnson, John Q., 123, 125
Judgment, 261–70

Kahn, Daisy K., 275
Kaleczka, John, 40, 60, 276
Kansas City *Star*, 269
Kaplan, Nathan, 19
Kaska, A. L., 62
Kemp, James C., 47
Kenna, "Hinky Dink," 171
Kenwood gang, 254
Kidnap note, 41–42, 56, 89–91
Kidnapped (Stevenson), 84
King, Alva Vest, 135

Kiwanis Magazine, 308
Klockzien, William, 130
Klon, Joe, 60–61
Knitter, George, 40, 60, 276
Knitter, Walter, 40, 43, 60, 276
Knowles, Victor I., 313
Korff, Claude, 59–60
Korff, Paul, 40–41, 42–43, 51, 59–60, 76, 276
Krauser, Walter, 282
Krohn, William O., 128, 129, 231
Krum, Tyrell, 134, 170, 181, 279–80
Ku Klux Klan, 233

Lahey, Edwin A., 297–98; quoted on Loeb's death, 298
Lang, William, 125
Laube, W., 62
Lazelle, Constance, 138–39
Leopold, Aaron, 65
Leopold, Babette, 65
Leopold, Foreman M., 66
Leopold, Henry, 65
Leopold, Louis, 65
Leopold, Mike, 79, 84, 122, 160, 161, 163, 182, 193, 204, 228, 263, 275, 287, 317, 322, 324; death of, 313
Leopold, Nathan F., 37, 106, 139, 145, 158, 160, 163, 187, 263, 275, 320; death of, 275; wealth of, 136
Leopold, Nathan F., Jr.: and ABCD crimes, 249–60; activities in prison education, 289–90; aliases, 24–25; alibi, 79–84, 86–87, 91–92, 111; appearance, 20; as arsonist, 151; attitude toward Loeb, 92–133; as burglar, 15–17, 151–52; as cardplayer, 19; college years, 18, 82, 199–200; confession of, 93–94; death of, 9, 34; early years, 18, 66–67; escape attempt, alleged, 284–85; hobbies and interests, 18–20; as law student, 19, 68; life after prison: 332–40; as linguist, 19, 82, 182–83; malaria cure project, 307–10; marriage, 336, 339; and Nietzschean philosophy, 19–20, 88,210; 1949 parole decision, 311–13; 1957 parole decision, 318–20; as ornithologist, 18–19, 82; personality and character, 18, 63, 86, 140, 145, 197–205, 206–31; physical health, 66; plea, 145, 160–68; planning and execution of Franks murder, 95–112; previous crimes, 143–56; in prison, 273–320; release of, 320–24; sentencing of, 267; sex life, 83–84, 146, 149, 201–2, 214–15, 306–7, 329–30; suicide fixation, 153–54; suit against Levin, 325–31
Leopold, Samuel, 65, 66, 275, 314, 334, 339
Leopold family, 275; history of, 65–66
"Leopold Should be Freed!" (Martin), 316
Levin, Meyer, 116, 139, 166, 276, 284, 314–17, 325–31, 339
Levinson, Johnny, 31–32, 93, 96, 100–1, 119
Levinson, Salmon O., 31–32, 119
Lewis, George Porter, 39, 49, 65, 67, 80, 183

Lewy, Leonard, 223
Life Plus 99 Years (Leopold), 284, 295, 304, 308, 317
Lincoln, Warren, 253
Lindsey, Ben B., 167–68
Loeb, Albert, 17, 65–66, 89, 96, 117–18, 119, 149, 158, 163, 182, 187, 227, 275; death of, 275; as a father, 194
Loeb, Allan, 87–88, 118, 119, 146, 148, 149, 160, 161, 163, 182, 193, 194, 203, 263
Loeb, Anna, 89, 145, 194, 196, 283–84
Loeb, Ernest, 118, 119, 194, 203, 283
Loeb, Jacob, 117, 122–23, 128, 160, 182, 193, 263, 268, 274
Loeb, Julius, 117
Loeb, Moritz, 117
Loeb, Richard: and ABCD crimes, 249–60; activities in prison education, 289–90; aliases, 25; alibi, 79–84, 86–87, 91–92, 111; appearance, 20; arrest of, 86–87; as arsonist, 151; attitude toward Leopold, 92–133; as burglar, 13–17, 151–52; college years, 18, 199–200; confession, 92–93; death of, 9, 294–95, 298–300; early years, 17, 18; hobbies and interests, 18–20; personality and character, 18, 20, 23–24, 62–63, 86–87, 140, 145, 194–97, 200–5, 206–31; planning and execution of Franks murder, 95–112; plea, 145, 160–68; previous crimes, 143–56; in prison, 273–300; sentencing of, 267; sex life, 55, 83–84, 146, 149, 214–15, 293–94, 329–30; suicide fixation, 153–54, view of Bobby Franks, 53
Loeb, Sidney, 117
Leob, Tommy, 31, 32, 57, 100, 118, 196; as potential murder victim, 96
Loeb family, history of, 117–18
Lohman, Joseph D., 312, 313
London, Ephraim, 251, 252, 327–29, 330
London, Jack, 305–6
Long, S. P., 135
Lovitz, Gene, 305–9, 320
Lucht, William, 60
Lundin, Fred, 78
Lundon, Dudley, 254
Lurie, Susan, 30, 49, 63, 67, 72, 325

Madhouse on Madison Street, The (Murray), 298
Mandel, Leon, 19, 90, 150–51, 182–83
Manke, Tony. *See* Mankowsky, Tony
Mankowsky, Tony, 39–41, 42, 43, 46, 276, 326
Mann Act, 123
Manson, Lewis L., 213
Manus, Albert, 312
Maremont, Arnold, 19–20, 89–90, 222–23
Marshall, Thomas, 172, 232, 263
Martin, John Bartlow, 316
"Mason, Louis" (Loeb alias), 25
Mayer, Howard, 52, 53, 55, 57, 86–88, 94, 325
McGuire, William Anthony, 185, 208

McFarland, Smuts, 142
MacGillivray, James, 19
McKeever, William A., 135
McKernan, Maureen, 194–95, 259
McNally, William D., 54, 177, 178
McPhaul, Jack, 94
Meiss, Edwin, 147, 222
Mengel, Jack, 148–49
Miranda rule, 231
Miss Spade's School, 198
Mitchell, Mott Kirk, 48, 57, 58, 71–73, 77
Moll, Philip, 59
Muhammad Ali, 10
Mulroy, James, 44, 45, 52, 53, 55, 57, 89, 94, 139, 275, 283, 326; Pulitzer Prize award, 276
Murphy, Daniel, 254
Murray, George, 269, 298

Nathan, Lorraine, 63, 220–21
Nelson, Oscar, 290
New York *Evening Sun,* 269
Newman, M.W., 337–38
Newman, Mary Lynn, 333
Newman, Ralph, 314, 315, 317, 322, 323, 333, 335
Nusbaum, Aaron, 118

O'Banion, Dion, 29
Obendorf, Howard, 19, 90
Obsession, The (Levin), 315
Oettinger, Mark, 289
O'Grady, Michael, 57, 59
Olejniczak, Stanley, 43, 177
Olejniczak, Mrs. Stanley, 43
O'Malley, Thomas, 125
Orr, Robert, 74
Oswald, Lee Harvey, 222

Papritz, Adolph, 61
Passmire, John, 278
Patrick, Hugh, 128, 129, 137, 228, 229
Peoria *Evening Star,* 99
Philson, Robert, 255
Pillsbury, Walter B., 135
Planning of Franks crime, 95–112
Plea, guilty, 145, 160–68
Princeton-Yale School, 34
Prohibition, 29
Prosecution of Leopold and Loeb, 169–87
Psychiatric evidence, 206–31
Pursifull, Joseph, 289
Puttkammer, Ernst W., 73, 171, 184, 268, 339

Quigg, Florence, 58

Ragen, Joseph, 292, 294, 300–1, 302, 309, 322
"Ragged Stranger." *See* "Handless Stranger"
Ream, Charles: castration of, 21, 23, 132, 250, 251–56; and lawsuit against Leopold and Loeb, 286–87
Reese, Harold, 278–79
Reinhardt, Germaine K., 55, 221
Remsberg, Charles, 308
Rewards, 275–76
Rizzo, G., 284–85
Roa, Bernardo, 284–85
Robberies, 14–17, 21–23, 252
Robinson, Charles, 46–47
Rosenwald, Julius, 96, 118, 119
Row, W. Harold, 324
Royal Typewriter Company, 90
Rubel, Dick, 96, 106–7, 119,

150–51, 325
Rudy, Elmer, 254
Rutledge, I. W. *See* Allen, I. W.

St. Xavier's School, 68
Sandburg, Carl, 320
Sanders, Ralph, 282
Sattler, Elizabeth, 77, 90–91
Saturday Evening Post, 315, 316
Savage, Joseph P., 76, 79–84, 90, 92, 93, 108, 125, 132, 145, 172, 185, 232, 236, 263, 274–75
Savage, Mrs. Joseph P., 187
Sbarbaro, John, 79–84, 88, 92–93, 108, 125, 145, 172, 176, 228, 263
Scherer, Ferdinand, 264
Schrayer, Max, 15, 16–18, 23–24, 26, 30–31, 72, 143–44, 146–47, 188, 220, 268
Schwab, Birdie, 67, 197, 325
Schwab, Joseph G., 301
Scopes, John T., 124, 273
Scott, Robert, 290
Sears, Roebuck, and Company, 118
Seass, J. T., 32, 100
Sea-Wolf, The (London), 305–6
Seldes, Timothy, 304
Sentencing, 267
Shackleford, John, 70
Shanberg, Maurice, 19, 90
Shapino, Tony, 43
Shoemacher, William, 37, 70, 90–91, 121, 125, 127, 248
Sigma Chi, 14, 257, 258
Sigma Nu, 257, 258, 259
Singer, Harold Douglas, 230
Skeplowski, Mr., 300
Skillman, Thomas, 36
Smith, John Justin, 323
Smith, Milton, 125, 145, 172, 263, 273
Social climate, of the 1920s, 29–30
South Side Academy, 34
Spanier, Seymour, 327
Spence, Charles E., 34, 35, 57
Springer, Joseph, 53–54, 87, 176–79, 230
Stand, Pudgy, 142
Starren, N. C., 58
Stein, Sidney, 65, 80
Stevenson, Robert Louis, 84
Stone, Irving, 124, 227, 274
Story of My Life, The (Darrow), 124, 319
Stratton, William, 312–13, 318
Strauss, Leo, 66
Struthers, Miss, 195–97, 202, 206–7, 226
Suicide fixation, 153–54
Sullivan, Lefty, 290
Sullivan, Wallace, 126, 128
Sunday, Billie, 134–35
Sutton, H. P., 51, 90
Swift, Charles H ., 74

Taylor, Thomas, 180
Taylor, William, 47
Thompson, "Big Bill," 78
Thompson, Hank, 278
To Life (Gertz), 333
Torrio, Johnny, 29, 142
Touhy, Roger, 292
Tracy, Freeman Louis, murder of, 21, 132, 250–54, 257
Trial of Leopold and Loeb, 160–270; cost of, 137; defense, 188–231; guilty plea, 160–68; judgment, 261–70; prosecution,

169–87; psychiatric evidence, 206–31
Trucklett, John, 142
True Detective magazine, 292, 294, 299–300, 302
Tuttle, Frank B., 85
Typewriter used in kidnap note, 89–91, 121

Ulgish, Carl, 183
Ulvigh, Carl, 319
Union League, 257
University of Chicago, 63, 64, 255, 257, 259, 260; crime wave at, 21–23
Unna, Johanna, 117

Van de Bogert, Percy, 47, 53, 58
Van de Vorrse, Philip, 60
Van den Bosch, Pauline, 197–98

Wade, Horace, 51
Wantz, Mathilda, 198–99, 226
Ward, Charles, E., 24
Ward, Daniel P., 331
Washington *Post,* 269
Webster, Ralph W., 178
Weinstein, Jacob, 276
Weir, Father Eligius, 293, 294–95, 301, 314
Weitzel, Tony, 314
Welling, Lieutenant, 37–38
Wellington, Edward, 70
Wenjenski, Sylvester, 61
Went, Sylvester. *See* Wenjenski, Sylvester
Wesner, John A., 178
Westbrook, Warden, 277, 278
Wharton, Charles S., 71, 72, 73
White, De Witt, 70
White, William Alanson, 137, 138, 144, 188, 206–21
Whitman, Warden, 280, 283
Wilkins, Professor, 19
Wilkinson, Janet, 78
Williams, Richard P., 36, 57–58
Wilson, Walter, 36–37, 57, 58, 71, 72, 73, 77, 285
Wolf, Melvin T., murder of, 23, 250–52, 256–57
Wolfe, Thomas C., 64–65, 77
Wolff, Oscar, 51, 54–55
Woods, Hubbard, 252, 256
Woodyatt, Rollin Turner, 229

Zeta Beta Tau, 14, 49, 52, 72, 143–44, 145, 147, 152, 222, 258; burglary of, 14, 252